Transfer Pricing and Developing Economies

DIRECTIONS IN DEVELOPMENT
Public Sector Governance

Transfer Pricing and Developing Economies

A Handbook for Policy Makers and Practitioners

Joel Cooper, Randall Fox, Jan Loeprick, and Komal Mohindra

 WORLD BANK GROUP

Contents

Boxes

Figures

Tables

Acknowledgments

This handbook is a product of the Global Tax Team in the Equitable Growth, Finance, and Institutions Vice Presidency. It draws on a range of the World Bank's operational engagements in the areas of tax policy and administration. The publication of this handbook was made possible by the generous support of the U.K. Department for International Development (DfID), by the government of Switzerland through the State Secretariat for Economic Affairs (SECO), and by the Ministry of Finance of the government of Luxembourg. The contents of this book were prepared over several years and as a result contain examples from countries' domestic laws and guidance that may have since been repealed, amended, or otherwise modified. In this regard, readers should acknowledge that examples are for illustrative purposes only and should not be taken as an accurate representation of the current law and or guidance in any particular country. The authors thank Daniel Alvarez, Melinda Brown, Michael Engelschalk, Sebastian James, Michael Jarvis and Michael Lennard for helpful comments and guidance as part of the peer-review process. Colin Clavey, Oscar Good, Arcotia Hatsidimitris, Ania Rajca, and Norbert Roller provided valuable contributions throughout the handbook. Rumit Pancholi and Ashish Sen edited the draft.

Joel Cooper worked as an international tax specialist at the World Bank Group, providing technical assistance on transfer pricing and related tax matters. This involved the development of appropriate policies, training tax officials and working with tax administrations to establish administrative processes and procedures. During this time, he was also involved in tax policy discussions with other international organizations, such as the Organisation for Economic Co-Operation and Development, the International Monetary Fund, and the World Customs Organization. Before joining the World Bank Group, Joel worked for the International Bureau of Fiscal Documentation in the Netherlands and for a tax advisory firm in Australia. He is currently co-head of international transfer pricing at a leading global law firm and is based in London.

Randall Fox worked as a transfer pricing and advance pricing agreement specialist for the World Bank Group, where he assisted tax administrations around the world with building capacity on transfer pricing and developing advance pricing agreement programs. He developed and led training workshops, drafted advance pricing agreement guidelines and worked directly with tax administrations, finance ministry officials as well as the Organisation for Economic Co-Operation and Development on numerous policy matters related to transfer pricing. Before his time at the World Bank Group, Randall was an advance pricing agreement team leader and competent authority analyst for the Internal Revenue Service in Washington, DC. Before joining the government, he started his career in transfer pricing at Ernst & Young in Cincinnati, Ohio. He holds a master of arts in economics from Miami University. Randall is currently co-head of international transfer pricing at a leading global law firm and is based in London.

Jan Loeprick works for the World Bank as a senior economist and covers a range of tax policy and administration issues, including the implementation of transfer pricing regimes. He previously coordinated the International Finance Corporation's business taxation advisory portfolio in Eastern Europe and Central Asia. Jan has also worked in the international tax department at the Austrian Ministry of Finance and has taught as a lecturer at Dresden University in Germany. He holds a PhD in economics from the Vienna University of Business and Economics and a master of arts in international relations from The Johns Hopkins University School of Advanced International Studies.

Komal Mohindra is a barrister and solicitor who has worked at the World Bank Group since 2008. Komal has provided technical assistance and training to governments around the world on a range of tax policy and tax administration issues, including transfer pricing. She represented the World Bank in policy discussions at multilateral global meetings, including at the Organisation for Economic Co-Operation and Development and the Global Forum for Transparency and Exchange of Information for Tax Purposes, and contributed on behalf of developing countries to G20 and G8 tax policies. Komal's current work focuses on innovation and entrepreneurship. Before joining the World Bank Group, Komal spent eight years working with the Toronto and London offices of a global firm, advising multinationals and other businesses on an array of corporate tax issues. Before that, she worked in the attorney-general's office.

Foreword

Multinational enterprises have been an important source of global innovation, growth, and government revenues. But, as the proportion of international trade taking place between members of multinational corporations grows, the scope for these companies to exploit differences between national tax systems and to reduce their tax bills also expands. Aggressive tax practices by multinationals undermine countries' tax bases and the fairness of tax systems. Transfer pricing, or rather, transfer mispricing, by multinationals is probably the most challenging global tax planning tool as highlighted during the Spring Meetings of the International Monetary Fund and World Bank Group earlier this year.[1]

The challenge of profit shifting through transfer mispricing is arguably even more pressing in developing economies because corporate tax tends to account for a larger share of their revenue. At the same time, concerns over double taxation stemming from aggressive and unilateral measures to counter mispricing are growing in the global business community and are particularly relevant for countries wanting to draw on global capital with an attractive business environment.

With the publication of *Transfer Pricing and Developing Economies*, the World Bank's Global Tax Team, housed in the Equitable Growth, Finance, and Institutions Vice Presidency, provides technical guidance on the main issues and ways for policy makers to protect their corporate tax bases from transfer mispricing. Building on a review of approaches to assess the magnitude of transfer mispricing risks and the formulation of a tailored transfer pricing policy, the book provides example-based guidance on the practical application of the arm's length principle, effective compliance management, and the development of requirements to disclose and document relevant information.

The authors provide compelling examples, illustrating that there are important short-term opportunities in catching up and introducing transfer pricing regimes tailored to country-specific risks. Importantly, however, transfer pricing, as part of wider efforts to improve tax systems in developing economies, is never just about raising more revenue. It is also about inclusive growth—promoting private sector development, improving the lives of the bottom 40 percent of the population, and thereby contributing to ending extreme poverty. Preventing double taxation, while ensuring that the playing field for business is not tilted away from domestic firms toward multinational companies, and ensuring that taxation fairly impacts wealthy and regular taxpayers alike, are important parts of the challenge before us. The handbook *Transfer Pricing and Developing Economies* adds to the tools at policy makers' and administrators' disposal to address this multifaceted challenge. It recognizes the importance of balancing revenue and investment climate objectives' and it discusses various domestic and international instruments and country experiences in avoiding and resolving transfer pricing disputes.

The book provides useful insight into understanding the challenges in different country situations and aims at providing lessons learned. It is noteworthy that the analysis draws on a range of operational engagements in the areas of tax policy and administration led by different practices in the World Bank Group, underscoring the importance of bringing together expertise across a broad range of topics to work effectively on international tax issues.

We hope that *Transfer Pricing and Developing Economies* will be of interest to policy makers and tax administrators, and researchers, as well as to development organizations looking for ways to support the implementation of effective transfer pricing regimes. We also invite readers to let us know how they think the World Bank Group and its development partners can further contribute to this important objective.

Note

1. See: Fiscal Forum. IMF and WBG Spring Meetings 2016, *Strengthening the International Tax System: Roundtable Discussion—Future of International Taxation*, April 17. Washington, DC: IMF. http://www.imf.org/external/POS_Meetings/SeminarDetails.aspx?SeminarId=128.

Jan Walliser
Vice President, Equitable Growth, Finance, & Institutions
World Bank Group

Introduction

Transfer Pricing and the Global Agenda to Mobilize Domestic Resources

Recent years have seen unprecedented public scrutiny over the tax practices of multinational enterprise (MNE) groups. Tax policy and administration concerning international transactions, aggressive tax planning, and tax avoidance have become an issue of extensive national and international debate in developed and developing economies alike. In this context, transfer pricing, historically a subject of limited specialist interest, has attained name recognition among a broader global audience that is concerned with equitable fiscal policy and sustainable development.

Abusive transfer pricing practices are considered to pose major risk to the direct tax base of many countries and developing economies, which are particularly vulnerable because corporate tax tends to account for a larger share of their revenue. There are short-term opportunities for countries to catch up and introduce common antiabuse provisions tailored to country-specific risks and an ever-increasing number of emerging and developing economies are following the example of Organisation for Economic Co-operation and Development (OECD) economies, which have introduced legislation specifically aimed at regulating transfer pricing for direct taxation purposes.

Transfer pricing is, however, only one of many priorities to strengthen domestic resource mobilization (DRM) as part of the post-2015 development agenda. Which areas matter most in addressing developing economies' financing needs for development, and whether and when an emphasis on international tax and transfer pricing is justified depends on country circumstances. This handbook therefore starts out by providing a high-level summary of issues to consider, including guidance on analytical steps that should be taken at the outset to understand a country's potential exposure to inappropriate transfer pricing, or rather "transfer mispricing" (discussed in chapter 1).

Where a focus on strengthening transfer pricing regimes is justified, it is important to manage expectations carefully. Building commensurate administrative capacity for transfer pricing is not a short-term endeavor. Country experience suggests that institution building for effective audit activities focused on transfer pricing takes a minimum of 3–5 years. To support and guide the capacity-building process, this handbook provides an outline of the main areas that require attention in the design and implementation of transfer pricing provisions. While a number of specific challenges and sector-specific dynamics are mentioned, the handbook does not offer detailed sectoral case studies. These will, however, be covered in separate sector-specific publications, such as the World Bank's reference guide on "Transfer Pricing in the African Mining Industry."

Transfer pricing regimes are often challenging to implement, in particular in countries where commensurate administrative capacity is yet to be developed. The development of such capacity for transfer pricing can be time consuming and resource intensive, and may be limited by various constraints. A lack of administrative capacity can lead to a disregard for the legislation, or, alternatively, may result in "innovative" and poorly targeted enforcement by the tax administration. The former may result in further erosion of the tax base, as a result of opportunistic investor behavior, or simply tax avoidance, or a bias toward risk aversion in countries with stronger administrative capacity. The latter can result in increased uncertainty, undermining investor confidence and it can raise transaction costs (for example, double taxation, penalties, or advisor fees). Recognizing the importance of transfer pricing regulation and administration for the business environment and investor confidence, this handbook aims to balance the general objective of protecting a country's tax base and raising additional revenue with investment climate considerations wherever appropriate.

The handbook is structured as follows: The first chapter provides a general overview on transfer pricing and the global policy debate. A discussion of the relevance of transfer pricing and the arm's length principle for developing economies is followed by a presentation of approaches to assess the magnitude of transfer mispricing risks, general preconditions for successfully implementing a regime, and a discussion of investment climate considerations.[1]

In the second chapter, we consider a broad range of aspects in countries' international legal framework relevant for transfer pricing. An overview of the key articles of tax treaties relevant to transfer pricing is followed by an introduction of the role of other relevant international sources, such as the OECD *Transfer Pricing Guidelines* and the UN *Practical Manual on Transfer Pricing for Developing Countries*. Subsequently, the third chapter is aimed at offering detailed guidance and country examples on drafting transfer pricing legislation for direct taxation purposes based on the arm's length principle. The chapter aims to touch on relevant aspects of the legislative process, including the formulation of a transfer pricing policy and the role and content of administrative guidance.

The practical application of the arm's length principle (comparability, transfer pricing methods, and the arm's length range concept) is presented in chapter 4 and followed in chapter 5 by a discussion of selected issues for specific transaction types or situations (intragroup services, financial transactions, intangibles, cost contribution arrangements, loss-making entities and start-up operations, business restructurings, location savings, government regulations, set-off arrangements, transfer pricing and customs valuation and value-added tax, and profit attribution to permanent establishments).

Promoting compliance among taxpayers through effective communication and outreach campaigns, and requirements to disclose and document transfer pricing-related information, is the focus of chapter 6. We examine the main issues to consider when introducing transfer pricing documentation rules and provide an overview of international and regional guidance as well as a range of country approaches to transfer pricing documentation requirements.

In chapter 7, different components of a successful dispute avoidance and resolution strategy are discussed. Various domestic and international instruments (advance pricing agreements and safe harbors) to help avoid disputes are discussed, and country experience with domestic appeals channels and the mutual agreement process are presented. Finally, chapter 8 discusses the necessary components to develop, implement, and continuously update an effective transfer pricing audit program.

This handbook is part of the wider World Bank Group engagement in supporting countries with domestic resource mobilization by protecting their tax base. It is complemented by the concurrently published reference guide, "Transfer Pricing in the African Mining Industry."

Note

1. The arm's length principle requires that transactions between associated parties should be consistent with those that would have prevailed between two independent parties in a comparable transaction under similar circumstances.

Abbreviations

AOA	Authorized OECD Approach
APA	Advance pricing agreement
ATAF	African Tax Administration Forum
ATO	Australian Taxation Office
BEPS	Base Erosion and Profit Shifting
CbC	Country-by-Country
CCA	Cost contribution arrangement
CCCTB	Common Consolidated Corporate Tax Base
CFC	Controlled Foreign Corporation
CFFR	Centre for Financial Reporting Reform
CUP	Comparable uncontrolled price
EBITDA	Earnings before interest, taxes, depreciation, and amortization
EU	European Union
EUJTF	European Union Joint Transfer Pricing Forum
EUJTPF	EU Joint Transfer Pricing Forum
FASB	Financial Accounting Standards Board
FDI	Foreign direct investment
FIE	Foreign Invested Enterprises
GATT	General Agreement on Tariffs and Trade
GDT	General Department of Taxation
IBFD	International Bureau of Fiscal Documentation
IFRS	International Financial Reporting Standards
IMF	International Monetary Fund
IRAS	Inland Revenue Authority of Singapore
ITL	Income Tax Law
KRA	Kenya Revenue Authority
LB&I	Large Business and International
LTO	Large Taxpayer Office
MAP	Mutual Agreement Procedure

MC	Model Conventions
MEMAP	Manual on Effective Mutual Agreement Procedures
MOU	Memorandum of understanding
OECD	Organisation for Economic Co-operation and Development
PATA	Pacific Association of Tax Administrators
PE	Permanent establishment
PITAA	Pacific Islands Tax Administrators Association
R&D	Research and development
RBA	Risk Based Assessment
SARS	South African Revenue Service
SGATAR	Study Group on Asian Tax Administration and Research
SME	Small and medium-size enterprises
TIEA	Tax Exchange of Information Agreements
TNMM	Transactional net margin method
TU	Taxable units
UN	United Nations
UNCTAD	United Nations Conference on Trade and Development
VAT	Value-added tax
WBG	World Bank Group

Transfer Pricing, Corporate Strategy, and the Investment Climate

The issue that has to be wrestled with is this: What is the fair price for those transactions, in particular (from the development perspective) when you bear in mind the real economic engagement of the multinational in a particular developing country, and where the multinational's profits are truly being made? If transfer pricing does not reflect the true profits earned in that country, the country is unfairly deprived of funds and opportunities for development. And, of course, it is ultimately the people of that country who bear the costs in food, water, health, and education, especially.

—Jomo Kwame Sundaram,
Assistant Secretary-General for Economic Development,
United Nations Department for Economic and Social Affairs, 2011

Globalization and trade liberalization, coupled with advances in information technology, have contributed to an increase in the number of enterprises expanding beyond their domestic markets. As a result, foreign direct investment (FDI) stocks and the number and size of multinational enterprise (MNE) groups have continued to increase. In 2000, the United Nations Conference on Trade and Development (UNCTAD) estimated that there were 63,000 parent firms with 690,000 foreign affiliates (UNCTAD 2000). By the end of 2007, UNCTAD estimated that there were 79,000 parent firms with 790,000 foreign affiliates (UNCTAD 2008).

This growth in FDI stocks and the number and size of MNE groups has not been limited to developed economies. There has been a general increase in south-south FDI flows. In 2014, their share in global FDI increased to 35 percent of total FDI (UNCTAD 2015). Of the 790,000 foreign affiliates estimated to have existed at the end of 2007, more than half were in developing economies (UNCTAD 2008). Imports and exports of merchandise and services have also continued to rise in both developed and developing economies.

What Is Transfer Pricing?

Upon entering a new market, an enterprise generally faces various options regarding the form the new business activity will take. These options include direct exportation, establishment of a local representative office or branch, and establishment or acquisition of a subsidiary that is wholly or substantially owned and controlled.

When an MNE group establishes itself in a new market by incorporating or acquiring a local subsidiary or establishing a branch, the local subsidiary or branch generally engages in transactions with other members of the group (see figure 1.1). As a result, a significant portion of international trade now takes place between members of MNE groups.[1]

As a result of the common ownership, management, and control relationships that exist among members of an MNE group, their transactions are not fully subject to many of the market forces that would have been at play had the transactions taken place among wholly independent parties. The prices charged—known as *transfer prices*—may be intentionally manipulated or set

Figure 1.1 Transactions within Multinational Enterprise Groups

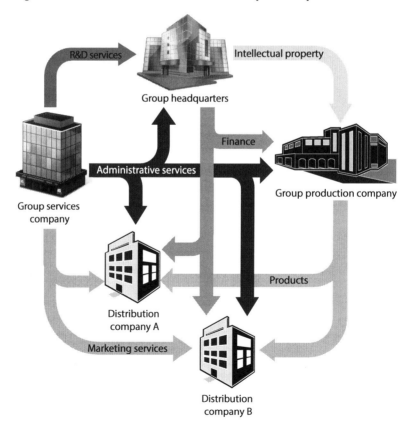

in a way that has the unintentional consequence of being unacceptable to external stakeholders.

This phenomenon is not limited to transactions within MNE groups. It also occurs in transactions between other parties—such as family members or companies and their substantial shareholders—whose relationship may allow them to influence the conditions of the transaction.

Transactions between parties whose relationship may allow them to influence the conditions of the transaction—associated parties—can involve the provision of property or services, the use of assets (including intangibles), and the provision of finance, all of which need to be priced. A range of regulatory and nonregulatory factors can influence the determination of transfer prices.

Transfer pricing is a neutral concept that simply refers to the determination of transfer prices for transactions between associated parties. As pointed out by the Tax Justice Network, "[t]ransfer pricing is not, in itself, illegal or abusive. What is illegal or abusive is transfer mispricing, also known as transfer pricing manipulation or abusive transfer pricing."[2]

Transfer mispricing arises as a result of abusive or inappropriate transfer pricing practices. Abusive practices include situations in which transfer prices are intentionally manipulated to achieve certain outcomes. Inappropriate practices include situations in which the parties unintentionally use transfer prices that external stakeholders find unacceptable because, for example, they are inconsistent with applicable laws, regulations, standards, or relevant commercial practices.

How and Why Are Transfer Prices Determined?

How transfer prices are determined is essential for defining the corporate tax base (direct taxation), but it can also be important for a range of other regulatory and nonregulatory purposes, including the following:

- Taxes and duties (for example, value-added tax [VAT], customs duties, mining royalties, and petroleum resource taxes)
- Corporate laws (for example, directors' duties and protection of minority shareholders)
- Contractual requirements (for example, investment contracts)
- Statutory accounting requirements
- Foreign exchange controls
- Management accounting
- Internal performance management and evaluation
- Employee profit sharing requirements
- Competition law
- Official trade statistics

From an accounting perspective, "transfer pricing is considered as a part of the management control system of the company with two main objectives: the promotion of goal congruence and the provision of a suitable system of performance measurement and evaluation" (Cools 2003, 136). Transfer prices must be determined so managers can measure the profitability of divisions, product lines, and subsidiaries and thus evaluate performance. Transfer pricing can thus serve as an important behavioral tool for motivating and evaluating the performance of managers, influencing behavior, and promoting goal congruence.

The determination of appropriate transfer prices is also often required for subsidiaries to prepare stand-alone statutory accounts to meet local reporting requirements. Although standards or methodologies for determining these transfer prices may or may not be provided for under local, generally accepted accounting principles, the value of associated party transactions will typically require separate disclosure in the notes to the accounts, as may any uncertain tax positions related to them (see box 1.1).

Regulation of transfer pricing for tax purposes generally involves the prescription of standards or methodologies, which must be complied with when determining transfer prices. Direct tax transfer pricing regulations, for example, usually require that transfer prices for transactions between associated enterprises be determined in accordance with the arm's-length principle. Noncompliance with these regulations will often result in adjustments to the tax liability and the imposition of penalties and interest.

Cools (2003, 139) found that "because of the real threat of audits and penalties, the tax requirements of transfer pricing play a prominent role in the

---

Box 1.1　Selected Accounting Disclosures Related to Transfer Pricing

International Accounting Standard 24: Related Party Disclosures

18. If an entity has had related party transactions during the periods covered by the financial statements, it shall disclose the nature of the related party relationship as well as information about those transactions and outstanding balances, including commitments, necessary for users to understand the potential effect of the relationship on the financial statements…

23. Disclosures that related party transactions were made on terms equivalent to those that prevail in arm's-length transactions are made only if such terms can be substantiated.

Financial Accounting Standards Board (FASB) Interpretation No. 48 (FASB ASC 740-1), Accounting for Uncertainty in Income Taxes (United States)

FIN 48 is an interpretation of FASB Statement 109, Accounting for Income Taxes, that prescribes a recognition threshold and measurement attribute for the financial statement recognition and measurement of a tax position taken or expected to be taken in a tax return.

6. An enterprise shall initially recognize the financial statement effects of a tax position when it is more likely than not, based on the technical merits, that the position will be sustained upon examination.

The definition of tax position encompasses positions taken for tax purposes with respect to transfer pricing.

Figure 1.2 The Role of Transfer Pricing in Corporate Strategy

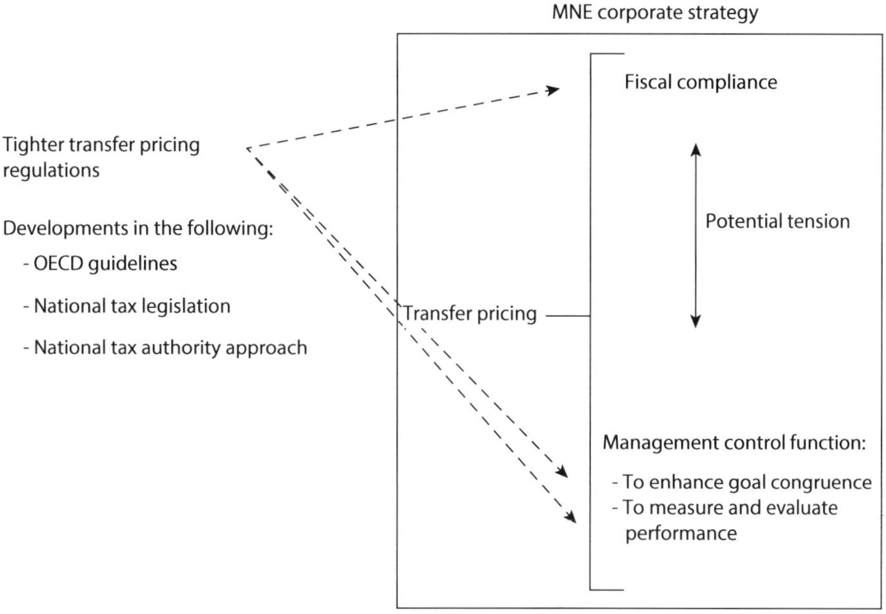

Source: Cools 2003.
Note: MNE = multinational enterprise; OECD = Organisation for Economic Co-operation and Development.

MNE's decision-making process" (see figure 1.2). As an increasing number of countries introduce transfer pricing legislation and increase audit capacity, this trend will only increase.

Regulation of transfer prices for customs purposes (i.e., determination of customs values) and VAT purposes generally involves the prescription of specific standards or methodologies that must be complied with. However, these standards or methodologies generally differ from those prescribed for direct tax purposes and have a narrower scope of application (see chapter 5).

In addition to taxes and duties, foreign exchange controls, contractual requirements, and other regulations and administrative practices can have a substantial impact on the determination of transfer prices.

As a result of the different regulatory and nonregulatory factors that can influence the determination of transfer prices, MNE groups sometimes face conflicting requirements. Although congruence is theoretically desirable, transfer prices may be recorded or reported for different purposes.

Transfer Mispricing

In the absence of clear regulatory requirements (or in situations in which the benefits of not complying with such requirements outweigh the potential costs), associated parties may have incentives to engage in transfer mispricing. The incentives to engage in transfer mispricing can be grouped under two broad headings (see table 1.1).

Table 1.1 Possible Incentives to Engage in Transfer Mispricing

Incentive	Example
Maximize the present value of the group's overall profits	• Reduce tax liabilities by taking advantage of differences in national tax rates.
	• Reduce customs duties on imports and exports.
	• Avoid profit remittance or foreign exchange restrictions; avoid withholding taxes on dividends or royalties.
	• Engage in exchange rate speculation to move profits from a devaluing currency into a stronger one.
	• Reduce profits of an entity that must be shared with minority (or state) shareholders.
Minimize the present and future risks of uncertainty regarding the value of profits	• Minimize the exposure of the firm's profits to governmental threats of expropriation or trade union activism.
	• Reduce apparent profitability of a subsidiary to deter competitors from entering the subsidiary's market.

Source: Based on Muchlinksi 2007 (p. 269), citing Lall 1980.

Regulation of Transfer Pricing for Direct Taxation Purposes

Over the past two decades, transfer pricing has become one of the most important international tax issues faced by MNE groups operating in developed, transition, and developing economies. To ensure that their tax policy is not undermined, an increasing number of countries have introduced transfer pricing legislation for direct taxation purposes and increased the resources allocated to building the capacity of their tax administrations. During the period 1994–2014, the number of countries with "effective" transfer pricing documentation rules increased from four to more than 80 (see figure 1.3).[3]

This trend continues with many developed and developing economies introducing comprehensive transfer pricing legislation, amending existing legislation, investing in tax administration resources, and introducing or updating compliance requirements.

Transfer pricing is of critical importance for direct tax purposes since transfer prices directly affect the allocation of profits and losses to resident enterprises upon which most countries levy a form of direct taxation (i.e., corporate income tax or profits tax). The transfer pricing practices of taxpayers can therefore have a direct impact on a country's tax base. For example, transfer prices for imported goods or services that are overstated can result in understatement of the local enterprise's taxable income. Transfer prices for exported goods or services that are understated can result in an understatement of the local enterprise's taxable income. The opposite effects are observed for the enterprise in the other country. Where the effective tax rates of the countries involved differ significantly, associated parties may have an incentive to determine their transfer prices in a way that allocates profits to the lower tax jurisdiction, reducing the overall worldwide tax liability (see table 1.2). Even if a country has a low tax rate, in the absence of appropriate transfer pricing

Figure 1.3 Timeline of Effective Transfer Pricing Documentation Rules, 1994–2014

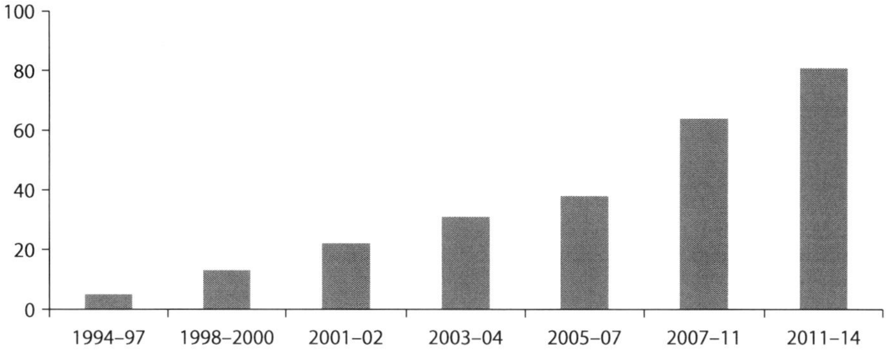

Source: Based on Oosterhoff 2008 and PwC 2014.

Table 1.2 Impact of Transfer Prices on Worldwide Tax Liability of a Multinational Enterprise Group and on the Allocation of Tax Revenues Between Countries

	Country A	Country B	
	Tax rate 30%	Tax rate 10%	Group Total
Scenario 1: transfer price of 1,000			
Sales	1,000	1,400	1,400
Cost of goods sold	(600)	(1,000)	(600)
Other expenses	(300)	(200)	(500)
Profit	100	200	300
Tax	(30)	(20)	**(50)**
Scenario 2: transfer price of 1,100			
Sales	1,100	1,400	1,400
Cost of goods sold	(600)	(1,100)	(600)
Other expenses	(300)	(200)	(500)
Profit	200	100	300
Tax	(60)	(10)	**(70)**

legislation and commensurate administrative capacity, transfer mispricing may result in significant tax revenues being foregone.

To protect its tax base from being eroded through transfer mispricing, a country needs to have appropriate transfer pricing legislation and take steps to ensure that it is effectively administered. The threat of a transfer pricing audit and a resulting transfer pricing adjustment, along with the possible imposition of interest and penalties, can go a long way toward discouraging taxpayers from engaging in transfer mispricing and toward promoting awareness and resulting self-compliance.

Country experience and various studies suggest that the introduction of a transfer pricing regime can play a significant role in reducing profit shifting. Lohse and Riedel's (2012, 15) analysis of profit shifting by MNE groups and the evolution of transfer pricing requirements in Europe suggests that "transfer price documentation rules are instrumental in limiting income shifting activities." Beer and Loeprick (2015) investigate the drivers of global profit shifting, showing that both intangible asset endowment and complexity of a particular MNE group's supply chain determine a subsidiary's reported profits' sensitivity to the corporate income tax rate differential with the rest of the MNE group. They also find the introduction of transfer pricing documentation rules has significant mitigation effects, reducing the estimated profit shifting on average by 52 percent two years after the rules are introduced (see figure 1.4).

In response to the introduction of transfer pricing legislation or an increase in administrative capacity in a country, MNE groups may adjust their transfer pricing policies, increasing their reported profits in the country in question to lower their tax risk profile. This phenomenon may have spillover effects on the tax bases of trading partner countries that have not yet introduced transfer pricing legislation or begun building administrative capacity.

Although the focus of most countries' transfer pricing regimes is on international transactions, transfer mispricing with respect to domestic transactions can also undermine the effectiveness of a country's tax system, particularly if

Figure 1.4 Mitigation Effect of Transfer Pricing Documentation Requirements

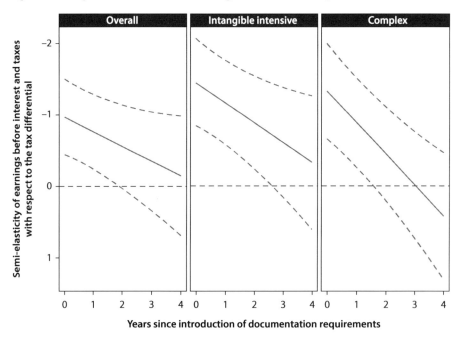

Years since introduction of documentation requirements

Source: Beer and Loeprick 2015.
Note: Mitigation effect for selected groups. This figure illustrates the estimated elasticity of taxable profits with respect to the tax differential as a function of the presence of documentation requirements. The first panel shows the effect of documentation requirements for the whole sample. The second (third) panel present the effect for intangible intensive (highly complex) subsidiaries with an average level of complexity (intangible intensity). The solid line is the expected value. The dashed lines are 95 percent confidence intervals.

taxpayers are subject to differential treatment. Examples in which domestic transfer mispricing may undermine the operation of a country's domestic tax system include the following:

- An enterprise that is subject to tax may make excessive payments for goods or services to a taxpayer that benefits from a tax exemption or lower tax rate.
- An enterprise may stream income to or reinvoice transactions through taxpayers benefiting from an exemption or lower tax rate.
- An enterprise may provide (noncommercial) interest-free loans or other benefits to a controlling shareholder.
- Property may be disposed of at values that are too high or too low to benefit from preferential tax rates, capital gains tax discounts, or accelerated capital allowances.
- An enterprise may make excessive payments for goods and services related to specific incentives (such as R&D incentives) to inflate its claim.

Regulation of domestic transfer prices may be necessary in some countries, while in other countries it may impose a significant, and possibly disproportionate, compliance burden on taxpayers. An Organisation for Economic Co-operation and Development (OECD) survey of member and nonmember countries found that in 26 out of 41 respondent countries, domestic transactions were subject to the arm's-length principle (OECD 2012a). In contrast, international transactions were subject to the arm's-length principle in all 41 countries. Many of the countries that subject domestic transactions to the arm's-length principle (the Russian Federation and Slovenia, for example) regulate only specific domestic transactions, such as those with enterprises located in special economic zones or where the aggregate value of such transactions exceeds a specified minimum threshold. Many countries do not have general legislation governing the pricing of domestic associated party transitions, relying instead on targeted rules to counter specific areas of risk (see chapter 3).

Many developing economies still lack effective transfer pricing regimes, typically due to inappropriate transfer pricing legislation and insufficient administrative capacity to effectively implement international tax provisions. These countries may thus be losing significant tax revenues as a result of both intentional and unintentional transfer mispricing (see box 1.2). Statistics reported by the tax administrations of countries with recently established transfer pricing regimes also provide insight into the important sums that are potentially involved.[4]

Of great concern to developing economies and the countries that provide aid to them is the use of transfer mispricing and fictitious transactions to shift profits to low tax jurisdictions or jurisdictions with relatively lax reporting requirements. Crevelli, De Mooij, and Keen (2015) demonstrate the importance of base spillovers in low- and middle-income countries (LMICs). Their findings suggest that revenue losses through avoidance activities associated with tax havens are larger for non-OECD countries than for OECD member states. Since 2008, increased international attention has been paid and an effort made to improve the transparency of and the exchange of information with tax havens.

Box 1.2 Estimates of Revenue Lost to Developing Economies as a Result of Transfer Mispricing

Several nongovernmental organizations (NGOs) have tried to quantify the tax revenues foregone by developing economies from transfer mispricing. However, as discussed in Fuest and Riedel (2010), the measurement approaches used in these studies have drawbacks that make the results difficult to interpret.

- Christian Aid estimates that capital flows from trade mispricing into the European Union (EU) and the United States from non-EU countries during the period 2005–07 exceeded US$1 trillion and that taxing these capital flows at current rates would have raised about US$121.8 billion a year in additional tax revenues (Christian Aid 2009).
- Oxfam estimates tax revenue losses from the shifting of corporate profits out of developing economies at about US$50 billion a year (Oxfam 2000).

The increased reporting requirements and enhanced data collection and management procedures within tax administrations associated with the introduction of a substantive transfer pricing regime will help provide tax administrations with the tools and data necessary to fulfill their exchange of information obligations, helping in the global fight against tax evasion. Moreover, the increase in the quantity and quality of information collected on international transactions and increased scrutiny of these transactions may also put countries in a better position to curb illicit flows of capital (greater scrutiny and monitoring of international transactions can assist in the prevention and detection of trade-based money laundering activities, for example).

The introduction of a transfer pricing regime based on generally accepted international principles and practices can also provide investors with increased certainty regarding the treatment of associated party transactions, thereby reducing their financial risk.[5] Legislation based on the arm's-length principle should also help to ensure fair competition through the equitable treatment of domestic and foreign investors. Finally, the adoption of legislation based on generally accepted international principles and practices can improve a country's ability to influence the development of international transfer pricing and intervene on behalf of local enterprises to protect them from unjustified transfer pricing adjustments by other countries and the resulting double (or unexpected) taxation that may arise.

Costs and Benefits of Regulating Transfer Pricing

The introduction or reform of a transfer pricing regime will require policy makers to assess its budgetary impact and

- Estimate potential tax revenues
- Consider the impact on the collection of customs duties

- Estimate the costs of implementation and ongoing administration
- Consider the potential impact on the investment climate

Tax Revenue Impact

In countries where little or no attention has been paid to transfer pricing, incidences of transfer mispricing may have resulted in lost tax revenues that are unlikely to be recoverable. However, the introduction and effective administration of a transfer pricing regime can assist in reestablishing and securing the tax base for future years. In countries where transfer pricing legislation is already in place but is not being effectively administered, an increase in administrative capacity may provide opportunities for the recovery of tax revenues previously foregone.

As a result of the introduction and administration of transfer pricing legislation, increased tax revenues may arise from a combination of enforcement activities and self-compliance. For example, of the ¥10.272 billion (about US$1.5 billion) reported as collected in 2010 as a result of the State Administration of Taxation's (China) transfer pricing approach, ¥7.268 billion (about US$1.1 billion) was attributable to administration (mainly voluntary adjustments)—far more than the ¥2.3 billion (about US$0.35 billion) attributable to investigations (PwC 2011b).

In addition to Beer and Loeprick's (2015) finding that transfer pricing documentation rules play a significant role in mitigating observable profit shifting, country experiences suggest that the introduction and administration of transfer pricing legislation based on the arm's-length principle can result in significant revenue collection (see box 1.3).

Box 1.3 Examples of Revenue Collection from Transfer Pricing Regulation in Selected Countries

China: China's tax authority, the State Administration of Taxation, is reported to have collected an additional ¥10.272 billion (about US$1.5 billion) as a result of its approach toward transfer pricing issues (PwC 2011b).

Hungary: The National Tax and Customs Administration has reported that an additional €370 million of tax difference was revealed due to transfer pricing audits during 2006–10 (see figure B1.3.1).

India: In India, reports indicate that about US$15.42 billion of transfer pricing adjustments were made during the period 2008–12 (Kapur 2012).

United Kingdom: In the United Kingdom, Her Majesty's Revenue and Customs reports transfer pricing yields of £519 million in 2007/08; £1,595 million in 2008/09; £1,039 million in 2009/10; and, £436 million in 2010/11, with fluctuations in annual yields primarily reflecting the small number of very large cases (HMRC 2011).

box continues next page

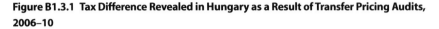

Box 1.3 Examples of Revenue Collection from Transfer Pricing Regulation in Selected Countries
(continued)

Figure B1.3.1 Tax Difference Revealed in Hungary as a Result of Transfer Pricing Audits, 2006–10

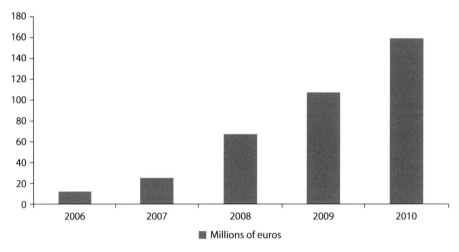

Source: Lanyfalvi 2012 (based on statistics from the National Tax and Customs Administration of Hungary).

The impact that transfer pricing legislation and administration may have on a country's tax revenues is often difficult (or impossible) to measure. In the absence of comprehensive reporting requirements for transfer pricing, the data required to derive detailed estimates are typically not available. It may, however, be possible to ascertain an indication of the revenue potentially at risk and identify the most problematic sectors by examining the composition of the country's tax base and other related macroeconomic data, such as foreign direct investment (FDI) stocks, the presence of MNE groups, and the extent of cross-border trade (see table 1.3). The more detailed and comprehensive the data that are available, the more sophisticated an analysis can be conducted.

Effect on Customs Revenues

Although the revenue raised from trade taxes has declined significantly since 1980, and will most likely continue to do so with further liberalization, trade taxes remain an important source of revenue for many developing economies. In Sub-Saharan Africa, for example, trade taxes still account for one-quarter of tax revenues (IMF 2011).

The introduction of a transfer pricing regime may affect customs revenue, since increased scrutiny of the prices local entities pay for goods acquired from associated parties will likely motivate MNE groups to revise their transfer pricing practices. If the net result of these revisions is a decrease in the prices actually paid by the local enterprises, resulting decreases in customs duties (where the transaction price method of customs valuation is applicable) may, to some extent, offset increases in income tax collections, as the example in box 1.4 shows.

Table 1.3 Data for Assessing a Country's Transfer Pricing Exposure

Data	Use	Possible source(s)
Taxpayer-specific data		
Economic activity (industry code or similar)	Compare taxpayer profitability with industry norms to identify outliers.	• Tax filings (such as tax returns, withholding tax returns) • Companies' register • Financial accounts
Resident versus permanent establishment	Identify transfer pricing issues versus profit attribution issues.	• Tax filings
Part of an MNE group (foreign-owned/controlled or foreign subsidiaries)	Identify taxpayers likely to be involved in associated party transactions and allow for comparisons between these taxpayers and independent taxpayers.	• Tax filings • Companies' register • Financial accounts
Location of related parties	Identify multinational enterprises with related parties in offshore financial centers or low tax jurisdictions, in which the incentive to engage in transfer mispricing may be increased.	• Tax filings • Companies' register • Financial accounts
Gross profit	Calculate financial indicators (gross margin, operating margin, net margin) to compare and quantify potential exposure.	• Tax filings • Financial accounts
Net profit (or loss)	Calculate financial indicators to compare and identify persistent loss-making taxpayers.	• Tax filings • Financial accounts
Interest income and expense	Calculate financial indicators and interest cover ratios (net profit + interest paid/payable)/(interest paid/payable) to identify tax-thin capitalization issues.	• Tax filings • Financial accounts
Interest paid/payable to nonresidents	Excessive interest payments to nonresidents can significantly erode a country's tax base, especially where such payments are fully deductible and are subject to low (or no) withholding tax rates. One indicator of thin capitalization or non–arm's-length interest payments is the interest coverage ratio of a company, which indicates the factor by which the earnings of the company exceed the interest payments made to service its debt. The lower the ratio, the greater the risk that the entity will not be able to meet its interest payment obligations out of current income. A ratio of 1 or less indicates that the entity has not generated sufficient profits to cover its interest expense for the period.	• Tax filings • Financial accounts • Foreign exchange control declarations
Services fees paid/payable to nonresidents	Payments for intragroup services, such as management services, administrative services, consulting services, and technical services, are generally deductible and subject to reduced or no withholding tax rates where an income tax treaty applies. The risk to a country's tax base arising from non–arm's-length service payments is generally considered to be high, since the provision of services can be difficult to document.	• Tax filings • Financial accounts • Central bank data
Royalties paid/payable to nonresidents	Non–arm's-length royalty payments to nonresidents can erode a country's tax base, particularly where such payments are deductible and subject to reduced or no withholding tax rates. As a result, non–arm's-length royalty payments are often identified by tax administrations as an area of concern.	• Tax filings • Financial accounts • Central bank data

table continues next page

Table 1.3 **Data for Assessing a Country's Transfer Pricing Exposure** *(continued)*

Data	Use	Possible source(s)
Details (type and amount) of associated party transactions	Details of taxpayers' associated party transactions provide an indication of the volume and type of transactions that may be potentially mispriced. Such information can also play an important role in risk-based assessment (see chapter 8); as a result, numerous countries have introduced requirements for taxpayers to disclose this information on an annual basis (see chapter 6).	• Tax filings • Financial accounts • Customs declarations • Central bank data
Macroeconomic/tax system data		
Cross-border trade statistics	Identify a country's key industries, country trading partners, level of cross-border trade, and any anomalies and potential risks (for example, high volumes of trade with low tax jurisdictions).	• National statistics office • Customs data • Central bank data • UNCTADstat
Number of multinational enterprise taxpayers	Assess resourcing requirements for tax administration.	• National statistics office • Companies' register • Tax filings • Development agency • Proprietary databases
Major sources and destination of FDI	Identify potential risks (for example, high volumes of FDI from or to low tax jurisdictions).	• National statistics office • UNCTADstat • Companies' register • Tax filings • Development agency • Proprietary databases
Existence of tax-free zones and special regimes	Mispricing of domestic transactions can pose a significant risk to a country's tax base when disparities in the treatment of resident taxpayers exist (as a result of tax exemptions and tax holidays, for example).	• Domestic legislation
Existence and rate of withholding taxes	Can reduce net revenue leakage from transfer mispricing.	• Domestic legislation • Bilateral tax treaties

Note: FDI = foreign direct investment; MNE = multinational enterprise.

Box 1.4   Effect of Change in Prices on Direct Tax Revenues and Customs Revenues

Where the transfer prices for imported goods are decreased to comply with the arm's-length principle, a decrease in the customs value (if the transaction value method is used) can be more than offset by the increase in direct tax revenues, provided that the direct tax rate is higher than the applicable customs rate of duty. The following example in figure B1.4.1 illustrates a scenario where the decrease in transfer price from scenario A to scenario B results in a reduction in customs duties collected. This revenue impact is more than offset by the significant increase in direct tax revenues. The net revenue impact for the country of import of the reduction in the transfer price of the imported goods is positive.

box continues next page

Box 1.4 Effect of Change in Prices on Direct Tax Revenues and Customs Revenues *(continued)*

Figure B1.4.1 Net Revenue Impact of Decreased Transfer Price for Imported Goods

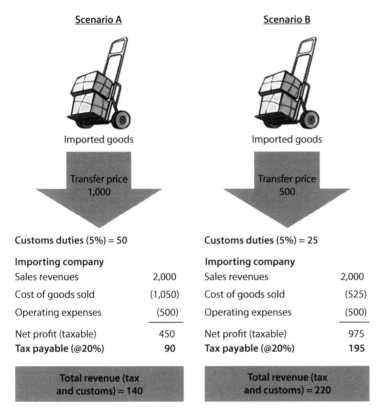

Scenario A		Scenario B	
Imported goods		Imported goods	
Transfer price 1,000		Transfer price 500	
Customs duties (5%) = 50		**Customs duties (5%) = 25**	
Importing company		**Importing company**	
Sales revenues	2,000	Sales revenues	2,000
Cost of goods sold	(1,050)	Cost of goods sold	(525)
Operating expenses	(500)	Operating expenses	(500)
Net profit (taxable)	450	Net profit (taxable)	975
Tax payable (@20%)	**90**	**Tax payable (@20%)**	**195**
Total revenue (tax and customs) = 140		**Total revenue (tax and customs) = 220**	

Where corporate tax rates are higher than customs rates of duty for the applicable goods, the revenue impact of a decrease in the transfer prices will generally be positive.

Despite the potential for reduced customs revenues, the introduction of a transfer pricing regime and the accompanying capacity building within the tax administration may provide incidental benefits in relation to customs administration. For example, greater scrutiny and understanding of associated party transactions may help tax administrations identify misclassifications of goods and services. More accurate customs values will also provide policy makers with more reliable trade statistics upon which to base economic forecasts. Ensuring an understanding of the relationship between direct taxation and customs revenues can also underscore the importance of information sharing between customs and direct taxation authorities. A clear protocol according to which customs authorities are automatically informed about a price adjustment made by the tax authorities and vice versa can be helpful.

Transfer Pricing and Developing Economies • http://dx.doi.org/10.1596/978-1-4648-0969-9

Net Benefits of Revising Transfer Pricing Laws and Regulations

Although the required investment in resources to effectively implement a transfer pricing regime may be significant and its direct revenue impact hard to quantify, the benefits of implementing a suitably tailored transfer pricing regime (i.e., tax revenues and investor-friendly framework) are likely to exceed total costs in most countries.

In addition to the drafting and implementation of the necessary laws and regulations, substantial capacity-building activities will be required within the tax administration, the ministry of finance, and the judiciary. Information technology upgrades, subscriptions to databases, and the introduction of e-filing may also be required to ensure efficient and effective administration (the suggested preconditions for transfer pricing reform are discussed in the next section). In this regard, policy makers need to ensure that the resources required for the efficient and effective administration of the transfer pricing regime are, or will be, available. The sequencing of transfer pricing reforms thus requires careful consideration.

Preconditions for Transfer Pricing Reform

To successfully implement and administer a transfer pricing regime that achieves the dual objective of protecting a country's tax base while maintaining an attractive investment climate, policy makers must try to ensure that certain preconditions are in place before a program of transfer pricing reform is commenced (see box 1.5).

Box 1.5 Basic Preconditions for Transfer Pricing Reform

Macroeconomic Context

- *Relevant foreign direct investment.* Important or growing FDI levels with significant involvement of MNEs in the economy
- *Substantial levels of cross-border trade*

Legal Preconditions

- *Accounting requirements.* Requirements for companies to maintain financial accounts in place
- *Comprehensive tax laws.* Profits, income taxes, or other taxes for which the revenues collected may be impacted by transfer mispricing, such as mining royalties based on sales
- *Open market economy.* Open to FDI with no or limited restrictions on import and export transactions

box continues next page

Box 1.5 Basic Preconditions for Transfer Pricing Reform *(continued)*

- *Dispute resolution mechanisms.* Taxpayer access to efficient and equitable dispute resolution procedures, including courts and appeals
- *Implementation of tax treaties.* Where applicable, implementation of key concepts into domestic law and procedures for dispute resolution in place

Administrative Preconditions

- *Relevant audit experience.* Experience with auditing multinational enterprise taxpayers
- *Availability of human resources.* Sufficient number of auditors available and willing to undergo specialist training on transfer pricing
- *Effective tax return filing and data processing*
- *Language abilities.* To monitor international developments

Source: Based on PwC 2011b and OECD 2011.

Approaches to Transfer Pricing Regulation

The primary objective of transfer pricing legislation is to provide the tax administration with the legal and administrative tools needed to protect the country's tax base. However, to attract foreign investment and international trade, protection of the tax base must be balanced by investment climate considerations. For example, the Australian Treasury (2011, iv.) stated in a consultation paper on proposed changes to Australia's transfer pricing rules that while "[t]ransfer pricing rules are designed to make sure Australia receives an appropriate share of tax from multinational firms… [a]n impor-tant consideration in designing these rules is that they should not unreason-ably inhibit Australia's attractiveness as a destination for new investment and business activity".

To meet this dual objective, an increasing number of countries have introduced transfer pricing legislation based on the arm's-length principle (see figure 1.5) in the belief that this approach should reduce instances of double taxation and prevent MNE groups from having to manage contrasting compliance obligations and associated costs.

The theoretical alternative to the arm's-length principle for addressing the allocation of profits between members of an MNE group is global formulary apportionment. Although several countries have experience with the use of formulary apportionment at the subnational level,[6] there have been no successful attempts to date to introduce it at the international level. The EU has recently relaunched[7] an initiative to introduce a Common Consolidated Corporate Tax Base (CCCTB) for the European internal market. This is the first of five high-lighted areas in the EU's 2015 Action Plan[8] on a fair and efficient corporate tax system in Europe.

Figure 1.5 Timing of Introduction of the Arm's-Length Principle in Selected Countries

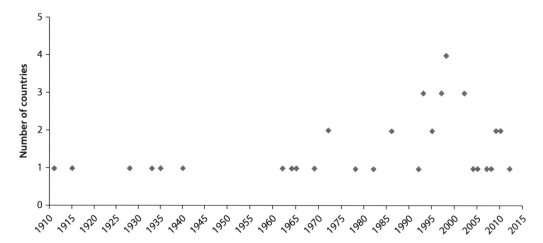

Source: OECD 2012a.
Note: Countries: Argentina, Australia, Austria, Belgium, Canada, Chile, China, Colombia, the Czech Republic, Denmark, Estonia, Finland, France, Germany, Hungary, India, Indonesia, Ireland, Israel, Italy, Japan, Luxembourg, Malaysia, Mexico, the Netherlands, New Zealand, Norway, Poland, Portugal, the Russian Federation, Singapore, the Slovak Republic, Slovenia, the Republic of Korea, Spain, South Africa, Sweden, Switzerland, Turkey, the United Kingdom, and the United States.

The Arm's-Length Principle: The Current International Consensus and Developments under the G20/OECD's Base Erosion and Profit Shifting Initiative

The arm's-length principle requires that transactions between associated parties should be consistent with those that would have prevailed between two independent parties in a comparable transaction under similar circumstances. This principle has been adopted, in one way or another, by all countries that have introduced transfer pricing regimes to date. The principle can be expressed and applied in various ways.[9] The most common expression is found in Article 9(1) of the OECD Model Tax Convention (2010) and Article 9(1) of the UN Model Tax Convention (2011), which both read as follows

> …where conditions are made or imposed between the two enterprises in their commercial or financial relations which differ from those which would be made between independent enterprises, then any profits which would, but for those conditions, have accrued to one of the enterprises, but, by reason of those conditions, have not so accrued, may be included in the profits of that enterprise and taxed accordingly.

Articles equivalent to Article 9(1) of the OECD and UN Model Tax Conventions are found in almost all comprehensive tax treaties currently in force.

In almost all countries that have introduced transfer pricing legislation on the basis of the arm's-length principle, the principle is applied by reference comparing the conditions in the associated party transactions under examination with conditions in comparable transactions between independent parties. (Brazil is one notable exception, as discussed in chapter 3.)

Notably, however, the implementation of the arm's-length principle has been vulnerable to manipulation as a result of the overemphasis on the contractual allocation of functions, assets, and risks. Actions 8, 9, and 10 in the G20/OECD Base Erosion and Profit Shifting (BEPS)[10] project were therefore focused on revising the OECD transfer pricing guidelines, focusing on problem areas such as transactions involving intangibles, allocation of risk, or profit allocation in contexts lacking a commercially viable rationale. The agreed revision of the guidelines emphasizes the need for a careful delineation of transactions, thus comparing contractual with actual conduct when reviewing transfer pricing arrangements (see discussion in chapter 4). In the case of intangibles, the result is that legal ownership alone should not necessarily generate a right to the return from the exploitation of an asset. Remuneration within a group will be based on the actual contribution by group members. Similarly, risks that are assumed by a party that cannot meaningfully control these risks or bear their financial consequences may be reallocated to a party that does or can; a clarification that is aimed at addressing excess profits being allocated to "cash boxes." Moreover, additional guidance on commodities and low-value-adding services is being developed in the context of the G20 developing working group.[11]

Global Formulary Apportionment: A Valid Alternative to the Arm's-Length Principle?

Global formulary apportionment refers to the distribution of profits between countries on the basis of a predetermined formula. Rather than regulating the determination of transfer prices on the basis of economic principles, global formulary apportionment requires that the worldwide profits of an MNE group be aggregated and apportioned between the jurisdictions in which it operates.

Proponents of global formulary apportionment commonly make reference to a formula based on sales, payroll, and property taxes. They favor formulary apportionment because it is simple and objective, removes incentives or possibilities for transfer mispricing, and does not rely on the identification of comparable information.

Irrespective of its theoretical merits, it is clear that the introduction of global formulary apportionment presents numerous practical difficulties, political[12] and otherwise. First, introduction of global formulary apportionment would require agreement by a significant proportion of countries regarding the appropriate formula,[13] the definition of a "unitary business" (for which profits should be aggregated), the basis on which profits are calculated (i.e., common accounting standards), the functional currency to be used, and other issues.

In addition to these challenges, international law obligations arising from tax treaties that include the arm's-length principle may pose a further barrier to implementation. If an agreement on these issues can be reached, implementation into domestic law would then be required by a critical mass of countries. Adoption by only a small number of countries would result in increased incidences of economic double taxation or less than singular taxation for MNE groups with operations in the countries that have adopted formulary apportionment, because profits taxed under global formulary apportionment in one country would likely be subject to the arm's-length principle in other jurisdictions and vice versa (see box 1.6).

Box 1.6 The Potential for Double Taxation if Conflicting Approaches Are Adopted

When conflicting approaches to transfer pricing are adopted by countries it will result in the inconsistent allocation of an MNE group's profits between the group members. This may give rise to economic double taxation or less than single taxation. For example, if country A adopts the arm's-length principle and country B adopts global formulary apportionment, the sum of the profits allocated to company A and company B may exceed their actual aggregate profit, giving rise to economic double taxation (see figure B1.6.1). Alternatively, if country A adopts the arm's-length principle and country B adopts global formulary apportionment, the sum of the profits allocated to company A and company B may be less than their actual aggregate profit, giving rise to less than single taxation (see figure B1.6.2).

Figure B1.6.1 Economic Double Taxation Arising from Conflicting Approaches

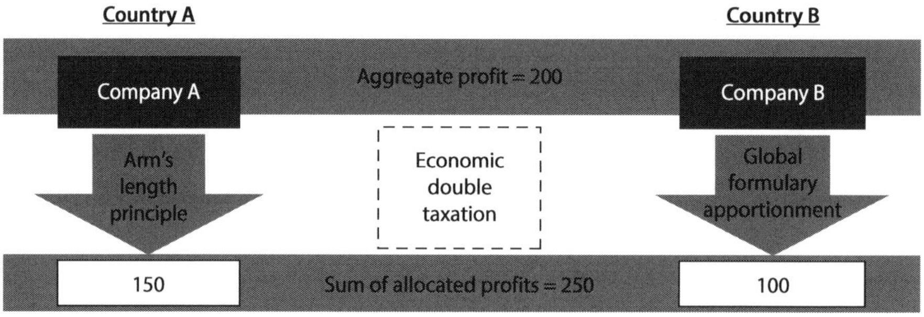

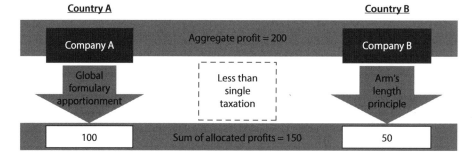

Figure B1.6.2 Less than Single Taxation Arising from Conflicting Approaches

If not relieved, economic double taxation imposes an additional transaction cost on MNE groups, hindering international trade and foreign investment. In addition, MNE groups that must apply two different approaches will face increased compliance costs.

Because of the various practical difficulties associated with the adoption of global formulary apportionment—in particular, the potential for significant incidences of double taxation or less than single taxation and the lack of consensus as to the detail—formulary apportionment has not yet been adopted at the international level for tax purposes. As a result, adoption of global formulary apportionment is likely not a realistic short- or medium-term option for developing economies, particularly as unilateral adoption by a country (or a handful of countries) would negatively affect a country's investment climate.

Is the Arm's-Length Principle Suitable for Developing Economies?
The aim of transfer pricing legislation based on the arm's-length principle is to ensure that the conditions of transactions between associated parties are not distorted by their relationship so as to adversely affect the determination of the relevant taxable base. In this regard, the arm's-length principle is a neutral concept that does not, in theory, favor developed or developing economies. In practice, however, it is often argued that developing economies are at a disadvantage in relation to developed countries because of the difficulties they face in implementing the principle. Difficulties typically arise due to a combination of capacity and informational constraints. Administrators in more developed economies may face the same challenges of incomplete or asymmetric information, but often have a more refined set of policy and administrative tools to address these challenges. It is worth noting that, as discussed in the remainder of this toolkit, access powers, reporting obligations, and audit regulation need to be well specified to meet the tax administrators' needs when administering transfer pricing legislation.

Whilst basing a country's transfer pricing legislation on the arm's-length principle has both advantages and disadvantages (see table 1.4), for the majority of countries, developed or developing, the practical difficulties associated with the implementation of the arm's-length principle will generally be significantly outweighed by the advantages of adopting the arm's-length principle, provided that the legislation is tailored to a country's specific circumstances; appropriate resources are made available to develop the capacity of the tax authorities; and enforcement activities target the sectors and transaction that pose the greatest risks. This is particularly the case given the current absence of a practical and realistic alternative.

Mitigating the Investment Climate Impact

Before introducing a new transfer pricing regime, policy makers should ensure that they understand the private sector's concerns. Reasonable concerns should be taken into account in the drafting and implementation process.

Table 1.4 Selected Advantages and Disadvantages of the Arm's-Length Principle for Transfer Pricing

Advantages	Disadvantages
• Provides the tax administration with the necessary legal basis to protect the tax base.	• Relies heavily on (comparable) information, which may not exist or be readily available.
• Reduces instances of economic double taxation.	• Results in the imposition of a significant administrative burden on the tax authorities.
• Creates a level playing field among associated and independent enterprises, foreign and domestic enterprises, and countries (limiting the potential for enterprises to obtain a competitive advantage through transfer mispricing).	• Results in the imposition of a significant compliance burden on taxpayers.
• Aligns with commitments a country may have made under international law (as a result of tax treaties in force that contain an Article 9 equivalent, for example; see chapter 2).	• Requires discretion by the tax administration, which if not properly controlled may provide opportunities for corruption or result in the imposition of unnecessary compliance costs.
• Reduces uncertainty for taxpayers and tax administrations, both of which can draw on an extensive body of internationally accepted principles and practices (see section "Approaches to Transfer Pricing Regulation").	• May result in some uncertainty for taxpayers and the tax administration with respect to the treatment of particular transactions and circumstances.
• Puts a country in a position to influence future developments in international transfer pricing and protect the interests of resident taxpayers in discussions with other tax authorities	• May require adjustments to uncontrolled transactions to improve comparability, which can be complex and somewhat arbitrary.
	• Use of one-sided methods may not take into account network profits and economies of scale.
• Reduces (global) compliance costs for MNE groups, which need to comply with only one approach to transfer pricing, making it more likely that they do so on a global or regional basis.	• Requires significant investment in capacity building within the tax authority.
	• Many developing economies have a limited number of tax treaties in force (which provide the legal basis for ensuring relief from economic double taxation).

Transfer pricing is currently one of the most important tax issues MNE groups face (see box 1.7). This is not surprising given the vast sums of money often involved, the potential for economic double taxation, and for the imposition of substantial penalties and interest. High compliance costs are often associated with preparing transfer pricing documentation and managing related investigations and inquiries, moreover MNEs are increasingly concerned about potential reputational risk associated with scrutiny over transfer pricing practices by civil society, and the financial impact of accounting requirements to book liabilities for certain uncertain tax positions.

Transfer pricing legislation is often associated with double taxation, high compliance costs, increased discretion for tax administrations and, as a result, heightened levels of uncertainty for taxpayers, all of which can have a negative effect on a country's investment climate. However, if appropriate steps are taken to address these issues when designing a country's transfer pricing regime, adverse effects can be limited—a well-designed regime may even be viewed favorably by current and potential investors because of the increased certainty it provides.

Practices that can help limit or avoid any adverse effects on the investment climate include the following:

- Adopting generally accepted international principles and practices;
- Engaging and communicating with private enterprises;

Box 1.7 Results of Ernst & Young's 2010 Global Transfer Pricing Survey

According to Ernst & Young's 2010 Global Transfer Pricing Survey, on the basis of interviews with 877 multinational enterprises in 25 countries, tax directors view transfer pricing as the most important tax issues they face, with 74 percent viewing it as very important or absolutely critical.

Figure B1.7.1 Most Important Tax Issues for Tax Directors (Parents), 2010

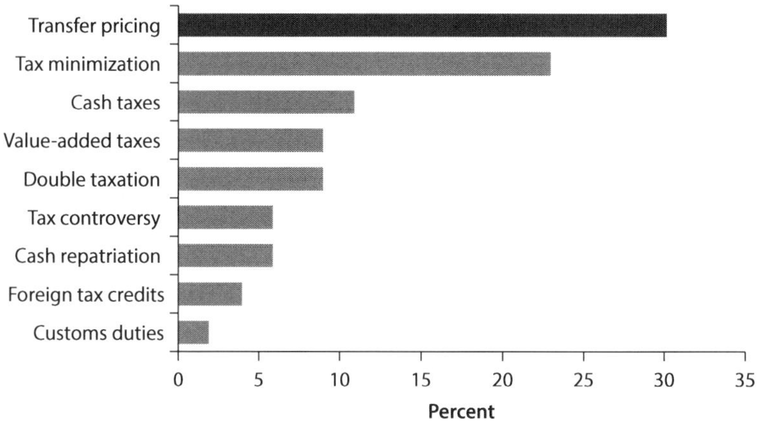

Table B1.7.1 Importance of Transfer Pricing in the Next Two Years (Parents), 2007 and 2010

percent

	2007	2010
Absolutely critical	29	32
Very important	45	42
Fairly important	18	21
Not very important	5	4
Not at all important	1	1

Source: Ernst & Young 2010.

- Limiting instances of unrelieved economic double taxation;
- Ensuring that the compliance burden imposed is not disproportionate or unreasonable;
- Providing access to effective and equitable dispute avoidance and resolution mechanisms;
- Ensuring that tax administration staff are adequately trained; and
- Ensuring that the law is applied consistently, minimizing uncertainty.

Adopting Generally Accepted International Principles and Practices

To limit instances of economic double economic taxation and to best achieve the dual objective of protecting their tax bases while maintaining attractive investment climates, most countries base their transfer pricing legislation on the arm's-length principle. Numerous international organizations and regional bodies have published general or specific guidance on transfer pricing and related topics (or are in the process of doing so), which can provide useful guidance for policy makers, tax administrations, and taxpayers alike.[14]

The OECD has published comprehensive transfer pricing guidelines. The *OECD Transfer Pricing Guidelines for Multinational Enterprises and Tax Administrations* (2010),[15] which were first published in 1979 and substantially revised and updated in 1995, provide detailed practical guidance regarding application of the arm's-length principle. The OECD transfer pricing guidelines are specifically referred to in the commentary for both the OECD Model Tax Convention on Income and Capital (2010)[16] and the United Nations Model Double Taxation Convention between Developed and Developing Countries (2011).[17] The basic principles elaborated in the OECD guidelines form the basis of almost all developed and developing economies' transfer pricing regimes. Numerous countries explicitly refer to them in their legislation or supporting administrative documents (see chapters 2 and 3).

Reference to generally accepted international principles helps reduce uncertainty by providing both taxpayers and the tax administration with a body of established knowledge and experience on which to draw. Adoption of internationally accepted principles may also signal to current and future investors that the country is adopting conventional approaches to foreign investment, thus having a positive effect on the country's investment climate.

Engaging and Communicating with the Private Sector

A strategic approach to communication and public consultation plays an important role in easing private enterprises' concerns regarding the introduction of a transfer pricing regime. It should be integrated into a reform project from the outset.[18] Introducing transfer pricing regulation as part of a wider investment climate reform package may also help ease private enterprises' concerns, ideally resulting in a focus on the positive aspects of the overall reform package rather than the increased compliance obligations that the introduction of a transfer pricing regime requires.

Limiting Instances of Unrelieved Economic Double Taxation

Economic double taxation refers to the inclusion of the same income in the taxable bases of two different taxpayers. In the context of transfer pricing, economic double taxation may result from a transfer pricing adjustment by one tax administration for which a corresponding adjustment is not granted in part or in full by the other (see figure 1.6) or as a result of a mismatch between two countries' transfer pricing regimes. If not relieved, economic

Figure 1.6 Economic Double Taxation Resulting from a Transfer Pricing Adjustment

To see how changes in transfer pricing can result in double taxation, consider the following example.

- A manufacturing company in country A manufactures goods that it sells to its associated distribution subsidiary in country B for 500

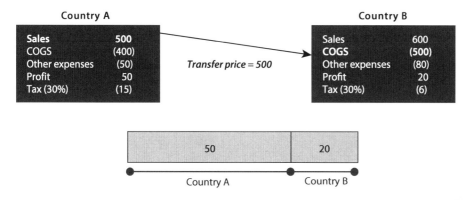

- Following a transfer pricing audit by country B's tax authority, the taxable profit of the distribution company is increased to 50, reflecting the tax authority's assessment that the transfer price for the goods should have been 470, as opposed to the 500 used

- If the tax authority of country A does not agree with the transfer pricing adjustment made by the tax authority in country B and therefore does not reduce the taxable profits of the company in country A accordingly, the group will be taxed in aggregate as if it made total profits of 100, despite only actually making total profits of 70. As a result, 30 of income/profits will be subject to economic double taxation.

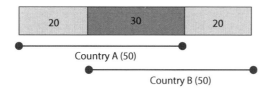

double taxation imposes an additional transactional cost on MNE groups, which hampers international trade and foreign investment. In this regard, the European Commission has stated that "[d]ouble taxation is one of the most onerous obstacles to international economic activity, with detrimental effects on efficiency and growth" (EC 2011).

Transfer Pricing and Developing Economies • http://dx.doi.org/10.1596/978-1-4648-0969-9

The Mutual Agreement Procedure (MAP) in tax treaties provides a mechanism for the relief of double taxation. However, few tax treaties require that countries eliminate economic double taxation unless an agreement can be reached as to the appropriate application of the arm's-length principle to the case. As a result, despite the apparent protections afforded by the applicable tax treaties, taxpayers can end up bearing the cost of economic double taxation. This problem can be serious. Ernst & Young's 2003 Global Transfer Pricing Survey reports that 40 percent of transfer pricing adjustments resulted in economic double taxation. Given that many developing economies have limited treaty networks or no treaties at all, relief from economic double taxation may not be available.

To reduce incidences of unrelieved economic double taxation, policy makers should ensure that appropriate processes are in place within the tax administration before implementing transfer pricing adjustments; that the tax administration is appropriately trained; and that taxpayers have access to effective and equitable dispute resolution procedures, including the MAP provided for under any tax treaties the country has signed. Where treaties do not exist, policy makers could also consider negotiating them with major trading partners. This will, however, require a careful assessment of the wider cost and benefits of giving up any taxing rights in a treaty (see chapter 2).

In the context of the BEPS process, the OECD developed a minimum standard with respect to dispute resolution mechanisms focusing on the access and effective implementation of the MAP process (Action 14).[19] A number of countries have also indicated a commitment to provide for mandatory binding MAP arbitration in their treaties to ensure a timely resolution of disputes. At the same time, several countries expressed skepticism with respect to mandatory binding arbitration.[20]

Ensuring That the Compliance Burden Imposed Is Not Disproportionate or Unreasonable

Transfer pricing documentation can be costly and time consuming for MNE groups to prepare and maintain. A 2011 survey by Deloitte conducted for the European Commission, for example, estimated that transfer pricing compliance costs (transfer pricing documentation, clearances and rulings, and MAPs) directly or indirectly account for about 60 percent of all corporate tax-related compliance costs for a new subsidiary in the EU of an MNE with a large parent (European Commission 2011).

Differing documentation requirements by different countries risk imposing an unnecessary compliance burden. As the International Chamber of Commerce notes, "Transfer pricing documentation requirements continue to spread from country to country… Unfortunately, the natural result of separate and uncoordinated national policies is ever-increasing and divergent documentation requirements and, in consequence, an inappropriate and unnecessary compliance burden on [multinational enterprises]" (ICC 2008).

Because of the somewhat subjective nature of the arm's-length principle, transfer pricing reviews and audits can also create significant compliance costs for MNEs, especially when the tax administration's lack of capacity leads to unnecessarily protracted disputes or the imposition of unreasonable transfer pricing adjustments.

To address the concerns of MNE groups, policy makers need to ensure that (a) taxpayers and transactions that pose the highest risk to revenue are targeted; (b) transfer pricing documentation and disclosure requirements do not impose informational requirements on taxpayers that exceed the needs and capacity of the tax administration or differ unnecessarily from the approaches adopted by their major trading partners; and (c) the tax administration is equipped to deal with transfer pricing issues effectively, efficiently, and consistently.

Following common standards for transfer pricing documentation, obligations can help address some of the concerns on compliance costs and burdens imposed on business. The agreement in the OECD's BEPS process on several core elements for the implementation of transfer pricing documentation (and country-by-country reporting), relying on a master and local file that will be prepared by MNEs for local tax administrations, is therefore a useful reference point (see chapter 6).[21]

Moreover, the introduction of simplification measures can play a role in limiting the compliance burden on taxpayers and the administrative burden on the tax administration. In this regard, an increasing number of countries have adopted measures that represent a compromise between the country's need to protect the tax base and the compliance burden imposed on taxpayers. Such measures generally relate to specific transactions types (for example, low-value-adding services or small loans) or specific classes of taxpayer (for example, small and medium enterprises[22]). They generally provide certainty regarding treatment or exemption from the rules. However, given that such measures are usually unilateral, they often do not provide protection against economic double taxation and may even provide possibilities for less than single taxation. The design of the measures is therefore of critical importance. The risk of double taxation linked to safe harbors, for instance, can be mitigated by adopting arm's-length ratios or prices, and by ensuring they are within scope of the MAP (see chapter 7). The concept of bilateral safe harbors also seeks to address this potential challenge (OECD 2012b).

Providing Access to Effective and Equitable Dispute Resolution Mechanisms

Transfer pricing disputes can involve vast sums of money and be extremely resource intensive for both tax administrations and taxpayers, particularly as it is not uncommon for the process to extend over multiple years. It is therefore important that effective and equitable dispute avoidance and resolution mechanisms be in place. At a minimum, appropriate domestic mechanisms should be in place (such as appeals procedures) and accessible. Given the international context of transfer pricing, where applicable, processes should also be in place to provide taxpayers with access to international dispute resolution procedures, such as the MAP provided for in tax treaties (see chapter 7).

Ensuring Tax Administration Staff Are Adequately Trained

The importance of the tax administration in limiting any adverse impacts on a country's investment climate when undertaking transfer pricing reform cannot be overestimated. A country's transfer pricing legislation can be appropriately designed to minimize the compliance burden, provide a level of certainty, and limit instances of unrelieved economic double taxation. However, this can be completely undermined by poor administration. For example, inconsistent and overly aggressive administration may increase uncertainty and compliance costs for taxpayers and result in instances of unrelieved economic double taxation. On the other hand, ineffective administration may result in decreased tax revenues, if, for example, MNEs assess the tax administrations' capabilities as lacking and adjust their transfer pricing policies accordingly.

To prevent these undesirable outcomes from occurring, tax administrations need to engage in substantial capacity building and develop appropriate administrative policies and procedures before a transfer pricing regime is introduced. Capacity building should encompass training on transfer pricing and related international tax issues (including tax treaties); soft skills; and, where necessary, English-language courses.

Moreover, administrations routinely invest in ongoing capacity-building activities to ensure that staff can address and stay up to date with local and international developments and, critically, that staff turnover can be addressed by training new generations of experts. High demand for transfer pricing expertise makes the latter component a crucial ingredient for long-term sustainability.

Ensuring That the Law Is Applied Consistently and Uncertainty Is Minimized

With discretion comes uncertainty. For a country that focuses on transfer pricing for the first time, this uncertainty will likely be exacerbated by the tax administration's limited experience. The adoption and consistent application of generally accepted international principles and practices helps limit uncertainty, as does the timely issuance by the tax administration of advice and guidance on general and specific transfer pricing matters, such as administrative bulletins, practice statements, or practical guidelines.

To provide the highest level of certainty for both the tax administration and taxpayers regarding the treatment of particular transactions or a group of transactions, the development of an advance pricing agreement (APA) program may be considered. The timing for introducing such a program will, however, require careful consideration to best allocate resources and avoid a situation in which wide-reaching agreements are concluded when the necessary administrative capacity is still being developed.

Chapter 1 Main Messages

- A substantial portion of international trade now takes place between members of MNE groups, the prices charged between them—known as transfer prices—may be intentionally manipulated or set in a way that has the unintentional consequence of being unacceptable to external stakeholders. Transfer mispricing may result in significant tax revenues being foregone.
- Over the past two decades, transfer pricing has become one of the most important international tax issues faced by MNE groups operating in developed, transition, and developing economies.
- How transfer prices are determined is essential for defining the corporate tax base, but it can also be important for a range of other regulatory and nonregulatory purposes.
- To protect its tax base from being eroded through transfer mispricing, a country needs to have in place appropriate transfer pricing legislation and must take steps to ensure that it is effectively administered.
- Country experiences suggest that the introduction and administration of transfer pricing legislation based on the arm's-length principle can result in substantial revenue collection. Increased tax revenues may arise from a combination of enforcement activities and self-compliance.
- Transfer pricing legislation is often associated with double taxation, high compliance costs, increased discretion for tax administrations (and, as a result, heightened levels of uncertainty for taxpayers), all of which can have a negative effect on a country's investment climate. If appropriate steps are taken to address these issues when designing a country's transfer pricing regime, adverse effects can be mitigated.
- There are several preconditions for a program of transfer pricing reform to be initiated, but the benefits of implementing a suitably tailored transfer pricing regime are likely to exceed total costs in most countries.

Notes

1. UNCTAD (1999) provides an estimate of one-third for the share of intra-firm trade in international trade. Forstater (2015) clarified that common references to a share of up to 60 percent of global trade taking place within Multinationals (Neighbour 2002) are based on a misunderstanding of UNCTAD's report from 1999.

2. See Tax Justice Network, "Transfer Pricing," at http://www.taxjustice.net/cms/front _content.php?idcat=139.

3. "Effective" indicates that the country has specific legislation, regulations, or other guidance that, at a minimum, strongly suggest that transfer pricing documentation should be in place.

4. In Vietnam, for example, transfer pricing adjustments made by the tax administration by end of 2013 accounted for US$110 million; the Kenya Revenue Authority collected US$85 million in additional tax revenues in 2013 from transfer pricing. See also box 1.4.

5. At an informal meeting on practical transfer pricing issues in June 2011 (UN 2011), an advisor to Chile's Internal Revenue Service noted that the private sector supported

the tax administration in sensitizing the Parliament to pass the transfer pricing law. The World Bank Group's Global Tax Team made similar observations during public consultations on transfer pricing in Albania.

6. Canada, Switzerland, and the United States have applied various forms of formulary apportionment to the allocation of profits between provinces, cantons, and states (Mayer 2009).

7. Relaunch of the Common Consolidated Corporate Tax Base (CCCTB). http:// ec.europa.eu/taxation_customs/common/consultations/tax/relaunch_ccctb_en.htm.

8. Communication from the Commission to the European Parliament and the Council. http://ec.europa.eu/taxation_customs/resources/documents/taxation/company_tax /fairer_corporate_taxation/com_2015_302_en.pdf.

9. Numerous countries' transfer pricing legislation uses terms such as "market price" or "fair market value." When used in a similar context, these terms are generally interpreted as equivalent, or similar, to the arm's-length principle. However, it should be noted that the terms "market price" and "fair market value" as used in financial valuations, etc. are concepts that differ from the arm's-length principle.

10. The G20/OECD project on base erosion and profit shifting (BEPS) was launched in 2013 to address a range of challenges in the international corporate tax system. The outcomes of the two year process were presented in a number of reports released in October 2015. The relevant measures proposed in the BEPS project are referenced throughout this handbook. See: http://www.oecd.org/tax/beps/beps-actions.htm

11. See BEPS 2015 Final Reports: http://www.oecd.org/ctp/beps-2015-final-reports.htm.

12. The political difficulties of adopting formulary apportionment at the international level are particularly evident in the EU, in which a policy for the introduction of a common consolidated tax base was first proposed in 2001. For further information, see http://ec.europa.eu/taxation_customs/taxation/company_tax/common_tax _base/index_en.htm.

13. Where the relative gain for many developing and emerging economies would likely depend on the weight placed on employment. See also IMF (2014).

14. For an overview of the transfer pricing activities of international organizations, financial institutions, and regional tax authorities' groupings' as of October 2012, see United Nations' Committee of Experts on International Cooperation in Tax Matters, "Secretariat Note: Transfer Pricing: Technical Assistance and Capacity Building Resources," October 11, 2012.

15. The current version of the guidelines was issued in 2010. Revisions are being finalized as part of the BEPS process. Unless specified otherwise, references to the OECD transfer pricing guidelines are to the 2010 version.

16. Unless specified otherwise, references to the OECD Model are to the 2010 version.

17. Unless specified otherwise, references to the UN Model are to the 2011 version.

18. For guidance on using strategic communication to engage stakeholders in tax reform generally, see Rahman (2010).

19. See Final Report on Action 14. "Making Dispute Resolution Mechanisms More Effective," October 2015. http://www.oecd.org/tax/making-dispute-resolution -mechanisms-more-effective-action-14-2015-final-report-9789264241633-en.htm.

20. This skepticism may be linked to negative experience with other investor-state arbitration, costs related to the process, and is a particular concern when administrators do not (yet) have the same experience to bring to negotiations with treaty partners and

where they perceive a risk that panels could be biased toward the views of capital exporters.

21. See Final Report on Action 13. "Transfer Pricing Documentation and Country-by -Country Reporting," October 2015.

22. The EU Joint Transfer Pricing Forum is particularly engaged in work on simplification. In 2011, it published recommendations concerning SMEs (http://ec.europa.eu /taxation_customs/resources/documents/taxation/company_tax/transfer_pricing /forum/jtpf/2011/jtpf_001_final_2011_en.pdf) and on low-value-adding services in 2010 (http://ec.europa.eu/taxation_customs/resources/documents/taxation /company_tax/transfer_pricing/forum/jtpf/2010/jtpf_020_rev3_2009.pdf). With regard to low-value-adding services the BEPS final report on Action 8-10 includes a simplified approach for low-value-adding services as well (http://www.oecd.org/tax /aligning-transfer-pricing-outcomes-with-value-creation-actions-8-10-2015-final -reports-9789264241244-en.htm).

Bibliography

Australian Treasury. 2011. "Income Tax: Cross Border Profit Allocation: Review of Transfer Pricing Rule." Consultation Paper, November. http://www.treasury.gov.au/~/media /Treasury/Consultations%20and%20Reviews/Consultations/2011/Transfer%20 Pricing%20Rules/Key%20Documents/PDF/Review_of_transfer_pricing_rules _CP.ashx.

Beer, S., and J. Loeprick. 2015. "Profit Shifting: Drivers of Transfer (Mis) Pricing and the Potential of Countermeasures." *International Tax and Public Finance* 22 (3): 426–51.

Casanegra de Jantscher, M. 1990. "Administering the VAT." In *Value-Added Taxation in Developing Countries*, edited by M. Gillis, C. S. Shoup, and G. Sicat, 171–79. Washington, DC: World Bank.

Christian Aid. 2009. *False Profits: Robbing the Poor to Keep the Rich Tax-Free*. London: Christian Aid. http://www.christianaid.org.uk/Images/false-profits.pdf.

Cools, M. 2003. "Increased Transfer Pricing Regulations: What about the Managerial Role of Transfer Pricing?" *International Transfer Pricing Journal* 10 (4): 134–40.

Crevelli, E., R. De Mooij, and M. Keen. 2015. "Base Erosion, Profit Shifting and Developing Countries." IMF Working Paper, WP/15/118.

Ernst & Young. 2003. *Global Transfer Pricing 2003 Global Survey 2003*. London: Ernst & Young. http://webapp01.ey.com.pl/EYP/WEB/eycom_download.nsf/resources/Transfer %20Pricing%20Survey%20Report_2003.pdf/$FILE/Transfer%20Pricing%20 Survey%20Report_2003.pdf.

Ernst & Young. 2010. *Global Transfer Pricing Survey–Addressing the Challenges of Globalization*. London: Ernst & Young. http://www.ey.com/Publication/vwLUAssets/Global_transfer _pricing_survey_-_2010/$FILE/2010-Globaltransferpricingsurvey_17Jan.pdf.

European Commission. 2011. *Impact Assessment: Accompanying Document to the Proposal for a Council Directive on a Common Consolidated Corporate Tax Base*. (CCCTB). http://eur-lex.europa.eu/LexUriServ/LexUriServ.do?uri=SEC:2011:0315:FIN :EN:PDF.

Forstater, M. "Can Stopping 'Tax Dodging' by Multinational Enterprises Close the Gap in Development Finance?" CGD Policy Paper 069. Washington, DC: Center for Global Development.

Fuest, C., and N. Riedel. 2010. *Tax Evasion and Tax Avoidance in Developing Countries: The Role of International Profit Shifting.* Oxford, U.K.: Oxford University Centre for Business Taxation.

Gurría, A. 2008. "The Global Dodgers." *Guardian*, November 26. http://www.guardian.co.uk/commentisfree/2008/nov/27/comment-aid-development-tax-havens.

HMRC (Her Majesty's Revenue and Customs). Internal Manual—International Manual. http://www.hmrc.gov.uk/manuals/intmanual/intm410000.htm.

———. 2011. *Transfer Pricing Statistics.* http://www.hmrc.gov.uk/international/transfer-pricingtransfer pricing-stats.pdf.

ICC (International Chamber of Commerce). 2008. *Transfer Pricing Documentation Model.* ICC. Paris. http://www.iccwbo.org/Data/Policies/2008/Transfer-PricingTransferpricing-Documentation-Model/.

IMF (International Monetary Fund). 2011. *Revenue Mobilization in Developing Countries.* Washington, DC: IMF. http://www.imf.org/external/np/pp/eng/2011/030811.pdf.

———. 2014. "Spillovers in International Corporate Taxation." Technical report, IMF, Washington, DC. http://www.imf.org/external/np/pp/eng/2014/050914.pdf.

Kapur, A. 2012. "Indian Transfer Pricing System." Presentation, Helsinki, May 13. http://www.taxjustice.net/cms/upload/pdf/Anita_Kapur_1206_Helsinki_ppt.pdf.

Lanyfalvi, S. 2012. "Transfer Pricing Compliance Management: Establishing and Strengthening- Gradual Implementation in Hungary." Presentation at International Tax Dialogue Conference "Transfer Pricing in ECA—Protecting the Tax Base and Building a Strong Investment Climate," Tirana, Albania, May 30 to June 1. http://www.itdweb.org/documents/Conferences/AlbaniaConference/Presentations/6a2_Transfer_Pricing_Hungary.pdf.

Lohse, T., and N. Riedel. 2012. "The Impact of Transfer Pricing Regulations on Profit Shifting Within European Multinationals." FZID Discussion Papers, No. 61–2012. Hohenheim, Germany.

Mayer, S. 2009. "Formulary Apportionment for the Internal Market." IBFD Doctoral Series 17. International Bureau of Fiscal Documentation, Amsterdam.

Muchlinksi, P. T. 2007. *Multinational Enterprises and the Law.* 2nd ed. Oxford, U.K.: Oxford University Press.

Neighbour, J. 2002. "Transfer Pricing: Keeping It at Arm's-Length." *OECD Observer.* http://www.oecdobserver.org/news/fullstory.php/aid/670/Transfer_pricing:_Keeping_it_at_arms_length.html.

OECD (Organisation for Economic Co-operation and Development). 2010. *OECD Transfer Pricing Guidelines for Multinational Enterprises and Tax Administrations.* Paris: OECD.

———. 2011. *Transfer Pricing Legislation: A Suggested Approach.* Paris: OECD. http://www.oecd.org/dataoecd/41/6/45765682.pdf.

———. 2012a. *Multi-country Analysis of Existing Transfer Pricing Simplification Measures.* Paris: Centre for Tax Policy and Administration, OECD.

———. 2012b. *Discussion Draft: Proposed Revision of the Section on Safe Harbours in Chapter IV of the OECD Transfer Pricing Guidelines and Draft Sample Memoranda of Understanding for Competent Authorities to Establish Bilateral Safe Harbours.* Paris: Centre for Tax Policy and Administration, OECD.

———. 2013. "Transfer Pricing: Progress and Next Steps (Session V, 4th Plenary Meeting OECD Task Force on Tax and Development." Seoul, October 30–31. http://www .oecd.org/ctp/tax-global/tf-on-td-sess-five-transferpricing.pdf.

Oosterhoff, D. 2008. "Global Transfer Pricing Trends." *International Transfer Pricing Journal* 15 (3): 119–25.

Oxfam. 2000. *Tax Havens: Releasing the Hidden Billions for Poverty Eradication*. Oxford, U.K.: Oxfam. http://www.taxjustice.net/cms/upload/pdf/oxfam_paper_-_final_version__06 _00.pdf.

PwC (PricewaterhouseCoopers). 2011a. *Pricing Knowledge Network: Focusing on the Impact of Major Intercompany Pricing Issues*. London: PricewaterhouseCoopers. http:// www.pwchk.com/webmedia/doc/634396822810797099_cn_tp_enforcement _apr2011.pdf.

———. 2011b. *Transfer Pricing and Developing Countries: Final Report*. London: PricewaterhouseCoopers. http://ec.europa.eu/europeaid/what/economic-support /documents/transfer-pricingtransferpricing-study_en.pdf.

———. 2014. "International Transfer Pricing." Transfer Pricing Requirements around the World. London: PricewaterhouseCoopers http://www.pwc.com/gx/en/services/tax /transfer-pricing/international-transfer-pricing-2013-14.html.

Rahman, S. 2010. *Using Strategic Communications to Engage Stakeholders in Tax Reform*. Washington, DC: World Bank. https://www.wbginvestmentclimate.org/uploads /Inpractice%20Communications.pdf.

UN (United Nations). 2011. *Informal Meeting on Practical Transfer Pricing Issues for Developing Countries*. New York: UN. http://www.un.org/esa/ffd/tax/2011_TP/2011 _TP-Report_Meeting7-8June.pdf.

UNCTAD (United Nations Conference on Trade and Development). 1999. *World Investment Report 1999: Foreign Direct Investment and the Challenge of Development*. New York and Geneva: UNCTAD. http://www.unctad.org/en/docs/wir1999_en.pdf.

———. 2000. *World Investment Report 2000: Cross-Border Mergers and Acquisitions*. New York and Geneva: UNCTAD. http://www.unctad.org/en/docs/wir2000_en.pdf.

———. 2008. *World Investment Report 2008: Transnational Corporations and the Infrastructure Challenge*. New York and Geneva: UNCTAD. http://www.unctad.org /en/docs/wir2008_en.pdf.

———. 2015. *World Investment Report 2015: Reforming International Investment Governance*. New York and Geneva: UNCTAD. http://unctad.org/en/PublicationsLibrary/wir2015 _en.pdf.

———. n.d. *Statistics*. New York and Geneva: UNCTAD. http://www.unctad.org /Templates/Page.asp?intItemID=1584 &lang=1.

The International Legal Framework

> International tax law is a term of art used to indicate a set of rules that affect the tax treatment of cross-border operations. This set of rules is constituted primarily by domestic tax rules, whose application is generally limited by double tax treaties and other international law instruments.
>
> *—Finnerty and others 2007*

While transfer pricing issues can, and do, arise in a purely domestic context, transfer pricing is predominately an international tax matter. Therefore, when considering the design, implementation, and application of a country's transfer pricing regime, it is important to refer to the relevant international legal framework. This chapter considers a range of aspects of the international legal framework. It starts by providing an overview of the key articles of tax treaties relevant to transfer pricing and then introduces the role of other relevant international sources, such as the *OECD Transfer Pricing Guidelines* and the *UN Practical Transfer Pricing Manual for Developing Countries*.

Tax Treaties

Tax treaties aim to prevent double taxation by clearly allocating taxation rights. For example, treaties usually impose a maximum tax rate for the most mobile investment income (investment income, dividends, and royalties) on the source state. Tax treaties often also contain Articles formalizing information exchange obligations and procedures for administrative assistance for the collection of taxes. Such articles, where included, are typically aimed at mitigating tax evasion. The impact of treaties thus depends on the details of each agreement and the envisaged division of taxation rights. While tax treaties may contribute to investment and growth by reducing risks of double taxation and providing certainty to investors, they restrict states' rights to tax foreign investors and foreign-owned companies, and may thus also lead to important tax revenue losses.

Most current comprehensive tax treaties are based on the current (2010) or an earlier version of the Organisation for Economic Co-operation and Development (OECD) Model Tax Convention on Income and on Capital[1] or the current (2011) or an earlier version of the UN Model Double Tax Convention between Developed and Developing Countries,[2] or a combination thereof. Both models contain articles important to international transfer pricing: Article 9 (Associated Enterprises), Article 25 (Mutual Agreement Procedure), and Article 26 (Exchange of Information). Other articles in the models refer to the arm's-length principle and are therefore also relevant to transfer pricing.[3]

Article 9 (Associated Enterprises)

Tax treaties that incorporate provisions based on Article 9(1) of the OECD and UN models set the arm's-length principle as the boundary for applying each of the contracting states' domestic transfer pricing legislation in relation to transactions that fall within their scope (see box 2.1).

Tax treaties are generally not considered to create taxation powers additional to those provided for under each contracting state's domestic law; rather, their role is to place limitations on the contracting states' taxation

---

Box 2.1 Article 9 of the OECD Model Tax Convention on Income and on Capital, 2010

1. Where
   a) an enterprise of a Contracting State participates directly or indirectly in the management, control or capital of an enterprise of the other Contracting State, or
   b) the same persons participate directly or indirectly in the management, control or capital of an enterprise of a Contracting State and an enterprise of the other Contracting State, and in either case conditions are made or imposed between the two enterprises in their commercial or financial relations which differ from those that would be made between independent enterprises, then any profits which would, but for those conditions, have accrued to one of the enterprises, but, by reason of those conditions, have not so accrued, may be included in the profits of that enterprise and taxed accordingly.

2. Where a Contracting State includes in the profits of an enterprise of that State—and taxes accordingly—profits on which an enterprise of the other Contracting State has been charged to tax in that other State and the profits so included are profits that would have accrued to the enterprise of the first-mentioned State if the conditions made between the two enterprises had been those which would have been made between independent enterprises, then that other State shall make an appropriate adjustment to the tax charged therein on those profits. In determining such adjustment, due regard shall be had to the other provisions of this Convention and the competent authorities of the Contracting States shall, if necessary, consult each other.

---

powers in accordance with the agreed allocation of taxation rights under the treaty. The dominant view is therefore that Article 9 of a tax treaty is not a legal basis for a transfer pricing adjustment (a "primary adjustment") to be made by a tax administration and that a domestic legal basis is required for a tax administration to make such an adjustment (Lang 2010). The role of treaty provisions based on Article 9(1) is therefore to provide taxpayers with certainty regarding the treatment of their associated party transactions that fall within its scope and to provide a level of protection from economic double taxation.

Although Article 9 is titled "Associated Enterprises," the term is not elaborated on beyond the reference to participating "directly or indirectly in the management, control or capital," and neither of the models nor their commentaries provide any further insight as to when this threshold is considered to have been met. In accordance with Article 3(2) of the models, where a term is not defined, reference to the countries' domestic law may be required,[4] which can lead to conflicting interpretations.[5]

Tax treaty provisions based on Article 9(2) of the OECD and UN models provide mechanisms for the relief of economic double taxation arising from a transfer pricing adjustment made in accordance with the arm's-length principle. The mechanism for relief from economic double taxation under Article 9(2) is generally referred to as a corresponding adjustment (or "correlative adjustment" under the UN model) and typically involves the other contracting state making an adjustment to the amount of tax charged to provide relief from economic double taxation (see figure 2.1).

Issues when considering permutations of associated enterprises articles in tax treaties include the following:

Mechanism for relief from economic double taxation (or lack thereof). Although the vast majority of treaties require relief from economic double taxation by way of an adjustment to the profits of the other enterprise, there is also the possibility of relieving economic double taxation through a credit for the additional taxes paid in the other state, as is the case in a limited number of current treaties.[6] The goal is to ensure that there is a mechanism for relief of economic double taxation since this is a priority for foreign investors. Some treaties, especially older ones, do not include wording in Article 9 to relieve double taxation; and furthermore, some countries, as a matter of their treaty policy, do not include it. As highlighted in paragraph 7 of the Commentary to Article 9 of the UN model, failure to provide for compensating (or correlative adjustment) will result in an outcome contrary to the intended purpose of tax treaties:

> The view has been expressed that a correlative adjustment under paragraph 2 could be very costly to a developing country, which may consider not including paragraph 2 in its treaties. However, paragraph 2 is an essential aspect of Article 9 and failure to provide a correlative adjustment will result in double taxation, which is contrary to the purpose of the convention.

Figure 2.1 Corresponding Adjustment Example

1. Enterprise A sells goods to its associated party, Enterprise B, for 1,000 and this is the transfer price reported by both Enterprise A and Enterprise B for direct taxation purposes.

2. Enterprise A is subject to a transfer pricing audit, and the tax authorities of State A make a transfer pricing adjustment that increases the taxable income of Enterprise A by 250, to reflect an arm's-length transfer price of 1,250 for the goods sold to Enterprise B. As a result of the different transfer prices now reflected in the determination of each party's taxable income, the group is subject to economic double taxation on 250.

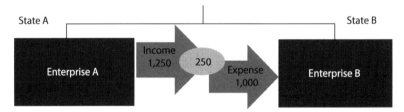

3. Insofar as State B's authority agrees that 1,250 is an appropriate arm's-length price and there are no other relevant limitations, it may grant a **corresponding adjustment** that has the effect of decreasing the taxable income of Enterprise B by 250 to reflect an increase in the transfer price to 1,250 for direct taxation purposes.

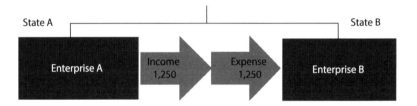

Requirement for agreement to the adjustment by the treaty partner. While wording of Article 9(2) appears to suggest that corresponding adjustment must be made (i.e., "that other State **shall** [emphasis added] make an appropriate adjustment"), paragraph 6 of the commentaries to Article 9 of both models make it clear that corresponding adjustments are not automatic or guaranteed and that a contracting state is required to make a corresponding adjustment only insofar as it agrees that the primary adjustment made in the other country is justified in both principle and amount:

> … an adjustment is not automatically to be made in State B simply because the profits in State A have been increased; the adjustment is due only if State B

considers that the figure of adjusted profits correctly reflects what the profits would have been if the transactions had been at arm's-length. In other words, the paragraph may not be invoked and should not be applied where the profits of one associated enterprise are increased to a level which exceeds what they would have been if they had been correctly computed on an arm's-length basis. State B is therefore committed to make an adjustment of the profits of the affiliated company only if it considers that the adjustment made in State A is justified both in principle and as regards the amount.

The treatment of corresponding adjustments is clarified by some countries during their treaty negotiations, typically by inserting an explicit requirement for agreement on the corresponding adjustment in the text of the treaty. For example, Article 9(2) of the 2001 tax convention between the United Kingdom and the United States includes the following language:

2. Where a Contracting State includes in the profits of an enterprise of that State, and taxes accordingly, profits on which an enterprise of the other Contracting State has been charged to tax in that other State, and **the other Contracting State agrees** [emphasis added] that the profits so included are profits that would have accrued to the enterprise of the first-mentioned State if the conditions made between the two enterprises had been those that would have been made between independent enterprises, then that other State shall make an appropriate adjustment to the amount of the tax charged therein on those profits. In determining such adjustment, due regard shall be paid to the other provisions of this Convention and the competent authorities of the Contracting States shall, if necessary, consult each other.

In addition, countries that have addressed corresponding adjustments in their domestic legislation may place specific administrative requirements on taxpayers regarding the application procedure and the information required.

Where there is no Article 9(2) equivalent in the applicable tax treaty or the other contracting state does not grant a corresponding adjustment (for various reasons, including disagreement with the adjustment in principle or the amount or domestic law restrictions), taxpayers may need to look to the mutual agreement procedure (MAP) to obtain relief from economic double taxation. In this regard, the commentary to Article 25 of the OECD model states that even in the absence of an Article 9(2) equivalent, most countries consider that cases of economic double taxation due to a transfer pricing adjustment are not in the spirit of the convention and thus fall within the scope of the MAP article.[7] Even in the case of an applicable Article 9(2), it will typically be necessary, however, to go through a MAP to obtain a corresponding adjustment.[8]

Limitations on relief from economic double taxation. Article 9(3) of the UN model, for which there is no equivalent provision in the OECD model, provides that Article 9(2) will not apply if one of the taxpayers is liable to a penalty with respect to the adjustment as a result of fraud, gross negligence, or willful default:

> 3. The provisions of paragraph 2 shall not apply where judicial, administrative or other legal proceedings have resulted in a final ruling that by actions giving rise to an adjustment of profits under paragraph 1, one of the enterprises concerned is liable to penalty with respect to fraud, gross negligence or willful default.

Time limitations on relief from economic double taxation. There are also examples of countries that have negotiated the associated enterprises articles of their tax treaties so as to include an additional paragraph that places a specific time limitation on adjustments for the relief of economic double taxation. For example, Article 9 of the Canada-Australia Income Tax Convention (1980) includes the following provision:

> 4. The provisions of paragraph 3 relating to an appropriate adjustment are not applicable after the expiration of six years from the end of the year of income or taxation year in respect of which a Contracting State has charged to tax the profits to which the adjustment would relate.

Availability of information. Associated enterprises articles can be negotiated to include provisions that provide greater flexibility for the contracting states to make transfer pricing adjustments in cases where there is inadequate information. For example, Article 9 of the Canada-Australia Income Tax Convention (1980) includes the following provision:

> 2. If the information available to the competent authority of a Contracting State is inadequate to determine the profits to be attributed to an enterprise, nothing in this Article shall affect the application of any law of that State relating to the determination of the tax liability of a person, provided that that law shall be applied, so far as the information available to the competent authority permits, in accordance with the principles of this Article.

Article 25: Mutual Agreement Procedure

The MAP article plays a crucial role in eliminating double taxation by providing a legal framework for the competent authority of one contracting state to join with the competent authority of the other contracting state to endeavor to remedy instances of "taxation not in accordance with the provisions of the Convention." While MAP is equally applicable to nontransfer pricing cases, such as disputes regarding the existence of and attribution of profits to a permanent establishment, residence, and withholding taxes, "historically the majority of these cases have been issues of transfer pricing where associated companies of a multinational enterprise group incurred economic double taxation due to an adjustment to their income from intragroup transactions by one or more tax administrations" (OECD 2007).

The outcome of a MAP may involve the contracting state that made the primary adjustment reducing or eliminating the adjustment, the other contracting state making the necessary corresponding adjustment to eliminate economic double taxation, or a combination thereof. However, MAP articles of most of the current comprehensive tax treaties do not require that the competent authorities reach an agreement, only that they endeavor to do so. Thus, under such agreements, there is no guarantee that any economic double taxation arising from transfer pricing adjustments will be eliminated.

In recent years, an increasing number of MAP articles have included binding arbitration provisions.[9] Where applicable, treaties containing such provisions may require that the contracting states implement a solution to eliminate double taxation. The European Arbitration Convention (1990) provides for compulsory binding arbitration regarding disputes between its contracting parties, which eliminates double taxation in connection with the adjusted profits of associated enterprises.

The 2015 minimum standard in the OECD/G20's base erosion and profit shifting (BEPS) strategies on the access and effective implementation of the MAP process (Action 14) is aimed at ensuring:[10]

- That treaty obligations related to MAP are fully implemented in good faith and that MAP cases are resolved in a timely manner;
- The implementation of administrative processes that promote the prevention and timely resolution of treaty-related disputes; and
- That taxpayers can access MAP when eligible.

While several countries have committed to providing for mandatory binding MAP arbitration in their treaties, others have indicated skepticism. In light of this skepticism, policy makers should carefully consider in treaty negotiations whether and when to opt for mandatory arbitration.

As well as providing a mechanism for resolving disputes, MAP articles provide the necessary legal basis for competent authorities to negotiate bilateral advance pricing agreements for specific taxpayers and, although much less common, more general agreements covering a transaction type or industry. The introduction of bilateral APA programs is one of the approaches recommended by the OECD/G20 as part of the BEPS outcomes.

Article 26: Exchange of Information

Most current tax treaties contain articles that provide the legal basis for the competent authorities of the contracting parties' countries to exchange information, as necessary, to carry out the provision of the tax treaty and enforce domestic tax laws. Similar provisions are also found in Tax Exchange of Information Agreements (TIEAs), which have become increasingly common in recent years as international efforts to address tax evasion and avoidance have gained momentum.

Exchange of information provisions provide the legal basis for a contracting state's competent authority to request information from the other contracting state, as required, to assess the proper allocation of profits in accordance with the application of the arm's-length principle. Because of the highly factual nature of transfer pricing cases and the growing importance of (and international focus on[11]) the exchange of information (which has resulted in a substantial increase in the number of TIEAs), the role and importance of exchange of information in transfer pricing enforcement is increasing. Depending on their scope, exchange of information articles can also provide a legal basis for carrying out simultaneous tax examinations by tax administrations through their competent authorities (see chapter 8).

Tax Treaties, Transfer Pricing, and the Protection of Investors in Developing Countries

Tax treaties provide taxpayers with a level of certainty regarding the treatment of their associated party transactions by setting boundaries for the application of the contracting states' domestic law and by providing an international legal framework for the avoidance and elimination of economic double taxation. Furthermore, tax treaties can provide a legal basis for contracting states to exchange information that can help them enforce their domestic tax laws, including laws relating to transfer pricing.

At the same time, tax treaties can generate important costs in terms of foregone revenue. Ongoing work led by the OECD as part of the BEPS project is aimed at limiting the abuse of tax treaty provisions, yet in many developing economies there is a more general need for a structured analysis of what a desirable treaty network would look like.[12] Improving treaty networks is an important policy area for developing economies (IMF 2014), which may require the revision of existing treaties.

Many developing economies have limited tax treaty networks (Thuronyi 2010), thereby limiting costs related to treaties, but also the protection from double taxation afforded to taxpayers operating there. Even where tax treaties are in force, tax administrations and policy makers often have limited experience as to the treaties' application. As a result, the necessary administrative procedures are often not in place, unable to be applied in practice, or are applied inconsistently. The resulting lack of access for taxpayers to the protections afforded by the tax treaties (that is, access to MAP) undermines the treaty's intended effect and may have a negative impact on a country's investment climate.[13]

To complement the introduction or reform of a country's transfer pricing regime, it is thus advisable to consider the effects of existing or potential tax treaties with key trading partners[14] and to ensure that the necessary administrative procedures are in place to administer existing treaties. Readily available access to the competent authority must also be ensured to allow taxpayers practical access to relief from double taxation through MAP (see chapter 6).

Where the negotiation of comprehensive tax treaties is not a desirable option, countries may consider negotiating "light treaties" that address exchange of information and MAP with respect to transfer pricing adjustments (see box 2.2; see also Thuronyi 2010).

Box 2.2 Example of a "Light" Treaty

In 2009, an agreement between the government of Australia and the Kingdom of the Netherlands in respect of Aruba on the allocation of taxing rights with respect to certain income of individuals and to establish a MAP with respect to transfer pricing adjustments was signed. Article 8 of this agreement—Mutual Agreement Procedure in Respect of Transfer Pricing Adjustments—reads as follows:

1. Where a resident of a Party considers the actions of the other Party results or will result in a transfer pricing adjustment not in accordance with the arm's-length principle, the resident may, irrespective of the remedies provided by the domestic law of those Parties, present a case to the competent authority of the first-mentioned Party. The case must be presented within 3 years of the first notification of the adjustment.
2. The competent authorities shall endeavour to resolve any difficulties or doubts arising as to the application of the arm's-length principle by a Party regarding transfer pricing adjustments. They may also communicate with each other directly for the purposes of this Article.

Other International Instruments and Sources

In addition to tax treaties, numerous other instruments of international law may have a direct or indirect impact on the design and application of a country's transfer pricing regime, depending on their applicability:

- *European Arbitration Convention.* Within the European Union (EU), the European Arbitration Convention establishes a procedure for resolving disputes between member states arising from transfer pricing adjustments. Recognizing that most current tax treaties do not impose a binding obligation on countries to eliminate double taxation, the convention "improves the conditions for cross-border activities in the Internal Market" by imposing a binding obligation with respect to transactions between enterprises of member states of the EU (EC 2011).
- *TIEAs and similar instruments.* Much like the exchange of information articles found in tax treaties, TIEAs are increasingly common. Multilateral conventions such as the Council of Europe and OECD Convention on Mutual Administrative Assistance in Tax Matters and the Nordic Convention on Mutual Assistance in Tax Matters provide a legal basis for the competent authorities of the contracting states to obtain information from other jurisdictions as necessary to enforce their domestic tax laws. Depending on their scope, these agreements can also provide the legal basis for tax administrations to conduct simultaneous or joint tax examinations.

Although not legally binding, numerous other international instruments can have a significant influence on the design and application of a country's transfer pricing regime. The *OECD Transfer Pricing Guidelines* (OECD 2010b) is the most influential of these instruments. In October 2012, the UN Committee of Experts on International Cooperation in Tax Matters adopted the *Practical Manual on Transfer Pricing for Developing Countries*.

Other regional bodies—including the African Tax Administration Forum (ATAF), the Pacific Association of Tax Administrators (PATA), and the EU Joint Transfer Pricing Forum (EUJTPF)—have also issued, or are in the process of issuing, guidance on transfer pricing and related matters.[15]

OECD Transfer Pricing Guidelines

The *OECD Transfer Pricing Guidelines* are the most influential source on transfer pricing; they provide guidance for multinational corporations and tax administrations regarding the practical application of the arm's-length principle. The 2010 version comprises nine chapters covering a range of transfer pricing issues (see figure 2.2). The guidelines are updated periodically to address new topics of concern or to better reflect developments in transfer pricing practices.[16]

The guidelines are not a legal instrument per se, and, as a result, their legal and practical relevance varies significantly between countries.

The OECD Council recommends that the *OECD Transfer Pricing Guidelines* be followed by the tax administrations of OECD countries and encourages taxpayers to follow them (OECD 2010b). In some OECD member countries, the status of the guidelines is clear since legislation makes explicit reference to them (see box 2.3). Despite having high practical relevance, the legal relevance of these guidelines is less certain in other countries.[17]

Figure 2.2 *OECD Transfer Pricing Guidelines* 2010

- Chapter 1 The Arm's-Length Principle
- Chapter 2 Transfer Pricing Methods
- Chapter 3 Comparability Analysis
- Chapter 4 Administrative Approaches to Avoiding and Resolving Transfer Pricing Disputes
- Chapter 5 Documentation
- Chapter 6 Special Considerations for Intangible Property
- Chapter 7 Special Considerations for Intra-group Services
- Chapter 8 Cost Contribution Arrangements
- Chapter 9 Transfer Pricing Aspects of Business Restructurings

---

Box 2.3 Reference to *OECD Transfer Pricing Guidelines* in the United Kingdom's Domestic Legislation, 2010

Section 164 of the Taxation (International and Other Provisions) Act 2010 (the United Kingdom) directly references the use of the *OECD Transfer Pricing Guidelines* for interpreting transfer pricing provisions:

164 Part to be interpreted in accordance with OECD principles

(1) This Part is to be read in such manner as best secures consistency between:
   (a) the effect given to Sections 147(1)(a), (b) and (d) and (2) to (6), 148 and 151(2), and
   (b) the effect which, in accordance with the transfer pricing guidelines, is to be given, in cases where double taxation arrangements incorporate the whole or any part of the OECD model, to so much of the arrangements as does so.

[...]

(3) In this section "the OECD model" means:
   (a) The rules which, at the passing of ICTA (which occurred on February 9, 1988), were contained in Article 9 of the *Model Tax Convention on Income and on Capital* published by the Organisation for Economic Co-operation and Development, or
   (b) Any rules in the same or equivalent terms.

(4) In this section "the transfer pricing guidelines" means:
   (a) All the documents published by the Organisation for Economic Co-operation and Development, at any time before May 1, 1998, as part of their Transfer Pricing Guidelines for Multinational Enterprises and Tax Administrations, and
   (b) Such documents published by that Organisation on or after that date as may, for the purposes of this Part, be designated by an order made by the Treasury as comprised in the transfer pricing guidelines.

Regardless of whether a direct reference to the guidelines exists in the domestic law, the guidelines are generally considered to be highly persuasive in OECD countries and are often referred to in practice by tax administrations and the private sector.

In numerous non-OECD countries, such as Namibia, the Philippines, and South Africa, the legislation or administrative guidance implicitly or explicitly refers to the OECD guidelines, making their relevance clear (see box 2.4). In other non-OECD countries, however, no reference is made to the guidelines, even though in many cases the domestic transfer pricing legislation is based on the same principles upon which the guidelines are based. In Turkey, for example, although the Turkish Revenue Administration considered the guidelines to be the main source of information during the preparation of Turkey's secondary legislation, domestic laws are considered the only legislative source; the guidelines thus have no direct legal impact relative to Turkish transfer pricing rules (Alioğlu and Aşkın 2011).

Transfer Pricing and Developing Economies • http://dx.doi.org/10.1596/978-1-4648-0969-9

Box 2.4 Relevance of International Guidelines in Selected Non-OECD Countries

Albania. Paragraph 2 of the Instruction on Transfer Pricing (No. 16, June 18, 2014) states that the instruction is based on the principles of the *OECD Transfer Pricing Guidelines* (2010), but that in the event of conflict between the *OECD Transfer Pricing Guidelines* (2010) and the Albanian Income Tax Law and Instructions, the Albanian law will take precedence. In addition, paragraph 15.4 of the instructions provides taxpayers with the possibility to prepare transfer pricing documentation based on the approach detailed in the "Code of Conduct on Transfer Pricing Documentation for Associated Enterprises in the European Union."

Georgia. Article 1(3) of Decree 423 "on the Approval of the Instructions on International Transfer Pricing" states that the *OECD Transfer Pricing Guidelines* (2010) are applicable to the extent that they do not conflict with Georgian transfer pricing legislation.

Namibia. Paragraph 3.2 of Practice Note 2 of 2006 (PN 2/2006) on the "determination of the taxable income of certain persons from international transactions: transfer pricing" makes explicit reference to the status of the OECD guidelines: "This Practice Note is based on and acknowledges the principles of the OECD Guidelines. Nothing in this Practice Note is intended to be contradictory to the OECD Guidelines and in cases where there is conflict, the provisions of the OECD Guidelines will prevail in resolving any dispute."

Pakistan. Rule 22 of the Income Tax Rules (2002), which applies for the purposes of section 108 of the Income Tax Ordinance (2001) to international standards and guidelines issued by various tax-related, internationally recognized organizations, reads: "Subject to the other rules ins this chapter, the Commissioner, in applying this chapter, shall also be guided by international standards, case law and guidelines issued by the various tax-related internationally recognized organizations."

The Philippines. In March 2008, the Philippine Bureau of Internal Revenue issued Revenue Memorandum Circular No. 026-08, formally adopting the OECD guidelines for resolving transfer pricing disputes in the Philippines, pending final issuance of its own comprehensive transfer pricing regulations, which were issued in January 2013.

Serbia. In December 2012, the Serbian Parliament adopted amendments to the Corporate Income Tax Law. These amendments included changes to the transfer pricing provisions, and, in particular, a new Article 61a was introduced that specifies that the Minister of Finance shall, relying on the *OECD Transfer Pricing Guidelines* and other international sources, specify more closely the manner of application of the articles concerning transfer pricing.

South Africa. Paragraph 3.2.1 of Practice Note No.7 states: "[A]lthough South Africa is not a member country of the OECD, the OECD Guidelines are acknowledged as an important, influential document that reflects unanimous agreement amongst the member countries, reached after an extensive process of consultation with industry and tax practitioners in many countries." In this regard, paragraph 3.2.3 states that the "OECD Guidelines should be followed in the absence of any specific guidance in terms of this Practice Note, the provisions of section 31 or the tax treaties entered into by South Africa."

Where a tax treaty containing an associated enterprises article based on Article 9 of the OECD or UN model tax conventions is applicable, reference will generally be made to the guidelines when applying that article (e.g., during a MAP). In this regard, paragraph 1 of the commentary to Article 9 of the OECD model notes that the guidelines represent "internationally agreed principles and [provide] guidelines for the application of the arm's-length principle of which [Article 9] is the authoritative statement." However, this reference is made in the commentary to the OECD model, the status of which can vary significantly as between countries and is the subject of much debate (on the legal status of the commentaries see: Engelen (2004) and Engelen and Douma (2008)).

Where no tax treaty is applicable and no reference is made in the domestic law, the relevance of the OECD guidelines can be unclear. However, in many instances, the guidelines will at least be considered as a relevant source of reference by taxpayers, the tax administration, and even the judiciary (see box 2.5). According to Judge Alnashir Visram in *Unilever Kenya Ltd v. the Commissioner of Income Tax* (Income Tax Appeal No. 752 of 2003): "[I]t would be foolhardy for any court to disregard internationally accepted principles of business as long as these do not conflict with our own laws. To do otherwise would be highly

---

Box 2.5 Judicial Reference to the *OECD Transfer Pricing Guidelines* in Selected Non-OECD Countries

Argentina. According to Ernst & Young (2012): "Argentina is not an OECD member, and the *OECD Transfer Pricing Guidelines* (OECD Guidelines) are not referenced in Argentina's Tax Law and Regulations. However, the tax authority usually recognizes the OECD Guidelines in practice, as long as they do not contradict the ITL [Income Tax Law] and Regulations.

A trial level court case, dated 15 August 2007, was based on OECD Guidelines provisions. Other, more recent, trial level court cases also recognize the use of the OECD Guidelines, insofar as they do not contradict the ITL and Regulations."

Colombia. According to Ernst & Young (2012): "Although Colombia is not a member of the OECD, its Guidelines are generally followed in the local regulations. According to Sentence C-690 of the Colombian Constitutional Court, issued on August 12, 2003, OECD Guidelines and Commentary are an auxiliary source of guidance and interpretation, but they are not mandatory for the tax authorities. However, the OECD Guidelines have been mentioned and have been used as a reference in recent audits."

Kenya. Unilever Kenya Ltd v. Commissioner of Income Tax (Income Tax Appeal No. 752 of 2003) was the first transfer pricing case to go to court in Kenya for which a judgment was delivered. One of the core issues was the relevance of the *OECD Transfer Pricing Guidelines*

box continues next page

Box 2.5 Judicial Reference to the *OECD Transfer Pricing Guidelines* in Selected Non-OECD Countries *(continued)*

in Kenya. The Kenya Revenue Authority (KRA) contended that the guidelines were not applicable because Kenya is not a member of the OECD, the guidelines were not incorporated into or adopted in the legislation, and the guidelines could be used only if Kenya had adopted the guidelines in a tax treaty with another country. For its part, Unilever Kenya contended that the guidelines were applicable because in the absence of specific guidelines by the KRA reference ought to be made to international best practice, as represented by the *OECD Transfer Pricing Guidelines*; guidelines adopted by other countries essentially endorse or adopt the principles set forth by the OECD guidelines; and countries that are not members of the OECD have adopted the guidelines.

The court found that where the legislation gives no guidelines, other guidelines should be looked at. It thus ruled that the OECD guidelines are applicable in Kenya. In reaching his conclusion, the judge stated: "[I]t would be foolhardy for any court to disregard internationally accepted principles of business as long as these do not conflict with our own laws. To do otherwise would be highly short-sighted." Kenya has revised its transfer pricing legislation since this decision.

short-sighted." In the absence of clearly conflicting legislation or guidance, it is therefore reasonable to assume that the OECD *Transfer Pricing Guidelines* will have a significant influence on the development and practical application of a developing country's transfer pricing regime.

UN Practical Manual on Transfer Pricing for Developing Countries

The UN Committee of Experts on International Cooperation in Tax Matters constituted the Subcommittee on Transfer Pricing–Practical Issues at its annual session in 2009. The subcommittee was given the mandate to produce a practical manual on transfer pricing based on the following principles (UN 2012):

(a) It should reflect the operation of Article 9 of the United Nations Model Convention, and the arm's-length principle embodied in it, and be consistent with relevant commentaries of the United Nations Model Convention;

(b) It should reflect the realities for developing countries at the relevant stages of their capacity development;

(c) Special attention should be paid to the experience of other developing countries; and

(d) It should draw upon the work being done in other forums.

The draft foreword to the manual notes that the guidelines are "a practical manual rather than a legislative model," that "a key 'value added' of the manual is to be its practicality," and that in developing the manual "consistency with the OECD *Transfer Pricing Guidelines* has been sought."[18]

During its October 2012 session, the Committee of Experts approved the draft practical manual and the final version was launched in May 2013.[19] The manual is described as "a living work, however, which will be improved and added to over time by drawing upon further experiences and expertise" (UN 2012a, 2).

The manual will play an influential role in the development of transfer pricing practices in transition and developing economies moving forward. Like the *OECD Transfer Pricing Guidelines*, it is, however, not a legal instrument. Its status and influence will therefore depend on domestic law references and practices in each country, taking into account that the manual was not adopted by consensus of all UN member states, but by the Committee of Experts (comprising 25 members nominated by governments and acting in their personal expert capacity).[20]

Chapter 2 Main Messages

- When considering the design, implementation, and application of a country's transfer pricing regime, it is important to refer to the relevant international legal framework.
- Tax treaties provide taxpayers with a level of certainty regarding the treatment of their associated party transactions by setting boundaries for the application of the contracting states' domestic law and by providing an international legal framework for the avoidance and elimination of economic double taxation.
- Tax treaties typically also provide a legal basis for contracting states to exchange information that can help them enforce their domestic tax laws, including laws relating to transfer pricing.
- At the same time, tax treaties can generate important costs in terms of foregone revenue and countries need to be careful and conduct a structured analysis of what a desirable treaty network would look like before signing any tax treaties.
- To complement the introduction or reform of a country's transfer pricing regime, it is advisable to consider the effects of existing or potential tax treaties with key trading partners and to ensure that the necessary administrative procedures are in place and the tax administration appropriately trained.
- Where the negotiation of comprehensive tax treaties is not a desirable option, countries can consider negotiating "light treaties" that address exchange of information and MAP with respect to transfer pricing adjustments
- In practice, the *OECD Transfer Pricing Guidelines* are the most influential source of guidance on transfer pricing. The UN *Practical Transfer Pricing Manual for Developing Countries* will also play an influential role in the development of transfer pricing practices in transition and developing economies. Both provide guidance for multinational corporations and tax administrations regarding the practical application of the arm's-length principle.

Notes

1. References to the OECD model are to the 2010 version, unless otherwise indicated.

2. References to the UN model are to the 2011 version, unless otherwise indicated.

3. For example, Article 7 (Business Profits) requires that the profits attributable to a permanent establishment be determined in accordance with the arm's-length principle, and Article 11 (Interest) and Article 12 (Royalties) are worded so as to apply only to the arm's-length amount of interest or royalty income.

4. The question of common management or control always depends very much on the facts and circumstances of a case, limiting the potential for formalistic definitions. Some countries provide specific guidance on thresholds regarding capital participation. In Austria, for example, a participation in capital of more than 25 percent leads to the assumption of association (Austrian Income Tax Code section 6, paragraph 6).

5. As countries' domestic law definitions can, and do, reasonably differ, situations can arise in which the contracting states have different positions regarding the applicability of the article, potentially resulting in instances of economic double taxation for which there is no clear or explicit solution provided (Rotondaro 2000). In practice, the occurrence of these situations is minimal.

6. See, for example, Article 23(4) of the Australia-Malaysia Double Tax Convention 1980.

7. Not all tax administrations share this view. Recognizing this reality, the Australian Taxation Office (ATO), for example, "does not consider that tax treaty partner countries have an obligation to provide relief from economic double taxation in the absence of a provision in a DTA (Double Taxation Agreement) specifically directed at the relief of economic double taxation [such as Article 9(3) of the Vietnamese agreement; see also Article 9(2) of the OECD model]. In these circumstances, the operation of the MAP article is limited to resolving taxation not in accordance with the DTA and does not extend to the provision of relief from economic double taxation" (ATO 2000, paragraph 2.3 of Taxation Ruling TR2000/16).

8. Article 9(2) does not oblige a country to make an automatic corresponding adjustment.

9. Examples of such provisions are found in Article 25(5) of the OECD model (2010) and Article 25B of the UN model (2011).

10. See Final Report on Action 14, "Making Dispute Resolution Mechanisms More Effective," October 2015, http://www.oecd.org/tax/making-dispute-resolution-mecha nisms-more-effective-action-14-2015-final-report-9789264241633-en.htm.

11. In particular, following a decision by the G20 to strengthen the standards on transparency and exchange of information, which are now being implanted through the Global Forum on Transparency and Exchange of Information for Tax Purposes. For more information refer to the OECD website at http://www.oecd.org/tax /transparency/.

12. Withholding instruments, which are typically limited by tax treaties, can in some cases be a simple safeguard for resource-constrained administrations that are not (yet) in a position to effectively implement transfer pricing provisions against international tax planning and profit shifting. At the same time, potential negative effects on the investment climate need to be considered.

13. For information on the design and drafting of domestic law to implement a tax treaty generally, see IMF (2011).

14. This should be done carefully considering the wider cost and benefits of giving up taxation rights in such a treaty. Where a tax treaty is deemed too costly, TIEAs provide a narrower option to ensure that information can be accessed.

15. For an overview of the activities of international organizations, financial institutions, and regional tax authorities' groupings' transfer pricing activities as of October 2012, see the UN Committee of Experts on International Cooperation in Tax Matters, "Secretariat Note: Transfer Pricing: Technical Assistance and Capacity Building Resources," October 11, 2012. Available at http://www.un.org/esa/ffd/tax/eighthsession/CRP14-TransferPricing-capacity-building.pdf.

16. The OECD guidelines are being revised as part of the ongoing BEPS project. Agreed upon revisions emphasize the need for a careful delineation of transactions, thus comparing contractual with actual conduct when reviewing transfer pricing arrangements. The envisaged outcome is to either supplement or replace contractual arrangements where required. See the OECD website, BEPS 2015 Final Reports, at http://www.oecd.org/ctp/beps-2015-final-reports.htm.

17. For example, in Australia, in the case of *SNF (Australia) Pty Ltd v FC of T [2010] FCA 635*, Middleton notes (at paragraph 58) that he referred to the 1995 OECD guidelines as a convenient reference to the various methods that have been adopted or referred to in determining arm's-length consideration, but that they "do not dictate to the Court any one or more appropriate methods, and are just what they purport to be, guidelines." In this regard, he distinguished the Australian transfer pricing legislation, which (at the time) contained no reference to the guidelines from that of the United Kingdom, where explicit reference is made to the guidelines (see box 2.5).

18. The "Practical Manual on Transfer Pricing for Developing Countries: Foreword" is available at the UN website, http://www.un.org/esa/ffd/tax/eighthsession/Foreword-20120928_v5_ML-accp.pdf.

19. See the UN website at http://www.un.org/esa/ffd/documents/UN_Manual_TransferPricing.pdf.

20. A revised version of the *UN Practical Manual on Transfer Pricing for Developing Countries* is expected to be finalized in 2017.

Bibliography

Alioğlu, O., and M. Aşkın. 2011. *IBFD Transfer Pricing Database (Turkey Chapter)*. Amsterdam: International Bureau of Fiscal Documentation.

ATO (Australian Taxation Office). 2000. *Taxation Ruling TR2000/16 Income Tax: International Transfer Pricing—Transfer Pricing and Profit Reallocation Adjustments, Relief from Double Taxation and the Mutual Agreement Procedure*. Canberra: ATO. http://law.ato.gov.au/atolaw/view.htm?dbwidetocone=06%3AATO%20Rulings%20and%20Determinations%20(Including%20GST%20Bulletins)%3ABy%20Type%3ARulings%3ATaxation%3A2000%3A%2305000160000%23TR%202000%2F16%20-%20Income%20tax%26c%20international%20transfer%20pricing%20transfer%20pricing%20and%20profit%20real...%3B.

EC (European Commission). 2011. *Transfer Pricing and the Arbitration Convention*. Brussels: EC. http://ec.europa.eu/taxation_customs/taxation/company_tax/transfer_pricing/arbitration_convention/index_en.htm.

Engelen, F. 2004. *Interpretation of Tax Treaties under International Law*. IBFD Doctoral Series. Amsterdam: International Bureau of Fiscal Documentation.

Engelen, F., and S. Douma, eds. 2008. "The Legal Status of the OECD Commentaries." In *Conflicts of Norms of International Law Series*, Vol. 1. Amsterdam: International Bureau of Fiscal Documentation. http://www.ibfd.org/sites/ibfd.org/files/content /pdf/Legal_Status_OECD_TOC.pdf.

Ernst & Young. 2012. *Transfer Pricing Global Reference Guide*. London: Ernst & Young. http://www.ey.com/Publication/vwLUAssets/2012-transfer-pricing-global-reference -guide/$FILE/Tranfer-Pricing-Reference-2012.pdf.

European Arbitration Convention. 1990. "90/436/EEC: Convention on the Elimination of Double Taxation in Connection with the Adjustment of Profits of Associated Enterprises." *Official Journal of the European Communities* 225: 10–24.

Finnerty, C., P. Merks, M. Petriccione, and R. Russo. 2007. *Fundamentals of International Tax Planning*. Amsterdam: International Bureau of Fiscal Documentation.

IMF (International Monetary Fund). 2011. *Tax Policy: Designing and Drafting a Domestic Law to Implement a Tax Treaty*. Washington, DC: IMF. http://www.imf.org/external /pubs/ft/tnm/2011/tnm1101.pdf.

———. 2014. Spillovers in International Corporate Taxation. IMF Policy Paper. Washington, DC: IMF. http://www.imf.org/external/np/pp/eng/2014/050914.pdf.

Lang, M. 2010. *Introduction to the Law of Double Taxation Conventions*. Amsterdam: International Bureau of Fiscal Documentation.

OECD (Organisation for Economic Co-operation and Development). 2007. *Manual on Effective Mutual Agreement Procedures*. Paris: Centre for Tax Policy and Administration, OECD.

———. 2010a. *Recommendation of the Council on the Determination of Transfer Pricing between Associated Enterprises* [C(95)126/Final], as amended April 11, 1996 [C(96)46 /FINAL]; July 24, 1997 [C(97)144/FINAL]; October 28, 1999 [C(99)138], July 16, 2009 [C(2009)88]; and July 22, 2010 [C(2010)99]. Paris: OECD.

———. 2010b. *Transfer Pricing Guidelines for Multinational Enterprises and Tax Administrations*. Paris: OECD.

Rotondaro, C. 2000. "The Application of Art. 3(2) in Case of Differences between Domestic Definitions of 'Associated Enterprises': A Problem of Treaty Interpretation and a Proposed Solution." *International Transfer Pricing Journal* 7 (5).

Thuronyi, V. 2010. "Tax Treaties and Developing Countries." In *Tax Treaties: Building Bridges between Law and Economics*, edited by M. Lang, P. Pistone, J. Schuch, C. Staringer, A. Storck, and M. Zagler. Amsterdam: International Bureau of Fiscal Documentation.

UN (United Nations). 2012. Provisional Agenda: *Practical Manual on Transfer Pricing for Developing Countries*. New York: UN. E/C.18/2012/CRP.1. http://www.un.org/esa /ffd/tax/eighthsession/CRP1-practical-manual-on-transfer-pricing-for-developing -countries.pdf.

———. 2013. *Practical Manual on Transfer Pricing for Developing Countries*. New York: UN. http://www.un.org/esa/ffd/documents/UN_Manual_TransferPricing.pdf.

CHAPTER 3

Drafting Transfer Pricing Legislation

At the theoretical level, the challenge for developing and transitioning countries in the development of transfer pricing legislation is in essence the same as for OECD countries: protecting their tax base while not creating double taxation or uncertainties that could hamper foreign direct investment and cross-border trade. The adoption of transfer pricing legislation embodying the arm's-length principle can be instrumental in achieving this dual objective.

—OECD (2011)

This chapter provides practical guidance on drafting transfer pricing legislation for direct taxation purposes based on the arm's-length principle. Examples from selected developing and developed countries' transfer pricing legislation and *Transfer Pricing Legislation: A Suggested Approach* (OECD 2011) are referred to throughout. While the focus of the chapter is on drafting transfer pricing legislation, relevant aspects of the legislative process, such as formulating a transfer pricing policy, are touched on, as is the role of administrative guidance and other practical considerations relevant to the drafting process. Other steps in the legislative process, such as the parliamentary process, private sector and intragovernmental consultants and adoption, and guidance on drafting tax legislation more generally, are necessarily outside the scope of this chapter.[1]

Formulating a "Transfer Pricing Policy"

Drafting transfer pricing provisions is an exercise of policy implementation. Before drafting a country's transfer pricing legislation, policy makers must make initial decisions concerning the country's "transfer pricing policy," recognizing, however, that throughout the process policy decisions can and often do evolve.

A needs assessment should inform initial policy decisions concerning transfer pricing[2] and reference a range of factors, including the country's broader economic policies (such as investment and tax policies), administrative capacity, and the structure of the economy. Table 3.1 sets out common considerations when

Table 3.1 Common Considerations When Formulating a Transfer Pricing Policy

Tax base protection	• Level of transfer pricing risk • Other mechanisms that counter profit shifting (withholding taxes, thin capitalization rules, etc.) • Tax rate in relation to main trading partners • Specific risk areas (special economic zones, etc.) • Industry-specific risks
Investment climate	• Importance of providing certainty • Limiting compliance costs • Signaling effect (adopting international standards) • Access to effective and efficient dispute resolution procedures
International aspects	• International law obligations (tax treaties, etc.) • Protection of local MNEs' operations abroad • Global and regional integration • Ability to influence international developments • Transfer pricing regimes of trading partners
Taxpayer characteristics	• Number and size of MNEs • Level of sophistication • Compliance behavior
Administration	• Capacity • Resources (human and technology) • Level of corruption

Note: MNE = multinational enterprise.

formulating a transfer pricing policy that can help to inform questions during the drafting process, such as appropriate scope and compliance requirements.

Table 3A.1 in annex 3A is a checklist designed to aid the design and drafting of transfer pricing legislation.

Drafting Approach

Countries have adopted a range of approaches to drafting transfer pricing legislation. These can be grouped into three main categories, each with different levels of reliance on primary legislation, secondary legislation, and administrative guidance:

• Separate legal act on transfer pricing
• Detailed provisions in primary legislation (for example in the tax code, corporate tax law, or profits tax law, as applicable) with or without secondary legislation (regulations, rule books, instructions, etc.), or administrative guidance
• Relatively brief provisions in primary legislation, which are elaborated on in secondary legislation or administrative guidance

With few exceptions, countries have tended to adopt one of the latter two approaches, with the majority introducing relatively brief provisions in their primary legislation that are then elaborated on in secondary legislation or administrative guidance.[3] However, the level of detail in the primary legislation can differ significantly. At one end of the spectrum are countries that have introduced very brief legislation that is limited to core provisions (such as scope, arm's-length principle, and an authority to make adjustments). Examples include the Arab Republic of Egypt (box 3.1), Ghana, Kenya (box 3.2), Malaysia, and the United States.[4] At the other end of the spectrum are countries that have adopted more detailed provisions in their primary law that deal with the core elements and a range of practical, administrative, and procedural aspects. Examples include Albania, Colombia, Georgia, Hungary, India, Mexico, Serbia, and Turkey. Table 3.2 summaries the drafting approach adopted in selected countries by reference to key elements of a country's legal framework for transfer pricing.

Different approaches to drafting result in multiple relative advantages and disadvantages (see table 3.3). In selecting an appropriate approach, trade-offs are typically required between flexibility and certainty. The appropriate drafting approach will depend on such factors as the legal system; drafting traditions; design of the tax system; legislative process; and the capacity of policy makers,

---

Box 3.1 Egypt's Transfer Pricing Legislation

Egypt's primary legislation is found in Article 30 of the Income Tax Law No. 91 of 2005, the application of which is elaborated on in Articles 38, 39, and 40 of the executive regulations and the transfer pricing guidelines issued by the Egyptian Tax Administration. Article 30 reads as follows:

> If related persons have set conditions for their commercial or financial transactions other than those operative among nonrelated persons, either to reduce the tax base or to shift the tax burden from a taxable person to an exempt or nontaxable one, the Authority is entitled to determine the taxable profit on the basis of the neutral price.
>
> The Commissioner may conclude agreements with such related persons to follow one or more ways in determining the neutral price in their transactions.
>
> The Executive Regulation of this Law shall determine methods of calculating the neutral price.

Box 3.2 Kenya's Transfer Pricing Legislation

Kenya's primary legislation is found in Article 18(3) of the Income Tax Act, the application of which is elaborated on in the Income Tax (Transfer Pricing) Rules, 2006. Article 18(3) reads as follows:

> Where a non-resident person carries on business with a related resident person and the course of that business is so arranged that it produces to the resident person either no profits or less than the ordinary profits which might be expected to accrue from that business if there had been no such relationship, then the gains or profits of that resident person from that business shall be deemed to be the amount that might have been expected to accrue if the course of that business had been conducted by independent persons dealing at arm's-length.

Table 3.2 Drafting Approach Adopted in Selected Countries

Country	Scope	Arm's-length principle	Comparability standard	Comparability factors	Transfer pricing methods	Selection of method	Arm's-length range
Albania	Primary legislation (elaborated on in secondary legislation)	Primary legislation	Primary legislation	Primary legislation (elaborated on in secondary legislation)	Primary legislation (elaborated on in secondary legislation)	Primary legislation (elaborated on in secondary legislation)	Primary legislation
Australia	Primary legislation	Primary legislation	Primary legislation	Primary legislation	Primary legislation	Primary legislation	Primary legislation
Colombia	Primary legislation	Primary legislation	Primary legislation	Primary legislation	Primary legislation	Primary legislation	Primary legislation
Georgia	Primary legislation (elaborated on in secondary legislation)	Primary legislation	Primary legislation (elaborated on in secondary legislation)	Primary legislation (elaborated on in secondary legislation)	Primary legislation (elaborated on in secondary legislation)	Primary legislation (elaborated on in secondary legislation)	Primary legislation (elaborated on in secondary legislation)
Ghana	Primary legislation	Primary legislation	Secondary legislation	Secondary legislation	Secondary legislation	Secondary legislation	Secondary legislation
India	Primary legislation	Primary legislation	Secondary legislation	Secondary legislation	Primary legislation (expanded on in secondary legislation)	Secondary legislation	Primary legislation
Kazakhstan	Separate law on transfer pricing	Separate law on transfer pricing	Separate law on transfer pricing	Separate law on transfer pricing	Separate law on transfer pricing	Separate law on transfer pricing	Separate law on transfer pricing
Kenya	Primary legislation	Primary legislation	Secondary Legislation	Secondary legislation	Secondary legislation	Secondary legislation	n.a.

table continues next page

Table 3.2 Drafting Approach Adopted in Selected Countries *(continued)*

Country	Scope	Arm's-length principle	Comparability standard	Comparability factors	Transfer pricing methods	Selection of method	Arm's-length range
Mexico	Primary legislation	Primary legislation	Primary legislation	Primary legislation	Primary legislation	Primary legislation	Primary legislation (further defined in secondary legislation)
Nigeria	Primary legislation (expanded on in secondary legislation)	Primary legislation (elaborated on in secondary legislation)	Secondary legislation	Secondary legislation	Secondary legislation	Secondary legislation	n.a.
South Africa	Primary legislation	Primary legislation	Administrative guidance	Administrative guidance	Administrative guidance	Administrative guidance	Administrative guidance
Ukraine	Primary legislation	Primary legislation	Primary legislation	Primary legislation	Primary legislation	Primary legislation	Primary legislation
United Kingdom	Primary legislation	Primary legislation	Explicit reference in primary legislation to OECD Transfer Pricing Guidelines	Explicit reference in primary legislation to OECD Transfer Pricing Guidelines	Explicit reference in primary legislation to OECD Transfer Pricing Guidelines	Explicit reference in primary legislation to OECD Transfer Pricing Guidelines	Explicit reference in primary legislation to OECD Transfer Pricing Guidelines
United States	Primary legislation (expanded on in secondary legislation)	Broad legal basis for adjustments in primary legislation	Secondary legislation	Secondary legislation	Secondary legislation	Secondary legislation	Secondary legislation

Note: This table is for illustrative purposes only and is based on information available as of June 30, 2014. n.a. = not applicable.

Table 3.3 Summary of Different Approaches to Drafting Transfer Pricing Legislation

Drafting approach	Primary legislation	Secondary legislation	Administrative guidance	Relative Advantages and disadvantages
Detailed primary legislation	Detailed	As required	As required	• High level of legal certainty for private sector and tax administration • Limited flexibility for application to specific circumstances and changes • Drafting appropriate detailed primary legislation can be very complex
Detail in secondary legislation	Brief	Detailed	As required	• Moderate flexibility for application to specific circumstances • Moderate legal certainty for taxpayers and tax administration
Detail in administrative guidance	Brief	As required	Detailed	• High level of flexibility for application to specific circumstances and for changes • Relatively simple to draft primary legislation • Less legal certainty for taxpayers and tax administration

legal drafters, and the tax administration. Experience suggests, however, that a relatively brief and principles-based approach to primary legislation can:

• Result in legislation that is easier to draft and is easier to understand
• Provide the flexibility to amend and adapt the transfer pricing legal framework as experience with its practical application develops
• Avoid the introduction of lengthy and overly detailed provisions into the tax legislation, reducing uncertainty over interpretation
• Allow for existing principles, definitions, and concepts embedded in the country's tax law to be drawn upon where appropriate, avoiding unintended conflicts
• Assist management of specific issues concerning the legislative process that can arise, such as time constraints and obtaining support from key stakeholders

Table 3.3 sets out some of the relative advantages and disadvantages of different drafting approaches.

Where relatively brief provisions are adopted in the primary law, policy makers should ensure that the necessary authority is provided to the ministry of finance or tax administration (or equivalent thereof) to enact suitable secondary legislation or guidelines.

Components of Transfer Pricing Legislation

Transfer pricing legislation is typically comprised of provisions that can be grouped as core, practical and administrative, and procedural (see figure 3.1). The core provisions are those that set the scope of the legislation, prescribe the

Figure 3.1 Components of Transfer Pricing Legislation

Administrative and procedural

Reporting requirements
Documentation
Penalties
Advance pricing agreements
Simplification measures

Core

Scope
Arm's-length principle
Adjustments

Practical

Comparability
Transfer pricing methods
Selection of method
Arm's-length range
Transaction specific

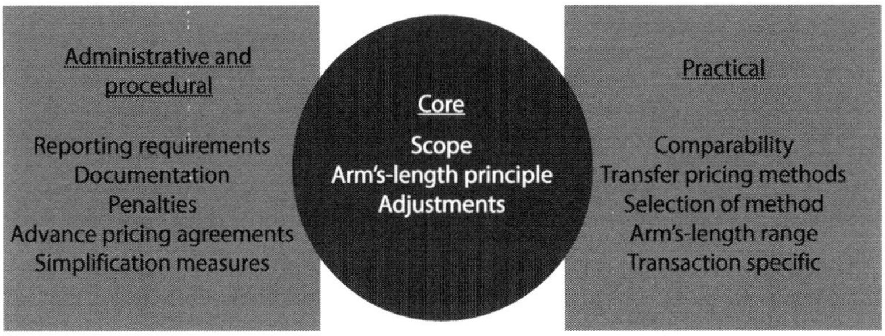

applicable benchmark or standard (for example the arm's-length principle), and provide the necessary authority to the tax administration to make transfer pricing adjustments. The practical provisions are those that guide the practical application of the arm's-length principle and include provisions dealing with comparability, transfer pricing methods, selection of method, etc. Administrative and procedural provisions are those that address matters of a procedural or administrative nature, such as compliance requirements (for example reporting and documentation), penalties, advance pricing agreements (APA), and information gathering powers, etc.

The extent to which the practical, administrative, and procedural provisions are in a country's primary legislation, secondary legislation, or administrative guidance will depend on the drafting approach adopted and the country's legal traditions. Core provisions, on the other hand, are necessarily included in a country's primary legislation.

Core Provisions

Core provisions set the framework for a country's transfer pricing legislation. Typically, they define the scope of the legislation, prescribe the applicable standard (for example arm's-length principle), and authorize types of adjustments.

Scope

The scope of a country's transfer pricing legislation is perhaps one of the most important aspects since it determines which parts of the tax law it will apply to and which classes of taxpayer and types of transactions will be regulated (see table 3.4). The scope of a country's transfer pricing legislation can have far-reaching implications in terms of providing the tax administration with the necessary legislative power to address transfer pricing risk, the level of certainty for taxpayers, and the related compliance costs and administrative burdens imposed on taxpayers and the tax administration.

Determination of the appropriate scope of a country's transfer pricing legislation requires policy makers to consider a range of factors, including the structure

Table 3.4 Determinants of the Scope of Transfer Pricing Legislation

Element		Considerations
Taxes covered		• Which taxes, or parts of the tax law, will be included in the scope?
Classes of taxpayer		• Which classes of taxpayer will the legislation apply to? • Exemption for small enterprises?
Controlled transactions	*Subject matter*	• Will all types of transactions be covered? • Special rules for specific transaction types?
	Size	• Is a threshold necessary or appropriate?
	Relationship between the parties	• How will related or associated parties be defined? • Extension of scope in specific cases (specific jurisdictions)?
	Residence of the parties	• Transactions between residents and nonresidents • Transactions involving permanent establishments • Will domestic transactions be included in the scope?

of the tax system (types of taxes, etc.); the types of transactions and classes of taxpayer that pose transfer pricing risks to the country's revenue; the extent of that risk; the potential compliance costs and administrative burdens imposed on taxpayers and the tax administration, respectively; and a balance between the need for a broad scope and the resulting compliance burden. The wider the scope, the greater the potential for unnecessary and unreasonable compliance costs to be imposed on taxpayers and for unnecessary enforcement costs incurred by the tax administration. However, an overly narrow scope may provide possibilities for circumventing the legislation or may miss certain significant transactions.

The following section sets out the various considerations for determining the appropriate scope for a country's transfer pricing legislation.

Taxes Covered

Depending on the design of a country's tax system, application of the arm's-length principle may be relevant in determining the taxable objects for one or more direct taxes (income tax, corporate tax, profits tax, etc.). Generally, most countries' transfer pricing legislation has broad application across direct taxes. One notable exception being Ireland, where the transfer pricing legislation introduced in 2010 applies only to certain classes of income for direct tax purposes.[5]

Countries with other specific types of direct taxes governing specific sectors or transactions types (such as a mining income tax)[6] may need to consider application of transfer pricing legislation to them. Typically, this would be achieved through separate provisions being inserted in the relevant taxing acts.[7] However, where a consolidated tax code has been adopted, a single set of legislation may be possible. Transfer pricing provisions may also be necessary for other types of taxes—such as a resources royalty—particularly where the base or rate of the tax is linked to income, expenses, or profits, and the value of which may be impacted by controlled transactions.[8]

General application of transfer pricing legislation designed for direct taxation purposes to indirect taxes (such as value added tax [VAT] and customs duties) is typically not appropriate. Customs legislation generally contains its own specific valuation methodologies, which in most countries will be based on the valuation agreement that is binding on World Trade Organization (WTO) members. Although sharing a similar objective to transfer pricing legislation,[9] the customs' valuation methodologies do not necessarily align with the arm's-length principle upon which the direct tax transfer pricing legislation is generally based. This is due to how customs duties are levied—on a transactional basis, at the time of import or export—and the differing requirements stemming from international law. VAT is typically calculated based on the transaction price used by the parties[10] or, as is often the case for imported goods, the customs value declared. Thus, in most circumstances the calculation of VAT does not require a substituted valuate based on objective criteria, except where special valuation rules for related party transactions exist.[11]

Classes of Taxpayer

Transfer pricing legislation may be drafted to apply to all classes of taxpayers or to exclude certain classes of taxpayers, as appropriate. In practice, countries have adopted a range of approaches, with some countries including all taxpayers, others focusing on enterprises and excluding private individuals,[12] and others, such as Ireland and the United Kingdom (see box 3.3), providing specific exclusions for small and medium enterprises (SMEs) from the scope of the legislation.[13] While exclusion of specific classes of transactions may limit the extent of the

---

Box 3.3 United Kingdom's Exemption for SMEs

166 Exemption for small and medium-sized enterprises

(i) Section 147(3) and (5) do not apply in calculating for any chargeable period the profits and losses of a potentially advantaged person if that person is a small or medium-sized enterprise for that chargeable period (see Section 172).

(ii) Exceptions to Subsection (1) are provided:

    (a) in the case of a small enterprise, by Section 167, and

    (b) in the case of a medium-sized enterprise, by Sections 167 and 168.

167 Small- and medium-sized enterprises: Exceptions from exemption

(i) Subsections (2) and (3) set out exceptions to Section 166(1).

(ii) The first exception is if the small or medium-sized enterprise elects for Section 166(1) not to apply in relation to the chargeable period. Any such election is irrevocable.

(iii) The second exception is if:

    (a) the other affected person, or

    (b) a party to a relevant transaction,

box continues next page

Box 3.3 United Kingdom's Exemption for SMEs *(continued)*

is, at the time when the actual provision is or was made or imposed, a resident of a non-qualifying territory (whether or not that person is also a resident of a qualifying territory).

(iv) For the purposes of Subsection (3):

   (a) a "party to a relevant transaction" is a person who, if the actual provision is or was imposed by means of a series of transactions, is a party to one or more of those transactions, and

   (b) "qualifying territory" and "non-qualifying territory" are defined in Section 173.

(v) In Subsection (3) "resident," in relation to a territory:

   (a) means a person who, under the law of that territory, is liable to tax there by reason of the person's domicile, residence or place of management, but

   (b) does not include a person who is liable to tax in that territory in respect only of income from sources in that territory or capital situated there.

Note: Small- and medium-sized enterprise is defined by reference to annex to Commission Recommendation: *2003/361/EC of May 6, 2003 (concerning the definition of micro-, small-, and medium-sized businesses) which defines the category of micro-, small-, and medium-sized business as those enterprises that employ fewer than 250 persons and which have an annual turnover not exceeding EUR50 million, and/or an annual balance sheet total not exceeding EUR43 million.*

---

compliance burden imposed, it comes at the cost of gaps in the legislation, which may be subject to abuse.

Transfer pricing legislation that is drafted to apply to all or most classes of taxpayer, but not necessarily all transactions, will provide the tax administration with a broad legal basis for addressing transfer pricing risks. Smaller taxpayers that pose less risk to the revenue may, as a consequence thereof, fall within the scope of the legislation. The administrative burden on such taxpayers can, however, be mitigated through appropriately designed documentation and reporting requirements.[14]

Controlled Transactions

Specifying the controlled transactions that are to be covered is central to determining the scope of a country's transfer pricing legislation. With some exceptions, countries will, at minimum, include within the scope all cross-border transactions between associated parties. However, this scope may be extended to include certain other transactions, such as domestic transactions between associated parties or transactions with parties in specified jurisdictions, and definitions of the term *associated party* (or similar) can differ markedly. The main determinants of what will be considered controlled transactions include

- Subject matter of the transaction
- Transaction size
- Relationship between the parties (i.e., definition of *associated parties*)
- Location of the parties

Subject matter of the transaction. Since the main objective of transfer pricing legislation is to protect the country's tax base, most countries draft their transfer pricing law to apply to all types of transactions that may affect a taxpayer's taxable income. For example, South Africa's legislation covers "supply of goods or services," which is interpreted as including financial transactions [paragraph 5 of Practice Note 7 (1999) (South Africa)], and Georgia's legislation broadly refers to "financial and commercial transactions" [section 127(1) Georgian Tax Code]. Similarly, in Albania, *transaction* has been defined broadly, including any direct or indirect agreements, understandings, or arrangements (see box 3.4).

Some countries have elected to adopt more elaborate specifications of the types of transactions covered in their primary or secondary legislation. For example, Kenya's primary legislation refers to situations in which "a nonresident person carries on business with a related resident person" [section 18(3) Income Tax Act (CAP.470 of the Laws of Kenya), as amended 2009], with section 6 of the Income Tax (Transfer Pricing) Rules 2006 providing a specific definition of the types of transactions this covers, but including a catchall for "any other transactions which may affect the profit or loss of the enterprise involved" (see box 3.5).

Similarly, in Ghana, Regulation 1(2) of Transfer Pricing Regulations contains a specific list of transaction types, with a catchall for "any other transaction that may affect the profit or loss of the entity."

Where specific legislation concerning the subject matter of the transactions (or types of transactions) is to be included, drafters should be careful to ensure

---

Box 3.4 Definition of *Transaction* in Albania's Transfer Pricing Legislation

Article 2(4)(dh) Law on Income Tax
Transaction includes a direct or indirect arrangement, understanding, agreement, or mutual practice whether or not legally enforceable or intended to be legally enforceable and includes any dealing between related persons.

Box 3.5 Transactions Subject to Kenya's Transfer Pricing Rules

Article 2(4)(dh) The Income Tax (Transfer Pricing) Rules, 2006
The transactions subject to adjustment of prices under these Rules shall include:
(a) the sale or purchase of goods;
(b) the sale, purchase or lease of tangible assets;
(c) the transfer, purchase or use of intangible assets;
(d) the provision of services;
(e) the lending or borrowing of money; and
(f) any other transactions which may affect the profit or loss of the enterprise involved.

---

that transaction types do not unintentionally fall outside the scope. If a country has specific legislation in place dealing with the treatment of certain transaction types, these transactions may require exclusion from the scope of the general transfer pricing legislation.[15]

Transaction size. To manage the compliance burden, some countries have elected to introduce size thresholds for certain transactions to be included in the scope of their transfer pricing legislation. In Ukraine, for example, aggregate controlled transactions with a counterparty had to exceed Hrv50 million (about US$3.9 million) before those transactions would be included in the scope of the transfer pricing provisions.[16] "Hard thresholds" such as these are atypical since they provide high potential for abuse. Taxpayers may, for example, enter into non–arm's-length transactions under but up to the limit of the threshold as a means of transferring profits out of the country. More commonly observed are "soft thresholds" based on transaction size that provide exclusions from compliance requirements on reporting and documentation (see also chapter 6).[17] Soft thresholds can be employed to balance the compliance burden imposed without generating the possibilities for abuse where hard thresholds exist. Where a hard threshold for application of the transfer pricing legislation is considered necessary, countries such as the United Kingdom and Ireland (see "Classes of Taxpayer") have based that threshold on the size of the taxpayer, rather than the object of the legislation (i.e., the transaction value).

Relationship between the parties. Transfer pricing risks arise where there is a relationship between the parties to the transaction that may influence the transfer price (other than in accordance with market forces). Countries have, therefore, tended to limit the scope of their transfer pricing legislation to transactions between "associated enterprises," or a similar concept, such as related, affiliated, or connected parties. Section 2(1) of *Transfer Pricing Legislation* (OECD 2011) adopts a definition of associated enterprises replicates the wording of Article 9(1) of the OECD model:

1. Two enterprises are considered to be associated where:
   (a) One enterprise participates directly or indirectly in the management, control or capital of the other, or
   (b) The same person or persons participate(s) directly or indirectly in the management, control or capital of both enterprises.

Section 2(2) (OECD 2011) further elaborates on this definition by defining when a "person or enterprise participates directly or indirectly in the management, control or capital of an enterprise":

2. A person or enterprise participates directly or indirectly in the management, control or capital of an enterprise where:
   (a) It owns, directly or indirectly, more than (50 percent) of the share capital of the enterprise, or
   (b) It has the practical ability to control the business decisions of the enterprise.

Countries have defined *associated parties* from brief, principles-based definitions to the more detailed and highly specific. The adopted definitions are influenced by a range of factors, including the classes of taxpayer that fall within the scope of the law and the perception of the relationships that pose a risk to revenue due to transfer mispricing, including any relationships of cultural or legal importance in the country. In Singapore, for example, *related parties* is defined as "any other person who, directly or indirectly, controls that person, or is controlled, directly or indirectly, by that person, or where he and that other person, directly or indirectly, are under the control of a common person" [section 13(16) of Singapore Income Tax Act]. In contrast, India defines *associated enterprise* in section 92(A) of the Income Tax Act of 1961 (India) with a high degree of specificity (see box 3.6).

The primary focus in most countries' definitions of associated parties is on formal relationships of ownership or control (de jure control), often with minimum

---

Box 3.6 India's Definition of *Associated Enterprise*

Article 2(4)(dh), the Income Tax (Transfer Pricing) Rules, 2006

1. For the purposes of this Section and Sections 92, 92B, 92C, 92D, 92E and 92F, associated enterprise, in relation to another enterprise, means an enterprise:
   a. which participates, directly or indirectly, or through one or more intermediaries, in the management or control or capital of the other enterprise; or
   b. in respect of which one or more persons who participate, directly or indirectly, or through one or more intermediaries, in its management or control or capital, are the same persons who participate, directly or indirectly, or through one or more intermediaries, in the management or control or capital of the other enterprise.

2. For the purposes of Subsection (1), two enterprises shall be deemed to be associated enterprises if, at any time during the previous year,
   a. one enterprise holds, directly or indirectly, shares carrying not less than 26 percent of the voting power in the other enterprise; or
   b. any person or enterprise holds, directly or indirectly, shares carrying not less than 26 percent of the voting power in each of such enterprises; or
   c. a loan advanced by one enterprise to the other enterprise constitutes not less than 51 percent of the book value of the total assets of the other enterprise; or
   d. one enterprise guarantees not less than 10 percent of the total borrowings of the other enterprise; or
   e. more than half of the board of directors or members of the governing board, or one or more executive directors or executive members of the governing board of one enterprise, are appointed by the other enterprise; or
   f. more than half of the directors or members of the governing board, or one or more of the executive directors or members of the governing board, of each of the two enterprises are appointed by the same person or persons; or

box continues next page

g. the manufacture or processing of goods or articles or business carried out by one enterprise is wholly dependent on the use of know-how, patents, copyrights, trademarks, licences, franchises or any other business or commercial rights of similar nature, or any data, documentation, drawing or specification relating to any patent, invention, model, design, secret formula or process, of which the other enterprise is the owner or in respect of which the other enterprise has exclusive rights; or

h. 90 percent or more of the raw materials and consumables required for the manufacture or processing of goods or articles carried out by one enterprise are supplied by the other enterprise, or by persons specified by the other enterprise, and the prices and other conditions relating to the supply are influenced by such other enterprise; or

i. the goods or articles manufactured or processed by one enterprise are sold to the other enterprise or to persons specified by the other enterprise, and the prices and other conditions relating thereto are influenced by such other enterprise; or

j. where one enterprise is controlled by an individual, the other enterprise is also controlled by such individual or his relative or jointly by such individual and relative of such individual; or

k. where one enterprise is controlled by a Hindu undivided family, the other enterprise is controlled by a member of such Hindu undivided family or by a relative of a member of such Hindu undivided family or jointly by such member and his relative; or

l. where one enterprise is a firm, association of persons or body of individuals, the other enterprise holds not less than 10 percent interest in such firm, association of persons or body of individuals; or

m. there exists between the two enterprises any relationship of mutual interest, as may be prescribed.

shareholding or control over of voting rights specified. These percentages can vary significantly between countries, for example, from 10 percent up to 50 percent and higher.

In many countries the definition has been expanded to include personal relationships; relationships of specific cultural importance; and relationships of practical control (de facto control), which generally focus on the ability of one enterprise to practically control or influence the business decisions of the other. Georgia has adopted this approach, with the definition of "associated enterprises" in Article 126(4) of the Tax Code making reference to a person who "practically controls the business decisions of an enterprise," which is then elaborated on in the secondary legislation (see box 3.7).

Including certain relationships of practical control within the scope is important because it limits opportunities for abuse and tax planning to which an otherwise purely de jure approach can be susceptible. For example, if the definition is limited to de jure relationships (such as percentages of voting rights or capital), it may be possible to avoid application of the law

Box 3.7 Georgia's Practical Control Definition

Article 3 Decree #423 on the Approval of the Instructions on International Transfer Pricing (2013)

For the purposes of Article 126(2)(b) of the tax code, a person is considered to "directly or indirectly practically control the business decisions of the enterprise" when one of the conditions listed below is met:

a) it directly or indirectly holds or controls a majority of stocks/shares of the company with the voting rights;
b) it can directly or indirectly control the composition of the board of directors;
c) it has a right to get directly or indirectly 50 percent or more of the profits of the enterprise;
d) the sum of loans directly or indirectly provided by it to the enterprise and the loans directly or indirectly borrowed by the enterprise guaranteed by it is greater than 50 percent of the book value of the enterprises' total assets;
e) a relative of a person directly or indirectly holds more than 50 percent of an enterprise or directly or indirectly manages the enterprise; and
f) control over the business decisions of the enterprise is otherwise evidenced by the facts and circumstances.

---

to certain transactions by routing them through (practically controlled) independent intermediaries (for example back-to-back loans through an intermediary). A definition that is too broad, however, has the potential to give rise to significant uncertainty and to impose an unnecessary compliance burden on taxpayers entering into, for example, arm's-length transactions with independent parties.

(*Table 3B.1 in annex 3B provides examples of types of relationships included in selected countries' definitions of* associated parties.)

Chile, France, Georgia, Mexico, Portugal, the Russian Federation, Serbia, and numerous other countries have extended the scope of their legislation to include transactions with parties located in specific jurisdictions, regardless of the existence of any specific relationship between the parties.[18] For example, the definition of *controlled transaction* under Albania's legislation includes transactions with residents of specified jurisdictions, regardless of the relationship (see box 3.8). Similarly, Serbia's legislation deems transactions with parties from jurisdictions with preferential tax regimes to be associated parties, with the definition of *preferential tax regime* specifically excluding tax treaty partners (see box 3.9).

The policy rationale underlying the deeming of such transactions as "controlled transactions" is to provide the tax administration with a tool to overcome information constraints when dealing with entities in "blacklisted" jurisdictions.

Administrators usually face difficulties in ascertaining and evidencing a relationship between a resident taxpayer and foreign parties in such jurisdictions. Where such a provision is adopted, the way in which the "specific jurisdictions" are defined or determined requires careful consideration. In addition to having potential political consequences, the definition may substantially impact the

---

Box 3.8 Albania's Definition of Controlled Transactions

Article 2(4)(c) Law on Income Tax
A **controlled transaction** is:
   i. any transaction between associated parties where:
      – one party to the transaction is a resident and the other party is a nonresident,
      – one party to the transaction is a nonresident that has a permanent establishment in Albania to which the transaction is attributable and the other party is another nonresident,
      – one party to the transaction is a resident and the other party is a resident that has a permanent establishment outside of Albania to which the transaction is attributable.
   ii. any dealings between a nonresident and a permanent establishment in Albania of that nonresident,
   iii. any dealings between a resident and its permanent establishment outside of Albania,
   iv. any transaction between a resident or a nonresident that has a permanent establishment in Albania to which the transaction is attributable with a resident of a jurisdiction, listed in the Instruction of the Minister of Finance.

Box 3.9 Serbia's Application of Its Transfer Pricing Legislation to Transactions with Entities from Jurisdictions with a Preferential Tax System

Article 59(7) Corporate Income Tax Law
Notwithstanding paragraphs 2 through 6 of this article, a party related to the taxpayer shall be understood to mean any nonresident legal entity from the jurisdiction with a preferential tax system.

Article 3A Corporate Income Tax Law
For the needs of application of the provisions of this law, the jurisdiction with a preferential tax system shall be understood to mean the territory with tax sovereignty which applies legislation that offer the possibilities for substantially lower tax burden on corporate income of legal entities, either all legal entities or those that meet particular requirements, as well as the dividend which they allocate to their founders in comparison with the one anticipated in the provisions of this law and the law which governs the taxation of income of citizens, or for preventing or obstructing the identification of the actual owners of legal entities by the tax

box continues next page

Box 3.9 Serbia's Application of Its Transfer Pricing Legislation to Transactions with Entities from Jurisdictions with a Preferential Tax System *(continued)*

authorities of Serbia and preventing or obstructing the identification of those tax facts, which would be of significance for assessing the tax liability under the regulations of Serbia (hereinafter the jurisdiction with the preferential tax system).

A nonresident legal entity from the jurisdiction with the preferential tax system shall be understood to mean the nonresident legal entity which:

1) is established in the territory of the jurisdiction with the preferential tax system, or
2) has a registered headquarters in the territory of the jurisdiction with the preferential tax system, or
3) has management headquarters in the territory of the jurisdiction with the preferential tax system, or
4) has a place of actual management in the territory of the jurisdiction with the preferential tax system.

Paragraph 2 of this article shall not apply in the case that the nonresident legal entity may be considered a resident of the other contracting country for the needs of application of the international agreement on avoidance of double taxation between that country and Serbia.

For the needs of application of paragraph 1 of this article the Minister of Finance shall determine the list of jurisdictions with the preferential tax system.

---

scope of the country's transfer pricing legislation and thus the potential compliance burden imposed on taxpayers. The inclusion of countries covered by tax treaties that have a comprehensive exchange of information article or by a tax exchange of information agreement would thus not usually be consistent with the aforementioned policy objective, since the provisions on the exchange of information should provide the tax administration with a channel for obtaining information.

Policy makers should be very cautious about introducing legislation with a scope that potentially includes transactions between independent parties. This approach is perhaps contrary to the purpose of transfer pricing legislation and has the potential to generate unnecessary uncertainty and impose an unnecessary compliance burden on taxpayers.

Residence of the parties. Although many countries apply their transfer pricing legislation to all transactions between associated parties, regardless of tax residence,[19] the focus of transfer pricing legislation is typically on "cross-border" or international transactions. Cross-border transactions will typically include transactions between

- A resident and a nonresident
- A local permanent establishment of a nonresident and a nonresident
- A resident and a foreign permanent establishment of a resident

In addition to including cross-border transactions in the scope of the legislation, some countries have included transactions between two nonresidents (for example, for the purposes of applying controlled foreign corporation [CFC] rules) and "dealings" between a permanent establishment and the rest of the entity of which it is a part.

Where a more limited scope is sought (i.e., limited or no coverage of domestic transactions), drafters should carefully consider the implications of the terminology. In such cases, failure to include permanent establishments of nonresidents within the scope of a country's transfer pricing legislation—that is, limiting the application of the legislation to transactions between a resident and a nonresident—may result in a significant gap in the legislation, potentially leading to lost tax revenues and issues of discrimination. South Africa has avoided this issue by drafting its transfer pricing legislation to specifically cover an international agreement, which, in turn, is broadly defined as (a) a transaction, operation, or scheme between a resident and a nonresident; (b) a South African permanent establishment of a nonresident and a resident; and (c) a nonresident and a foreign permanent establishment of a resident (see box 3.10). Albania has adopted a similar approach to its definition of *controlled transaction* (see box 3.8).

Where a broad scope is considered appropriate (for example, including domestic transactions), compliance obligations (reporting and documentation) should be tailored appropriately. To manage the uncertainty and potential compliance burden associated with full-scale application of the transfer pricing legislation to domestic transactions, some countries have excluded such transactions from reporting and documentation requirements, while others have limited the types of domestic transactions that are included within the

---

Box 3.10 South Africa's Definition of "International Agreement"

Article 31(1) Income Tax Act No. 58 of 1962 (as amended, South Africa)

"International agreement" means a transaction, operation or scheme entered into between

(a) (i) a resident; and
    (ii) any other person who is not a resident; or

(b) (i) a person who is not a resident; and
    (ii) any other person who is not a resident,

for the supply of goods or services to or by a permanent establishment of either of such persons in the Republic; or

(c) (i) a person who is a resident; and
    (ii) any other person who is a resident,

for the supply of goods or services to or by a permanent establishment of either of such persons outside the Republic.

---

scope of the law. In the latter case, typically only domestic transactions that pose a risk to the tax base are included, such as transactions with tax-exempt entities or entities subject to reduced tax rates.[20] For example, in Egypt, although the primary legislation applies to both domestic and international transactions, its scope is limited to transactions that "reduce the tax base or to shift the tax burden from a taxable person to an exempt or nontaxable one" (see box 3.1).

Similarly, in Russia, domestic transactions between related parties are subject to transfer pricing legislation only if they fulfill specific criteria. For example, transactions between residents where one of the parties is exempt from paying profit tax, pays tax at a 0 percent rate,[21] or is registered in a special economic zone—and for domestic-related party transactions generally—if the aggregate exceeds a Rub 3 billion (about US$108 million) threshold; the threshold was reduced to Rub 2 billion in 2013 and Rub 1 billion in 2014, with some exceptions (Ernst & Young 2011).

Arm's-Length Principle

Transfer pricing legislation requires that a specific standard be prescribed for the transactions that fall within the scope of the legislation. International practice is to adopt the arm's-length principle (as elaborated in Article 9 of OECD and UN models) as the applicable standard (see chapter 1). In this regard, a country's legislation will typically implement the arm's-length principle by prescribing that conditions in transactions falling within the scope of the legislation should be consistent with the conditions observed in comparable transactions between independent parties. For example, section 1(1) of *Transfer Pricing Legislation* (OECD 2011) reads:

> 1. For purposes of [relevant provisions of Country's tax law], where an enterprise engages in one or more commercial or financial transactions with an associated enterprise that is not an enterprise of [Country], each such enterprise shall determine the amount of its taxable profits in a manner that is consistent with the arm's-length principle. The amount of taxable profits derived by an enterprise that engages in one or more commercial or financial transactions with an associated enterprise shall be consistent with the arm's-length principle if the conditions of those transactions do not differ from the conditions that would have applied between independent enterprises in comparable transactions carried out under comparable circumstances.

Country experience suggests that, as in preceding examples, legislation should focus on *conditions* (for example prices, margins, and profit split) as opposed to *prices*. Legislation that focuses only on prices can unnecessarily limit the scope of the legislation and can give rise to practical difficulties (for example in determining actual prices when using transactional profits-based methods, which compare margins; see chapter 4). Ghana's transfer pricing regulations ensure a broad scope and avoid the practical issues associated with legislation focused on prices by focusing on the "terms" of the transaction (see box 3.11).

Box 3.11 Ghana's Legislation Is Focused on "Terms" as Opposed to "Price"

Ghana: Article 2 of Transfer Pricing Regulations (2012)

(1) A person who engages in a transaction with another person with whom that person has a controlled relationship shall compute the profit or loss arising from that transaction on the basis that it is conducted at arm's-length.

(2) A transaction is conducted at arm's-length between persons in a controlled relationship if the terms of the transaction do not differ from the terms of a comparable transaction between independent persons.

In some countries, use of terminology other than *arm's-length* or *arm's-length principle* may be necessary due to local language terminology or drafting style. The actual terminology used is not of great importance; rather, it is the way in which the standard is defined and interpreted that is important. For example, Article 36 of Law on Income Tax of Albania uses the term *market principle* as opposed to *arm's-length principle*; the legislation, however, defines *market principle* to be consistent with the generally accepted interpretation of the arm's-length principle.

Legislation that introduces a standard that differs from the generally accepted interpretation of the arm's-length principle, such as "open market value" or "competitive market price," can give rise to unnecessary uncertainty and disputes. Further, adoption of a different standard may result in legislation that is inconsistent with the country's international legal obligations (for example under tax treaties; see chapter 2) and may give rise to instances of economic double taxation.

Adjustments

In addition to providing the tax administration with the necessary authority to make primary adjustments, a country's transfer pricing legislation may provide other types of adjustments, discussed below (see also summary in table 3.5).

Primary Adjustments

To enforce compliance with the legislation where the conditions in transactions falling within the scope of the legislation are not consistent with the arm's-length principle, the tax administration needs the ability to adjust a taxpayer's taxable income. Such adjustments are typically referred to as "primary adjustments."

The authority for the tax administration to make a primary adjustment may be explicitly granted in the legislation, as is the case in Ethiopia (see box 3.12). Alternatively, the power to make an adjustment may be implicit, in that the legislation merely requires that taxable income be determined consistently with the arm's-length, and the authority for the tax administration to make adjustments will flow from the tax administration's general competency to administer the tax law.

Table 3.5 Main Types of Transfer Pricing Adjustments

Type of adjustment	Description
Primary	Adjustment made by the tax administration to increase the taxable income of a taxpayer in accordance with the arm's-length principle
Compensating	Adjustment in which a taxpayer reports an (arm's-length) transfer price for tax purposes that differs from the amount actually charged between the associated enterprises
Corresponding	Adjustment to the tax liability of an associated enterprise corresponding to a primary adjustment made with respect to another associated enterprise in relation to a transaction with the first associated enterprise so that the allocation of profits between the enterprises is consistent
Secondary	Adjustment that arises from imposing a tax on a secondary transaction (i.e., a constructive transaction asserted to make the actual allocation of profits consistent with the primary adjustment)

Box 3.12 Example: Explicit Adjustment Power

Ethiopia: Article 29(1) of Income Tax Proclamation No. 286/2002

Where conditions are made or imposed between persons carrying on business in their commercial or financial relations, which differ from those which would be made between independent persons, the Tax Authority may direct that the income of one or more of those related persons is to include profits which he or they would have made but for those conditions. The Tax Authority shall do so in accordance with the directives to be issued by the Minister.

Transfer pricing legislation that prescribes the arm's-length principle as the applicable standard should be neutral in its applicability: that is, the legislation, and the authority to make adjustments, should apply regardless of the intentions or motivations of the taxpayer. Where legislation is drafted so as to require the tax administration to demonstrate that the transfer prices were deliberately manipulated or that there is a tax avoidance motive, the legislation will be extremely difficult to administer successfully.

Typically, transfer pricing legislation will provide for only upward adjustments (i.e., adjustments that increase taxable income), with downward adjustments provided for only in limited situations, such as a corresponding adjustment under a tax treaty (see "Corresponding Adjustments"). For example, Article 36(3) of Albania's Law on Income Tax specifically requires that adjustments may be made only where they increase taxable profits (see box 3.13), while Article 36/6 provides the possibility for corresponding adjustments where a tax treaty is applicable (see box 3.16).

Box 3.13 Example: Legislation Allowing for Upward Adjustments Only

Albania: Article 36(3) of Law on Income Tax (1998, as amended)
Where the conditions made or imposed in one or more controlled transactions entered into by a taxpayer are not consistent with the market principle, then the taxable profits of that taxpayer may be increased so as to be consistent with the market principle.

Importantly, transfer pricing legislation applies for the purpose of adjusting taxable profit and income. This is typically the case: adjustments made for direct taxation transfer pricing purposes will affect only the computation of direct taxation liabilities and will not affect the transfer price for other regulatory purposes such as customs valuation, VAT, or foreign exchange requirements. (On the interface of transfer pricing, customs valuation, and VAT, see chapter 5.)

In addition to ensuring that there is a clear legal basis for the tax administration to make primary adjustments, other issues directly related to the exercise of this power, such as the statute of limitations, requirements of internal approval, and selection of point within the arm's-length range require due consideration when designing a country's transfer pricing legislation. These issues and others are discussed below in "Practical Provisions" and "Administrative and Procedural Provisions."

Compensating Adjustments
With compensating adjustments, a taxpayer reports an arm's-length transfer price for tax purposes that differs from the amount actually charged between the associated enterprises. Such adjustments, also referred to as year-end adjustments or self-adjustments, are often necessary where a taxpayer is using an ex post or arm's-length outcome testing approach to its transfer pricing (i.e., where the analysis is on ensuring that the outcome of the transactions is consistent with the arm's-length principle, as opposed to ensuring that the conditions of the transactions are arm's-length at the time at which the transactions are entered).

In practice, compensating adjustments may be made for tax purposes only (i.e., tax-only adjustments) or may involve actual price adjustments (i.e., actual price adjustments whereby payments are made or received by the taxpayer from the associated parties). The approach by a taxpayer will typically depend on the design of a country's transfer pricing legislation (i.e., what is acceptable, including to the tax administration) and the transfer pricing policy of the taxpayer. The approaches adopted by countries differ significantly, from wholesale acceptance of compensating adjustments (both tax-only and actual) to nonacceptance, or acceptance only in exceptional cases. It is primarily a matter of administrative practice, with relatively few countries having specific legislation or guidance.

Box 3.14 Example: Provision for Use of Arm's-Length Values in Lieu of Actual Values

United Kingdom: Section 147(1)-(3) "Tax calculations to be based on arm's-length, not actual, provision" of the Taxation [International and Other Provisions] Act 2010

(1) For the purposes of this Section "the basic pre-condition" is that:

   (a) provision ("the actual provision") has been made or imposed as between any two persons ("the affected persons") by means of a transaction or series of transactions,

   (b) the participation condition is met (see Section 148),

   (c) the actual provision is not within Subsection (7) (oil transactions), and

   (d) the actual provision differs from the provision ("the arm's-length provision"), which would have been made as between independent enterprises.

(2) Subsection (3) applies if:

   (a) the basic pre-condition is met, and

   (b) the actual provision confers a potential advantage in relation to the United Kingdom taxation on one of the affected persons.

(3) The profits and losses of the potentially advantaged person are to be calculated for tax purposes as if the arm's-length provision had been made or imposed instead of the actual provision.

Whether values can be declared for tax purposes that differ from the actual prices used in the transaction will be a matter of policy and legal tradition. Of the countries that allow for such adjustments, they are typically allowed only where they result in an increase in taxable income. Such is the case in the United Kingdom, where the arm's-length value may be used instead of the actual value, but only where use of the actual value would have resulted in a tax advantage for the affected persons (see box 3.14). U.S. Internal Revenue Code (IRC) 482 regulations, on the other hand, provide general scope for taxpayers to report arm's-length prices that differ from the amount actually charged if done so in a timely filed U.S. income tax return, but do not permit adjustments that decrease taxable income if made by way of an untimely or amended return.[22] In countries that specifically allow tax-only adjustments, officials should be aware of and monitor any potential abuses (such as schemes designed to repatriate funds while avoiding dividend withholding taxes).[23]

Recognizing the difficulties faced by taxpayers in the EU due to countries' different approaches to the acceptance of corresponding adjustments, the EU Joint Transfer Pricing Forum (EUJTPF) published the results of its study in *Report on Compensating Adjustments* in November 2013. This report recommended specific conditions under which compensating adjustments should be accepted (see box 3.15).

Box 3.15 EUJTPF: Practical Solution to Compensating Adjustments in the EU

[Member States] agree that: (i) the profits of the related enterprises with respect to the commercial or financial relations between them need to be calculated symmetrically, i.e., enterprises participating in a transaction should use the same price for the respective trans-actions, and that (ii) a compensating adjustment initiated by the taxpayer should be accepted if the conditions listed below are fulfilled. This means that if the [Member States] involved have less-prescriptive rules on compensating adjustments, these less-prescriptive rules apply; furthermore, this report does not encourage [Member States] to introduce more conditions for compensating adjustments than currently apply. The conditions are:

- Before the relevant transaction or series of transactions, the taxpayer made reasonable efforts to achieve an arm's-length outcome. This would normally be described in the transfer pricing documentation of the taxpayer.
- The taxpayer makes the adjustment symmetrically in the accounts in both [Member States] involved.
- The taxpayer applies the same approach consistently over time.
- The taxpayer makes the adjustment before filing the tax return.
- The taxpayer is able to explain for what reasons his forecast did not match the result achieved, when it is required by internal legislation in at least one of the [Member States] involved.

—EUJTPF (2013)

Corresponding Adjustments

A primary adjustment may result in economic double taxation if there is no corresponding adjustment made with respect to the tax liability of the other party to the transaction. Corresponding adjustments, or correlative adjustments, may be provided for with respect to international transactions, domestic transactions, or both, depending on the scope of the country's domestic law.[24]

In the international context, such adjustments are envisaged under tax treaties containing an article based on Article 9(2) of either the OECD or UN model tax conventions (see chapter 2). To implement this, numerous countries, such as Albania, Mexico, and Nigeria (see box 3.16), have included provisions in their legislation concerning corresponding adjustments.

Where a corresponding provision is included in a country's legislation, its application will typically be limited to situations in which a tax treaty is applicable and the tax administration agrees with the primary adjustment made by the other tax administration. Countries generally do not enact legislation that provides for a corresponding adjustment in the absence of an applicable tax treaty. Instead, they provide such relief only when the situation is covered by a tax treaty, thus providing for reciprocal treatment and the legal basis to obtain information regarding the primary adjustment and to enter into negotiations regarding the adjustment.

Box 3.16 Example: Corresponding Adjustment Provisions

Albania: Article 36/6 "Corresponding Adjustments" of the Law on Income Tax (No. 8438)

Where an adjustment to the conditions of a controlled transaction is made by a tax administration in another country, and this adjustment results in the taxation in that country of profits on which the taxpayer in Albania has already been charged to tax in Albania and the country that has made the adjustment has a treaty with Albania that reflects an intention to provide for the relief of double taxation, then, in such circumstances, the tax administration of Albania, after a request is made by the Albanian taxpayer, shall examine the consistency of that adjustment with the market principle, as defined in Article 36, point 2. If the tax administration concludes that the adjustment is consistent with the market principle, it makes an appropriate adjustment to the amount of the tax charged to the Albanian taxpayer. Procedure for request for a corresponding adjustment under this article will be specified in the instruction of the Minister of Finance.

Mexico: Section 217 of the Income Tax Law

When, in accordance with an international tax treaty concluded by Mexico, the competent authorities of the other country make an adjustment to the prices or consideration of a taxpayer residing in such country and, when such adjustment is accepted by the Mexican tax authorities, the related party residing in Mexico may file a supplementary tax return in which the corresponding adjustment is reflected. This supplementary tax return will not be calculated under the limit established by Art. 32 of the Federal Fiscal Code.

—(IBFD 2011)

Nigeria: Regulation 8 of the Income Tax (Transfer Pricing) Regulations, No. 2012

Where

(a) an adjustment is made to the taxation of a transaction or transactions of a connected taxable person by a competent authority of another country with which Nigeria has a Double Taxation Treaty; and

(b) the adjustment results in taxation in that other country of income or profits that are also taxable in Nigeria;

the Service may, upon request by the connected taxable person subject to tax in Nigeria, determine whether the adjustment is consistent with the arm's-length principle and where it is determined to be consistent, the Service may make a corresponding adjustment to the amount of tax charged in Nigeria on the income so as to avoid double taxation.

Provisions specifying the availability for corresponding adjustments can help avoid uncertainty and increased compliance costs that may be faced by taxpayers seeking to obtain the benefits afforded to them under an applicable tax treaty. Clear guidance on the procedure for seeking corresponding adjustments can also play an important role in this regard by, for example, specifying the information to be provided when seeking an adjustment (see box 3.17).

Box 3.17 Georgia's Corresponding Adjustment Request Procedure

Georgia: Article 37 "Corresponding Adjustment Procedure" of Decree on Approval on Instructions on International Transfer Pricing (#423, December 2013)

1. A request by a Georgian enterprise for a corresponding adjustment to be made in accordance with Article 129(2) of the Georgian Tax Code (GTC) must be made in writing to the Revenue Service and must include (or be accompanied by) the information necessary for the Revenue Service to examine consistency with the market principle:

   a) The name and registration details of the associated enterprise;

   b) The year in which the adjusted transaction took place;

   c) The amount of the requested corresponding adjustment and the amounts of the adjustment made by the tax administration of the tax treaty partner;

   d) Evidence of the tax residence of the associated enterprise (i.e., a letter or residency certificate provided by the tax administration of the tax treaty partner country);

   e) Evidence of the adjustment made by the tax administration of the tax treaty partner and the basis for the adjustment (i.e., a copy of the assessment and supporting analysis and details of any administrative appeals or litigation proceedings undertaken, where applicable);

   f) Details of comparability factors, the transfer pricing method applied, etc.;

   g) Confirmation that the associated party will not, or is unable to, pursue any further recourse under the domestic law of the tax treaty partner that may result in the adjustment made by the tax administration of the tax treaty partner being reduced or reversed;

   h) Any other information that may be relevant for examining the consistency of the adjustment with the market principle.

2. The request must be made within the applicable time period for making a request for the case to be resolved by way of mutual agreement procedure under the applicable tax treaty.

3. The Revenue Service will, within six months from the date of receiving a request that satisfies this article, notify the Georgian enterprise as to whether or not the requested corresponding adjustment under Article 129(2) of the GTC will be granted in part or in full.

4. Where the Revenue Service has rejected a Georgian enterprise's request for a corresponding adjustment to be granted under Article 129(2) of the GTC in part or in full, written reasons for this decision shall be provided to the Georgian enterprise at the time of the Georgian enterprise being notified of the decision. Such reasons may include, but are not limited to:

   a) The request does not satisfy the requirements of this article;

   b) The Georgian enterprise has failed to provide the Revenue Service with the information necessary for him to examine the consistency of the adjustment with the market principle;

   c) The Revenue Service is of the view that the adjustment is not consistent with the market principle, and provides an explanation to this effect.

5. Further clarification of the required procedure for a request for a corresponding adjustment under Article 129(2) of the GTC may be notified by the Revenue Service.

Box 3.18 Corresponding Adjustments for Domestic Transactions in the United Kingdom

Section 174 (1)-(2) of the Taxation [International and Other Provisions] Act 2010
174 Claim by the affected person who is not potentially advantaged

(1) Subsection (2) applies if:

(a) only one of the affected persons (in this chapter called "the advantaged person") is a person on whom a potential advantage in relation to the United Kingdom taxation is conferred by the actual provision, and (b) the other affected person (in this chapter called "the disadvantaged person") is within the charge to income tax or corporation tax in respect of profits arising from the relevant activities (see Section 216).

(2) On the making of a claim by the disadvantaged person:

(a) the profits and losses of the disadvantaged person are to be calculated for tax purposes as if the arm's-length provision had been made or imposed instead of the actual provision, and

(b) despite any limit in the Tax Acts on the time within which any adjustment may be made, all such adjustments are to be made in the disadvantaged person's case as may be required to give effect to the assumption that the arm's-length provision was made or imposed instead of the actual provision.

In some countries, the implementation of tax treaties may provide sufficient basis without the need for specific legislation. In such situations, clear guidance regarding the applicable procedure for seeking a corresponding adjustment is still necessary.

Where domestic transactions are included in the scope of a country's transfer pricing legislation, provision should be made for corresponding adjustments, except, perhaps, in cases of fraud or abuse. In the United Kingdom, for example, where domestic transactions fall within the scope of the transfer pricing legislation, provision is made through compensating adjustments (see box 3.18).

Secondary Adjustments

Secondary adjustments arise from the imposition of a tax on a secondary transaction (i.e., a constructive transaction asserted to make the actual allocation of profits consistent with the primary adjustment). The rationale for secondary adjustments is that when a primary adjustment is made, the resulting situation will not reflect the situation had the transaction originally taken place at arm's-length, even if a corresponding adjustment is made. This is because primary and corresponding adjustments affect only the calculation of taxable income, not the actual monies transferred (or assets and liabilities booked), which will still reflect the original (non–arm's-length) transaction. As a result, some countries recognize constructive transactions (for example deemed dividends, loans, or capital contributions), which are commonly referred to as "secondary transactions." The imposition of taxes, such as withholding taxes, with respect to a secondary transaction is referred to as a "secondary adjustment."

Examples of countries with explicit legislation concerning secondary adjustments are limited. While several countries, such as the Netherlands and the Republic of Korea, have provisions for "secondary adjustments,"[25] most countries have not introduced the concept in their legislation to date. Where secondary adjustments are provided for and are compulsory, this may lead to economic double taxation. Where secondary adjustments are provided for but are not compulsory, countries may refrain from making the adjustment where it will lead to double taxation.[26]

As an alternative to secondary transactions and adjustments, countries may agree to the repatriation of monies as part of the outcome of a successful mutual agreement procedure (MAP) (see chapter 7). Under this arrangement, the taxpayers party to the controlled transaction that has been adjusted book a payment that balances the books, but has no tax effects.

Practical Provisions

Prescription of the arm's-length principle as the relevant benchmark or standard on its own is typically not sufficient for ensuring the necessary level of certainty. Provisions that elaborate on the practical application of the principle are typically necessary and are, to differing degrees, included in the legislation or guidance of almost all countries with developed transfer pricing legislation.

The following contains descriptions of practical provisions typically found in transfer pricing legislation, along with examples and explanations of approaches observed in practice.

Comparability

The concept of "comparability" is fundamental to the application of the arm's-length principle since its application is generally based on comparison of the conditions in the controlled transaction with the conditions in comparable uncontrolled transactions. The importance of understanding or "delineating" the actual transaction in question, i.e., to what extend actual behavior of related parties corresponds to their written contractual agreements is emphasized as a critical element of a comparability analysis in the recent revisions to chapter 1 of the OECD *Transfer Pricing Guidelines for Multinational Enterprises and Tax Administrations* (2010b).

According to international practice and the guidance in the OECD *Transfer Pricing Guidelines* (2010b)[27] and the UN *Practical Manual* (2013), the concept of "comparability" does not require that the transactions being compared are identical. Rather, paragraph 1.33 of the OECD *Transfer Pricing Guidelines* (2010b) provided that "[t]o be comparable means that none of the differences (if any) between the situations being compared could materially affect the condition being examined in the methodology (for example price or margin), or that reasonably accurate adjustments can be made to eliminate the effect of any such differences."

Equivalent standards of comparability to that in the OECD *Transfer Pricing Guidelines* (2010b) are referred to, either explicitly or implicitly, in the primary or secondary legislation or administrative guidance of most countries with transfer pricing regimes (see table 3.6).[28]

Table 3.6 Comparability in Selected Countries

Country	Source type	Source	Standard or definition
Albania	Primary legislation	Article 36/1(1) Law on Income Tax	An uncontrolled transaction is comparable to a controlled transaction for the purposes of this chapter: a) when there are no significant differences between them that could materially affect the financial indicator being examined under the appropriate transfer pricing method; or b) where such differences exist, a reasonably accurate comparability adjustment is made to the relevant financial indicator of the uncontrolled transaction in order to eliminate the effects of such differences on the comparison.
Australia	Primary legislation	Section 815-125(4) Income Tax Assessment Act 1997	For the purposes of this section, circumstances are comparable to actual circumstances if, to the extent (if any) that the circumstances differ from the actual circumstances: (a) the difference does not materially affect a condition that is relevant to the method; or (b) a reasonably accurate adjustment can be made to eliminate the effect of the difference on a condition that is relevant to the method.
Kenya	Secondary legislation	Rule 1 of the Income Tax (Transfer Pricing) Rules 2006	"Comparable transactions" means transactions between which there are no material differences, or in which reasonably accurate adjustment can be made to eliminate material differences.
Singapore	Administrative guidance	Paragraph 3.2.4.1 of the IRAS Circular on Transfer Pricing Guidelines	The arm's-length principle is based on a comparison of the prices or margins adopted or obtained by related parties with those adopted or obtained by independent parties engaged in similar transactions. For such price or margin comparisons to be meaningful, all economically relevant characteristics of the situations being compared should be sufficiently similar so that: a) None of the differences (if any) between the situations being compared can materially affect the price or margin being compared or b) Reasonably accurate adjustments can be made to eliminate the effect of any such differences.
South Africa	Administrative guidance	Paragraph 8.1.2. of Practice Note 7	To be comparable means that none of the differences (if any) between the situations being compared could materially affect the condition being examined in the method (for example, price or margin) or that reasonably accurate adjustments can be made to eliminate the effect of any such differences. If suitable adjustments cannot be made, then the dealings cannot be considered comparable.

In addition to specifying the standard of comparability, most countries specify the factors to consider when assessing whether the applicable standard of comparability is met (the "comparability factors"). The factors typically specified by countries (see table 3.7) are largely consistent with the five comparability factors specified in the OECD *Transfer Pricing Guidelines* (2010b)[29] as important:

- Characteristics of the property or service
- Functional analysis
- Contractual terms
- Economic circumstances
- Business strategies

Some countries, such as Albania and Georgia (see box 3.19), have provided more detailed guidance on the comparability factors in their secondary legislation by including examples for each factor. Other countries have also provided detailed guidance and examples in their administrative guidance (see table 3.7).

Example of wording for a provision that introduces a standard of comparability consistent with the OECD *Transfer Pricing Guidelines* (2010b) and that specifies the five comparability factors in section 3 of *Transfer Pricing Legislation* (OECD 2011):

1. An uncontrolled transaction is comparable to a controlled transaction within the meaning of Section 1:
   (a) when there are no significant differences between them that could materially affect the financial indicator being examined under the appropriate transfer pricing method, or
   (b) when such differences exist, if a reasonably accurate comparability adjustment is made to the relevant financial indicator of the uncontrolled transaction in order to eliminate the effects of such differences on the comparison.
2. To determine whether two or more transactions are comparable, the following factors shall be considered to the extent that they are economically relevant to the facts and circumstances of the transactions:
   (a) characteristics of the property or services transferred;
   (b) functions undertaken by each enterprise with respect to the transactions (taking into account assets used and risks assumed);
   (c) contractual terms of the transactions;
   (d) economic circumstances in which the transactions take place; and
   (e) business strategies pursued by the associated enterprises in relation to the transactions.

Table 3.7 Comparability Factors in Selected Countries

Country	Source type	Source	Comparability factors
Albania	Primary legislation	Article 36/1(2) Law on Income Tax	To determine whether two or more transactions are comparable, the following factors shall be considered to the extent that they are economically relevant to the facts and circumstances of the transactions: a) the characteristics of the property or services transferred; b) the functions undertaken by each party with respect to the transactions, taking into account assets used and risks assumed; c) the contractual terms of the transactions; d) The economic circumstances in which the transactions take place; and e) the business strategies pursued by parties in relation to the transactions.
Australia	Primary legislation	Section 815-125(3) Income Tax Assessment Act 1997	In identifying comparable circumstances for the purpose of this section, regard must be given to all relevant factors, including the following: a) functions performed, assets used, and risks borne by the entities; b) characteristics of any property or services transferred; c) terms of any relevant contracts between the entities; d) economic circumstances; e) business strategies of the entities.
Bangladesh	Income Tax Rules	Section 71(1)	(1) The following factors shall be considered in judging the comparability of an uncontrolled transaction with the international transaction under the different methods as mentioned in Rule 70: (a) the characteristics of property, services or intangible properties involved in the transaction: (i) the case of tangible property: physical features, quality and reliability, availability, volume, and timing of property transferred; (ii) in the case of services provided: the nature and extent of the services; (iii) in the case of intangible property: the type of intangible, the form of transaction, the expected benefits, the duration of protection, the degree of protection, etc.; (b) the functions performed, the risks assumed, and the assets employed, especially the functions, risks, and assets that are materially significant in determining the price or margin in relation to the international transaction; (c) the contractual terms (whether or not such terms are formal or written) dictating the allocation of responsibilities, risks, and benefits between enterprises involved in the international transaction; (d) economic circumstances that affect the international transaction and uncontrolled transactions, including geographic location, the size and level of markets; the extent of competition in the market; the availability of substitute goods and services; the purchasing powers of consumers; government orders and policies; and the timing of the transaction; (e) any other factors that have material effect on the international transaction and uncontrolled transaction.

table continues next page

Table 3.7 Comparability Factors in Selected Countries *(continued)*

Country	Source type	Source	Comparability factors
Ghana	Secondary legislation	Section 2(3) Transfer Pricing Regulations 2012	The Commissioner-General shall, in selecting a comparable transaction, consider: a) whether there exist economically relevant characteristics of the transactions to be compared, in relation to: i. characteristics of the goods, property or services transferred; ii. relative importance of functions performed; iii. the contractual terms and conditions of the transactions; iv. assets used; v. relative risk assumed by the associated persons and any independent party, where the independent party is considered as a possible comparable; vi. economic and market circumstances in which the transaction takes place; vii. the business strategies pursued by the connected persons in relation to the transactions
Hong Kong SAR, China	Administrative guidance	Practice Note 46 Transfer Pricing Guidelines (paragraphs 48–62)	• Characteristics of the property or services • Functions performed, assets or resources contributed, risks assumed • Contractual terms (duration, rights, payment options) • Economic and market circumstances • Business strategies (market penetration, research development commitments, market positioning)
South Africa	Administrative guidance	Practice Note 7 (chapter 8, paragraph 8.1.6)	• Characteristics of goods and services • Relative importance of functions performed • Terms and conditions of relevant agreements • Relative risk assumed by the taxpayer, connected enterprises, and any independent party considered as a possible comparable • Economic and market conditions • Business strategies

---

Box 3.19 Georgia's Detailed Provision on Comparability Factors

Article 5 of Decree #423 on Approval of the Instructions on International Transfer Pricing (2013)

1. In determining whether or not two or more transactions are comparable for the purposes of Article 127(4) of the GTC, the following shall be considered to the extent that they are economically relevant to the facts and circumstances of the transactions:

   a) The characteristics of the property or services transferred, including:

      (i) in the case of tangible assets: the physical characteristics, quality, reliability, availability of supply, etc.

      (ii) in the case of services: the nature and extent of the service, whether or not the service involves specific experience, technical know-how or the use of intangibles, etc.

box continues next page

Box 3.19 Georgia's Detailed Provision on Comparability Factors *(continued)*

(iii) in the case of financing transactions: the amount of the principle, the period, guarantees, currency, solvency of the debtor, security, interest rate, etc.

(iv) in the case of intangible assets: the form of transaction (for example licensing or sale), the type of property (for example patent, trademark, or know-how), the duration and degree of protection, the anticipated benefits from the use of the property, etc.

(v) in the case of alienation of shares: the updated capital account of the issuer, the present value of the profits or projected cash flow, a stock market quotation at the time of the transfer of the shares, etc.

b) The functions undertaken, assets employed, and risks assumed by each enterprise with respect to the transactions, including:

(i) Functions: design, manufacturing, assembling, research and development, servicing, purchasing, distribution, marketing, advertising, transportation, financing, management, etc.

(ii) Assets: plant and equipment, the use of valuable intangibles, financial assets, etc., and the nature of the assets used, such as the age, market value, location, property right protections available, etc.

(iii) Risks, for example: market risks, risks of loss associated with the investment in and use of property, plant, and equipment; risks of the success or failure of investment in research and development; financial risks such as those caused by currency exchange rate and interest rate variability; credit risks, etc.

c) The contractual terms of the transactions, taking into account that:

(i) where there is not written contract, the terms of a transaction may be evidenced by correspondence/communications between the parties;

(ii) where no written terms exist, the contractual relationships of the parties must be deduced from their conduct and the economic principles that generally govern relationships between independent enterprises;

(iii) for controlled transactions, an examination should be undertaken to determine whether the conduct of the parties conforms to the terms of the contract or whether the parties' conduct indicates that the contractual terms have not been followed or are a sham. In case of the latter, further analysis is required to determine the true terms of the transaction.

d) The economic circumstances in which the transactions take place, in particular those that are relevant to determining market comparability, for example, such as geographic location; the size of the markets; the extent of competition in the markets and the relative competitive positions of the buyers and sellers; the availability of substitute goods and services; the levels of supply and demand in the market as a whole and in particular regions, consumer purchasing power, the nature and extent of government regulation of the market, costs of production (including costs of land, labor, and capital); transport costs; the level of the market (for example retail or wholesale); the date and time of transactions; etc.

e) The business strategies pursued by the parties to the transactions, including strategies relating to market penetration, diversification, innovation, product development, risk aversion, political changes, etc.

In addition to including provisions concerning the standard of comparability and comparability factors, some countries include in their legislation provisions concerning comparability adjustments (see box 3.20) and typical processes for undertaking a comparability analysis (see box 3.21). With respect to the latter, the process adopted tends to mirror the nine-step typical process

---

Box 3.20 Georgia's Provision on Comparability Adjustments

Article 6 of Decree #423 Approving the Instruction on International Transfer Pricing (2013)

For the purposes of Article 127(4)(b) of the GTC:

a) reasonably accurate adjustment should be considered only if it is expected to increase the reliability of the results, taking into account considerations such as the:
   (i)   materiality of the difference for which the comparability adjustment is being considered;
   (ii) quality of the data subject to comparability adjustment;
   (iii) purpose of the comparability adjustment;
   (iv) reliability of the approach used to make the comparability adjustment.

b) reasonably accurate comparability adjustment may include:
   (i)   adjustments for accounting consistency designed to eliminate differences that may arise from differing accounting practices between the controlled transaction and uncontrolled transaction;
   (ii) segmentation of financial data to eliminate significant non-comparable transactions;
   (iii) adjustments for the elimination of differences in capital, functions, assets, risks;
   (iv) adjustments for the elimination of differences in geographic markets.

Box 3.21 Albania's Provision on Typical Process for Comparability Analysis

Paragraph 5.7 of Instruction No.16 on Transfer Pricing (2014)

5.7 The following process (adapted from the nine-step process in the *OECD TPG* (2010b) is recommended when assessing comparability. However, following this process is not compulsory. It is the outcome rather than the process that is of importance.

1) determination of years to be covered;
2) broad-based analysis of the taxpayer's circumstances;
3) understanding the controlled transaction(s) under examination, based in particular on a functional analysis, in order to help choose the tested party in accordance with this Instruction (where needed); select the most appropriate transfer pricing method to the circumstances of the case in accordance with this Instruction; select the financial indicator

box continues next page

Box 3.21 Albania's Provision on Typical Process for Comparability Analysis *(continued)*

that will be tested (where needed); and, to identify the significant comparability factors that should be taken into account;

4) review of existing internal comparable uncontrolled transactions, if any;

5) determination of available sources of information on external comparable transactions where such external comparable transactions are needed taking into account their relative reliability;

6) the selection of the most appropriate transfer pricing method in accordance with this Instruction and, depending on the method, determination of the relevant financial indicator;

7) identification of potential comparable transactions: determining the key characteristics to be met by any uncontrolled transaction in order to be regarded as potentially comparable, based on the relevant factors identified in Step 3 and in accordance with the comparability factors specified in Article 36/1, paragraph 2;

8) determination of and making comparability adjustments where appropriate, taking into account paragraph 6 below;

9) interpretation and use of data collected, determination of conditions consistent with market principle.

---

introduced in the OECD *Transfer Pricing Guidelines* in the 2010 update. Where these issues are not addressed in primary or secondary legislation, practical guidance is often provided in administrative guidelines.

Chapter 4 provides a basic introduction to comparability in practice.

Transfer Pricing Methods

Most countries prescribe the five transfer pricing methods detailed in the *OECD Transfer Pricing Guidelines* as the applicable methods for determining consistency with the arm's-length principle (although they may use different nomenclature):[30,31]

- Comparable uncontrolled price method
- Resale price minus method
- Cost-plus method
- Transactional net profits method
- Profit split method[32]

In the OECD *Transfer Pricing Guidelines*, the first three methods are referred to collectively as "traditional transactional methods"; the last two methods are referred to as "transactional profit methods." The same five methods are detailed in the *UN Practical Manual*.

While some countries specify these methods in their primary legislation (for example Georgia; see box 3.20), others countries refer instead to the methods in secondary legislation (for example, Ghana; see box 3.22) or administrative guidance (for example, South Africa). Countries that make explicit reference to the *OECD Transfer Pricing Guidelines* in their legislation (see table 3.2 and chapter 2) incorporate the methods through this reference. Where the methods are specified in the legislation, definitions may be required in either the primary or the secondary legislation. Numerous countries have included illustrative examples of the application of each of the methods in their administrative guidelines.

Box 3.22 Examples of Provisions Specifying Approved Transfer Pricing Methods

Ghana: Article 3(1) of Transfer Pricing Regulations (2012)

(1) For purposes of these Regulations, the transfer pricing methods approved by the Commissioner-General are:
   a. The comparable uncontrolled price method;
   b. The resale price method;
   c. The cost-plus method;
   d. The transactional profit split method; and
   e. The transactional net margin method.

Georgia: Article 128 of the Tax Code of Georgia

1. The approved methods for pricing the international controlled transactions for the purpose of determining the consistency of the taxable profit with the market principle are:
   a. Comparable uncontrolled price method: This method compares the price charged for the goods and services transferred in an international controlled transaction to the price charged for the goods and services transferred in a comparable uncontrolled transaction.
   b. Resale price method: This method compares the margin obtained by reselling a product purchased in an international controlled transaction in an independent transaction to a margin obtained by reselling a product purchased in a comparable uncontrolled transaction in a comparable uncontrolled transaction.
   c. Cost-plus method: This method compares the markup applied to direct and indirect costs incurred in the supply of goods or services in an international controlled transaction with the markup applied to direct and indirect costs incurred in the supply of goods or services in a comparable uncontrolled transaction.
   d. Transactional net margin method: This method compares the net profit margin relative to an appropriate base (for example costs, sales, assets) obtained by an enterprise in an international controlled transaction with the net profit margin relative to the same base obtained in comparable uncontrolled transaction.
   e. Transactional profit split method: According to this method, each associated party participating in an international controlled transaction is allocated such share of profit/loss in this transaction, which an independent enterprise would expect to earn in a comparable independent transaction.

In some countries where the methods are specified in the legislation, such as Belarus,[33] only the traditional transactional methods are prescribed. This approach typically reflects the guidance in the 1995 version of the *OECD Transfer Pricing Guidelines*, which attributed "last resort" status to profit-based methods. In the 2010 update to the guidelines, this "last resort" status was removed to reflect the frequent use of the transaction profits methods in practice, and their acceptance by taxpayers and tax administrations around the world (Cooper and Agarwal 2011). Legislation that does not provide for the possibility for taxpayers to apply the transactional profits methods is inconsistent with current international practice and is likely to lead to uncertainty, increased compliance costs, and instances of economic double taxation, particularly since taxpayers will often still seek to apply the methods where they are appropriate or are adopted by the taxpayer as part of their global transfer pricing policy. Recognizing this, several countries have, in recent years, updated their legislation to reflect possibility for application of all of the five methods (for example Serbia) or have removed the "last resort" status for the transactional profits methods (for example Korea and Indonesia).

Whether both traditional transactional methods and transactional profits methods are specified, most countries also provide for the use of "other methods" (see box 3.23). As long as the outcome is consistent with the arm's-length principle, provision for the prescription or application of other methods will provide taxpayers and tax administrations with the flexibility to prescribe and use other methods that may be more appropriate to a transaction type or set of facts and circumstances (for example when valuing transfers of intangible property other methods are sometimes relied upon in practice). Section 4(5) of *Transfer Pricing Legislation* (OECD 2011) includes sample wording for the use of other methods:

> The taxpayer may apply a transfer pricing method other than the approved methods contained in paragraph 2 where it can establish that (i) none of the approved methods can be reasonably applied to determine arm's-length conditions for the controlled transaction, and (ii) such other method yields a result consistent with that which would be achieved by independent enterprises engaging in comparable uncontrolled transactions under comparable circumstances. The taxpayer asserting the use of a method other than the approved methods contained in paragraph 2 shall establish that the requirements of this paragraph 5 have been satisfied.

Some countries have also elected to prescribe special methods for specific transaction types; the most prominent example is the "sixth method." This method, which originated in Argentina, provides for the use of publicly quoted prices (for example from international exchanges) to determine transfer prices for specified commodities (PwC 2013). It has since been adopted in many other Latin American countries, including Brazil, the Dominican Republic, and El Salvador. A similar concept has been adopted in Zambia, whereby a "reference price" method is imposed for exports of base metals (see box 3.24). Some countries consider the method as a variant on the comparable uncontrolled price method, and others consider it an "other method." While the sixth method can

---

Box 3.23 Provisions Allowing for the Prescription or Use of Other Methods

Albania: Article 36/2 (2) of the Law on Income Tax (No. 8438)

The taxpayer may apply a transfer pricing method other than the approved methods when it proves that none of the above methods can be reasonably applied to determine consistency with the market principle for the controlled transaction, and such other method yields a result consistent with the market principle. The taxpayer asserting the use of a method, other than the approved methods, given in point 1 of this article, shall bear the burden of demonstrating that the requirements of this paragraph have been satisfied.

Egypt: Article 40 of Executive Regulation of the Income Tax Law Promulgated by Law No. 91 of 2005

In the case of an inability to apply any of the methods mentioned in the preceding article, the market price may be determined by any other method described by the Organisation for Economic Co-operation and Development or any other method suitable for the taxpayer.

Kenya: Article 7(f) of Income Tax (Transfer Pricing) Rules, 2006

Such other method as may be prescribed by the Commissioner from time to time, where in his opinion and in view of the nature of the transactions, the arm's-length price cannot be determined using any of the methods contained in these guidelines.

Nigeria: Regulation 5(4) of the Income Tax (Transfer Pricing) Regulations No. 2012

(4) A connected taxable person may apply a transfer pricing method other than those listed in this regulation, if the person can establish that:

    (a) none of the listed methods can be reasonably applied to determine whether a controlled transaction is consistent with the arm's-length principle; and

    (b) the method used gives rise to a result that is consistent with that between independent persons engaging in comparable uncontrolled transactions in comparable circumstances.

Portugal: Article 63(3) of the Corporate Income Tax Code

The methods employed must be:

    (a) the comparable uncontrolled price method, resale price method, or the cost-plus method;

    (b) the profit split method, the transactional net margin method, or another, when the methods listed in the preceding subparagraph cannot be used, or, if they can, they do not lead to the most reliable measure of the terms and conditions that independent entities would normally agree, accept, and practice.

---

be a powerful tool for countries where exports of commodities are significant to protect their tax base, there are valid concerns that legislation concerning application of this method doesn't typically take into account critical determinants of prices (such as geography, volume, and trade terms) and does not clearly specify the acceptable sources of publicly quoted prices (PwC 2013).

Box 3.24 Example: Zambia's "Reference Price" Method for Base Metal Exports

Zambia: Articles 2 and 97(13)-(14) of the Income Tax Act (2012 edition)
Article 2(1)
Base metal means a non-precious metal that is either common or more chemically active, or both common and chemically active and includes iron, copper, nickel, aluminum, lead, zinc, tin, magnesium, cobalt, manganese, titanium, scandium, vanadium and chromium

Article 97A (13) and (14)

(13) Notwithstanding any provision in this Act, for any transaction for the sale of base metals or any substance containing base metals or precious metals, directly or indirectly, between related or associated parties, the applicable sale price of such metals or recoverable metals shall be the reference price.

(14) For the purposes of Subsection (13), *reference price* means:
  – the monthly average London Metal Exchange cash price;
  – the monthly average Metal Bulletin cash price to the extent that the base metals or precious metal prices are not quoted on the London Metal Exchange;
  – the monthly average cash price of any other metal exchange market as approved by the Commissioner-General to the extent that the base metal price or precious metal price is not quoted on the London Metal Exchange or Metal Bulletin; or
  – the average monthly London Metal Exchange cash price, average monthly metal market exchange cash price approved by the Commissioner-General, less any discounts on account of proof or low quality or grade.

Selection of Transfer Pricing Method

Depending on the facts and circumstances, there may be the possibility to apply more than one of the transfer pricing methods. Therefore, legislation should provide guidance on how to select the transfer pricing method. Countries have tended to adopt one of three main approaches in this regard:

- Most appropriate method to the circumstances of the case
- Hierarchy of methods
- Best method rule

The "most appropriate method to the circumstances of the case" is the standard endorsed in the OECD *Transfer Pricing Guidelines* (2010b). Prior to 2010, the guidelines contained an explicit hierarchy of methods. After substantial public consultations and more than a decade's practical experience, the 2010 update to the guidelines replaced the explicit hierarchy of methods, and, in particular, the "last resort" status assigned to the transactional profits methods, with this standard. The "most appropriate method to the circumstances of the case" standard requires that a range of factors be considered when selecting a method, such as the nature of the transaction, the availability of information, the relative strengths and weaknesses of the methods, and the degree of comparability of the controlled and uncontrolled transactions. The "most appropriate method to the circumstances of the case" is the most commonly adopted approach to the selection of transfer pricing method. Examples of the many countries that have adopted this approach include Albania, Australia, Georgia, India, Ireland, Kenya, Nigeria (see box 3.25), South Africa, and the United Kingdom.

Section 4(1) of *Transfer Pricing Legislation* (OECD 2011) contains sample wording for a provision on the selection of method that adopts the "most appropriate method to the circumstances of the case" standard as detailed in the OECD *Transfer Pricing Guidelines* (2010b):

> 1. The arm's-length remuneration of a controlled transaction shall be determined by applying the most appropriate transfer pricing method to the circumstances of the case. Except to the extent provided in paragraph 5, the most appropriate transfer pricing method shall be selected from among the approved transfer pricing methods set out in paragraph 2, taking into consideration the following criteria:
>
> (a) Respective strengths and weaknesses of the approved methods;
>
> (b) Appropriateness of an approved method in view of the nature of the controlled transaction, determined, in particular, through an analysis of the functions undertaken by each enterprise in the controlled transaction (taking into account assets used and risks assumed);

Box 3.25 Nigeria's Provisions on Selection of Transfer Pricing Method

Regulation 5(2)–(3) of the Income Tax (Transfer Pricing) Regulations No. 1 2012

(2) In each case, the most appropriate transfer pricing method shall be used taking into account:
    (a) the respective strengths and weaknesses of the transfer pricing method in the circumstances of the case;
    (b) the appropriateness of a transfer pricing method having regard to the nature of the controlled transaction determined, in particular, through an analysis of the functions performed, assets employed and risks assumed by each person that is a party to the controlled transaction;
    (c) the availability of reliable information needed to apply the transfer pricing method; and
    (d) the degree of comparability between controlled and uncontrolled transactions, including the reliability of adjustments, if any, that may be required to eliminate any differences between comparable transactions.

(3) When examining whether or not the taxable profit resulting from a taxpayer's controlled transaction or transactions is consistent with the arm's-length principle, the Service shall base its review on the transfer pricing method used by the taxable person if such a method is appropriate to the transaction.

(c) Availability of reliable information needed to apply the selected transfer pricing method and/or other methods; and

(d) Degree of comparability between the controlled and uncontrolled transactions, including the reliability of comparability adjustments, if any, that may be required to eliminate differences between them.

The *UN Practical Manual* (2013) endorses an analogous standard for selection of transfer pricing method, noting in paragraph 6.1.2 that "[t]he selection of method serves to find the most appropriate method for a particular case," and in paragraph 6.1.3.2 that "[t]he most suitable method should be chosen taking into consideration the facts and circumstances."

The countries that have adopted this rule, consistent with the *OECD Transfer Pricing Guidelines* (2010b), have typically included a "tiebreaker" provision that provides a preference for the comparable uncontrolled price method, followed by the resale price method and cost-plus method, in cases where more than one method can be applied with equal reliability. Section 4(3) of *Transfer Pricing Legislation* (OECD 2011) contains sample wording for a tiebreaker provision:

3. Where, taking account of the criteria described in paragraph 1, a comparable uncontrolled price method described in subparagraph 2(a) and an approved method described in subparagraphs 2(b) to 2(e) can be applied with equal reliability, the determination of arm's-length conditions shall be made using the comparable uncontrolled price method. Where, taking account of the criteria described in paragraph 1, an approved method described in subparagraphs 2(a) to 2(c) and an approved method described in subparagraphs 2(d) to 2(e) can be applied with equal reliability, the determination of arm's-length conditions shall be made using the method described in subparagraphs 2(a) to 2(c).

However, not all countries have adopted the "most appropriate method to the circumstances of the case" standard. A declining number of countries prescribes an explicit hierarchy of methods.[34] This approach reflected the *OECD Transfer Pricing Guidelines* prior to the 2010 update, when other methods (namely, the transactional profit methods) were to be applied only "when traditional transaction methods cannot be reliably applied alone or exceptionally cannot be applied at all" (OECD 1995, paragraph 3.1). Prescription of an explicit hierarchy of methods limits the necessary flexibility for applying the arm's-length principle and does not reflect practical realities (i.e., concerning information availability; see chapter 4) and may give rise to economic double taxation and the imposition of an unnecessary compliance burden on taxpayers. Since the update to the guidelines, many countries, including Japan and Korea, have amended their legislation, replacing the explicit hierarchy with the most appropriate method to the circumstances of the case standard.[35]

The "best method rule," which has its roots in the United States' transfer pricing practice, requires that the arm's-length result of a controlled transaction must be determined under the method that, under the facts and circumstances, provides the most reliable measure of an arm's-length result (see box 3.26).

Although in theory the best method can be determined without checking the result under other methods, if the tax authority considers another method to be the best method, the taxpayer will be faced with the burden of proof to prove the authority wrong or face substantial penalties. In practice, therefore, although largely similar to the "most appropriate method to the circumstances of the case" as prescribed in the *OECD Transfer Pricing Guidelines* (2010b), the best method rule is slightly different and may impose a greater compliance burden on taxpayers.

Many countries prescribe that taxpayers are not required to apply more than one method,[36] and that where a taxpayer has selected the method consistently with the relevant standard, the tax administration's examination shall be based on the application of that method (this is the case in Nigeria, for example; see box 3.25). Section 4(6) of *Transfer Pricing Legislation* (OECD 2011) contains sample wording for such provisions:

> Where a taxpayer has used a transfer pricing method to establish the remuneration of its controlled transactions and that transfer pricing method is consistent with the provisions of this Section 4, then the tax administration's examination of whether the conditions of the taxpayer's controlled transactions are consistent with the arm's-length principle shall be based on the transfer pricing method applied by the taxpayer.

Box 3.26 United States' "Best Method Rule" for Selection of Transfer Pricing Method

Treas. Reg. §1.482-1(c)

(c) *Best-method rule*—(1) *In general.* The arm's-length result of a controlled transaction must be determined under the method that, under the facts and circumstances, provides the most reliable measure of an arm's-length result. Thus, there is no strict priority of methods, and no method will invariably be considered to be more reliable than others. An arm's-length result may be determined under any method without establishing the inapplicability of another method, but if another method subsequently is shown to produce a more reliable measure of an arm's-length result, such other method must be used. Similarly, if two or more applications of a single method provide inconsistent results, the arm's-length result must be determined under the application that, under the facts and circumstances, provides the most reliable measure of an arm's-length result. See §1.482-8 for examples of the application of the best-method rule. See §1.482-7 for the applicable method in the case of a qualified cost sharing arrangement.

(2) *Determining the best method.* Data based on the results of transactions between unrelated parties provides the most objective basis for determining whether the results of a controlled transaction are arm's-length. Thus, in determining which of two or more available methods (or applications of a single method) provides the most reliable measure of an arm's-length result, the two primary factors to take into account are the degree of comparability between the controlled transaction (or taxpayer) and any uncontrolled comparables, and the quality of the data and assumptions used in the analysis. In addition, in certain circumstances, it also may be relevant to consider whether the results of an analysis are consistent with the results of an analysis under another method. These factors are explained in paragraphs (c)(2)(i), (ii), and (iii) of this section.

Selection of Tested Party

Application of a one-sided transfer pricing methodology (the resale price method, cost-plus method, or transactional net margin method) requires the selection of a tested party—i.e., the party for which the relevant condition being examined (for example gross profit margin, gross profit markup, and net margin) is tested under the method. In practice, the tested party will usually be the one with the simplest functional profile and most reliable information. In theory, this may be the local taxpayer or the foreign party to the controlled transaction(s). In practice issues can arise in some countries about the acceptability of a foreign tested party. Recognizing this, some countries, such as Albania, have elected to introduce specific provisions that guide the selection of the tested party, and confirm the acceptability of foreign tested parties, where appropriate (see box 3.27).

Aggregation of Transactions

Transfer pricing legislation is typically drafted so as to require consistency with the arm's-length principle on a transactional basis (see "Arm's-Length Principle"). In practice, however, situations can, and do, arise in which transactions are best evaluated on an aggregate basis. For example, the transactions are priced as a package and cannot be reasonably disaggregated. A country's legislation or the administrative guidance may provide guidelines on the acceptability of such

---

Box 3.27 Albania's Provision on Selection of Tested Party

Paragraph 10 of Instruction (No. 16) on Transfer Pricing (2014)

10.1 When applying the cost-plus method, resale price method or transactional net margin method, it is necessary to select a tested party. The tested party being the party to the controlled transaction for which the financial indicator is tested.

10.2 The selection of which should be consistent with the functional analysis of the controlled transaction(s). As a general rule, the tested party is the party to the controlled transaction to which one of the transfer pricing methods in Article 36/2, paragraph 1 of the law, can be applied in the most reliable manner and for which the most reliable comparable uncontrolled transactions can be identified, i.e., it will most often be the party that has the less complex functions with respect to the controlled transaction and does not contribute any valuable intangibles.

10.3 The use of a foreign tested party, for example a tested party that is not the Albanian Taxpayer, will be accepted by the tax authority provided that the following requirements are met:

a) the transfer pricing method applied is an approved transfer pricing method that is the most appropriate transfer pricing method;
b) the tested party has been selected in accordance with this article; and
c) the taxpayer provides the tax authority with sufficient information regarding the tested party so as to allow for an assessment as to the conformity of the conditions of the controlled transaction with the market principle.

Box 3.28 Aggregation of Transactions under the IRC Sec. 482 Regulations

United States: 1.482-1(f)(2)(i)(A) of the Section 482 Regulations

Aggregation of transactions—(A) *In general.* The combined effect of two or more separate transactions (whether before, during, or after the taxable year under review) may be considered if such transactions, taken as a whole, are so interrelated that consideration of multiple transactions is the most reliable means of determining the arm's-length consideration for the controlled transactions. Generally, transactions will be aggregated only when they involve related products or services, as defined in §1.6038A–3(c)(7)(vii).

---

aggregation (see box 3.28). Section 5 of *Transfer Pricing Legislation* (OECD 2011) contains sample wording for such a provision:

> If a taxpayer carries out, under the same or similar circumstances, two or more controlled transactions that are economically closely linked to one another or that form a continuum such that they cannot reliably be analyzed separately, those transactions may be combined to (i) perform the comparability analysis set out in Section 3 and (ii) apply the transfer pricing methods set out in Section 4.

Arm's-length Range

Application of the arm's-length principle will very often result in a range of acceptable arm's-length prices or margins (typically referred to as an "arm's-length range"). This range may arise due to multiple comparable transactions being observed or from the application of more than one transfer pricing method. The OECD *Transfer Pricing Guidelines* (2010b) recommend that where the relevant price or margin of the controlled transaction falls within such an arm's-length range, no adjustment should be made. Most countries have adopted this approach in their legislation, administrative guidance, or in practice.[37] However, the approach as to how the arm's-length range is defined or determined differs across countries.

In line with the OECD *Transfer Pricing Guidelines*, many countries, including Albania, Australia, Canada, and South Africa,[38] have adopted the "full" arm's-length range: the range is determined based on the full range of "arm's-length" observations derived from the comparable transactions. This approach provides the greatest flexibility for tax administrations and taxpayers, and since it is in line with international practice, its adoption should reduce instances of economic double taxation. Section 6 of *Transfer Pricing Legislation* (OECD 2011) contains sample wording for a provision that defines arm's-length range and makes clear that adjustments should not be made whereby the financial indicator being tested is within the arm's-length range:

> 1. An arm's-length range is a range of relevant financial indicator figures (for example prices, margins or profit shares) produced by the application of the most appropriate

transfer pricing method as set out in Section 4 to a number of uncontrolled transactions, each of which is relatively equally comparable to the controlled transaction based on a comparability analysis conducted in accordance with Section 3.

2. A controlled transaction, or a set of transactions that are combined according to Section 5, shall not be subject to an adjustment under Section 1, paragraph 2 where the relevant financial indicator derived from the controlled transaction or set of transactions and being tested under the appropriate transfer pricing method is within the arm's-length range.

The use of statistical measures, such as the interquartile range (see figure 3.2), to determine a narrower range is also common practice in many countries, although it is not generally prescribed in legislation.[39] Some countries, such as Georgia, Mexico, and the United States, have, however, prescribed its use in their legislation. According to section 216 of Mexico's Income Tax Law, where two or more comparable transactions exist resulting in a range of prices, amounts of consideration, or profit margins, statistical methods are to be applied to determine the arm's-length range; the statistical method specified in Article 276 is the interquartile range. IRC section 482 regulations also provide for the use of the interquartile range, although they also provide for a full range (i.e., not reduced to the interquartile) whereby all material differences between the controlled transaction and the uncontrolled transactions are identified and quantified and reasonable adjustments made in relation to the differences [Treasury Regulation §1.482-1(e)(2)(iii)(B)-(C)]. Georgia's legislation is similar to that of the United States.

Figure 3.2 Interquartile Range Example

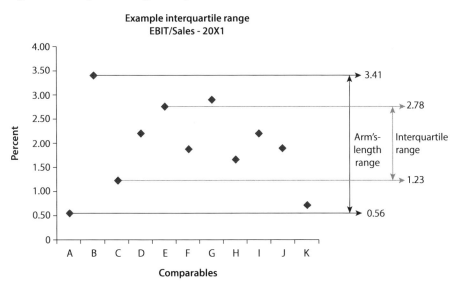

Note: EBIT = Earnings Before Interest and Taxes.

Some countries have adopted alternative approaches to the concept of arm's-length range. In India, for example, Section 92C(2) of the Income Tax Act 1961 requires that where more than one arm's-length price is observed, the arm's-length price shall be the arithmetical mean; if the price used in the controlled transaction falls outside a specified percentage variance of that price, it will be deemed not to be arm's-length. Historically, the percentage variance specified was 5 percent. The law was amended through the Finance Act 2011 (India), however, and the percentage is now that which is notified by the central government in the official gazette. In Belarus, the range of acceptable prices is determined by a 20 percent deviation from the market price (Strachuk 2012). As these "unique" approaches differ quite significantly from those adopted by most countries and may result in a different "arm's-length range," the potential for economic double taxation is increased.

Selection of a Point within the Range

Inherent in the power to make a transfer pricing adjustment is a requirement to determine the quantum of the adjustment. In this regard, countries that have adopted the arm's-length range concept (see "Arm's-Length Range") typically specify that when the condition being examined (for example price or margin) falls outside of the arm's-length range an adjustment may be made to a specific point within that range. Consistent with the OECD *Transfer Pricing Guidelines*, section 6(3) of *Transfer Pricing Legislation* (OECD 2011) suggests that in such cases the adjustment "shall be to a point in the arm's-length range that best reflects the circumstances of the case." While this approach provides flexibility to ensure that the adjustment is reasonable given the facts and circumstances, it may not be considered by some countries as providing sufficient certainty.

Although the legislation of some countries is conspicuously silent on this issue, numerous countries have specified in their legislation that the adjustment shall be to the median of the range, unless the facts and circumstances support an adjustment to a different point (for example Georgia, box 3.29). This approach provides certainty while retaining some flexibility. Other countries, such as Serbia,[40] have specified a point within the range to which the adjustment is to be made, but do not provide the possibility for either the taxpayer or the tax administration to demonstrate that another point may be more appropriate.

Sources of Information

The sources that can identify comparable uncontrolled transactions are generally not restricted or specified in a country's transfer pricing legislation. A multitude of sources may typically be relevant, depending on the specific transaction type and because the prevailing requirement in most country's transfer pricing legislation is consistency with the arm's-length principles as opposed to the use of one or more sources of information. That said, some countries have elected to include specific provisions in their legislation that define acceptable sources of comparable information. These provisions typically address key issues such as the use of foreign comparables (i.e., comparables from different geography markets;

Box 3.29 Selection of a Point within the Market Range in Georgia

Article 10 of Decree #423 on Approval of the Instructions on International Transfer Pricing

3. Where the relevant financial indicator derived from a controlled transaction, or from a set of controlled transactions that are combined according to Article 11 of these Instructions, falls outside the market range, the Revenue Service may make an adjustment to the taxable profits of the Georgian enterprise pursuant to Article 127(3) of the GTC. The adjustment shall be to the median of the market range unless the facts and circumstances clearly support an adjustment to a different point within the market range.

4. Burden of proof for showing that the facts and circumstances support an adjustment to a point in the market range that is different from the median is to be borne by:

a) the Georgian enterprise, when the Georgian enterprise asserts that the facts and circumstances indicate about the equality of the financial indicator to the point different from the market range median;

b) the Revenue Service, when the Revenue Service asserts that the facts and circumstances indicate about the equality of the financial indicator to the point different from the market range median.

---

see chapter 4) and the use of secret comparables (for example information not publicly available).

The acceptability of foreign comparables varies among countries. Out of necessity, most countries accept foreign comparables when no local comparables are available, with some countries, such as Albania, electing to confirm this in their legislation (see box 3.30). Although many countries adopt this approach, few provide any specific guidance on using foreign comparables in their primary or secondary legislation. Failure to allow for the use of foreign comparables where domestic comparables are not available may make the transfer pricing legislation difficult or impossible to apply in some situations, thereby increasing compliance costs and uncertainty for taxpayers.

The use of information available to the tax administration or other government agencies, but not to the public, is commonly referred to as relying on "secret comparables" and can be a source of tension between tax administrations and taxpayers. Although most countries do not explicitly prohibit the use of secret comparables by the tax administration, secret comparables are not often relied on in practice because of both practical problems and legal constraints. They can be used, however. In China, for example, Article 37 of the State Administration of Taxation's "Measures for the Implementation of the Special Tax Adjustment (trial)," states that "the tax authorities may use public information and nonpublic information." In Japan, if information listed under Article 22-10 of the Special Taxation Measures Law Ministerial Order is not duly provided by the taxpayer, Article 66-4 contains a clause on the presumptive taxation

Box 3.30 Provision Concerning Sources of Comparable Information in Albania

Paragraph 7 of Instruction No. 16 on Transfer Pricing (2014)

7.1 Comparable uncontrolled transactions may be:

   a. *Internal comparable uncontrolled transactions*, which are comparable uncontrolled transactions where one of the parties to the controlled transaction is also a party to the comparable uncontrolled transaction.

   b. *External comparable uncontrolled transactions*, which are comparable uncontrolled transactions where neither of the parties to the controlled transaction is a party to the comparable uncontrolled transaction.

7.2 An uncontrolled transaction may only be relied upon by the tax authority for the purposes of making an adjustment under Article 36, paragraph 3, if the relevant details of the transaction do not comprise a tax secret and there are other information sources for such transaction.

7.3 In the absence of domestic comparable uncontrolled transactions the use of foreign comparable uncontrolled transactions will be accepted by the tax authority provided that the impact of geographic differences and other factors on the financial indicator being examined under the appropriate transfer pricing method are analyzed, and that, where appropriate, comparability adjustments are made.

7.4 In the absence of information concerning external comparable uncontrolled transactions, from the same fiscal year as the controlled transaction(s), being available at the time of preparing the transfer pricing documentation specified in the Article 36/5, the taxpayer may rely on information concerning external comparable uncontrolled transactions from the most recent period for which such information is available, provided the standard of comparability in Article 36/1 is met.

rule that enables the tax authorities to make transfer pricing assessments based on undisclosed comparable information (i.e., secret comparables). Historically, Japan's National Tax Agency has used secret comparables on occasion, but their use has declined in recent years largely in response to intense criticism of the practice (Gruendel, Okawara, and Newman 2011). Other countries, such as Albania, have explicitly prohibited the use of secret comparables by the tax administration (see box 3.30).

Transaction-Specific Provisions

Although most countries address specific transactions types and situations in administrative guidance, many include provisions in their legislation. Because of the specificity of such provisions, the detail is generally found in secondary legislation, providing more flexibility for amendments. Countries that have introduced provisions dealing with specific transaction types include Albania, Georgia, and Ghana, each of which has provisions in its secondary legislation dealing specifically with services and intangibles transactions; Germany, which introduced specific legislation dealing with business restructurings in 2007[41]; and the United States, whereby regulations dealing with specific topics such as cost contribution arrangements, intragroup services, and intangibles have been introduced and amended over the years. *Transfer Pricing Legislation* (OECD 2011) includes examples of provisions on intragroup services and intangibles and the revisions to chapter 6 of the *OECD Transfer Pricing Guidelines* agreed in October 2015 introduce better tailored guidance for intangibles and hard-to-value intangibles aimed at ensuring remuneration is linked to value creation and providing remedies for tax administrators facing information asymmetries in valuing intangible assets.[42]

The export and import of certain commodities are often covered by specific provisions aimed at protecting revenue collection. Argentina, followed by other countries in Latin America, introduced requirements to refer to quoted prices of selected commodities at the time of their shipment (the "sixth method"). The application of similar requirements has been adopted by an increasing number of countries. Ukraine, for instance, introduced an anti-avoidance measure for specific commodities in transactions with affiliates operating in tax havens, requiring taxpayers to apply the comparable uncontrolled price method using the average price in a specified commodities market over 10 days as the starting point. Subsequently, transaction-specific adjustments can be made where necessary, such as for volume difference and transportation costs.[43]

Many countries have introduced safe harbors and simplification measures that target specific transaction types and situations. For example, Hungary and the United States have introduced specific safe harbor measures for intragroup services (see chapters 5 and 7), a concept, named "elective simplified method," that is now being added to the *OECD Transfer Pricing Guidelines* as a safe harbor for low value adding services.[44]

Relevance of the "OECD Transfer Pricing Guidelines" and Other Sources of International Guidance

The *OECD Transfer Pricing Guidelines* (2010) are the most influential source of guidance on international transfer pricing, and as a result have substantial impact on the design and implementation of countries' transfer pricing legislation (see chapter 2). Recognizing this, numerous countries have elected to make specific reference in their legislation or administrative guidance to the guidelines as a relevant source of guidance and interpretation. This may involve a specific requirement for the ministry of finance to develop implementing regulations consistent with the principles of the guidelines, as is the case in Serbia (see box 3.31), or may be a reference in the secondary legislation or administrative guidance to the guidelines as a relevant source of interpretation, as is the case in Albania (see box 3.32). Where the guidelines are referenced directly in the legislation, countries should consider their ability to influence developments in the guidelines against the legal status attributed to the guidelines in regard to other sources.

Box 3.31 Serbia's Requirement That Secondary Legislation Be Based on International Guidance

Article 61a of Corporate Income Tax Law

The Minister of Finance shall, relying on the sources related to taxation of transaction among related parties of the Organisation for Economic Co-operation and Development (OECD), as well as other international organizations, specify more closely the manner of application of the provisions of Article 10(a) and Articles 59 through 61 of this law.

Box 3.32 Albania's Reference to the 2010 *OECD Transfer Pricing Guidelines*

Paragraph 2 of Instruction (No. 16) on Transfer Pricing (2014)

2.1 These instructions are based on the principles in the *OECD Transfer Pricing Guidelines for Multinational Enterprises and Tax Administrations* (*OECD Transfer Pricing Guidelines* 2010).

2.2 In case of differences or conflicts between the *OECD TPG* 2010 and Albanian Income Tax Law and Instructions, the Albanian Income Tax Law and Instructions will take precedence.

Box 3.33 Nigeria's Reference to the *OECD Transfer Pricing Guidelines* and the *UN Practical Manual*

Part IV of the Income Tax (Transfer Pricing) Regulations No.1 2012

11. Application of UN and OECD Documents

Subject to the provisions of Regulation 12 of these Regulations, this regulation shall be applied in a manner consistent with:

(a) the arm's-length principle in Article 9 of the UN and OECD Model Tax Conventions on Income and Capital for the time it has been in force; and

(b) the *OECD Transfer Pricing Guidelines for Multinational Enterprises and Tax Administrations* approved by the Council of the OECD approved for publication on July 22, 2010 (otherwise referred to as annex I to C (2010) 99) as may be supplemented and updated from time to time.

12. Supremacy of relevant tax law provisions

(1) Where any inconsistency exists between the provisions of any applicable law, rules, regulations, the *UN Practical Manual on Transfer Pricing*, the OECD documents referred to Regulation 11 of these Regulations, the provisions of the relevant tax laws shall prevail.

(2) The provision of this regulation shall prevail in the event of inconsistency with other regulatory authorities' approvals.

A few countries have elected to make reference to other sources of international or regional guidance in addition to the *OECD Transfer Pricing Guidelines*. For example, paragraph 15.4 of Albania's Instruction No. 16 on Transfer Pricing (2014) makes reference to the EU code of conduct on transfer pricing documentation, and the Nigerian Transfer Pricing Regulation makes reference to the *UN Practical Manual* (2013) (box 3.33).

Administrative and Procedural Provisions

In addition to provisions guiding the practical application of the arm's-length principle, provisions concerning administrative and procedural matters are necessary. Such provisions are necessarily specific to transfer pricing (i.e., reporting requirements, documentation, and APA), while others may be either specific or general in scope (i.e., statute of limitations, penalties, or authority to issue secondary legislation). The following contains descriptions and examples of administrative and procedural provisions typically found in countries' transfer pricing legislation.

Reporting Requirements

Many countries have introduced additional disclosures in the income tax return concerning controlled transactions as part of the introduction or reform of a transfer pricing regime. Alternatively, an increasingly popular approach is to introduce a requirement for taxpayers to complete an additional disclosure schedule.

In addition to providing the tax administration with the basic information necessary to identify transfer pricing risks, and thus to identify and select taxpayers for transfer pricing audits, the imposition of disclosure requirements relating to transfer pricing can have a positive effect on taxpayer compliance.

To ensure that taxpayers comply with such requirements, the authorities may need to apply penalties for failure to disclose all relevant information. Additionally, or alternatively, the applicable statute of limitations may not come into effect until full and complete disclosure is made.

Where an additional disclosure requirement is introduced, a provision in the legislation may be required along with penalties for noncompliance (see box 3.34), especially where the tax administration or ministry of finance does not have a general power to introduce and amend reporting requirements. Where disclosure requirements are introduced as part of the income tax return (for example as an annex or additional schedule) lawmakers will typically not need to introduce a specific legislative basis and related penalties.

(*Chapter 6 provides guidance on the design and use of forms and schedules to collect information and promote compliance.*)

Box 3.34 Albania's Annual Controlled Transactions Notice Provisions

Article 36/5(2) Law on Income Tax
Taxpayers engaging in controlled transactions above a specified threshold are required to submit an annual controlled transactions notice/form. The Minister of Finance, by instruction, will define the abovementioned specified threshold, format, and deadline for submission of the controlled transactions notice.

Article 115/1(1) Law on Tax Procedures
In the case of failure to submit in time the "Annual Controlled Transaction Notice" in conformity with the related provisions of the Instruction of the Minister of Finance "On Transfer Pricing," the taxpayer shall be punished with a fixed fine of ALL10.000 for each month of delay.

Transfer Pricing Documentation and Country-by-Country Reporting

Transfer pricing documentation provides tax administrations with the information they need to assess taxpayer compliance with the transfer pricing legislation.[45] To limit the compliance costs imposed on taxpayers, transfer pricing documentation rules should ideally seek to balance the legitimate requirements of the tax administration to assess compliance with the burden imposed on taxpayers.

The approach to legislating transfer pricing documentation requirements varies from country to country, with some countries electing to introduce explicit transfer pricing documentation requirements in their primary legislation (see box 3.35) and others relying on the allocation of burden of proof or the interaction with penalty provisions to encourage taxpayers to prepare and make available sufficient documentation.

Countries participating in the G20/OECD base erosion and profit shifting (BEPS) process agreed on core documentation requirements covering three related information sources: (a) a master file with high-level information on the global business operations and transfer pricing policy of a multinational enterprise (MNE); (b) a local file containing the detailed country specific transaction-based transfer pricing information; (c) a global report providing country-by-country (CbC) information on key performance and input measures of an MNE's activities in all jurisdictions of the group's operations.[46]

An explicit documentation requirement in the primary legislation can have the effect of placing the initial burden of proof for demonstrating that the conditions in controlled transactions are consistent with the arm's-length principle on the taxpayer. This can be particularly important in countries where the tax administration faces difficulties in obtaining information from taxpayers. In addition, ensuring that compliance or noncompliance with the documentation requirement has a penalty impact (such as an increase or decrease in penalty rate) can be critical for ensuring compliance.

Box 3.35 Examples of Provisions Requiring Transfer Pricing Documentation

Albania: Article 36/5(1) Law on Income Tax

A taxpayer must have in place sufficient documented information and analysis to verify that the conditions of its controlled transactions are consistent with the market principle. Transfer pricing documentation shall be provided to the tax administration at its request within 30 days of receiving the tax administration's request. The content and form of the transfer pricing documentation will be specified by instruction of the Minister of Finance.

Serbia: Article 63(2) Corporate Income Tax Law

Alongside the tax return and the tax balance sheet, the taxpayer shall be required to submit to the competent tax authority documentation prescribed under this Law, as well as the documentation which the competent authority requires in accordance with the regulations which govern tax procedure and tax administration.

The specific details of a country's documentation requirement (for example content, language, form, etc.) are typically addressed in secondary legislation or administrative guidance.

Documentation requirements are discussed in detail in chapter 6.

Penalties

Penalties can help ensure taxpayer compliance with a country's transfer pricing legislation. A specific penalty regime may be introduced for transfer pricing, or, as is the case in many countries, the general penalty regime may be used. Penalties applicable for transfer pricing will typically be linked to compliance with the documentation requirement or to a transfer pricing adjustment being made under the legislation. Countries have adopted a range of approaches (see table 3.8 for selected examples and box 3.36 for legislative wording from Albania).

Penalties are typically imposed as fixed amounts, as percentages of the tax unpaid or adjustment made, or as combinations thereof. Where the penalties are based on the tax unpaid or the adjustment made, the penalties payable can be substantial, especially given the vast sums often involved in transfer pricing adjustments. In the member countries of the European Union (EU), for example, penalties are 10–200 percent of the tax unpaid or 5–30 percent of the adjustment made (EUJTPF 2009). Where penalties are fixed amounts, it is important to ensure that the cost versus benefit for taxpayers is appropriately balanced to result in a sufficient level of compliance. Further, where a fixed penalty is imposed regardless of whether an adjustment is made, exemptions or simplified requirements for SMEs or de minimis transactions may be necessary (see chapter 6).

Table 3.8 Approaches to Transfer Pricing Penalties

Approach	Examples
Penalties may be imposed for failure to fulfill documentation requirements, regardless of whether adjustment is made	Denmark, France, Finland, India, Spain, Hungary
Taxpayers that fail to fulfill documentation requirements may be subject to increased penalties should a transfer pricing adjustment be made	Canada, New Zealand
Taxpayers fulfilling documentation requirements are not subject to penalties, or are subject to reduced penalties, should a transfer pricing adjustment be made	Albania,[a] Italy, United States
Penalties are imposed when an adjustment is made, regardless of whether documentation requirement is fulfilled	Georgia, South Africa

Note: a. See box 3.36.

Box 3.36 Albania's Exemption from Penalties Where Documentation Requirement Met

Article 115/1(3) Law on Tax Procedures

In case of adjustment of tax dues for transfer pricing purpose under Article 36 of the Law No. 8438, dated December 28, 1998, "On Income Tax, amended" for the taxpayers which have filed and sent to the tax authorities the transfer pricing documentation as defined in Article 36/5 of the abovementioned law and the Instruction of the Minister of Finance "On Transfer Pricing," those taxpayers are required to pay only the additional tax obligation and interests, but not penalties.

Section 9 of *Transfer Pricing Legislation* (OECD 2011) contains sample wording for a provision that imposes penalties in the absence of documentation when the adjustment made to the taxpayer's taxable income exceeds a certain threshold:

If:

(a) A taxpayer fails to satisfy the provisions of paragraph[s] 1 [and 2] relating to transfer pricing documentation on a timely basis; and

(b) An adjustment under Section 1, paragraph 2 [in excess of _] is ultimately sustained with respect to the taxpayer;

Then a penalty in the amount of [_] percent of [the additional tax resulting from such adjustment] [the amount of the adjustment to income] may be imposed in addition to the tax otherwise due.

(Further guidance on penalties is provided in chapter 6.)

Requirements for Internal Approval

In some countries, the assessing officer must seek specific approval before a tax assessment arising from a transfer pricing adjustment can be made. Although such internal procedural requirements are typically administrative, some countries, such as Albania and Georgia (see box 3.37), have included a specific provision in their legislation. Where a tax administration's experience with and capacity for dealing with transfer pricing issues is limited, such a provision can provide some reassurance to the private sector since it can help safeguard the quality and consistency of the approach adopted by the tax administration toward transfer pricing matters. It can also help prevent unnecessary compliance costs from being imposed on taxpayers as a result of overzealous or inexperienced tax officials or pursuance of frivolous cases. Such provisions may additionally play a role in limiting opportunities for corruption.

Authority to Issue Secondary Legislation

Countries adopt a range of drafting approaches for transfer pricing legislation. Where secondary legislation is relied upon to introduce or elaborate on specific concepts, the body that will issue that secondary legislation needs authorization. In some countries, the ministry of finance or tax administration may have general power to issue secondary legislation (or administrative guidance) relating to the interpretation and application of provisions of the tax law. Where this is the case, a specific provision is likely not needed.[47] In other countries, such as Serbia, specific authority is provided to the minister of finance to issue secondary legislation clarifying the interpretation and application of the primary legislation on transfer pricing (see box 3.31).

Audit and Information Gathering Powers

While procedures and processes for administration of transfer pricing legislation should be approached in largely the same way as the administration of the rest of the tax law, it is important to consider that transfer pricing audits can differ somewhat from audits of other tax matters. In particular, transfer pricing audits

---

Box 3.37 Examples of Legislative Requirements for Internal Approval

Albania: Article 12(1) of Instruction (No.16) on Transfer Pricing (2014)

An adjustment pursuant to Article 36, paragraph 3 of the law, shall only be made by the tax authority with the written approval of the Director General of the GDT.

Georgia: Article 128(4) of Tax Code of Georgia

The decision about the audit of international controlled transactions is made by the Head of the Revenue Service and it will be performed in accordance with the provisions of this chapter.

---

can be fact intensive and time consuming. As a result, transfer pricing audits often run over longer periods than audits of other tax matters. While some of the simpler and more clear-cut transfer pricing cases can be dealt with in relatively short periods of time (i.e., 12 months or less), it is not atypical for a transfer pricing audit to continue for several years. According to the OECD (2012), the average elapsed time for transfer pricing audits was around 540 days.

It is important to ensure that any restrictions on audit times periods (where applicable) do not unnecessarily hinder the ability of the tax administration to properly develop and close transfer pricing audits. To address concerns that audits may drag on unnecessarily, internal procedures and guidance can be developed and even elaborated upon in a secondary law that, for example, requires periodic updates to the taxpayer as to the status of their case; this step is in addition to having an appropriate statute of limitations.

Ensuring that the tax administration has the necessary information gathering powers is crucial to the successful introduction of transfer pricing legislation. In addition to reporting requirements and a transfer pricing documentation obligation, to properly undertake a transfer pricing audit, the tax administration will for instance need the power to request business records, interview relevant personnel, conduct site inspections.

Statute of Limitations

Typically, a general or issue-specific statute of limitations will constrain the ability of the tax administration to issue revised tax assessments, including transfer pricing adjustments (see examples in table 3.9). Determination of the appropriate

Table 3.9 Statute of Limitations for Transfer Pricing Adjustments in Selected Countries

Country	Time limit
Australia	Seven years (unlimited in the case of fraud or evasion)
Belgium	Three years from end of tax year, seven years in cases of fraud
Canada	Private Canadian corporations: Six years from date of initial assessment after return filing; foreign-controlled corporations and public corporations: seven years from date of initial assessment after return filing
China	10 years
Kenya	Seven years, unlimited in cases of fraud
Russian Federation	Three years from tax year-end
South Africa	Three years from date of assessment if full and accurate disclosure made; no time limit if inaccurate or incomplete disclosure
Turkey	Five years from end of tax year
Uruguay	Five years, 10 years in cases of fraud
United Kingdom	Four years from end of accounting year, six years if company has acted "carelessly," and 20 years in cases of fraud or negligence
United States	Three years from due date or filing of the return, six years if substantial omissions, unlimited in cases of nonfiling or fraud

Source: Based on Deloitte 2014.

time period will require a balancing of the tax administration's need to protect the tax base and the need to provide taxpayers with certainty by allowing them to "close" prior years.

Advance Pricing Agreements

An increasing number of countries have introduced advance pricing agreement (APA) programs. APAs are agreements concerning the application of a country's transfer pricing legislation to specific controlled transactions undertaken by a taxpayer that will take place in future years. These agreements may be unilateral (i.e., between the taxpayer and the tax administration) or bilateral or multilateral (i.e., between two or more tax administrations). Unilateral APAs typically require specific legislative authority to be granted to the tax administration to enter into such agreements. Bilateral and multilateral APAs, on the other hand, typically derive their legal basis from the MAP article in applicable tax treaties.

Introduction of an APA program requires not only a basic legislative authority for the tax administration to conclude such agreements but also the development of relevant procedures and processes governing a range of matters (such as eligibility, user fees, process, etc.). The latter issues are typically addressed in detail in secondary legislation or administrative guidance,[48] while the basic legislative authority for APAs may be relatively short and is typically required to be specified in the primary legislation (see box 3.38).

(Development of an APA program is discussed in detail in chapter 7.)

Box 3.38 Provisions Providing Authority for APAs

Albania: Article 36/7 of Law on Income Tax

1) A taxpayer may request that the tax administration enter into an advance pricing agreement to determine an appropriate set of criteria for the determination of conditions that are consistent with the market principle for certain future controlled transactions over a defined period of time.

2) Where the tax administration enters into an advance pricing agreement with a taxpayer, no adjustment will be made under Article 36, point 3, to controlled transactions that are within the scope of the agreement as long as the terms and conditions set by the advance pricing agreements are satisfied.

3) The Minister of Finance is due to issue a specific instruction concerning Advance Pricing Agreements.

An adjustment pursuant to Article 36, paragraph 3 of the law, shall only be made by the tax authority with the written approval of the Director General of the GDT.

box continues next page

Malaysia: Section 138C of Malaysia's Income Tax Act 1967

(1) Subject to this Section, and any rules prescribed under this Act, on the application made to the Director General by any person who carries out a cross-border transaction with an associated person:

    (a) the Director General may enter into an advance pricing arrangement with that person; or

    (b) in the case where Section 132 applies, the competent authorities may enter into an advance pricing arrangement in order to determine the transfer pricing methodology to be used in any future apportionment or allocation of income or deduction to ensure the arm's-length transfer prices in relation to that transaction.

(2) An application under Subsection (1) shall be made in the prescribed form and shall contain particulars as may be required by the Director General.

(3) The transactions referred to in Subsection (1) shall be construed as a transaction between:

    (a) persons one of whom has control over the other;

    (b) individuals who are relatives of each other; or

    (c) persons both of whom are controlled by some other person.

(4) In this Section, "relative" and "transaction" have the same meanings assigned to them under Subsection 140(8).

Simplification Measures

The use of safe harbors and simplification measures, especially for small or low-risk transactions and taxpayers, can help ensure that the resources of the tax administration and taxpayers are efficiently allocated to areas of high risk, reducing taxpayer compliance costs, increasing certainty, and improving administrative efficiency (see chapter 7). In 2011, the OECD published a survey on the use of simplification measures in OECD and OECD observer countries. It found that of the 33 respondent countries, 27 had simplification measures in place, 70 percent of which were directed at SMEs, small transactions, and low value added services. Despite concerns about double taxation often expressed by commentators and in the *OECD Transfer Pricing Guidelines* (2010b), none of the countries that responded to the OECD survey reported instances of double taxation as a result of such measures. The most recent revision of the guidelines draws on the experience of member countries and includes a safe harbor (named "elective simplified approach") for low value adding services.[49]

Countries have introduced a range of different simplification measures and safe harbors that can be broadly grouped into five categories, as set out in table 3.10.

Where safe harbors are introduced that involve simplified transfer pricing methods or safe harbor arm's-length ranges, prices, margins, or rates, it advisable to introduce such measures through secondary legislation or administrative guidance in order to provide increased flexibility for the measures to be modified as experience with transfer pricing develops. Where such an approach is adopted, authority for the relevant body to introduce and amend such measures may need to be provided for in the primary legislation (see box 3.39).

Table 3.10 Categories of Simplification Measures and Safe Harbors

Type of simplification measure/safe harbor	Cross-reference
Exemptions from scope of transfer pricing legislation	Chapter 3 ("Classes of Taxpayer")
Simplified transfer pricing methods, safe harbor arm's-length ranges, prices, margins, rates	Chapter 7
Exemptions from or simplified documentation requirements	Chapter 6
Exemptions from or reduced penalties	Chapter 6
Simplified APA procedures or reduced APA charges	Chapter 7

Note: APA = advance pricing agreement.

Box 3.39 Provisions Providing Authority for Safe Harbors

India: Section 92CB of the Income Tax Act

(1) The determination of arm's-length price under Sec. 92C or Sec. 92CA shall be subject to safe harbour rules.

(2) The Board may, for the purposes of Subsec. (1), make rules for safe harbour.

Explanation. For the purposes of this Section, "safe harbour" means circumstances in which the income-tax authorities shall accept the transfer price declared by the assesse.

Serbia: Article 61 Corporate Income Tax Law

For the needs of determining the amount of interest that would be calculated under the arm's-length principle on loans or credits among related parties, the Minister of Finance may prescribe the amounts of interest rates which will be regarded as being in accordance with the arm's-length principle.

The taxpayer is entitled to apply the general rules on determining the transaction price under the arm's-length principle referred to in Articles 60 and 61 paragraphs 1 and 2 of this law instead of the interest rate amount referred to in paragraph 3 of this Article for the purpose of determining the amount which would be calculated on loan or credit with the related party under the arm's-length principle.

The taxpayer who decides to exercise the right foreseen in paragraph 4 of this Article shall be responsible to apply the general rules on determining the transaction price under the arm's-length principle referred to in Articles 60 and 61, paragraphs 1 and 2 of this law on all loans or credits with the related parties.

If the taxpayer decides to exercise the right foreseen in paragraph 4 of this Article, the tax administration, for the needs of determining the amount of interest which would be under the arm's-length principle calculated on loans or credits between that taxpayer and the parties related to it, shall not be bound by the amounts of interest rates referred to in paragraph 3 of this Article.

Other measures, such as exemptions from the scope of the legislation and reductions in penalties, may require specific provisions in the primary legislation. Others, such as simplified documentation requirements, may be provided for in secondary legislation or even administrative guidance.

Role of Administrative Guidance

Administrative guidance on the application of a country's transfer pricing legislation can be instrumental in reducing uncertainty, building awareness, and encouraging self-compliance. Recognizing this, administrations of numerous countries have issued detailed and practical guidance on transfer pricing that assists taxpayers and tax officials in applying the country's transfer pricing legislation. An important feature of administrative guidance is the possibility to present detailed practical examples that are otherwise generally not appropriate for inclusion in legislation.

Administrative guidance may address application of the transfer pricing legislation generally, or may address in detail one or more specific aspects of transfer pricing, such as intragroup services, intragroup finance, business restructurings, documentation, advance pricing arrangements, or other substantive or procedural issues.

Administrative guidance may take the form of a ruling, instruction, guideline, practice note, circular or communiqué, or otherwise, depending on the country's laws, traditions, and practices. Its legal status will depend on the country's legal system and the form the guidance takes. For example, public taxation rulings issued by the Australian Taxation Office are considered an expression of the commissioner of Taxation's opinion about the way in which a provision applies and are not legally binding on taxpayers.[50] These rulings may, however, bind the commissioner, provided certain criteria are fulfilled.[51] In contrast, interpretive decisions issued by the commissioner are not binding on the commissioner, but do provide penalty protection for taxpayers who have relied on them. In South Africa, the South African Revenue Service Practice Note 7 on transfer pricing serves merely as an indication of the commissioner's interpretation of the relevant law and its practical application; it is not legally binding (Horak 2011). Regardless of the legal status, drafters of administrative guidance are advised to consider that any guidance published by the tax administration is likely to be highly influential on the development of transfer pricing practices in the country.

Drafting administrative guidance on transfer pricing typically requires a thorough understanding of a country's legislation and the issues faced in practice, and can therefore be very resource intensive. Where a country has recently introduced transfer pricing legislation, preparation and publication of such guidance may thus be delayed until practical experience with applying the legislation has been developed or where appropriate resources are available. To bridge the gap, and provide tax officials and taxpayers with a level of certainty during the interim period, the tax administration may opt to issue interim guidance that endorses international guidelines such as the OECD *Transfer Pricing Guidelines* or the *UN Manual*.

In the Philippines, for example, the commissioner of Internal Revenue issued a revenue memorandum circular stating that until the revenue regulations on transfer pricing were finalized, the Bureau of Internal Revenue would subscribe to the guidelines (see box 3.40). As an alternative (or in addition) to preparing administrative guidance, several OECD member countries (including Australia, Ireland, Mexico, and the United Kingdom) have made direct reference to the guidelines in their primary legislation.[52] Other non-OECD member countries, such as Albania and Georgia, have made references to the guidelines as an interpretive aid in their secondary legislation. While these approaches may be appropriate for some countries, each country should carefully consider

---

Box 3.40 Example: The Philippines' Interim Transfer Pricing Guidelines

On March 24, 2008, the Philippines' Commissioner of Internal Revenue issued a revenue memorandum circular stating that until the revenue regulations on transfer pricing were finalized and issued, the Bureau of Internal Revenue subscribes to the *OECD Transfer Pricing Guidelines*. Final regulations were issued in early 2013.

REPUBLIC OF THE PHILIPPINES
DEPARTMENT OF FINANCE
BUREAU OF INTERNAL REVENUE
Quezon City

March 24, 2008

REVENUE MEMORANDUM CIRCULAR NO. 26 - 2008

SUBJECT: Interim Transfer Pricing Guidelines

TO   :   All Internal Revenue Officials, Employees, and Others Concerned.

For the guidance and information of all internal revenue officials, employees and others concerned, please be notified that the Bureau of Internal Revenue (BIR) is revising the final draft of the Revenue Regulations on Transfer Pricing. In view of the upcoming tax filing season and in order to preclude any issue that may arise in the interim, the BIR, as a matter of policy subscribes to the OECD Transfer Pricing Guidelines.

Accordingly, until the said Regulations are issued, any and all concerns shall be resolved in accordance with the principles laid down by the said guidelines.

All revenue officers and employees are enjoined to give this Circular as wide a publicity as possible.

(Original Signed)
LILIAN B. HEFTI
Commissioner of Internal Revenue

---

language and translation issues, the appropriateness of the guidelines in regard to the domestic law, and the ability of the country to influence the development of these guidelines in deciding whether to give the guidelines legal status.

(*Annex 3C lists examples of selected countries' administrative guidance on transfer pricing.*)

Practical Considerations when Drafting Transfer Pricing Legislation

This section outlines practical issues that are commonly encountered when drafting transfer pricing legislation, and provides examples of how countries have dealt with them.

Interaction with Other Tax Laws

Since transfer pricing legislation concerns the pricing of transactions, it is important to consider whether the legislation will impact, or be impacted by, other provisions of the country's tax law. For example, where "alternative assessment" provisions provide the tax administration with wide powers to make adjustments to transactions between related parties, this may undermine the practical application of the transfer pricing legislation.

Another issue relates to overlaps in the terminology. For example, where the term *related parties* is generally defined in the tax law, careful assessment of other provisions that use that term is required before modifying the definition. For example, where the country has a single tax code that covers VAT, income tax, corporate tax, and so on, and the definition proposed for transfer pricing may not be suitable, one solution may be to "ring fence" the definition used for transfer pricing by using different terminology.

Language Considerations

Transfer pricing has its own lexicon of specific terminology. Many of these terms, which have specific meaning in select languages, such as English, may not translate well into other languages. For example, in several languages, such as Albanian and Georgian, the direct translation of *arm's-length principle* is not acceptable for drafting purposes; thus, different terminology was used in drafting the legislation (i.e., a translation of *market principle*). Similar situations can arise regarding the translation of the terminology assigned in the OECD *Transfer Pricing Guidelines* (2010b) to the five transfer pricing methods. Use of alternative terminology, where necessary, is not problematic provided that, to the extent that the alternative term is intended to have an "international meaning," the drafter takes care to define the term analogously.

Great care should be taken to ensure that where phrases and terms from legislation drafted in another language are used that the meaning is not lost or altered. As Gordin and Thuronyi (1996, p.11) point out "translation is a cumbersome process, and problems of ambiguity or terminology are often obscured by translators, sometimes even by those of the highest quality and longest experience."[53] Where foreign advisors and nonnative language speakers are assisting with the drafting process, they must ensure that the intended meaning and context are discussed and clarified and that the final local language draft is clear and will operate as intended.

Use of Foreign Advisors and Other Countries' Transfer Pricing Legislation

Despite the benefit that foreign advisors' input and reference to other countries' legislation can provide, use of these resources should be approached with care. Because transfer pricing legislation needs to fit within the broader context of a country's tax legislation and economic policy, those involved in the policy design and drafting process must have knowledge of the general tax system, how the judiciary is expected to interpret the law, and the broader economic and legal environment. This is particularly important where an advisor's prior experience is in a country with a different legal system, different drafting traditions and approaches, and a different economy. Caution is also advised when looking to other countries' legislation and concepts (including the examples in this handbook) as a source of reference; drafters need to ensure that the broader context is understood.

Chapter 3 Main Messages

- Initial policy decisions concerning transfer pricing should be informed by a needs assessment and reference a range of different factors, including the country's broader economic and administrative capacity and the structure of the economy.
- The appropriate drafting approach for a particular country will depend on a variety of factors, but a relatively brief and principles-based approach to primary legislation is preferable to very detailed and thereby less flexible primary legislation.
- The scope of transfer pricing legislation needs to be carefully determined. The wider the scope, the greater the potential for unnecessary and unreasonable compliance costs to be imposed on taxpayers and for unnecessary enforcement costs incurred by the tax administration. At the same time, an overly narrow scope may provide possibilities for circumventing the legislation or may miss certain significant transactions.
- Legislation that introduces a standard that differs from the generally accepted interpretation of the arm's-length principle, such as "open market value" or "competitive market price," can give rise to unnecessary uncertainty and disputes.
- Prescription of the arm's-length principle as the relevant benchmark or standard on its own is typically not sufficient for ensuring the necessary level of certainty. Provisions that elaborate on the practical application of the principle need to be included in the legislation or related guidance.
- Provisions concerning administrative and procedural matters are critical for the practical implementation of transfer pricing. These include reporting and disclosure requirements, documentation obligations, and, where applicable, guidance on special processes such as safe harbors or the conclusion of advance pricing agreement.

Annex 3A: Transfer Pricing Legislation Checklist

Table 3A.1 Transfer Pricing Legislation Checklist

Item		Preparatory considerations
Transfer pricing policy		Has an appropriate transfer pricing policy been developed and agreed upon that will guide the drafting process?
Drafting approach		What is the most appropriate drafting approach that takes into account legal system, traditions, existing tax laws, capacity, etc.? (i.e., what will be included in primary legislation, secondary legislation, or administrative guidance?)
Core provisions		
Scope		What is the appropriate scope for the transfer pricing legislation (i.e., that appropriately balances the need to protect the tax base with investment climate considerations)?
	Taxes covered	Which taxes, and parts of the tax law, will the legislation apply to?
	Classes of taxpayer	Which classes of taxpayer will the legislation apply to?
		Will there be exemptions from the legislation for any specific classes of taxpayer (such as SMEs)?
	Controlled transactions	Will all types of transactions (arrangements, dealings, etc.) that may affect the taxable profit be included in the scope? Or is it necessary to exclude specific transaction types that are regulated elsewhere?
		Will there be any thresholds for application of the law based on transaction size?
		How will associated and related parties be defined with respect to both legal control (percentage of ownership, etc.) and practical (de facto) control?
		Will the legislation apply to any transactions between parties that are not demonstrated to be associated/related parties (i.e., where one party is from a specified jurisdiction)?
		Will the legislation apply to cross-border and domestic transactions? If it will apply to domestic transactions, will it apply to all domestic transactions or only in specific cases?
Arm's-length principle		How will the arm's-length principle be implemented?
		Will the definition be based on conditions of the transaction or on prices?
Adjustments	*Primary*	How will the legislation provide authority for the tax administration to make adjustment to ensure consistency with the arm's-length principle?
		Will that power be limited to adjustments that increase taxable income or profits?
	Compensating	Will specific provisions be introduced allowing taxpayers to self-adjust?
		Will both upward and downward adjustments be allowed, or only adjustments that increase taxable income or profits?
		Will safeguards be put in place to prevent possible abuses?
	Corresponding	Is a specific provision for corresponding adjustments under tax treaties necessary?
		Are there clear procedures for seeking relief under tax treaties, or are specific procedures for corresponding adjustments necessary?
		Will domestic corresponding adjustments be provided for where the legislation covers domestic transfer pricing?
	Secondary	Will provisions be introduced for secondary adjustments?

table continues next page

Table 3A.1 Transfer Pricing Legislation Checklist *(continued)*

Item	Preparatory considerations
Practical provisions	
Comparability	What will be the applicable standard of comparability (i.e., how will *comparability* be defined)?
	Will comparability factors be specified in the legislation? If so, which ones?
	Will there be any specific provisions on comparability adjustments (when they can be made, or types, etc.)?
	Will the process for comparability analysis be guided or regulated in any way?
Transfer pricing methods	Will the transfer pricing methods that can be applied be specified? If so, how will they be defined?
	Will provision be made for the use of other methods?
	Will any specific methods be introduced for certain transaction types?
Selection of method	How will the selection of transfer pricing method be legislated?
	Will the tax administration be required to accept the method used by the taxpayer, provided it was appropriately selected?
Selection of tested party	Will the selection of the tested party be legislated? If so, will the possible use of a foreign tested party be specifically provided for?
Aggregation of transaction	Will the circumstances under which controlled transactions can be aggregated be specified?
Arm's-length range	How will the arm's-length range be defined (whole range, interquartile, etc.)?
Selection of point within range	Will the point within the arm's-length range that adjustments must be made to be specified? If so, what will it be?
Sources of information	Will there be any specific provisions concerning the sources of information that can be used?
	Will the use of foreign comparables be specifically provided for?
	Will the use of secret comparables be prohibited?
Transaction-specific	Will any transaction-specific provisions be included in the legislation (i.e., provisions concerning the application of the arm's-length principle to specific transactions types, such as those involving services, intangibles, restructurings, etc.)?
Relevance of international guidance	Will any reference be made in the legislation to the *OECD Transfer Pricing Guidelines*, or other sources of international guidance (such as the *UN Practical Manual*), as a relevant source of interpretation or guidance?
Administrative and procedural provisions	
Reporting requirements	Will a specific reporting requirement for transfer pricing be introduced (i.e., a controlled transactions notice, or transfer pricing schedule)?
	Will there be a threshold for which taxpayers are required to fulfill this requirement?
	What will be the consequences of noncompliance (i.e., penalties)?
Transfer pricing documentation	Will a requirement be introduced for taxpayers to prepare transfer pricing documentation?
	What will be the prescribed content, form, and acceptable language(s)?
	Will there be any thresholds for this requirement?
	Will there be simplification measures for SMEs or de minimis transactions?
	How will the documentation requirement impact burden of proof?
	What are the consequences of noncompliance (i.e., penalties, burden of proof)?
Penalties	Will specific penalties for transfer pricing be introduced?
	Will penalties be linked to the documentation requirement? If so, how?
	Will the penalties be fixed or dependent on transaction or adjustment volume?
Internal approval requirement	Is it necessary to have a requirement in the legislation for approval of the commissioner (or similar) to undertake transfer pricing audits or make adjustments?
Authority to issue secondary legislation	Is it necessary to have a specific legislative authority for secondary legislation on transfer pricing to be issued?

table continues next page

Table 3A.1 **Transfer Pricing Legislation Checklist** *(continued)*

Item	Preparatory considerations
Audit and information-gathering powers	Are there any specific audit timeframe limits that may exist that are appropriate for transfer pricing? Does the tax administration have the necessary information-gathering powers to administer the transfer pricing legislation?
Statute of limitations	Is the current statute of limitations appropriate for transfer pricing?
Advance pricing agreements	Will an advance pricing agreement program be introduced in the near future? If so, is specific legislative authority for advance pricing agreements needed? Is legislation or guidance on the processes and procedures for advance pricing agreements needed?
Simplification measures (safe harbors)	Is it planned to introduce any safe harbors now or in the near future? If yes, is specific legislative authority for introducing such measures needed?
Administrative guidance	
General	Will practical guidance on the application of the transfer pricing legislation, including practical examples, be developed? Will this be for internal use only, or will it be made public? What will be the legal status of this guidance, i.e., will it be binding on the tax administration?
Specific	Is any guidance on specific issues required (for example applications for mutual agreement procedure to competent authority, advance pricing agreements, transaction specific, or industry-specific)?

Note: SMEs = small and medium enterprises.

Annex 3B: Examples of "Relationships" from Selected Countries' Legislation

Table 3B.1 **Examples of "Relationships" from Selected Countries' Legislation**

Nature of relationship	Selected country examples
Personal or family relationships	**Denmark:** Taxpayer's spouse, parents, and grandparents, as well as children and grandchildren and their spouses, or the estates of such persons. Any stepchildren and adopted children shall be comparable to children related by blood.
	India: Where one enterprise is controlled by an individual, the other enterprise is also controlled by such individual or his relative or jointly by such individual and relative of such individual.
	Indonesia: Family relationship either through blood or through marriage within one degree of direct or indirect lineage.
Common or joint management	**Finland:** It is under joint leadership with the other party or it otherwise has control over the other party.
	India: Control of composition of board.
Power to appoint or remove the board or executive officers	**Finland:** Directly or indirectly has the power to appoint the majority of the members of the board of directors or corresponding organ of the other party or to an organ that has this power.
	Hungary: A member or shareholder of the company is entitled to appoint or dismiss the majority of executive officers or supervisory board members of another company.

table continues next page

Table 3B.1 Examples of "Relationships" from Selected Countries' Legislation *(continued)*

Nature of relationship	*Selected country examples*
	India: More than half of the board of directors or members of the governing board, or one or more executive directors or executive members of the governing board of one enterprise, are appointed by the other enterprise; or more than half of the directors or members of the governing board, or one or more of the executive directors or members of the governing board, of each of the two enterprises are appointed by the same person or persons.
Voting rights	**Czech Republic:** One person participates in the capital or voting rights of multiple persons and this person has a holding of at least 25 percent in the other's or others' registered capital or voting rights.
	Denmark: Disposal of more than 50 percent of the votes.
	Finland: Directly or indirectly has more than half of the voting power of the other party.
	India: Any person or enterprise holds, directly or indirectly, shares carrying not less than 26 percent of the voting power.
	Slovak Republic: Any direct, indirect, or indirect derivative holding of more than 25 percent of the registered capital or voting rights.
Equity, capital, shareholding	**Czech Republic:** One person participates in the capital or voting rights of multiple persons and this person has a holding of at least 25 percent in the other's registered capital or voting rights.
	Denmark: Direct or indirect ownership of more than 50 percent of the share capital.
	Finland: Directly or indirectly owns more than half of the capital of the other party.
	Indonesia: Owns, directly or indirectly, at least 25 percent of the equity.
	Japan: 50 percent or more of the issued shares of either corporation is, directly or indirectly, owned by the other corporation.
	Latvia: Parent and subsidiaries, in cases where the parent company holds more than 50 percent of the subsidiary's share capital or voting rights.
	Malaysia: The same persons hold more than 50 percent of the shares in each of two or more companies.
	Portugal: Hold, directly or indirectly, a stake of not less than 10 percent of the capital or voting rights
	South Africa: At least 20 percent and no other shareholder with majority.
	Spain: An entity and its shareholders, generally when the participation is at least 5 percent (1 percent in the case of quoted stock companies).
	Thailand: A juristic person is a shareholder or partner holding more than 50 percent of the value of the total capital of another juristic person.

table continues next page

Table 3B.1 Examples of "Relationships" from Selected Countries' Legislation (continued)

Nature of relationship	Selected country examples
Right to share in profits	**Israel:** Holding, directly or indirectly, 50 percent or more of the right to profits.
Financial dependence	**India:** A loan advanced by one enterprise to the other enterprise constitutes not less than 51 percent of the book value of the total assets of the other enterprise. One enterprise guarantees not less than 10 percent of the total borrowings of the other enterprise.
	Japan: A substantial portion of the funds required for the business activities of either corporation is procured through borrowing(s) or with the benefit of guarantee(s) from the other corporation.
	Rep. of Korea: When one party borrows 50 percent or more of the funds necessary for its business from another party or under the other party's guarantee.
Transactional dependence	**Argentina:** One party is an exclusive agent or distributor of another for the sale of goods, services, or rights.
	India: The manufacture or processing of goods or articles or business carried out by one enterprise is wholly dependent on the use of know-how, patents, copyrights, trademarks, licences, franchises, or any other business or commercial rights of similar nature, or any data, documentation, drawing or specification relating to any patent, invention, model, design, secret formula or process, of which the other enterprise is the owner or in respect of which the other enterprise has exclusive rights.
	– 90 percent or more of the raw materials and consumables required for the manufacture or processing of goods or articles carried out by one enterprise are supplied by the other enterprise, or by persons specified by the other enterprise, and the prices and other conditions relating to the supply are influenced by such other enterprise;
	– the goods or articles manufactured or processed by one enterprise are sold to the other enterprise or to persons specified by the other enterprise, and the prices and other conditions relating thereto are influenced by such other enterprise.
	Japan: A substantial portion of the business activities of either corporation depends on transactions with the other corporation.
	– either corporation conducts its business based on copyrights, industrial property rights or know-how (which form the basis of its business activities) provided by the other corporation.
	Rep. of Korea: When one party depends on another party for 50 percent or more of its business.
	– when 50 percent or more of the business of one party relies on intangible property provided by another party.

Source: IBFD Transfer Pricing database country chapters: Argentina, Chile, Czech Republic, Denmark, Finland, Hungary, India, Indonesia, Israel, Japan, Republic of Korea, Latvia, Malaysia, Pakistan, Portugal, Slovak Republic, South Africa, Spain, Thailand.
Note: Database accessed on February 22, 2012.

Annex 3C: Selected Examples of Administrative Guidance on Transfer Pricing

This is a noncomprehensive list of administrative guidance available in English. Numerous other countries have administrative guidance (in English or other languages) that can typically be accessed via the tax administration website.

Canada

The Canada Revenue Agency has issued a circular that provides guidance on the application of its transfer pricing legislation. This circular can be accessed at http://www.cra-arc.gc.ca/E/pub/tp/ic87-2r/README.html.

Fiji

The Fiji Revenue and Customs Authority has issued transfer pricing guidelines, which are available at http://www.frca.org.fj/wp-content/uploads/2012/11/Transfer _Pricing.pdf.

Hong Kong SAR, China

The Inland Revenue Department of Hong Kong SAR, China, has issued transfer pricing guidelines, which are available at http://www.ird.gov.hk/eng/pdf/e _dipn46.pdf.

Japan

The National Tax Agency of Japan has issued a Commissioner's Directive on the Operation of Transfer Pricing (Administrative Guidelines), which is available at http://www.nta.go.jp/foreign_language/07.pdf, and a supplement containing numerous case studies, which is available at http://www.nta.go.jp/foreign _language/08.pdf.

Malaysia

The Inland Revenue Board of Malaysia has issued transfer pricing guidelines, which are available at http://www.hasil.gov.my/pdf/pdfam/garispanduanpin dahanharga_bm.pdf.

New Zealand

The New Zealand Inland Revenue Department has issued transfer pricing guidelines, which are available at http://www.ird.govt.nz/forms-guides/number/forms -unnumbered/guide-transfer-pricing.html.

Singapore

The Inland Revenue Authority of Singapore (IRAS) has issued a circular on transfer pricing guidelines and two supplementary circulars: an e-tax guide on transfer pricing guidelines for related party loans, and services and supplementary administrative guidance on advance pricing arrangements. The guides can be accessed at http://www.iras.gov.sg/.

South Africa

The South African Revenue Service issued a practice note on transfer pricing in 1999 (Practice Note 7) to which an addendum was issued in 2005. These documents are available at http://www.sars.gov.za/.

Notes

1. For guidance on drafting tax legislation generally, see Gordin and Thuronyi (1996).
2. A diagnostic based on firm-level and macro economic data that are undertaken to identify, understand, and quantify transfer pricing risks specific to a country's economy and the design of its tax system.
3. Russia, Ukraine, and Kazakhstan are noteworthy exceptions; Russia and Ukraine have adopted extremely detailed provisions on transfer pricing in their tax codes, and Kazakhstan has adopted a separate law on transfer pricing. See Article 39 of Tax Code of Ukraine (as amended in 2011), section V.1 of the Tax Code of the Russian Federation (as amended), and Law No. 67-IV of 5th July 2008 of the Republic of Kazakhstan Concerning Transfer Pricing.
4. Egypt: Article 30 of the Income Tax Law No. 91 of 2005; Ghana: section 70 of the Internal Revenue Act 2000 (Act 592); Kenya: section 18(3) of the Income Tax Act (CAP.470 of the Laws of Kenya), as amended (2009); Malaysia: section 140A of the Income Tax Act 1967; United States: section 482 of the Internal Revenue Code.
5. Ireland introduced transfer pricing legislation in 2010 that applies only to profits or losses arising from certain trading activities and professional operations (chargeable to tax under Case I or II of Schedule D of the Income Tax Consolidation Act, 1997). The new law does not apply to certain royalty and lease arrangements or to special purpose companies (see Part 35A Income Taxes Consolidation Act 1997 [Ireland]), which are taxed at different rates.
6. For a general discussion of the transfer pricing challenges in the extractive industries, please refer to "Transfer Pricing in Mining: An African Perspective" (International Mining for Development Centre and World Bank 2014).
7. For example, in Ethiopia, Articles 5 and 6 prescribe the arm's-length principle as applicable to income from and expenditure paid to affiliates.
8. For example, Australia's mineral resource rent tax includes an arm's-length requirement when determining the relevant supply consideration, which is used to determine the taxable base [section 30-25(2) of the Minerals Resource Rent Tax Act 2012 (Cth)].
9. An objective of transfer pricing legislation is the negation of the effect that any relationship between the parties may have had on the price for the purposes of determining the relevant taxable base.
10. See, for example, Article 73 of the EU VAT Directive 77/388/EEC.
11. For example, to combat VAT-avoidance schemes, in 2006 the EU enacted Council Directive 2006/69/EC, which opened up the possibility for tax authorities to adjust the valuation of certain transactions where the value declared differs from the open market value. Australia, Canada, China, Israel, Japan, New Zealand, and Norway have similar provisions (Lucas Mas 2009).
12. Georgia's legislation, for example refers to "Georgian enterprises," thus excluding from its scope private individuals acting as such. Similarly, *Transfer Pricing Legislation* (OECD 2011) uses the term *enterprises*.

13. Ireland: section 835E of the Taxes Consolidation Act 1997; United Kingdom: sections 166–68 of the Taxation (International and Other Provisions) Act 2010.

14. For example, many countries include a transactional threshold for the requirement to make annual disclosures or have simplified documentation requirements for small taxpayers and de minimis transactions.

15. In the United Kingdom, for example, the general transfer pricing legislation does not apply to certain transactions involving oil-related ring-fence trades, which are regulated by another provision [section 205 of the Taxation (International and other Provisions) Act 2010]. Brazil's transfer pricing legislation contains specific provisions for certain transaction types. Its core transfer pricing provisions are applicable only to imports and exports of certain goods and services; interest on loans and certain payments of the use of intangibles are covered by other specific provisions.

16. Article 3.2.1.4 of the Tax Code of Ukraine (as amended, 2013).

17. For example, in Hungary, "transactions with an arm's-length consideration net of VAT not exceeding the threshold of HUF50 million accumulated during the period of the date of the contract to the last day of the tax year" ((IBFD Transfer Pricing Database – Hungary Chapter, accessed in 2012) are not subject to the transfer pricing documentation requirements.

18. Chile: Article 38 of the Income Tax Law; France: Article 238-A of the Code Général des Impôts; Mexico: Article 125 of the Income Tax Law. Portugal: Article 63 of the Corporate Income Tax Code. Russia's new transfer pricing legislation applies to "third-party transactions where the counterparty is located in a blacklisted jurisdiction if the aggregate annual amount of income, as a result of all transactions between such parties, exceeds Rub 60 million (approximately US$2.2 million)" (Ernst & Young 2011).

19. See, for example, Hungary, Russia, Serbia, Ukraine, and the United Kingdom.

20. Domestic transfer pricing (i.e., transfer pricing as it relates to transactions between resident taxpayers or local permanent establishments of nonresidents) can, however, have a significant impact on a country's tax base when disparities in the treatment of resident taxpayers exist as a result of exemptions, tax holidays, or differences in tax rates, or where there is no possibility for fiscal unity or transfer of losses under a country's domestic law. Where such disparities exist, extending the scope of a country's transfer pricing legislation to certain domestic transactions may be necessary. In this regard, a 2010 survey of 33 OECD member and nonmember countries found that all countries surveyed applied the arm's-length principle to international transactions, but that in just 20 of the 33 countries it was applicable to domestic transactions (OECD 2010a). In most of the countries that did not apply the arm's-length principle to domestic transactions, the pricing of domestic transactions is either not regulated or is regulated by specific targeted measures.

21. That is, participants of "Skolkovo" innovation center projects.

22. S1.482-1(a)(3) section 482 regulations (United States).

23. For example, although a deduction may only be claimed for the arm's-length amount, actual payments for services to a parent company may be inflated to repatriate capital and avoid the withholding tax that would have been payable had the profits been distributed dividends.

24. Where domestic transaction falls within the scope of a country's transfer pricing legislation, provision for corresponding adjustments requires consideration.

25. In the Netherlands, Decree 295M states that "the Dutch tax authorities always require a transfer pricing adjustment to be processed by means of a secondary

transaction," which may, for example, result in a deemed dividend subject to with-holding tax. Similarly, Article 9 of Korea's International Tax Coordination Law (Law 9266) provides that "unless it is confirmed as provided by the Presidential Decree that the amount added to the resident's taxable income will be returned to the domestic corporation from the Foreign-Related Party, that amount shall be treated as a dividend, other outflow outside the company, or as an additional capital contribution to the Foreign-Related Party, notwithstanding Article 67 of the Corporate Income Tax Law" (IBFD Transfer Pricing Database – Korea Chapter, accessed in 2011).

26. For example, in the Netherlands, Dutch tax authorities can waive the withholding tax if, for example, the taxpayer can demonstrate it will not be credited in the other country.

27. Amended in October 2015 to further specify (among other changes) that the first step is the careful delineation of the actual transaction between the associated enterprises by analyzing the actual the conduct of the parties. See Final Reports on BEPS Actions 8-10: "Aligning Transfer Pricing Outcomes with Value Creation."(2015)

28. In many countries, a standard of comparability is not specified per se. Instead, a similar standard is implicit in the guidance provided on the comparability factors to be considered and the transfer pricing methods that can be applied.

29. Being slightly revised to:

    • The contractual terms of the transaction;
    • The functions performed by each of the parties to the transaction, taking into account assets used and risks assumed, including how those functions relate to the wider generation of value by the MNE group to which the parties belong, the circumstances surrounding the transaction, and industry practices;
    • The characteristics of property transferred or services provided;
    • The economic circumstances of the parties and of the market in which the parties operate;
    • The business strategies pursued by the parties.

    See: Amendments in October 2015 by the Final Reports on BEPS Actions 8-10: "Aligning Transfer Pricing Outcomes with Value Creation."

30. For example, in the U.S. transfer pricing regulations, a variant of the transactional net margin method (TNMM), referred to as the comparable profits method (CPM), is prescribed. Although there are some theoretical differences, the practical application of the TNMM and the CPM is similar.

31. Brazil being the notable exception—for a summary of the Brazilian transfer pricing regime see section 10.2 of the UN Practical Manual 2013.

32. The OECD has announced plans to revise the current guidance on the application of the transactional profit split method by 2017. The objective is to clarify some practical challenges raised in public consultation processes during the BEPS project. See Final Reports on BEPS Actions 8-10: "Aligning Transfer Pricing Outcomes with Value Creation" and revisions to chapter 6 of the OECD Transfer Pricing Guidelines, October 2015.

33. Article 30-1 Belarusian Tax Code (2002, as amended by law 330-Z of December 30, 2012).

34. Latvia: Government Regulation 556; and Turkey: Article 13 of the Corporate Income Tax Law.

35. Japan: Article 64-4 of the Special Measures Concerning Taxation (amended June 30, 2011, with effect October 1, 2011) (PwC 2013); Korea: in December 2010, the Law for Coordination of International Tax Affairs was amended, replacing the previous hierarchy of methods with a requirement to use the most reasonable transfer pricing method (PwC 2012).

36. For example, Article 36/2(3) of Law on Income Tax (Albania) states: "It is not required to apply more than one method to determine consistency with the market principle for a given controlled transaction."

37. In Hungary, for example, no specific legislative provisions deal with arm's-length range. In practice, however, transfer prices are assessed with reference to a range of prices rather than a single price (Deloitte 2011).

38. Australia: paragraphs 2.83-2.95 of Taxation Ruling TR97/20; Canada: section 16 of Circular IC 87-2R; South Africa: section 11.4 of Practice Note 7.

39. The interquartile range is a statistical measure that discards the top 25 percent and bottom 25 percent of observations. The definition in the IRC section 482 regulations differs from the definition commonly found in statistics textbooks because of differences in rounding.

40. Article 60 of the Corporate Income Tax Law (Serbia) specifies that the adjustment shall be to the average of the range.

41. In 2007, Germany amended section 1 of the Foreign Tax Code (Außensteuergesetz), regarding the transfers of functions. In 2008, the Bundesrat approved a decree law concerning the application of the arm's-length principle in the case of a cross-border transfer of functions.

42. See section 7 (Services between Associated Enterprises) and section 8 (Transactions Involving Intangible Property) of the OECD Secretariat's suggested approach to transfer pricing legislation and final report on BEPS Actions 8-10: "Aligning Transfer Pricing Outcomes with Value Creation," Revisions to chapter 6 of the OECD *Transfer Pricing Guidelines*, October 2015.

43. See: Article 39.2.1.3 of the Ukrainian Tax Code, following amendments in December 2014.

44. See: Final Reports on BEPS Actions 8-10: "Aligning Transfer Pricing Outcomes with Value Creation," Revisions to chapter 7 of the OECD *Transfer Pricing Guidelines*, October 2015.

45. In addition, documentation may serve as a prompt to ensure taxpayers turn their minds to better transfer pricing compliance and the information on documentation can be used for risk assessment by tax administrations (see chapter 8).

46. See: OECD Action 13, Final Report: "Transfer Pricing Documentation and Country-by-Country Reporting." The introduction of the CbC report is aimed at improving tax administrator's information for risk assessment purposes. It has drawn significant public attention and some criticism related to the high exemption threshold for entities with consolidated group revenue below a750 million (the threshold will be reconsidered in a review of the reporting standards scheduled for 2020), which may exclude critical taxpayers in many emerging and developing economies. Moreover, some countries have indicated a preference for a wider scope for the CbC report than what is currently covered in the agreed reporting template (covering additional transaction data such as interest and royalty payments). Finally, there are questions regarding the overall relevance and cost-effectiveness of the contribution of CbC reporting requirements in countering profit shifting (Evers, Meier, and Spengel 2014).

47. Such is the case in Albania, where Article 40 of the law in Income Tax states that the Ministry of Finance is responsible for issuing sublegal acts under and for implementation of the law.

48. See, for example, Georgia: chapter 5 of Decree 423 of Finance Minister on Approval of Instructions on International Transfer Pricing (2013); Nigeria: Regulation 8 of the Income Tax (Transfer Pricing) Regulations No. 1, 2012.

49. See: Final Reports on BEPS Actions 8–10: "Aligning Transfer Pricing Outcomes with Value Creation," Revisions to chapter 7 of the OECD *Transfer Pricing Guidelines*, October 2015.

50. Appendix B lists examples of taxation rulings issued by the Australian Taxation Office relevant to transfer pricing.

51. Australian Taxation Office Taxation Ruling TR2006/10 "Public Rulings."

52. Ireland: section 835D of the Taxes Consolidation Act 1997; Mexico: Article 215 Income Tax Law; United Kingdom: section 164 of the Taxation (International and Other Provisions) Act 2010.

53. See IMF website, http://www.imf.org/external/pubs/nft/1998/tlaw/eng/ch1.pdf.

Bibliography

Cooper, J., and R. Agarwal. 2011. "The Transactional Profit Methods in Practice: A Survey of APA Reports." *International Transfer Pricing Journal* 18(1).

Deloitte. 2011. Global Transfer Pricing Desktop Reference. Deloitte, London. http://www .deloitte.com/assets/DcomGlobal/Local%20Assets/Documents/Tax/dttl_tax _strategymatrix_2011_180211.pdf.

Deloitte. 2014. *2014 Global Transfer Pricing Country Guide*. London: Deloitte. http:// www2.deloitte.com/content/dam/Deloitte/global/Documents/Tax/dttl-tax-global -transfer-pricing-guide-2014.pdf.

Ernst & Young. 2011. "New Transfer Pricing Law in Russia." Ernst & Young, London. http:// www.ey.com/Publication/vwLUAssets/EY_Russia_Transfer_Pricing_Russia%27s _new_transfer_pricing_law/$FILE/TP_Russia_new_transfer_pricing_law.pdf.

EUJTPF. 2009. "Commission Staff Working Document: EU Joint Transfer Pricing Forum— Summary Report on Penalties." http://ec.europa.eu/taxation_customs/sites/taxation /files/resources/documents/taxation/company_tax/transfer_pricing/summary_report .pdf

EUJTPF (EU Joint Transfer Pricing Forum). 2013. "EU Joint Transfer Pricing Forum Report on Compensating Adjustments in November." JTPF/009/REV1/2013/EN, http://ec .europa.eu/taxation_customs/sites/taxation/files/resources/documents/taxation /company_tax/transfer_pricing/forum/jtpf/2013/jtpf_009_rev1_2013_en.pdf.

Evers, M., I. Meier, and C. Spengel. 2014. "Transparency in Financial Reporting: Is Country-by-Country Reporting Suitable to Combat International Profit Shifting?" ZEW - Centre for European Economic Research Discussion Paper No. 14-015. Centre for European Economic Research, Mannheim, Germany.

Gordin, R., and V. Thuronyi. 1996. "Tax Legislative Process." In *Tax Law Design and Drafting*, edited by V. Thuronyi, 1–13. Washington, DC: IMF. http://www.imf.org /external/pubs/nft/1998/tlaw/eng/index.htm.

Gruendel, K., K. Okawara, and, C. Newman. 2011. "Japan." *IBFD Transfer Pricing Database*. Amsterdam: International Bureau of Fiscal Documentation.

Horak, W. 2011. "South Africa." *IBFD Transfer Pricing Database*. Amsterdam: International Bureau of Fiscal Documentation.

International Mining for Development Centre and World Bank. 2014. "Transfer Pricing in Mining: An African Perspective." Briefing note, September, International Mining for Development Centre and World Bank, Washington, DC. http://im4dc.org/wp -content/uploads/2013/07/Transfer-pricing-in-mining-An-African-perspective-A -briefing-note1.pdf.

Lucas Mas, M. 2009. "Value Added Tax." In A. Bakker and B. Obuoforibo, eds. *Transfer Pricing and Customs Valuation: Two World to Tax as One*. Amsterdam: IBFD.

OECD (Organisation for Economic Co-operation and Development). 1995. *OECD Transfer Pricing Guidelines for Multinational Enterprises and Tax Administrations*. Paris: OECD.

———. 2004. "Peer Review of Mexican Transfer Pricing Legislation and Practices." OECD, Paris. http://www.oecd.org/dataoecd/56/41/38665215.pdf.

———. 2010a. "Multi-country Analysis of Existing Transfer Pricing Simplification Measures." OECD, Paris. http://www.oecd.org/dataoecd/55/41/48131481.pdf.

———. 2010b. *OECD Transfer Pricing Guidelines for Multinational Enterprises and Tax Administrations*. Paris: OECD.

———. 2011. *Transfer Pricing Legislation: A Suggested Approach*. Paris: OECD. http:// www.oecd.org/dataoecd/41/6/45765682.pdf.

———. 2012. "Dealing Effectively with the Challenges of Transfer Pricing." OECD, Paris. http://dx.doi.org/10.1787/9789264169463-en.

———. 2015. Action 13, Final Report: "Transfer Pricing Documentation and Country-by -Country Reporting." OECD, Paris. http://www.oecd.org/tax/transfer-pricing -documentation-and-country-by-country-reporting-action-13-2015-final-report -9789264241480-en.htm.

PwC (PricewaterhouseCoopers). 2012. International Transfer Pricing 2012. Pricewater houseCoopers, London. http://www.pwc.com/en_GX/gx/international-transfer -pricing/pdf/27185-ITP-2012.pdf.

PwC (PricewaterhouseCoopers). 2013. Transfer Pricing Requirements Around the World. PricewaterhouseCoopers, London. http://www.pwc.com/gx/en/services/tax/transfer -pricing/international-transfer-pricing-2013-14.html.

Strachuk, V. 2012. "Belarus" International Transfer Pricing Journal, Volume 19, No 4. IBFD.

United Nations. 2013. *UN Practical Manual on Transfer Pricing for Developing Countries*. New York: UN, Department of Economic & Social Affairs. http://www.un.org/esa/ffd /documents/UN_Manual_TransferPricing.pdf.

CHAPTER 4

Applying the Arm's-Length Principle

> Transfer pricing is largely a question of facts and circumstances coupled with a high dose of common sense.
>
> *—Justice Robert Hogan (2009)*

This chapter introduces the practical application of the arm's-length principle, focusing on issues of concern in developing countries. The main topics addressed are: comparability, transfer pricing methods, and the arm's-length range concept. This chapter is based predominately on the guidance found in the *OECD Transfer Pricing Guidelines for Multinational Enterprises and Tax Administrations* (2010a) and its amendments from 2015, with reference to the *UN Practical Manual on Transfer Pricing* (2013), other international and regional guidance, and country-specific examples.

Comparability

Market forces may not be fully at play where transactions take place between associated parties. When independent parties, acting as such, transact with one another, market forces will determine the conditions of the transactions. The arm's-length principle, applied to controlled transactions, draws on this by requiring a comparison of the conditions in a controlled transaction with the conditions in "comparable" transactions between independent parties. In this regard, comparability may be considered a cornerstone of the application of the arm's-length principle as applied by the vast majority of countries.

According to the *OECD Transfer Pricing Guidelines* (2010a), the *UN Practical Manual*, and the vast majority of countries' transfer pricing legislations (see chapter 2), controlled and uncontrolled transactions are considered to be "comparable" if there are no differences between them that materially affect the condition being examined in the transfer pricing method to be applied (e.g., price or margin), or, where such differences do exist, reasonably accurate adjustments can be made to eliminate the material effects of any such differences (see figure 4.1)

Comparability does not, therefore, require that the transactions being compared are identical, but rather that none of the differences between the transactions being compared *materially* impact on *the condition being examined* in the transfer pricing method applied; or, that where such differences do exist, reasonable adjustments can be made.

The condition being examined will depend on the transfer pricing methodology being applied (see table 4.1). Hence, the method being applied will directly impact whether or not differences between the transactions being compared impact comparability. For example, although significant product differences between transactions may materially impact the price, these same differences

Figure 4.1 Flow Chart for Assessing Comparability

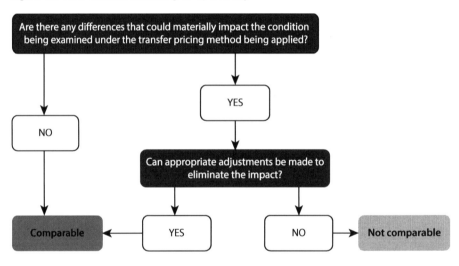

Table 4.1 Transfer Pricing Methods and the Condition Being Examined

Transfer pricing method	Condition being examined
Comparable uncontrolled price	Actual price charged for property or services (including interest rates, royalty rates, and commission rates, etc.)
Resale price	Resale price margin (gross profit level)
Cost-plus	Cost-plus markup (gross profit level)
Transactional net margin	Net profit margin (relative to an appropriate base)
Profit split	Division of profits or losses (can be based on gross margins, net margins, or other, depending on how the method is applied)

may not materially impact the gross or net profit margins relating to the sale of such products. Therefore, transactions that are not considered comparable for the purposes of applying one method (i.e., the CUP method in this example) may be considered sufficiently comparable for the purposes of applying another transfer pricing method.

Comparability Factors

When assessing comparability there are five factors that the *OECD Transfer Pricing Guidelines* (2010a), the *UN Practical Manual* (2013), and the vast majority of countries' transfer pricing legislations (see chapter 2) specify as important to consider (see figure 4.2).

To address vulnerability to manipulation of the purported contractual allocation of functions, assets, and risks in practice, recent revisions of the first chapter of the *OECD Transfer Pricing Guidelines* put further emphasis on a careful delineation of transactions in comparability analysis. This requires a determination of actual functions performed, risks assumed and controlled, and assets used by the relevant parties. The revisions highlight the importance of proper fact finding and looking beyond mere contracts in undertaking a comparability analysis.

Contractual Terms

Contractual agreements are commonly the starting point for delineating a transaction, but may need to be supplemented (or replaced) by information

Figure 4.2 Comparability Factors

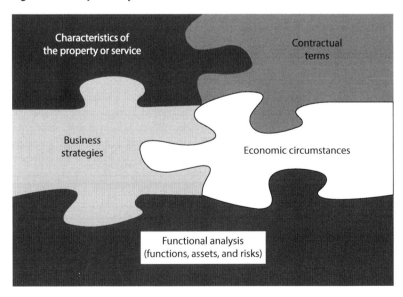

on the actual conduct of related entities in their commercial or financial relations (actual functions performed, assets used, risks assumed, etc.). The contractual terms of a transaction will influence the allocation of functions and risks between independent parties and, therefore, the prices charged and margins earned. Accordingly, differences in the contractual terms applicable to the controlled transaction and uncontrolled transactions require identification and analysis.

One of the benefits of forming a multinational enterprise (MNE) group, besides creating synergies, is a reduction in transaction costs (i.e., costs of negotiating and drawing up agreements). It is, therefore, not uncommon that MNE groups do not have formal contractual arrangements in place for some of their intragroup dealings. Where formal contractual arrangements are not in place, for transfer pricing purposes the terms may need to be deduced from the economic relationships of the parties and their conduct. This may be best evidenced by correspondence and communication between the parties. It is important to check whether the terms of the contract are actually adhered to in practice where formal contracts are in place. Where formal contracts are not, the conduct of the parties will usually provide a more reliable basis for comparison.

Details of the contractual terms of transactions between third parties will often be limited or unavailable. The impact of such informational deficiencies on comparability will depend on the method being applied, the transactions under examination, and the facts and circumstances. Informed judgment is required.

Examples of contractual terms that may influence the price or margin may include, but are not limited to[1]

- Differences in volumes
- Differences in payment terms (e.g., net 30 days as compared to net 90 days)
- Shipping terms (e.g., "free on board" [FOB] as compared to "cost, freight" [CFR] and "cost, freight, insurance" [CIF])[2]
- Geographic area, exclusivity, and duration in relation to the licensing of intangibles
- Currency, security, and call and repayment options in relation to financial transactions. See also Box 4.1.

Box 4.1 Examples of Contractual Terms in Internal Revenue Code (IRC) Section 482 Regulations

Extract is from *LMSB International Program Audit Guidelines*

Reg. 1.482–1(d)(3)(ii)(A) provides examples of contractual terms. These include the following:

· Form of consideration charged or paid,
· Sales or purchase volume,

box continues next page

Box 4.1 Examples of Contractual Terms in Internal Revenue Code (IRC) Section 482 Regulations *(continued)*

- Scope and terms of warranties provided,
- Rights to updates, revisions, or modifications,
- Duration of the agreement, including termination or renegotiation rights,
- Collateral services relating to the agreement, and
- Extension of credit and payment terms.

Functional Analysis

Compensation in transactions between independent parties will usually reflect the functions that each party to the transaction performs, the assets it employs, and the risks it assumes. For example, the more functions a party performs, the greater risks it bears; the higher the value of the assets it employs in relation to a transaction, the greater the remuneration it would expect to receive from the other party. As a result, the remuneration of a party, and therefore its profit potential, with respect to a transaction or set of transactions will generally be correlated with the functions it performs, the risks it bears, and the assets that it employs (see figure 4.3).[3]

An analysis of the economically significant functions performed, risks borne, and assets employed by the parties in relation to the transactions being examined is necessary not only to assess comparability but also to accurately delineate and characterize the transactions in selecting the appropriate transfer pricing method and, where applicable, the tested party.

The functions, assets, and risks requiring consideration will vary significantly depending on the type of transactions being analyzed, the point in the supply chain at which the transactions take place, and the industry within which the parties operate. When reviewing transactions, the capabilities of the parties involved will need to be understood to determine the options available. It is, therefore, important to ensure that a thorough functional analysis is undertaken, documented, and reviewed to ensure that important functions, assets, and risks are not overlooked. Table 4.2 provides examples of common functions, assets, and risks that require consideration in transactions between manufacturers and distributors.

Undertaking a functional analysis will often involve significant research and analysis and is highly reliant on the collection of accurate and sufficiently detailed information obtained from a variety of sources (see box 4.3). Typically, this will involve more than a desk review and may require interviews of relevant personnel (e.g., operational personnel) and site visits. Where informational deficiencies exist, as is often the case when analyzing external comparables, professional judgment may be required as to whether those transactions are sufficiently comparable.

The identification and quantification of risks assumed can present a significant practical challenge when conducting a functional analysis. Consequently,

Figure 4.3 Functions, Assets, and Risks and Their Impact on Profit Potential

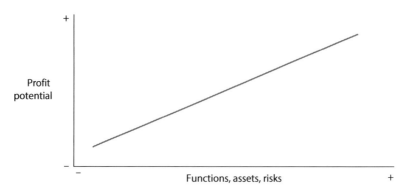

Table 4.2 Common Functions, Assets, and Risks of Manufacturers and Distributors

Functions	Assets[a]	Risks
• Design	• Plant and equipment	• Market risks such as input and output price fluctuations
• Manufacturing	• Valuable intangibles	
• Assembling	• Financial assets	
• R&D		• Risks of loss associated with investment in and use of property, plant, and equipment
• Servicing		
• Purchasing		
• Distribution		
• Marketing		• Risks of failure or success in research and development
• Advertising		
• Transportation		• Financial risks such as those caused by currency exchange rate and interest rate variability
• Financing Management		
		• Credit risks

Source: Based on OECD 2010a, paragraphs 1.43–1.50/ OECD 2015, paragraphs 1.54–1.55.
Note: R&D = research and development.
a. The age, market value, location, property right protections, etc., may also require consideration, along with the legal, economic, and beneficial ownership of valuable intangibles (see chapter 5 for further discussion regarding intangibles).

Box 4.2 Six-Step Process for Analyzing Risk in Revised *OECD Transfer Pricing Guidelines* (2015)

Extract is from OECD (2015, chapter 1, section D1.60) and Final Reports on BEPS Actions 8–10: "Aligning Transfer Pricing Outcomes with Value Creation."

1. Identify the economically significant risks with specificity;
2. Determine how specific, economically significant risks are contractually assumed by the associated enterprises under the terms of the transaction;

box continues next page

Box 4.2 Six-Step Process for Analyzing Risk in Revised *OECD Transfer Pricing Guidelines* (2015)
(continued)

3. Determine, through a functional analysis, how the associated enterprises that are parties to the transaction operate in relation to assumption and management of the specific, economically significant risks, and, in particular, which enterprise or enterprises perform control functions and risk-mitigation functions, which enterprise or enterprises encounter upside or downside consequences of risk outcomes, and which enterprise or enterprises have the financial capacity to assume the risk;

4. Steps 2 and 3 will have identified information relating to the assumption and management of risks in the controlled transaction. The next step is to interpret the information and determine whether the contractual assumption of risk is consistent with the conduct of the associated enterprises and other facts of the case by analyzing (i) whether the associated enterprises follow the contractual terms; and (ii) whether the party assuming risk, as analyzed, exercises control over the risk and has the financial capacity to assume the risk;

5. Where the party assuming risk under Steps 1–4 does not control the risk or does not have the financial capacity to assume the risk, apply the guidance on allocating risk;

6. The actual transaction as accurately delineated by considering the evidence of all the economically relevant characteristics of the transaction should then be priced taking into account the financial and other consequences of risk assumption, as appropriately allocated, and appropriately compensating risk management functions.

Box 4.3 United States: IRS Large- and Medium-Size Business International Audit Program Guidelines on Functional Analysis

4.61.3.5.1 (05-01-2006)
Extract is from IRS (2006).[a]

Functional Analysis
1. Determining whether controlled and uncontrolled transactions are comparable requires a comparison of functions performed. [International examiners] must, therefore, analyze the functions performed in both the controlled and uncontrolled transactions. See Reg. 1.482–1(d)(3)(l).

2. A functional analysis identifies the economically significant activities performed in connection with the transaction. An economically significant activity is one that, at arm's-length, materially affects the following:
   A. The price charged in a transaction, and
   B. The profits earned from a transaction

3. A functional analysis involves determining the following:
   A. What functions were performed by the transacting parties concerning the transaction?
   B. Who performed the functions?
   C. When were the functions performed?
   D. Where were the functions performed?
   E. How were the functions performed?

box continues next page

Box 4.3 United States: IRS Large- and Medium-Size Business International Audit Program Guidelines on Functional Analysis *(continued)*

      F. Why were the functions performed?

      G. What intangibles were employed in the performance of functions?

      H. How were intangibles employed in the performance of functions?

      I. Why was the transaction structured the way it was?

4. A functional analysis involves tracing the flow of products and services within the organization. Delivering products to a market generally involves various stages. These may include the following:

      A. Conceptualization

      B. Research and development

      C. Manufacturing

      D. Testing

      E. Marketing

      F. Sales

      G. Internal usage

5. In performing a functional analysis, additional considerations include:

      A. Did the taxpayer or another affiliate sell product in the controlled entity's market: Before the controlled entity's formation? After the controlled entity's formation? If sales were to unrelated distributors, what resale margins did the unrelated distributors earn?

      B. Does the controlled entity actively perform sales or marketing functions?

      C. Does the controlled entity rely on a distribution network that was previously established by the parent?

      D. Did the subsidiary develop new customers for the product it purchases from the parent?

      E. Have sales of the parent's product in the subsidiary's market increased following the subsidiary's formation?

      F. Has the subsidiary entered into any exclusive or nonexclusive distribution agreements with the parent?

      G. Are there any intangibles associated with the parent's sales of products to the subsidiary?

      H. Has the subsidiary entered into any license agreements with the parent?

6. Performing a functional analysis involves more than a review of the books and records. It involves active interaction with the taxpayer. Interaction with the taxpayer should go beyond the tax department. The tax department generally lacks the knowledge needed to complete a functional analysis. [International examiners should interview the taxpayer's operational personnel most familiar with the taxpayer's operations. International examiners should also consider conducting on-site visitations.] On-site visitations enable [international examiners] to do the following:

      A. View the taxpayer's operations and the functions performed

      B. Gain an understanding of the technical jargon used by the taxpayer

      C. Gain an understanding of the dependence or independence of the operation

      D. Discover additional facts

a. See IRS website, available at http://www.irs.gov/irm/part4/irm_04-061-003.html#d0e644.

the most recent revision to the *OECD Transfer Pricing Guidelines* provides expanded guidance on risk assumption in a transaction.[4] In line with the general emphasis on economic substance and the accurate delineation of transactions, these revisions emphasize that contractual allocation of risks is accepted only when it corresponds to actual control and capacity to bear the formally allocated risk. With respect to financing, for instance, the revisions clarify that a legal entity that controls a funding risk is not entitled to the returns associated with operational risks, unless it exercises control over those operational risks. The new guidelines propose six steps for analyzing risk in a controlled transaction (see box 4.2).

As part of its *International Program Audit Guidelines*, the U.S. Internal Revenue Service (IRS) has published a sample functional analysis questionnaire that can serve as a useful reference when undertaking a functional analysis. A copy of this questionnaire is provided in annex 4A.

Characteristics of the Property or Service

The specific characteristics of a product or service that is the object of a transaction will impact upon the value attributed to that product or service by the parties to the transaction. Therefore, when assessing the comparability of transactions, it is important to consider the characteristics of the products or services in transactions being compared. Table 4.3 contains examples of typical characteristics that may be important to consider.

Differences in characteristics of the property or services may or may not materially impact comparability since different weighting may need to be attached to the characteristics of the goods and or services in relation to other comparability factors depending on the transfer pricing method being applied, and thus the condition being examined. For example, differences in the characteristics of products or services are more likely to have material impact on the price and are, therefore, of importance when applying the comparable uncontrolled price (CUP) method. However, such differences may be less likely to have a material impact on gross or net profit margins and, therefore, may not materially affect comparability for the purposes of applying the cost-plus method, resale price method, or transactional net margin method (TNMM). It does not follow, however, that differences in the

Table 4.3 Sample Characteristics of Tangible Property, Services, and Intangible Property

Tangible property	Services	Intangible property
• Physical features • Quality and reliability • Availability and volume of supply	• Nature of the services • Extent of the services	• Form of the transaction (e.g., sale or license) • Type of property (e.g., patent, trademark, or know-how) • The duration and degree of protection • Anticipated benefits from use

Source: Based on OECD 2010, para. 1.39 (para. 1.107 following 2015 amendments).

Box 4.4 United States: IRS Large- and Medium-Size Business International Audit Program Guidelines on Comparability of Property and Services

4.61.3.5.6 (05-01-2006) Property or Services
Extract is from IRS (2006).[a]

1. Another factor for determining whether controlled and uncontrolled transactions are comparable is the property or services involved. [International examiners] must, therefore, analyze the property or services involved in both the controlled and uncontrolled transactions.
2. [International examiners] should consider obtaining the following information to analyze property or services:
   • Sales catalogs, brochures, pamphlets and other sales literature,
   • Technical literature describing the property or services, and
   • Descriptions of competing products or services.
3. [International examiners] should consider interviewing sales and marketing personnel employed by the taxpayer. Sales and marketing personnel can generally describe the taxpayer's products or services in detail.

a. See IRS website, available at http://www.irs.gov/irm/part4/irm_04-061-003.html#d0e644.

---

characteristics of the product or service can simply be ignored when applying methods that examine gross or net profit margins. Differences in the characteristics of the product or services may, for example, have broader implications, particularly in relation to determining the economically significant functions, assets, and risks of the parties, and understanding the economic circumstances and business strategies.

Analysis of the characteristics of a product or service will often require detailed examination of various sources of information, such as sales catalogues, brochures, and technical literature. Interviews with sales and marketing personnel, product designers, engineers, and so forth may also be necessary. Box 4.4 provides sources of information that international examiners in the United States will look toward.

Economic Circumstances

The market within which a transaction takes place can have a significant influence on its pricing. In the open market, for example, the price paid for the same goods or services can differ significantly based on the location, industry, or subindustry in which they take place. Accordingly, it is important to consider the *economic circumstances* applicable to the controlled transactions to determine whether potentially comparable uncontrolled transactions are sufficiently similar.

Whether differences in the market in which the controlled transactions and the uncontrolled transactions take place have a material impact on the condition being examined will depend on the facts and circumstances. For example, some products and services have global markets, thus location may have limited or no impact on the pricing.[5] However, for many products and services, differences in market size, competition, and regulation can have a significant impact on pricing at the regional or country levels. In practice, adjustments may be possible for certain market differences. This can be important to consider if information regarding comparable uncontrolled transactions in the same or similar markets is not available or does not exist and, as a result, transactions from different markets or industries are required to be considered. This situation is common in developing countries where there is often a lack of information on potentially comparable uncontrolled transactions.

Information regarding the relevant characteristics of the industry and market in which the controlled transaction takes place is generally obtained in an industry analysis. Relevant factors that may require further consideration in relation to potentially comparable uncontrolled transactions (so as to identify whether they materially impact the condition being examined) include[6]:

- Geographic location
- Market size
- Barriers to entry
- Level of the market (wholesale, retail, etc.)
- Competition
- Existence and availability of substitutes
- Location-specific costs
- Government regulation
- Economic condition of the industry
- Consumer purchasing power
- Economic, business, or product cycles

Business Strategies

Adoption of particular *business strategies* may have an impact on the pricing of products or groups of products over their life cycle. Such strategies may include, inter alia, market penetration, market expansion, market maintenance, and diversification strategies depending on the facts and circumstances (see box 4.5).

A market penetration or expansion strategy may require that products are sold at a reduced price into the market at the outset in anticipation of future profits, or certain products may be sold at cost or a loss to develop or maintain a market for related products (e.g., razors and razor blades, printers and ink cartridges, or coffee machines and coffee capsules).

Consideration of business strategies pertaining to the controlled transactions and any potentially comparable uncontrolled transactions therefore require identification and analysis since they may have a material impact on the condition

Box 4.5 Ansoff's Growth Matrix

Ansoff's growth matrix is a tool that can be used by businesses to help determine their product and market growth strategies (figure B4.5.1).

Figure B4.5.1 Ansoff's Growth Matrix

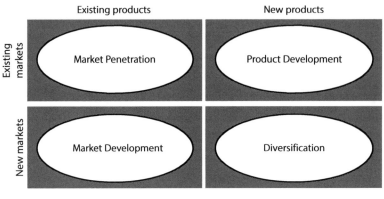

Source: Ansoff 1957.

being examined (i.e., it would most likely not be appropriate to compare a transaction involving the sale of an established product to an established market participant with the sale of a new product to a new venture undertaking a market penetration strategy).

Sources of Comparable Data

Application of one of the transfer pricing methods generally requires that potentially comparable uncontrolled transactions are identified and then an analysis is undertaken to assess the comparability thereof. The sources of information for identifying and analyzing potentially comparable transactions will vary depending on, inter alia, the type of controlled transactions being examined, the transfer pricing method being applied, the location of the tested party (where applicable), and the market within which the controlled transactions took place.

A broad distinction can be made between "internal comparables" and "external comparables" (see figure 4.4):

- *Internal comparables.* Comparable transactions that have taken place between one party to the controlled transaction and another independent party
- *External comparables.* Comparable transactions that have taken place between two independent parties, which are not associated with each other or party to the controlled transactions

Figure 4.4 Internal and External Comparable Uncontrolled Transactions

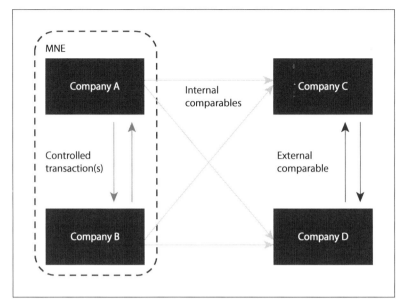

Note: Company A and B belong the the same MNE; Company C and D are independent of each other.
MNE = multinational enterprise.

Internal Comparables

Internal comparables, where they exist, may have a more direct relationship to the transaction being examined. Furthermore, it is likely that the necessary information to perform the comparability analysis will be more readily available and complete. As a result, internal comparables can be easier and less expensive to identify and obtain information in relation thereto as opposed to that of external comparables. However, since most MNE groups are highly integrated, internal comparables are uncommon. Often, where an entity engages in potentially comparable uncontrolled transactions these uncontrolled transactions do not, upon closer examination, meet the comparability standard. This can be due to differences in comparability factors such as market level, geographic market, contractual terms, and quantities sold or purchased. Therefore, possible internal comparables should not automatically be assumed to be more reliable or even to be comparable—a thorough comparability analysis is required. That said, however, identification of and an analysis of any possible internal comparables should precede the search for external comparables.

External Comparables

Various sources can be used to identify and obtain information on external comparables. The availability of such information, however, will be dependent on numerous factors, including the type of transaction being examined, the methodology being applied, and, where applicable, the country (or region) of the tested party.

Commonly used sources of information include commercial databases, government bodies that collect and publish statutory accounts of local entities, company websites, and the Internet (which can be used, for example, to obtain copies of annual reports and general information about business activities and strategies of enterprises). These sources are used by both taxpayers and tax administrations.[7]

Commercial databases collate accounts or details of transactions that are otherwise publicly available and present this data in an easily searchable format. Although these databases require a paid subscription (which can be a constraint in developing countries with limited resources), they generally provide a cost-effective way for identifying external comparables.[8] Such databases might present whole of entity financial data (i.e., company financial accounts) or data on specific transactions types (such as loans, royalty agreements, and other financial transactions). One limitation is that the information is based on publicly available information, which may not exist in many developing countries, thus requiring reliance on the use of so-called "foreign comparables."

Comparable information may also be identified and obtained using other sources, such as government bodies that collect and publish information.[9] However, in many countries this information often not presented in an easily searchable format, is not required to be prepared, or is not collected. Policy makers in developing countries should therefore consider establishing ecouraging financial transparency in the corporate sector (see box 4.6). Where other publications, such as industry periodicals and other reports are available, analysis of the source of the information should be undertaken before relying on it (i.e. is it based on actual transactions between independent parties, or is based on estimates, forecasts and or rumors).

Box 4.6 Improving Access to Commercial Information and Comparables in Developing Countries

An obligation for companies to prepare financial accounts and to file them with a central registry (or similar) or otherwise make them publicly available is a prerequisite for access to any financial information contained therein. In the absence of a general obligation to prepare financial accounts and make them publicly available, the necessary data to assess comparability and apply the arm's-length principle may not exist. The importance of reliable corporate financial reporting has been broadly recognized and initiatives such as the Centre for Financial Reporting Reform (CFFR) of the World Bank are providing countries assistance in building institutional frameworks and developing capacity in financial reporting.

Transfer pricing applications are a secondary consideration of such reforms, which are implemented with the objective of giving "investors and owners an accurate understanding of the financial viability and performance of the business, provid[ing] the detailed information for

box continues next page

Box 4.6 **Improving Access to Commercial Information and Comparables in Developing Countries**
(continued)

creditors to make informed lending decisions to help businesses develop and grow, and giv[ing] regulators a clear picture of financial institutions' credit exposure. Trust in the accuracy of financial information expands the access to and reduces the cost of credit, and enables the efficient operation of private and state-owned enterprises. Enhanced supervision reduces the risk of crises in the financial sector and increases financial stability, allowing capital markets to develop and flourish." Quote taken from CFRR Mission Statement (2016): http://siteresources.worldbank .org/EXTCENFINREPREF/Resources/CFRR_brochure_spreads.pdf.

Use of Nontransactional Data

In practice, reliable transactional data for external comparables are often not available. Therefore, information in statutory accounts, which generally comprises aggregate data (at the divisional or whole of entity level), is often necessarily relied upon. Where such information is used, caution must be taken to ensure that the aggregate data comprise transactions comparable to the transactions under review, and where division information is being relied upon, that the information has been reliably and accurately prepared.[10]

In practice, available third-party data are often aggregated data at a company-wide or segment level, depending on the applicable accounting standards. Whether such nontransactional third-party data can provide reliable comparables for the taxpayer's controlled transaction or set of transactions aggregated depends on whether the third party performs a range of materially different transactions. Reliable segmented data can provide a better comparable than companywide, nonsegmented data, although segmented data can raise issues related to the allocation of expenses to various segments. Similarly, companywide third-party data may provide better comparables than third-party segmented data in certain circumstances, such as where the activities reflected in the comparables correspond to the set of controlled transactions of the taxpayer transactions.

Annex 4B contains a nonexhaustive list of commercial databases.

Dealing with the Dearth of Comparable Information

The identification of comparables can create particular difficulties for developing countries wanting to undertake effective transfer pricing audits and enquiries.

—*OECD Forum on Tax Administration (FTA) Report: Dealing Effectively with the Challenges of Transfer Pricing 2012*

The experience of many developed and developing economies suggests that the lack of availability of comparable information is a major constraint faced in effectively applying transfer pricing legislation based on the arm's-length principle. Application of a principle that is centered largely on a comparison of the conditions (i.e., price or margin) observed in transactions between associated parties with the conditions observed in comparable transactions between independent parties is extremely difficult, if not impossible, where the requisite information for undertaking such comparisons is not available or does not exist.

The problem arises at both ends of the transfer pricing spectrum. In the context of highly complex transactions involving unique and valuable intangibles, comparable transactions often simply do not exist due to the unique nature of the transactions. This is a major concern across Organisation for Economic Co-operation and Development (OECD) and G20 economies and is at the core of a range of measures covered in the OECD's base erosion and profit shifting (BEPS) project. In many countries, especially developing economies, the dearth of comparable information is, however, of general "day-to-day" concern and not limited to specific transactions of high complexity. The difficulty often faced in developing economies in this regard is twofold. First, many tax administrations face difficulties funding access to commercial databases. Second, even where they can be accessed, such databases often contain limited, or no, data concerning "local" economic operators that may potentially serve as potential "comparables." Surprisingly, despite the significance and widespread awareness of the lack of comparable data and the issue it poses in practice, to date, practical and policy guidance is largely nonexistent at both the international and national levels.[11]

The dearth of comparables is a practical issue, particularly acute in many developing economies where such information is often not available due to the lack of financial reporting requirements or due to comparable transactions simply not existing in the domestic market (i.e., due to an industry, or country, only recently being opened up or liberalized by the government, or due to significant levels of consolidation or vertical integration). The absence of comparables does not mean, however, that the controlled transactions are not arm's-length.

There is a need to find an answer for all transfer pricing problems.

—*Australian Taxation Office TR 97/20*

Aside from addressing the issue at the regulatory level (i.e., by putting in place a reporting system that encourages greater transparency, see box 4.6), practical solutions are required that allow for the efficient and effective administration of a country's transfer pricing regime. Although by no means perfect, possible solutions and alternative approaches are set out in table 4.4, followed by a high-level discussion of some relative advantages and disadvantages.

Table 4.4 Potential Alternative Approaches

Solution or alternative approaches	Advantages	Disadvantages
Use of foreign comparables (i.e., use of comparables from other geographic markets)	• Widens the pool of potential comparables	• Access to databases containing foreign comparables may not be available or can be expensive • Complex (and somewhat arbitrary) comparability adjustments may be required

table continues next page

Table 4.4 Potential Alternative Approaches (continued)

Solution or alternative approaches	Advantages	Disadvantages
Use of comparables from other industries or with different functional profiles	• Widens the pool of potential comparables	• Requires that comparables exist for which differences that materially affect the condition being examined can be appropriately adjusted for • Complex (and somewhat arbitrary) comparability adjustments may be required
Safe harbors (with fixed margins)	• Safe harbors can increase certainty for both taxpayers and the tax administration, and can increase administrative efficiency • No reliance on comparables information required - Design can draw on administrative data, which is readily available	• Where safe harbors are unilateral, there is a risk of economic double taxation (if not optional) or foregone revenues • Scope for safe harbors may be limited (i.e., generally used for low value add services, small loans, etc.)
Rebuttable fixed margins	• Simple to administer • No reliance on comparables (except for initial determination of margins) • Certainty	• Similar to safe harbors: Risk of double taxation; limited scope • Complacent tax administration may ignore arguments for rebuttal
Advance pricing arrangements[a]	• Can provide a solution where no comparables are available • Provides certainty for taxpayer and the tax administration • Bilateral or multilateral advance pricing arrangements can limit instances of economic double taxation	• Arrangement should be based on the arm's-length principle, which generally requires comparables • Can be resource intensive for the tax administration • Unilateral advance pricing agreements do not prevent economic double taxation • Needs capacity and skilled staff
Use of internal rates of return[b]	• Provides a solution where no comparables are available	• Relies upon subjective assumptions • Rate of return can be influenced by a range of different factors other than transfer prices
Lower independence requirements for uncontrolled transactions	• Widens the pool of potential comparables	• Transactions between associated parties may be influenced by those parties' transfer pricing policies
Use of secret comparables	• Greater availability of information for the tax administration	• Not equitable, as information cannot generally be disclosed to taxpayers, hence taxpayer is unable to defend its position • Information cannot generally be disclosed in mutual agreement procedures, hence may lead to cases of unrelieved economic double taxation
Use of customs valuations	• Access to vast amounts of transactional data	• Generally, information required to conduct a comparability analysis is unavailable • Customs valuation methods and transfer pricing operate differently and have different objectives • Only limited transactions types are dutiable
Use of industry average returns	• Greater availability of information	• Limited information as to composition of industry average, hence can't assess comparability • Industry averages generally include data from controlled transactions

a. See chapter 7.
b. See box 4.7.

Box 4.7 Australia: Use of Internal Rates of Return in Difficult Transfer Pricing Cases

Extract from Australian Taxation Ruling TR 97/20 reads as follows[a]:

Internal rates of return may provide a suitable benchmark

3.94. Some enterprises establish criteria to evaluate the non-portfolio investment (where the taxpayer holds at least 10 percent of the voting interest in a company), opportunities or strategic initiatives available to them. These criteria are then used, in particular, to evaluate the performance of the various business units, to assess future expansion opportunities (those that arise from internal search, and those that arise externally), and to consider the sale of units that are underperforming or which no longer fit the purposes of the enterprise.

3.95. The criteria may include (but are not limited to) the following:

(1) payback period;

(2) rates of return on invested capital, equity, sales, etc.;

(3) net present value of a specified cash flow;

(4) strategic net present value—an option-based approach;

(5) internal rate of return;

(6) shareholder value analysis; and

(7) economic value added.

3.96. If a discount rate is required, this may be the risk-free rate, a weighted average cost of capital, or a risk-adjusted rate, depending upon the purpose of the analysis. In each case, either industry practice or intra-company hurdle levels of performance may influence management attitudes to a proposed investment.

3.97. If external comparisons are not available, or if it is important to consider the internal viability of a specific deal, transaction, or profit flow, an evaluation of the choice represented by the offer (implied or actual) to the controlled enterprise involved in the transaction, deal or profit flow, using one or more of the criteria noted above, may assist in identifying the likely response of an arm's-length participant.

3.98. The 1979 OECD Report "Transfer Pricing and Multinational Enterprises," which formed the starting point for the 1995 OECD Report discusses such other approaches (1979 OECD Report, paragraphs 70–74). While the use of such methods is significantly qualified in the 1979 OECD Report and the 1995 OECD Report does not canvass these other approaches, Australia's transfer pricing rules do permit recourse to them in extremely difficult cases (paragraph 1.23).

However, while use of internal rates of return is discussed in this Australian ruling, no practical applications have been reported of its use to support a transfer pricing adjustment. In practice, internal rates of return have been sometimes used to do an additional "sense check."

a. See Australian Taxation Ruling TR 97/20, available at http://law.ato.gov.au/atolaw/DownloadNoticePDF.htm?DocId =TXR%2FTR9720%2FNAT%2FATO%2F00001&filename=pdf/pbr/tr1997-020.pdf&PiT=99991231235958.

Use of So-Called Foreign Comparables

Since information regarding comparable transactions (or entities) may be limited or unavailable in the country, the search may need to be expanded to include information regarding uncontrolled transactions in different geographic markets, or *foreign comparables* (figure 4.5).

Figure 4.5 Domestic and Foreign Comparables

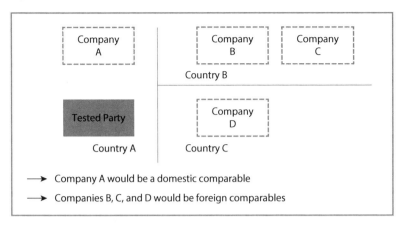

Note: Company A is a domestic comparable. Companies B, C, and D are foreign comparables.

The use of foreign comparables in practice is very common, particularly due to inadequate information being available. In a survey conducted by the World Bank in Eastern European and Central Asian Economies in 2013, tax practitioners in the region indicated that when domestic comparables are not available, the most common approach adopted is to use "foreign comparables."[12] Among the 51 practitioners surveyed, 67 percent reported that they regularly observe challenges in obtaining domestic comparable information, and 57 percent reported that they often, very often or always use or observe the use of "foreign comparables." Similarly, according to a EuropeAid and PwC (2011) case study, Kenyan taxpayers report relying on European databases given the limitations in domestic information sources when searching for comparable uncontrolled transactions.

Another common reason for MNE groups to use foreign comparables is the reduction of compliance costs. Where MNE groups have similar operations in a number of countries in a region, they will often undertake and rely upon *regional comparability studies* for those regions (see figure 4.6), thus avoiding the cost of undertaking tailored studies for each country in which they operate.

Where foreign comparables are being relied upon it is important to consider that the geographic market is an economic circumstance that can affect comparability. Where the domestic market and foreign markets are relatively homogeneous or where regional or global markets exist, foreign comparables are more likely to meet the applicable comparability standard without the need for comparability adjustments. Where market differences do exist, however, comparability adjustments may be required to account for country-specific risk and other factors (see annex 4C).

Tax administrations' position regarding the acceptability of foreign comparables varies among countries. However, in most countries using foreign comparables is generally accepted where no local comparables are available and provided that the

Figure 4.6 Approach to Comparables Sets (Parents)

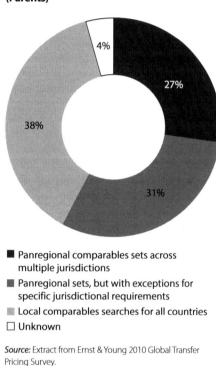

- ■ Panregional comparables sets across multiple jurisdictions
- ■ Panregional sets, but with exceptions for specific jurisdictional requirements
- ▨ Local comparables searches for all countries
- ☐ Unknown

Source: Extract from Ernst & Young 2010 Global Transfer Pricing Survey.

foreign comparables meet the applicable comparability standard. For example, the OECD Secretariat's Guidance Note on "comparability" states that in instances where there is a lack of public data available in a country "it may be possible to use comparables data from other countries where more public information is available, subject to the markets being sufficiently comparable."[13]

In South Africa, the South African Revenue Service (SARS) has formally acknowledged that there is a lack of local comparable information available, and has provided specific guidance on the use of foreign comparables in section 12 of Practice Note 7 (see box 4.8). The Russian Federation has adopted a similar approach in its new transfer pricing legislation (see chapter 3).

The introduction of International Financial Reporting Standards (IFRS) globally is an attempt to harmonize disclosure and reporting standards. In practice, however, different accounting standards and approaches are still adopted, which can impact the financial information that is reported, resulting in timing differences (i.e., due to different depreciation or amortization methods, or different inventory accounting systems[14]), permanent differences (due to the recognition of certain income or expense), or classification differences (e.g., capitalization of certain expenditures or inclusion in cost of goods sold). These differences can have a material impact on the condition being examined depending on the transfer method being applied, etc.

Box 4.8 SARS Guidance on the Use of Foreign Comparables

Extract from SARS Practice Note 7 reads as follows[a]:

11.2 The availability of information

11.2.1 In the light of the difficulties which may be encountered in obtaining information on uncontrolled transactions in South Africa, the Commissioner will accept the use of foreign country comparables (e.g., data from the Australian, British, and U.S. markets) in taxpayers' transfer pricing analyses. However, taxpayers using such comparables would be expected to assess the expected impact of geographic differences and other factors on the price.

11.2.2 For example, data may be available to indicate that the gross margin paid to distributors of a particular product in the United Kingdom is 20 percent. This does not mean that 20 percent will necessarily be an appropriate gross margin for South African distributors. There are a number of factors which may indicate an alternative gross margin to be more appropriate. For example:

a) Consumer preferences may result in different retail prices for a product in the two countries. This raises the question of which party to the transaction should capture any premium in price.

b) Higher transport costs may be associated with one of the markets. The relative gross margins may be affected by who bears this cost.

c) The relative competitiveness of the distribution industries in South Africa and the United Kingdom may differ. This could result in lower gross margins being paid in the more competitive market.

d) There may be differences in accounting standards that, if not adjusted for, could distort the relative margins of the parties being compared.

11.2.3 Thus, while foreign comparables may be useful, taxpayers will need to exercise caution to ensure that appropriate adjustments reflect differences between the South African and foreign markets.

a. See SARS Practice Note 7, available at http://www.sars.gov.za/AllDocs/LegalDoclib/Notes/LAPD-IntR-PrN-2012-11%20-%20 Income%20Tax%20Practice%20Note%207%20of%201999.pdf.

Accounting differences that result in timing differences may be addressed through the use of multiple year data, since this may smooth out the impact of the different depreciation or amortization policy. Or they may be addressed through the selection of a different financial indicator (see "Transactional Net Margin Method"), for example, by using a gross margin or a net profit-based indicator that excludes amortization or depreciation expense (such as earnings before interest, taxation, depreciation, and amortization [EBITDA]). Differences in accounting treatment that result in classification differences and permanent differences, however, may require adjustments to ensure comparability (see annex 4C).

Use of Secret Comparables

Tax administrations will generally have access to information regarding taxpayers and their transactions that is not publicly available and is the subject of domestic confidentiality requirements. Use of such information (which are generally referred to as "secret comparables") to determine and support transfer pricing adjustments is a contentious issue, and may or may not be possible under a country's domestic law. In this regard, the *OECD Transfer Pricing Guidelines* (2010a) recommend against the use of secret comparables:

> Tax administrators may have information available to them from examinations of other taxpayers or from other sources of information that may not be disclosed to the taxpayer. However, it would be unfair to apply a transfer pricing method on the basis of such data unless the tax administration was able, within the limits of its domestic confidentiality requirements, to disclose such data to the taxpayer so that there would be an adequate opportunity for the taxpayer to defend its own position and to safeguard effective judicial control by the courts.[15]

Both in legislation (see chapter 3) and in practice, countries have adopted different approaches to the use of secret comparables. A summary of approaches is provided in table 4.5.

Table 4.5 Use of Secret Comparable in Practice

Country	Position
Austria	Use of secret comparables is seen as a potential violation of fundamental taxpayer rights in Austria. According to Austrian law, every taxpayer has the right to defend its position before an adjustment is made, and this right would be undermined by the use of secret comparables.
China	Circular 2/2009 explicitly states that the tax authorities may use nonpublic information.[a]
Mexico	A domestic law provision specifically allows the use of secret comparables by the SAT provided that disclosure of the details of the comparables is made to an elected "representatives" of the taxpayer under examination.[b]
South Africa	Practice Note 7 states that SARS does not intend to use secret comparables, but does not rule out the possibility.
Turkey	"When determining transfer pricing-related assessments Turkish tax auditors would highly tend to use their own 'secret comparables' to which only they have access, by virtue of their public authority."[c]
United Kingdom	HMRC does not rely on secret comparables, except as a basis for rejecting a potential comparable (see box 4.9).
United States	The IRS strongly opposes the use of secret comparables and routinely objects to their use in mutual agreement proceedings.[d]

Note: HMRC = Her Majesty's Revenue and Customs; IRS = Internal Revenue Service; SARS = South African Revenue Service; SAT = Servicio de Administración Tributaria.
a. 2009 Special Measures.(SAT's "Measures for the Implementation of the Special Tax Adjustment (trial)", 1 January 2009 2009,Guo Shui Fa [2009] 2).
b. See "Controlled Transactions" in chapter 3.
c. From Özlem Güç Alioğlu and Mehmet Devrim Aşkın, in Turkey chapter of *IBFD Transfer Pricing Database;* last reviewed October 24, 2011.
d. Joseph Andrus in IBFD Transfer Pricing Database, United States chapter, last reviewed 2008.

Box 4.9 Use of Secret Comparable in the United Kingdom

From HMRC's *International Manual:*[a]

INTM467110: Establishing the arm's-length price: Gathering your own evidence Searching for comparables: Public information

Probably the best potential source of comparable information is HMRC. We hold a detailed breakdown of accounts for every company in the UK, and generally a good amount of detail about the business activities of medium, large, and very large companies. Given a sufficient amount of time, an Officer could probably find either a comparable transaction or a good set of comparable companies.

This information is not available to the taxpayer. The *OECD Transfer Pricing Guidelines* do not sanction the use of hidden comparables and so you should not use information that is only available to HMRC.

You can object to the use of particular companies presented as comparables from the results of a search of a commercial database if you hold information that suggests conclusively that the company is not actually comparable. You cannot tell the taxpayer why it shouldn't be used, unless the information you hold is actually within the public domain, but was not available (or was unknown to the researcher) at the time the comparable search was being made.

In practice, an enquiry should not be dependent on such secret comparables. From the facts available to both HMRC and the taxpayer, it should be possible to consider the arm's-length price.

a. See HMRC, *International Manual,* available at http://www.hmrc.gov.uk/manuals/intmanual/intm467110.htm.

Although secret comparables are not often relied upon in practice by tax administrations to determine and support transfer pricing adjustments, non-public information regarding taxpayers and their transactions is often used for risk-assessment purposes, and can inform the design of safe-harbor margins (see chapter 7).

Conducting a Comparability Analysis

The objective of a comparability analysis is to identify uncontrolled transactions that are sufficiently comparable to the controlled transactions under examination so as to be able to apply a transfer pricing method and make a determination of the arm's-length price or margin, or as is more common, a range of arm's length prices or margins (*arm's-length range*).

This, initially, requires an analysis of the economically relevant characteristics of the controlled transactions. Based on this analysis, potentially comparable uncontrolled transactions are then identified and subject to a similar analysis. Based on these analyses, the economically relevant characteristics of the controlled and the uncontrolled transactions are compared, with reference to the five comparability factors, to determine whether they meet the applicable standard of comparability. Where no differences exist that materially impact the condition being examined, the appropriate transfer pricing method can be applied and an arm's-length price or range of prices established. Where such differences do exist, adjustments (so-called comparability adjustments) may be possible to achieve a sufficient level of comparability. If such adjustments cannot be made, these new, potentially comparable transactions must be identified or a different approach (i.e., transfer pricing method) adopted.

The actual process adopted will depend on the facts and circumstances of a case and the resources available. The *OECD Transfer Pricing Guidelines* (2010a) provide a *typical nine-step process* that is considered good practice (see box 4.10). The chapter on comparability analysis in the *UN Transfer Pricing Manual* details a similar, although slightly different, process. While these typical processes provide a good reference point, it should be noted that following such a process does not guarantee that the outcome will be arm's-length, and failure to follow the process does not imply that the outcome will not be arm's-length. Simply put, the outcome matters more than the process.

Annex 4C contains a sample search process for external comparables, and annex 4D depicts a flowchart for the whole comparability analysis.

Box 4.10 Comparability Analysis: Typical Nine-Step Process in the *OECD Transfer Pricing Guidelines*

The *OECD Transfer Pricing Guidelines* outline a typical nine-step process that can be followed when performing a comparability analysis (OECD 2010a):

- Step 1: Determination of years to be covered.
- Step 2: Broad-based analysis of the taxpayer's circumstances.
- Step 3: Understanding the controlled transaction(s) under examination, based in particular on a functional analysis, in order to choose the tested party (where needed), the most appropriate transfer pricing method to the circumstances of the case, the financial indicator that will be tested (in the case of a transactional profit method), and to identify the significant comparability factors that should be taken into account.
- Step 4: Review of existing internal comparables, if any.
- Step 5: Determination of available sources of information on external comparables where such external comparables are needed taking into account their relative reliability.
- Step 6: Selection of the most appropriate transfer pricing method and, depending on the method, determination of the relevant financial indicator (for example, determination of the relevant net profit indicator in case of a transactional net margin method).
- Step 7: Identification of potential comparables: determining the key characteristics to be met by any uncontrolled transaction in order to be regarded as potentially comparable based on the relevant factors identified in Step 3 and in accordance with the comparability factors set forth at paragraphs 1.38–1.63 of the guidelines.
- Step 8: Determination of and making comparability adjustments where appropriate.
- Step 9: Interpretation and use of data collected, determination of the arm's-length remuneration.

Comparability Adjustments

[A] comparability adjustment is an adjustment made to the conditions of uncontrolled transactions in order to eliminate the effects of material differences which exist between them and the controlled transaction being examined.

— *OECD (2010a)*

As discussed in "Comparability" in chapter 3, transactions will generally be considered to be comparable if "none of the differences between the transactions could materially affect the factor being examined in the methodology (e.g., price or margin), or if reasonably accurate adjustments can be made to eliminate the material effects of any such differences" (paragraph 1.33 of the *OECD Transfer Pricing Guidelines)*. With regard to the latter, such adjustments are referred to as *comparability adjustments*.

Comparability adjustments include ones aimed at eliminating differences that may arise as a result of the following[16]:

- Differing accounting practices (i.e., to provide consistency with the tested party)
- Segmentation of financial data
- Differences in capital, functions, assets, and risks (see also box 4.11)

Box 4.11 Country Experience with Comparability Adjustments: India

Extract from OECD Secretariat Note on Comparability Adjustments (2010), which reads as follows[a]:

Indian courts have released several decisions relevant to comparability adjustments and, in particular, to the extent to which comparability adjustments performed are sufficiently reliable.

The need to perform in certain cases comparability adjustments to eliminate differences in working capital, risk, growth and R&D expenses was laid down in *Mentor Graphics [Mentor Graphics (Noida) (P.) Ltd. v. DCIT, Circle 6(1), New Delhi (2007) 109 ITD 101 (DELHI)/112 TTJ 408]* and confirmed in several decisions since. In Philips Software Centre [*Philips Software Centre (P.) Ltd. v. ACIT, Circle 12(2) [2008] 26 SOT 226 (BANG.)]* ITAT approved comparability adjustments being made to eliminate differences on account of different functions, assets and risks, and specifically for differences in risk profile, working capital and accounting policies. On the other hand, if the differences between the companies or transactions are so material that it is not possible to perform a reasonably accurate adjustment, then the "comparables" should be rejected [*Mentor Graphics (ibid) and Egain Communication (P.) Ltd. v. Income-tax Officer, Ward 1(4), Pune [2008] 23 SOT 385 (PUNE)]*. Furthermore, a working capital adjustment should not be performed in a particular case if its effect would be very marginal [*Sony India (P.) Ltd. v. Deputy Commissioner of Income-tax, Circle 9(1) [2008] 114 ITD 448 (DELHI)]*.

A remaining difficulty is the subjective question of determining what a "reasonably accurate comparability adjustment" is. In Sony India (ibid), ITAT upheld an overall flat adjustment of

box continues next page

Box 4.11 Country Experience with Comparability Adjustments: India *(continued)*

20 percent proposed by the Transfer Pricing Officer for differences in intangible ownership and risks assumed in the controlled transaction and "comparables" as being "fair and reasonable." By contrast, in *CIT v. Philips Software Centre [CIT v. Philips Software Centre Pvt. Ltd. (2009) TIOL-123-HC-KAR-IT]*, the High Court of India examined whether the Tribunal was correct in allowing a flat comparability adjustment of 11.72 percent (6.46 percent working capital adjustment +5.25 percent risk adjustment) "ignoring all important issues like the quality of adjustment data, purpose and reliability of the adjustment performed to be considered before making adjustment on account of capital and risk," and found this contrary to Rule 10B(3)(ii), which provides for only reasonably accurate adjustment, and accordingly stayed the operation of judgement of ITAT.

Other questions addressed in Indian decisions with respect to comparability include the use of data from other years than the year of the controlled transaction [Mentor Graphics (ibid)]; acceptability as comparables of companies in startup years and of loss-making companies [*Mentor Graphics (ibid) and Skoda Auto India Pvt. Ltd. v. ACIT (2009-TIOL-214-ITAT-PUNE)*]; acceptability as comparables of companies with low employee costs [Mentor Graphics (ibid)]; exclusion from the set of comparables of companies with significant "other income" such as interest, dividends, licenses [Egain Communication (ibid)]; treatment of "pass-through costs" [Sony India (P.) Ltd. (ibid)]; underutilization of capacity [Sony India (P.) Ltd. (ibid) and Skoda Auto India (ibid)]; acceptability of a comparability adjustment for a very material difference [*Essar Shipping Limited v. Deputy Commissioner of Income Tax (2008-TIOL-652-ITAT-MUM)*]; selection of the point of adjustment within the arm's-length range [Mentor Graphics (ibid) and Sony India (P.) Ltd. (ibid)]; use of multi-year data in case of different product cycles [Skoda Auto India (ibid)]; etc."

a. See OECD Secretariat Note on "Comparability Adjustments," available at http://www.oecd.org/dataoecd/41/3/45765353.pdf.

The day-to-day practice differs regarding the use of comparability adjustments (particularly between countries, but also between tax officers and tax advisors within a country), yet the prevailing view is that comparability adjustments should be made only with respect to differences that have a material impact on the condition being examined and where they are expected to increase the reliability of the results.[17] They should not be made routinely without considering applicable facts and circumstances. Furthermore, whether or not comparability adjustments are made in practice will often require a cost-benefit analysis since some adjustments can be very resource-intensive.

(Descriptions and examples of possible adjustments that can be made for differences in accounting treatment, working capital differences, and country-specific risk are provided in annex 4C.)

Transfer Pricing Methods

The OECD *Transfer Pricing Guidelines* (2010a), the *UN Practical Manual* (2013), and most countries' transfer pricing legislations (see chapter 3) detail five transfer pricing methods that can be used to establish whether the conditions imposed

Figure 4.7 Transfer Pricing Methods

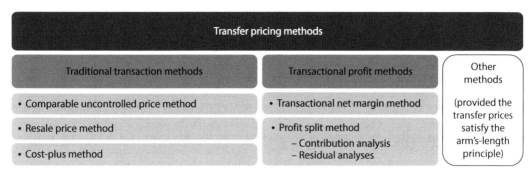

in controlled transactions are consistent with the arm's-length principle (see figure 4.7). Reference is also commonly made to the use of "other methods" to establish transfer prices, provided that one of the five methods cannot be applied and that the outcome is consistent with the arm's-length principle. The five methods and some of the "other methods" observed in practice are summarized in this section.

Comparable Uncontrolled Price Method

Application of the CUP method involves a comparison of the prices charged in the controlled transactions with the prices charged for comparable goods or services (including the provision of finance and intangible property) in uncontrolled transactions (see box 4.12). Prices that differ may indicate that the conditions of the controlled transaction are not consistent with the arm's-length principle.

This price comparison may be made between internal uncontrolled transactions (see figure 4.8) or external uncontrolled transactions (see figure 4.9), depending on the existence of such transactions and availability of related information.

Since the price is the condition being examined when applying the CUP method, when assessing comparability, it is important to consider that even minor price differences may have a material impact on the condition being examined. In this regard, the required standard of comparability for applying the CUP method is generally considered to be high relative to the other transfer pricing methods.

The main strengths of the CUP method are (a) it requires a detailed transaction analysis, and (b) because the price in the transaction is the subject of the analysis, it is not a one-sided analysis. There is, therefore, no requirement to select a tested party. However, it can be difficult to apply this method because detailed information about transactions is often not publicly available. Moreover, even where detailed data on internal uncontrolled transactions exist, such transactions often are not comparable for the purposes of applying the CUP method. For example, similar transactions with independent parties may have been entered into at a different level in the market or in different geographic markets.

Box 4.12 Sample Application of the CUP Method

Background Information

- Company A and Company B are associated parties.
- Company A manufactures pillows (Type A and Type B), which it sells to Company B, which distributes the pillows in its local market.
- Company A also sells Type A pillows to Company X and Type B pillows to Company Y, both of which are independent distributors in the same local markets (quantities and prices as specified). (See figure B4.12.1.)
  - A comparability analysis reveals that
  - The sales of Type A pillows to Company X are comparable to the sales of Type A pillows to Company B.
  - The sales of Type B pillows to Company Y are comparable to the sales of Type B pillows to Company B, except for a 10 percent quantity discount that was provided to Company Y. Further research reveals that this discount is provided to all independent customers purchasing over 100,000 units per annum.

Observations

- The price charged for the sales of Type A pillows to Company B appears to satisfy the arm's-length principle— *no adjustment required.*
- The price charged for the sales of Type B pillows to Company B does not appear to satisfy the arm's-length principle— *adjustment may be required.*
  - Possible adjustment: Reduction in price charged by 10 percent (resulting in the arm's-length price being US$9) to afford Company B the same quantity discount that independent parties are afforded, i.e., decrease total price charged by US$150,000, increasing Company B's profit by US$150,000 and decreasing Company A's profit by US$150,000.

Figure B4.12.1 Application of the CUP Method

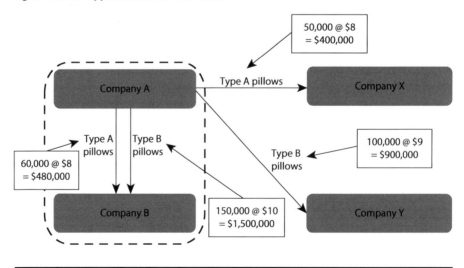

Figure 4.8 Application of the Comparable Uncontrolled Price Method Based on Internal Comparables

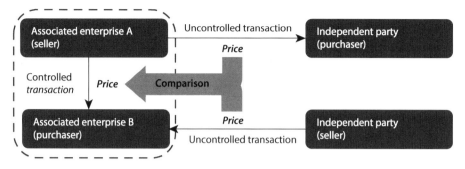

Figure 4.9 Application of the Comparable Uncontrolled Price Method Based on External Comparables

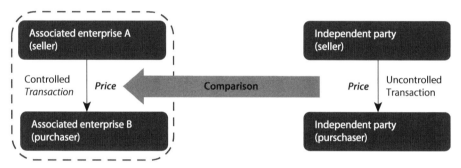

Where potentially comparable transactions are identified, but there are one or more differences that materially affect the price, comparability adjustments may be possible to neutralize this effect. Examples may include the effect of quantity discounts, delivery terms, contractual terms, and minor product differences. Some differences may be impossible to account for by making adjustments, such as differences in geographical market, branding (trademarks) or valuable intangibles, functional differences, and significant contractual differences.

The most common examples of the CUP method being successfully applied in practice include

- Cases where internal comparables exist (tangible goods, services, royalty rates, etc.)
- Certain commodities transactions
- Financial transactions (interest rates on loans, etc.)

Resale Price Method

The resale price method starts with the price at which the product that is the object of the controlled transaction is resold to an independent enterprise (the "resale price"), which is then reduced by an appropriate gross profit margin (the "resale price margin") to determine an arm's-length price. The appropriate resale price margin is determined by reference to the gross margins in comparable uncontrolled transactions. Accounting consistency is, therefore, paramount to the reliable application of the resale price method.

$$\text{Arm's-length price} = \text{resale price} \times (1\text{-resale price margin})$$

Where resale price margin = gross profit margin, defined as ratio of gross profit to revenues

The resale price margin represents the margin that a reseller of the relevant products would seek to make to cover operating expenses, taking into account the functions performed, assets employed, and risks assumed. The appropriate resale price margin may be determined by reference to the gross profit margins earned in internal uncontrolled comparable transactions (see figure 4.10) or by reference to the gross profit margins earned by independent parties (external comparables. See figure 4.11). Comparable resale price margins may be used to test compliance with the arm's-length principle or as a reference point for setting the prices in the controlled transactions.

Figure 4.10 Example: Application of the Resale Price Method Based on Internal Uncontrolled Comparables

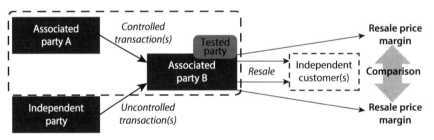

Figure 4.11 Example: Application of the Resale Price Method Based on External Uncontrolled Comparables

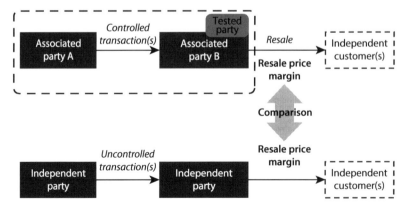

The condition being examined when applying the resale price method is the resale price margin earned by the reseller of the goods; hence, it is a one-sided method that requires the selection of a tested party. Since the resale price is the starting point for application of the resale price method, the tested party will necessarily be the party that purchases the product in the controlled transaction that it then resells (see also box 4.13).

Box 4.13 Example: Application of the Resale Price Method

Background Information
- Company A and Company B are associated parties.
- Company A manufactures canned soup, which it sells to Company B.
- Company B is a distributor of canned foods and resells the canned soup in its local market for 10,000 per palette.
- Company B does not modify the products or undertake any marketing activities in relation thereto.
- Since Company B is the reseller of the goods, it is necessarily the tested party for the purposes of applying the resale price method.
- Company X, Company Y, and Company Z are independent distributors of canned food products in the same local market that Company B operates. A comparability analysis determines that their business activities are comparable to those performed by Company B in relation to the canned soup that it purchases from Company A and resells. (See figure B14.3.1.)

Observations
- The resale price margin earned by Company B (25 percent) is within the arm's-length range of resale price margins (22 percent to 26 percent)—*no adjustment required.*

Figure B14.3.1 Application of the Resale Price Method

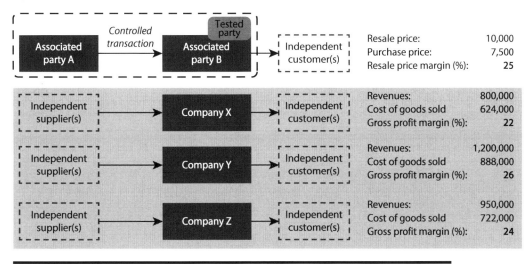

When assessing comparability for the purposes of applying the resale price method it is important to consider that minor differences in the characteristics of the product may not materially affect the condition being examined—the resale price margin—since, for example, minor product differences are more likely to materially impact price as opposed to a net profit margin. Functional comparability is very important, however, since the main premise underlying the resale price method is that parties with comparable functional profiles will be compensated similarly.

The main strengths of the resale price method are that (a) since the condition being examined is at the gross margin level there is less scope for variables unrelated to the transfer price in the controlled transaction to have an affect in regard to the TNMM (see "Transactional Net Margin Method"), (b) the starting point is a market price (the resale price) and availability of comparable information in relation to the CUP method (see "Comparable Uncontrolled Price Method"). Since the resale price method is a one-sided method, the arm's-length resale margin for one party may result in an extreme result for the other party to the controlled transactions (i.e., a loss or extreme profitability). Issues can arise where a tax administration is presented with an analysis that relies on a foreign-tested party. Furthermore, since gross margin data may not be reported, and where there are differences in accounting treatment that cannot be reliably adjusted for, such data may not be available or may be rendered unsuitable for the application of the resale price maintenance (RPM). As a result, availability of reliable gross margin data for the purposes of applying the resale price method can be problematic in practice.

Common examples of the resale price method being successfully applied in practice include situations in which

- A reseller purchases products for resale from associated parties and independent parties, but due to product differences the CUP method cannot be applied
- Products are purchased from associated parties for resale by a reseller (i.e., a distributor) that does not add significant value by, for example, making physical modifications, contribution of valuable intangible property, or significant marketing activities.
- Commissionaires and agents are not undertaking significant marketing activities.

Cost-Plus Method

The cost-plus method starts with the costs incurred by the supplier of the property or services that are the object of the controlled transaction, which are then appropriately marked up to determine an arm's-length price (see box 4.14). The appropriate markup ("cost-plus markup") is determined by reference to the margins earned in comparable uncontrolled transactions.

Figure 4.12 Example: Application of the Cost-Plus Method Based on Internal Uncontrolled Comparables

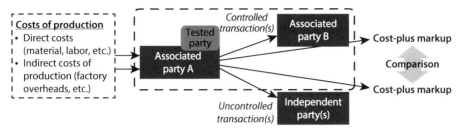

Figure 4.13 Example: Application of the Cost-Plus Method Based on External Uncontrolled Comparables

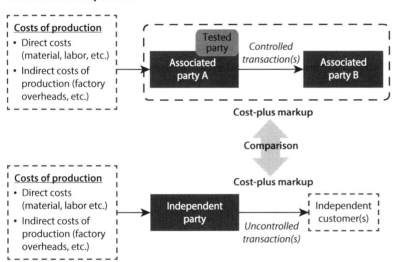

Accounting consistency—particularly the composition of the relevant cost base—is therefore paramount to the reliable application of the cost-plus method.

$$\text{Arm's-length price} = \text{Cost base} \times (1 + \text{cost-plus markup})$$

Where cost-plus markup = gross profit margin, defined as ratio of gross profit to the relevant cost base

The cost-plus markup represents the margin that a supplier of the relevant goods or services would seek to make to cover operating expenses, taking into account the functions performed, assets employed, and risks assumed. The appropriate cost-plus margin may be determined by reference to the gross profit margins earned in internal uncontrolled comparable transactions (see figure 4.12) or by reference to the gross profit margins earned by independent parties (external comparables; see figure 4.13). Comparable cost-plus margins may be used as either a comparison to test compliance with the arm's-length principle or a reference point for setting the prices in the controlled transactions.

The condition being examined when applying the cost-plus method is the cost-plus markup earned by the supplier of the products or services; hence, it is a one-sided method that requires the selection of a tested party. Since the costs incurred by the supplier of the goods and services are the starting point for application of the cost-plus method, the tested party must necessarily be the party that supplies the product or service in the controlled transaction. The costs to be considered are the direct and indirect costs of producing the product or service, excluding operating costs.[18]

The approach to assessing comparability, as well as advantages and disadvantages of the cost-plus method are similar to the resale price method.

Common examples of the cost-plus method being successfully applied in practice include

- Situations where a supplier of the goods or services in the controlled transactions supplies similar goods or services to independent parties, but due to differences in the product or service the CUP method cannot be applied
- Sales of products where the manufacturer, such as a contract manufacturer, does not contribute valuable intangible property or incur substantial risks
- Intragroup services (e.g., contract R&D, toll manufacturing, etc.)

Box 4.14 Example: Application of the Cost-Plus Method

Background Information

- Company A and Company B are associated parties.
- Company A manufactures clothing, which it sells to Company B (its only customer) based on the specifications in the orders placed by Company B. In this regard Company A is considered a "contract manufacturer."
- Company B designs the clothing, owns the relevant intangible property, and places orders with Company A, specifying design, quantities, and quality.
- Company B distributes the clothing purchased from Company A around the world.
- Since Company A is the supplier of the products, it is necessarily the tested party for the purposes of applying the cost-plus method.
- Company X, Company Y, and Company Z are independent contract manufacturers that operate in the same local market in which Company A operates. A comparability analysis determines that their business activities are comparable to those performed by Company A in relation to the clothing it manufactures and sells to Company B. (See figure B4.14.1.)

box continues next page

Box 4.14 Example: Application of the Cost-Plus Method *(continued)*

Figure B4.14.1 Application of the Cost-Plus Method

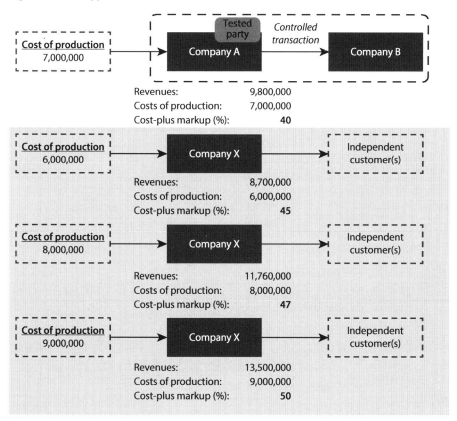

Revenues:	9,800,000
Costs of production:	7,000,000
Cost-plus markup (%):	**40**

Revenues:	8,700,000
Costs of production:	6,000,000
Cost-plus markup (%):	**45**

Revenues:	11,760,000
Costs of production:	8,000,000
Cost-plus markup (%):	**47**

Revenues:	13,500,000
Costs of production:	9,000,000
Cost-plus markup (%):	**50**

Observations:

- The cost-plus markup earned by Company A (40 percent) does not fall within the arm's-length range of cost-plus markups (45–50 percent)— *adjustment may be required.*

   Possible adjustment: increase the transfer price to put the cost-plus markup to within the range—if the median is selected as the appropriate point within the range (i.e., 47 percent) this would result in the total transfer price charged increasing to 10,290,000 (7,000,000* [1+0.47 percent]), increasing Company A's profit by 490,000 and decreasing Company B' s profit by 490,000, respectively.

Transactional Net Margin Method

The TNMM examines an appropriate financial indicator (based on net profit) that the tested party realizes in controlled transactions and compares it with that realized in uncontrolled transactions. The appropriate financial indicator will

Table 4.6 Example of Financial Indicators Used When Applying the Transactional Net Margin Method

Financial indicators		Tested party	Examples of use
Operating profit margin (also "EBIT/sales ratio") ROS	Operating profit[a]/sales	Party earning sales income	Distribution enterprises
Return on total costs (also "full cost-plus markup") FCM	Operating profit/total costs	Party incurring costs	Service providers and manufacturers
Berry ratio	Gross profit/operating expenses	Party incurring operating expenses	Distribution enterprises
ROA	Operating profit/assets[b]	Party holding and employing assets	Asset-intense activities
ROCE	Operating profit/capital employed[c]	Party with capital employed	Asset/capital-intense activities

Note: See annex 4D for example of calculations of operating profit margin, return on total costs, and Berry ratio. EBIT = earnings before interest and tax; FCM = full cost markup; ROA = return on assets; ROCE = return on capital employed; ROS = return on sales.

a. Net margin, excluding taxes and interest, also referred to as EBIT.

b. Generally tangible operating assets.

c. For example, total assets less current liabilities or fixed assets plus working capital.

differ depending on the facts and circumstances and the selection of the tested party. Examples of financial indicators commonly used are set out in table 4.6.

The appropriate financial indicator is determined with reference to the net profit (operating margin) earned in comparable uncontrolled transactions (as opposed to the gross margin, as used when applying the resale price or cost-plus methods).

Since the condition being examined when applying the TNMM is the net profit (relative to an appropriate base, dependent on the financial indicator being applied), accounting consistency is typically of less importance regarding the classification of revenues and expenses in relation to the resale price method and the cost-plus method.[19]

When assessing comparability for the purposes of applying the TNMM functional comparability is very important since the main premise underlying the TNMM is that parties with comparable functional profiles will be compensated similarly. At the same time, relatively minor differences in functional comparability may not have a material impact on the net margin, or may be able to be appropriately adjusted for.

The main strengths of the TNMM are that as the condition being examined is at the net margin level there is a greater pool of potential comparable information available in relation to the CUP, resale price, and cost-plus methods (see "Comparable Uncontrolled Price Method," "Resale Price Method," and "Cost-Plus Method"). This is due to the net margin being less likely to be materially affected by differences in the product or service or minor functional differences, and that the net margin information is commonly reported on in financial accounts—with a much broader coverage of information on most commercial databases. TNMM is often applied in practice based on a comparison to the net margin's earned by whole entities, as opposed to the individual uncontrolled transactions (see box 4.15). The TNMM is also very flexible in its application, in that the net margin can be compared to different bases depending on the financial indicator

Box 4.15 Example: Application of the TNMM Using a Sales-Based Financial Indicator

Background Information

- Company A and Company B are associated parties.
- Company A manufactures home hardware products, which it sells to Company B.
- Company B is a distributor of home hardware products and resells the products in its local market.
- Company B does not modify the products or undertake any marketing activities in relation thereto.
- Since Company B is the reseller of the goods, it is necessarily the tested party for the purposes of applying the TNMM, with operating profit or sales selected as the financial indicator.
- Comparables A, B, C, D, and E are independent distributors of home hardware products in the same local market in which Company B operates. A comparability analysis determines that their business activities are comparable to those performed by Company B in relation to the products that it purchases from Company A and distributes. (See figure B4.15.1.)

Observations

- The operating profit or sales margin earned by Company B (2.75 percent) is within the arm's-length range of operating profit or sales ratios (2.00–3.50 percent)—*no adjustment required.*

Figure B4.15.1 Application of the TNMM Using a Sales-Based Financial Indicator

Revenues:	25,000,000
Cost of goods sold:	20,000,000
Operating costs:	5,312,500
Operating profit:	687,500
Return on sales (%):	2.75

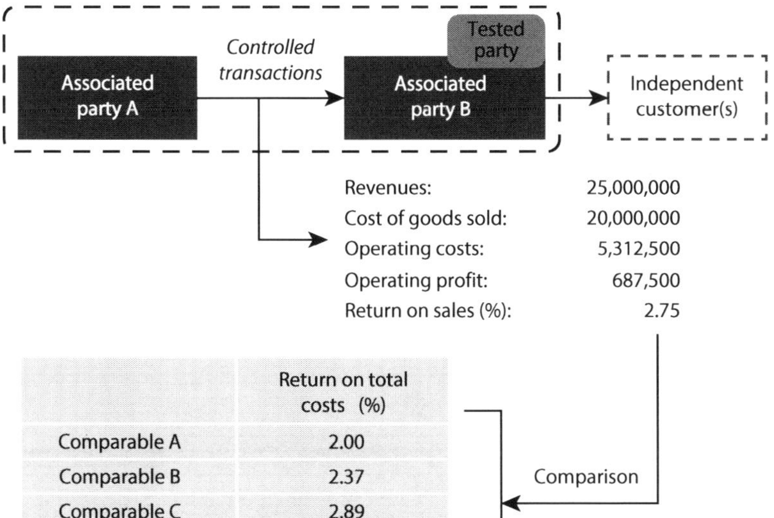

	Return on total costs (%)
Comparable A	2.00
Comparable B	2.37
Comparable C	2.89
Comparable D	3.5
Comparable E	3.11

Arm's-length range: 2.0–3.5%

Note: TNMM = transactional net margin method.

selected (see table 4.6), allowing, for example, for the selection of the supplier or the purchaser in the controlled transactions as the tested party. As a result of this flexibility (see also box 4.16) and the relative availability of information, the TNMM is one of the most commonly applied methods in practice (Cooper and Agarwal 2011).

Since the TNMM is a one-sided method, there is the possibility that the selected financial for one party may result in an extreme result for the other party to the controlled transactions (i.e., a loss or extreme profitability). Issues can also arise with analysis that relies on a foreign-tested party. A major criticism of the TNMM is that net margins are affected by factors other than the transfer price(s). It is therefore important to ensure that during the comparability analysis these other factors, unrelated to the controlled transaction, are considered.

Common examples of the TNMM method being applied in practice include

- Sales of tangible products by distributors (not performing significant marketing functions or contributing valuable intangibles) where the data are not available to use the resale price method
- Sales of tangible products by manufacturers (performing routine manufacturing functions and not contributing valuable intangibles or bearing significant risk) where the data are not available to use the cost-plus method
- Where gross margin data are available, but are not reliable due to accounting differences
- Intragroup services, including contract research and development arrangements

---

Box 4.16 Example: Application of the TNMM Using Cost-Based Financial Indicator

Background Information

- Company A and Company B are associated parties.
- Company A manufactures paper products, which it sells to Company B (its only customer) based on the specifications in the orders placed by Company B. In this regard, Company B is considered a "contract manufacturer."
- Company B designs the products, owns the relevant intangible property, and places orders with Company A specifying quantities and quality.
- Company B distributes the paper products purchased from Company A around the world.
- Since Company A is the supplier of the products, it is necessarily the tested party for the purposes of applying the TNMM, with return on total costs selected as the financial indicator.
- Comparables A, B, C, D, and E are independent contract manufacturers that operate in the same local market in which Company A operates. A comparability analysis determines that their business activities are comparable to those performed by Company A in relation to the clothing it manufactures and sells to Company B. (See figure B4.16.1.)

box continues next page

Box 4.16 Example: Application of the TNMM Using Cost-Based Financial Indicator *(continued)*

Figure B4.16.1 Application of the TNMM Using Cost-Based Financial Indicator

Arm's-length range: 8.13–11.10%

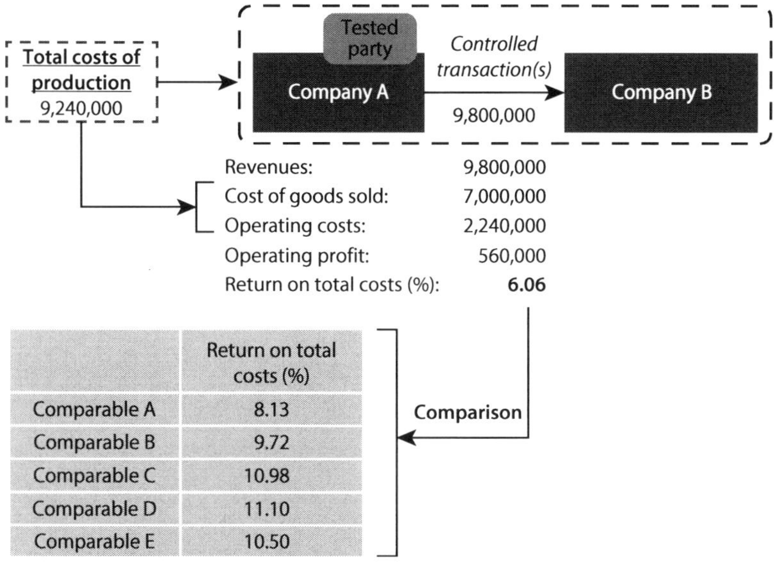

Observations

- The return on total costs earned by Company A (6.06 percent) does not fall within the arm's-length range (8.13–11.10 percent)—*adjustment may be required.*
  - Possible adjustment: Increase the transfer price to put the cost-plus markup to within the range, as follows: (Please refer to "Selecting a Point Within the Range" for a discussion of the arm's-length range and median).

Adjustment to median (10.50%)
= 9,240,000 × [10.50%-6.06%]
= 410,200

Revenues:	$9,800,000	$+**410,200**	$10,210,200
Cost of production:	$7,000,000		$7,000,000
Operating cost:	$2,240,000		$2,240,000
Operating profit	$560,000	$+**410,200**	$970,200
Return on total cost (%):	**5.71**		**10.50**

▶ **Increase in company A's profit by 410,200**
▶ **Decrease in company B's profit by 410,200**

Profit Split Method

The profit split method begins with the combined profit (or loss) arising from the controlled transactions and then attempts to split the profits between the associated enterprises party to those transactions on an economically valid basis. Where possible, this economically valid basis should be supported by market data. However, this is not always possible and thus internal data, applied objectively using, for example, allocation keys, may need to be relied upon.

The application of the profit split method is an important building block to implement the arm's-length principle and align profits with value creation in situations where the scope for application of other methods is limited due to the features of a transaction. More detailed guidance on the method is expected to be developed by the OECD's *Working Party* 6 and to be finalized by 2017.[20] When applying the profit split method, different approaches may be used for determining the appropriate (arm's-length) split of profits between the parties:

- Contribution analysis: Combined profits from the controlled transactions allocated between the associated parties on the basis of their relative contributions
- Comparable profit split: Combined profit (or loss) is split by reference to comparable splits between independent enterprises
- Residual analysis: Two-step approach that first allocates profits to nonunique (routine) activities and then splits the residual profit on an economically valid basis

Since the condition being examined when applying the profit split method is the split of the combined profits, the profit split method is not a one-sided method—the results of all parties to the controlled transactions are considered. Depending on the approach adopted, the application of the profit split method may require the application of other one-sided methods (such as the resale price method, cost-plus method, and TNMM) as one of the steps in determining the appropriate split.

The profit split method is used in situations where the controlled transactions are highly interrelated and therefore cannot be reliably considered on a separate basis or situations where both parties to the transaction contribute valuable intangible property.[21]

Contribution Analysis

Application of the profit split method based on a contribution analysis requires that the combined profits from the controlled transactions are determined and then allocated between the associated parties on the basis of their relative contributions to the derivation of those combined profits. The allocation should be determined based on sound economic principles and should reflect an approximation of the division of the profits that would have been agreed by independent parties.

The profits will generally be split at the operating profit level. However, a split of gross profits or otherwise may be appropriate depending on the facts and circumstances. Consistency as to the accounting treatment of the parties is necessary to calculate the combined profit for this split, and allocation of costs and expenses to the controlled transactions, where necessary, must be done on a reasonable and objective basis.

Gonnet and Fris (2007) describe four approaches that could be applied (either alone or in combination) to quantitatively evaluate the contributions of the parties based on[22]

- *Capital investment.* Assessment of the relative contributions of the parties based on the capital they have invested in intangibles
- *Compensation.* Use of labor cost data to quantify the parties' contributions
- *Bargaining theory.* Application of bargaining theory (such as game theory and sharply theory) to evaluate the relative bargaining positions of the parties and thus obtain insight into their respective contributions
- *Survey.* Use of expert opinions of internal and external observers regarding the assumptions for the split

This list is not exhaustive. Other approaches or techniques may be suitable and the bottom line is that approaches need to be consistent, logical, and supportable, based on the facts and circumstances of a specific case.

Comparable Profit Split

Application of the profit split method based on comparable profit split requires that the profits be allocated between the parties to the controlled transactions with reference to similar splits of profits between independent parties. In this regard, the "comparable profit split," which is otherwise similar to the contribution analysis,[23] requires the existence and identification of one or more comparable profit split between independent parties engaged in comparable uncontrolled transactions. Due to the limited existence and availability of sufficient information on such arrangements, the comparable profit split is not often reliably applied in practice.

Residual Analysis

The residual analysis (see figure 4.14) involves a two-step approach for determining the allocation of the combined profits from the controlled transactions:

1. Each party is allocated profits based on their non unique (or routine) contributions (e.g., basic manufacturing or distribution activities) by reference to comparable uncontrolled transactions (or entities); and
2. The residual profits (profits remaining after step 1) are allocated on an economical basis with reference to the particular facts and circumstances.

Figure 4.14 Example of Application of the Profit Split Method Based on a Residual Analysis

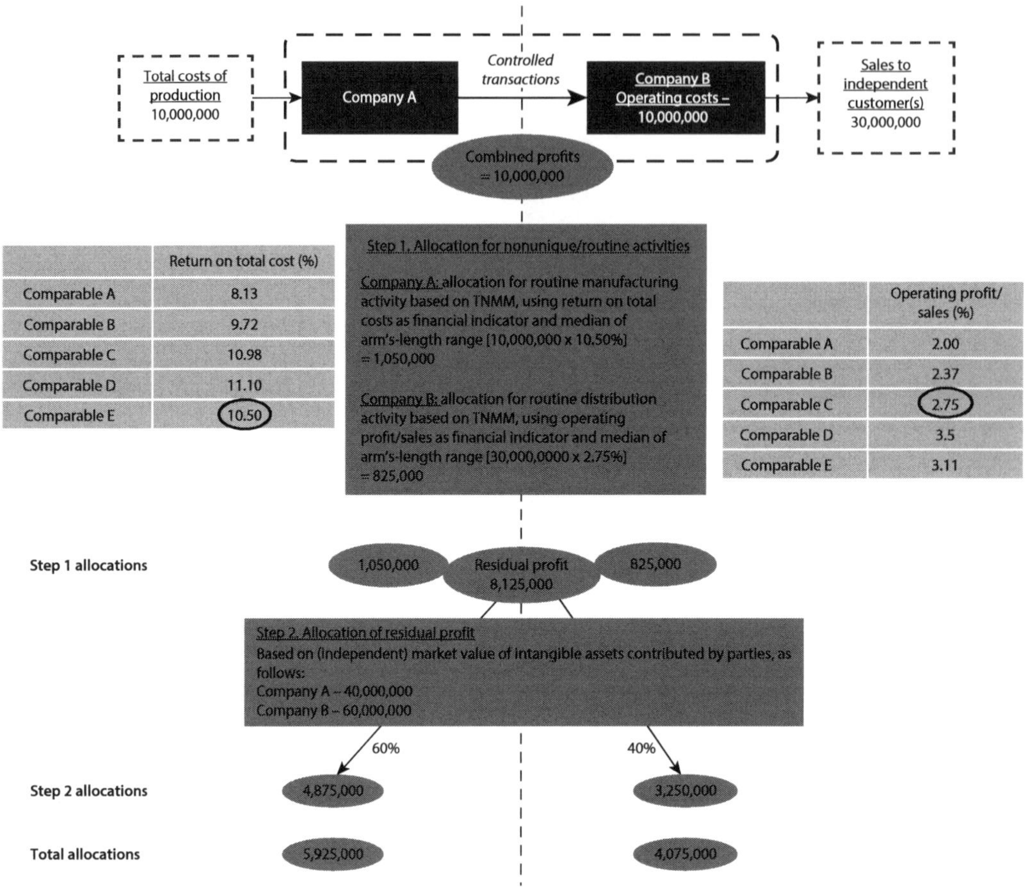

Note: TNMM = transactional net margin method.

The allocation of the profits for nonunique activities in step 1 is determined by way of application of one of the other transfer pricing methods. Since the focus is on the nonunique contributions, unique and valuable contributions (e.g., those relating to valuable intangibles) are disregarded for this step.

The allocation of the residual profits (step 2) should be determined based on sound economic principles. Reference to comparable uncontrolled transactions may be made where available, or allocation keys or the techniques discussed previously for the application of the contribution analysis may be appropriate, depending on the facts and circumstances (e.g., market value of intangible property contributed, capitalized costs of developing intangible property contributed, or expenditure on intangible development).

As with the contribution analysis, the residual analysis profits generally split profits at the operating profit level. However, a split of gross profits (or otherwise) may be appropriate depending on the particular facts and circumstances. Consistent accounting treatment is necessary to calculate the combined profit to be split.

Other Methods

Other methods may be necessary in practice due to particular facts and circumstances. Their use is often provided for under a countries' domestic law, and in some countries other methods are specified (see chapter 3). The *OECD Transfer Pricing Guidelines* (2010a, paragraph 2.9) provides the following regarding the use of "other methods":

> MNE groups retain the freedom to apply methods not described in these Guidelines (hereafter 'other methods') to establish prices provided those prices satisfy the arm's-length principle in accordance with these Guidelines. Such other methods should, however, not be used in substitution for OECD-recognized methods where the latter are more appropriate to the facts and circumstances of the case. In cases where other methods are used, their selection should be supported by an explanation of why OECD-recognized methods were regarded as less appropriate or nonworkable in the circumstances of the case and of the reason why the selected other method was regarded as providing a better solution.

Examples of other methods used in practice and included in countries' domestic laws are set out in table 4.7.

Table 4.7 Other Methods

Comparable profits method	A method described in IRC section 482 regulations that is very similar to the TNMM. The main difference is that CPM is described in the U.S. regulations as providing for a comparison with the results of uncontrolled entities, whereas the TNMM, as described in the *OECD Transfer Pricing Guidelines*, refers to a comparison of the controlled transaction with uncontrolled transactions. The distinction is clear in theory. However, in practice, the TNMM is, out of necessity, often applied using whole of entity or segmented data (provided the comparability requirements are still met)
Services cost method	A method described in IRC section 482 regulations that allows for the charging out of certain (covered) services on a cost basis.
Brazilian transfer pricing methods	Brazil's unique transfer pricing regime specifies several methodologies that are not consistent with the arm's-length principle (in the traditional sense).
Methods based on internal rates of return	Methods based on a targeted internal rate of return. See, for example, Australian Taxation Office guidance for dealing with difficult transfer pricing cases.
Corporate finance valuation approaches	Cost-based, market-based, and income-based methods from corporate finance theory are often used when dealing with transactions involving intangibles.

Note: CPM = cost-plus method; TNMM = transactional net margin method.

Selecting the Transfer Pricing Method

When undertaking a transfer pricing analysis, the transfer pricing methods to be applied will need to be selected. When determining which method to apply or which can be applied, reference should first be made to the relevant domestic law requirements, if any. In this regard, domestic law may dictate a hierarchy of methods: a "best method" standard or, as is more commonly the case, a standard of "most appropriate method to the circumstances of the case." The latter of which is the approach provided for in the *OECD Transfer Pricing Guidelines* (2010a). Regardless of the domestic law requirements, practical realities and constraints such as the information available, the functional profiles of the parties to the controlled transactions and hence the tested party, and the type of transactions will generally dictate the methods available.

Although theoretically more than one method can be applied, this is not commonly done (due to the additional compliance costs involved) and is not generally a requirement under domestic law.[24] In this regard the *OECD Transfer Pricing Guidelines* (2010a), recognizing the compliance burden of applying more than one method, state in paragraph 2.11:

> [t]he arm's-length principle does not require the application of more than one method for a given transaction (or set of transactions that are appropriately aggregated…) and in fact undue reliance on such an approach could create a significant burden for taxpayers.

Application of more than one method may, however, be advisable in complicated and controversial circumstances where the approach would give rise to an arm's-length range from which an appropriate point may need to be selected.

The guidance provided in the *OECD Transfer Pricing Guidelines* (2010a) on the selection of the most appropriate method to the circumstances suggests that the following be taken into account[25]:

i.   The respective strengths and weaknesses of the OECD recognised methods;
ii. The appropriateness of the method considered in view of the nature of the controlled transaction, determined in particular through a functional analysis;
iii. The availability of reliable information (in particular on uncontrolled comparables) needed to apply the selected method and/or other methods; and
iv. The degree of comparability between controlled and uncontrolled transactions, including the reliability of comparability adjustments that may be needed to eliminate material differences between them.

Furthermore, the *OECD Transfer Pricing Guidelines* (2010a) express a preference for the CUP method where it and another method can be applied "in an equally reliable manner." This same preference is also relevant regarding the cost-plus method and the resale price method when either can be applied in an equally reliable manner to the TNMM.

Table 4.8 Extract from OECD Secretariat Note on "Transfer Pricing Methods," 2010a

Illustration, of the selection of the most appropriate method to the circumstances of the case		
If CUP and another method can be applied in an equally reliable manner	• CUP	
	If not:	
Where one party to the transaction performs "benchmarkable" functions (e.g. manufacturing, distribution, services for which comparables exist) and does not make any valuable, unique contribution (in particular does not contribute a unique, valuable intangible)	• One sided method • Choice of the tested party (seller or purchaser): generally the one that has the less complex functional analysis.	
*The tested party is the seller (e.g. contract manufacturing or provision of services)	• Cost plus • Cost-based TNMM (i.e. the net profit/costs) • Asset-based TNMM (i.e. testing the net profit/assets)	• If cost plus and TNMM can be applied in an equally reliable manner: cost plus
*The tested party is the buyer (e.g. marketing/distribution)	• Resale price • Sales based TNMM (i.e. testing the net profit/sales)	• If resale price and TNMM can be applied in an equally reliable manner: resale price
Where each of the parties makes valuable, unique contributions to the controlled transaction (e.g. contributes valuable unique intangibles)	• Two-sided method • Transactional profit split	
MNEs retain the freedom to use "other methods" not listed above, provided they satisfy the arm's-length principle. In such cases, the rejection of the above-described methods and selection of an "other method" should be justified.	• Other methods	

Note: CUP = comparable uncontrolled price; MNE = multinational enterprise; TNMM = transactional net margin method.

Selecting the Tested Party

The choice of the tested party should be consistent with the functional analysis of the transaction. As a general rule, the tested party is the one to which a transfer pricing method can be applied in the most reliable manner and for which the most reliable comparables can be found, i.e. it will most often be the one that has the less complex functional analysis.

— *OECD Transfer Pricing Guidelines (2010a)*

Application of one-sided transfer pricing methodology (i.e., the resale price method, the cost-plus method, and the TNMM; see "Resale Price Method," "Cost-Plus Method," and "Transactional Net Margin Method," respectively) requires the selection of a tested party. The tested party is the party for which the relevant condition being examined (i.e., gross profit margin, gross profit markup, net margin, etc.) is being tested. The selection of the tested party is crucial to the selection of the transfer pricing method to be applied and, in the case of the TNMM, the financial indicator to be used (see "Transactional Net Margin Method").

In practice, the tested party will generally be the party to the transaction with the least complex functional profile and for which the most reliable information is available. For example, when examining the sale of products by a complex manufacturer that owns valuable intangible property (such as patents and trademarks) to a distributor that undertakes general routine functions, bears minimal risks, and that does not own any valuable intangible property, it is likely that the distributor would be the appropriate tested party and the resale price method or the TNMM would be applied accordingly. If, however, the factual situation is reversed and the manufacturer undertakes general routine functions, bears minimal risks, and the distributor undertakes high value added functions (such as extensive marketing) and owns valuable intangibles (e.g., a valuable trademark), then it is likely that the manufacturer would be the appropriate tested party, and the cost-plus method or TNMM would be applied accordingly. Likewise, when examining the provision of a service, such as technical services, the service provider will generally be selected as the tested party, and the cost-plus method or the TNMM will be applied.

In theory, the tested party may be the local party or the foreign party to the controlled transactions. However, in practice, issues can arise in some countries regarding the acceptability of a tested party not located in that country, i.e., a foreign-tested party (see box 4.17). Where a foreign-tested party is relied upon, the identification of comparable uncontrolled transactions should be approached taking into account the economic circumstances of the country in which the foreign party is located.

Obtaining an understanding of the controlled transactions will help to provide the necessary background for the selection of the tested party, and thus will assist with identifying which transfer pricing methods may be applicable. Identification of the appropriate tested party is also necessary for narrowing the focus of the search for comparables.

Box 4.17 Acceptability of Foreign-Tested Parties

Since international transfer pricing necessarily involves parties in more than one country, where a one-sided transfer pricing method is being applied, it may be that the appropriate tested party is a party not located in the country where examination is being undertaken. For example, where the tax administration of Country A is examining the sale of products manufactured by an entity resident in Country A (Company A) that are sold to an associated party resident in Country B (Company B), which then distributes the products in the local market, application of a transfer pricing method that relies on the party in Country B as the tested party may be appropriate based on the facts and circumstances (figure B4.17.1).

While in theory the use of a foreign-tested party should be acceptable, in practice some tax administrations are averse to, or suspicious of, their use. Generally, this is due to concerns regarding the availability and reliability of information regarding the foreign-tested party and the foreign comparables, or a lack of experience and thus confidence on the part of the tax administration. Provided that sufficient information can be obtained and/or is provided

box continues next page

Box 4.17 Acceptability of Foreign-Tested Parties *(continued)*

regarding the foreign-tested party and the applicable comparables, and that the foreign party has been appropriately selected as the tested party, the use of a foreign party should be acceptable to a tax administration. A systematic failure to accept foreign-tested parties can create further practical difficulties for application of the arm's-length principle by unnecessarily limiting the transfer pricing methods that can be applied to a particular situation and thus the pool of potential comparable uncontrolled transactions available. This may result in the imposition of unnecessary compliance costs and instances of economic double taxation, particularly whereby different transfer pricing analyses are required for each party to the transaction as a result.

Figure B4.17.1 Acceptability of Foreign-Tested Parties

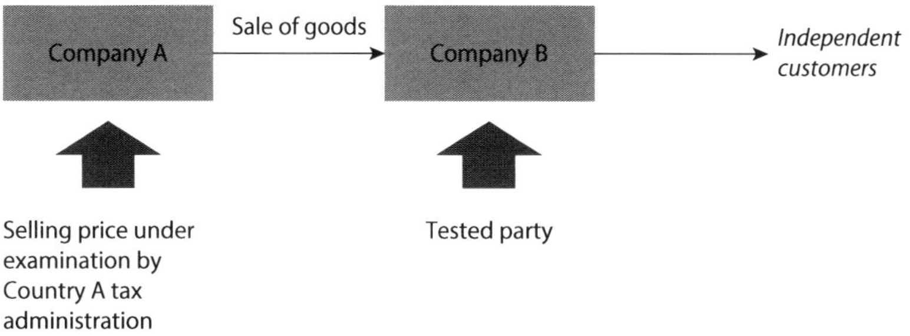

Arm's-Length Range

> As transfer pricing is not an exact science, the application of the most appropriate method or methods will often result in a range of justifiable transfer prices.
>
> *—South Africa Practice Note 7*

Although application of the most appropriate transfer pricing methods can give rise to a single arm's-length price or margin, in practice it is commonly the case that application of the most appropriate methods will give rise to a range of arm's-length results (an arm's-length range). This range may come about because[26]

- In using a single method, the arm's-length principle produces only an approximation of conditions that may be established between independent enterprises, and for this reason the comparables examined may lead to different results
- When using more than one method, differences in the nature of the methods and data relevant to applying each method may produce different results

In practice, an arm's-length range is more likely to arise due to multiple comparables (of equal reliability) that give rise to different arm's-length prices or margins (see figure 4.15), as opposed to the use of more than one method, since it is not common that more than one method is applied.

The relevance of the arm's-length range, and how it is determined, and, where necessary, how the appropriate point within the range is selected will depend on the relevant domestic law (see chapter 3).

Figure 4.15 Arm's-Length Range (EBIT/Sales)

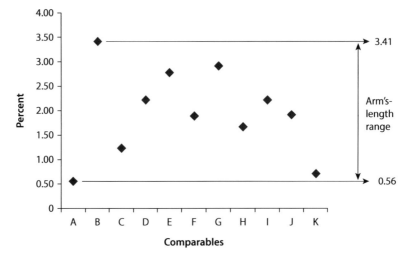

Note: EBIT = earnings before interest and tax.

Narrowing the Range

In some situations, it may be considered necessary to try to narrow the arm's-length range. In situations where a large pool of comparables with questionable comparability due to a lack of information is relied upon, statistical tools (such as the interquartile range) are sometimes used to narrow the range.

The acceptability of the use of statistical tools to narrow the range differs among countries. In some countries, the use of such statistical tools is accepted or even mandated, while in others the full range is to be considered (see chapter 3). Regardless of the approach adopted, there is a general consensus that when trying to narrow the range, the relative comparability of the uncontrolled transactions should be the starting point, before the use of statistical tools is contemplated, if at all (see box 4.18).

The most commonly used statistical tool for narrowing the range is the interquartile range (see figure 4.16). In the United States, for example, the arm's-length range will consist of the results of all of the uncontrolled comparables that meet the following conditions: (a) the information on the controlled transaction and the uncontrolled comparables is sufficiently complete that it is likely that all material differences have been identified; (b) each such difference has a definite and reasonably ascertainable effect on price or profit; and (c) an adjustment is made to eliminate the effect of each such difference.

Where these conditions are not met (i.e., where comparable information is constrained), the arm's-length range may need to be determined through applying statistical tools, namely the interquartile range. While there are different ways of calculating the interquartile range in practice,[27] in the IRC section 482 regulations the interquartile range is defined as follows:

> [T]he interquartile range is the range from the 25th to the 75th percentile of the results derived from the uncontrolled comparables. For this purpose, the

Box 4.18 HMRC Guidance on Narrowing the Range

HMRC International Manual reads as follows[a]:

Factors to take into account when trying to narrow the range

To narrow the range of results, you have to consider the comparable companies put forward very carefully. This involves looking at the available information about the comparable companies, in particular, what they say about themselves on their own websites. Think about the following points:

- Should any of the companies obviously be excluded? Are there any companies which should be included? This will involve you carrying out your own search of commercial databases. Companies do get missed out.
- Is there a subset of comparables within the larger range? For example, consider a company carrying out contract R&D in the field of computer software. You may find that the transfer pricing report contains 16 comparable companies carrying out contract R&D in the computer field (ranging from hardware, operating systems, communications, switching, and software), but that there are three companies involved in just software R&D. Why not use just those three companies as a starting point? These companies should, in theory, be more comparable to the tested party.

a. For more information, see the HMRC website at http://www.hmrc.gov.uk/manuals/intmanual/intm467150.htm#IDAXJJHG.

Figure 4.16 Interquartile Range (EBIT/Sales)

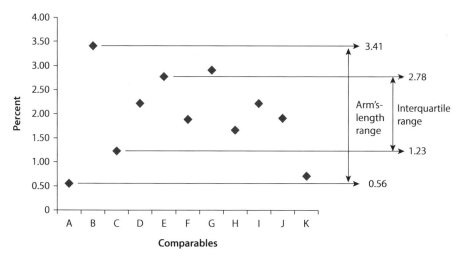

Note: EBIT = earnings before interest and tax.

25th percentile is the lowest result derived from an uncontrolled comparable such that at least 25 percent of the results are at or below the value of that result. However, if exactly 25 percent of the results are at or below a result, then the 25th percentile is equal to the average of that result and the next higher result derived from the uncontrolled comparables. The 75th percentile is determined analogously.

The position in the *OECD Transfer Pricing Guidelines* (2010a) is that statistical tools such as the interquartile range may be used to enhance the reliability of the analysis where the dataset is sufficiently large and comparability deficiencies remain, but only after attempts are made to exclude comparables that are less comparable.

It may also be the case that while every effort has been made to exclude points that have a lesser degree of comparability, what is arrived at is a range of figures for which comparability defects remain, that cannot be identified or quantified, and are therefore not adjusted. This may be due to the process used for selecting comparables and limitations on information availability. In such cases, if the range includes a sizeable number of observations, statistical tools to narrow the range (e.g., the interquartile range or other percentiles) might help to enhance the reliability of the analysis. Narrowing of the range is, however, not necessary where the observations all meet the standard of comparability and are equally reliable. In such cases, the use of the full range is most appropriate.

Selecting a Point within the Range

In most countries, where the price or margin used in the controlled transaction falls within the arm's-length range, no transfer pricing adjustment will generally be made (see chapter 3). However, where the price or margin falls outside of the arm's-length range, or where the MNE group is attempting to establish an arm's-length price or margin, then an appropriate point within the range will need to be selected.

In practice, various approaches are adopted to the selection of the appropriate point within the range. The *OECD Transfer Pricing Guidelines* (2010a) in paragraph 3.62, state that "[in] determining this point, where the range comprises results of relatively equal and high reliability, it could be argued that any point in the range satisfies the arm's-length principle." Therefore, in practice, the selection of the appropriate point in the range should be based on the facts and circumstances, weighing qualitative factors. However, in the absence of any factors or circumstances in favor of a particular point in the range, or where there are comparability defects (i.e., due to a lack of information or the use of "inexact" comparables), using measures of central tendency, such as the average (mean), median or weighted average, is recommended (see figure 4.17).

For example, the South African Revenue Service's Practice Note 7 states that "the Commissioner concurs with the view of the OECD that the adjustment should reflect the point in the range that best accounts for the facts and circumstances of the controlled transaction. However, in the absence of persuasive evidence for the selection of a particular point in the range, the Commissioner may select the mid-point in the range."[28] Similarly, in the United Kingdom, the *HMRC International Manual* states that "if unidentifiable or unquantifiable comparability defects remain (e.g., due to limitations in information available on the comparable transactions) the use of measures of central tendency such as the median, mean or weighted average, etc. may be useful in deciding where to set the transfer price. In all cases, selecting the appropriate measure of central tendency maximizes the likelihood that the adjusted price falls within the true arm's-length range."[29]

Figure 4.17 Example of Median, Average, and Weighted Average (EBIT/Sales)

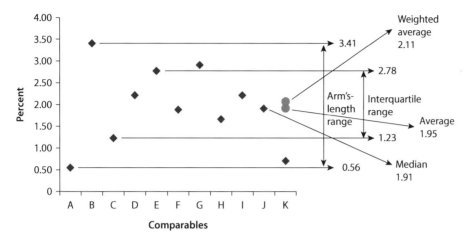

Note: EBIT = earnings before interest and tax.

Chapter 4 Main Messages

• Comparability is a cornerstone of the application of the arm's-length principle. Controlled and uncontrolled transactions are considered to be "comparable" if there are no differences between them that materially affect the condition being examined.

• Proper fact-finding to look beyond mere contracts is critical when undertaking a comparability analysis. This entails a determination of actual functions performed, risks assumed and controlled, and assets used by the relevant parties.

• The sources of information for identifying and analyzing potentially comparable transactions will vary and include internal and external comparables. Commonly used external sources of information include commercial databases, government bodies that collect and publish statutory accounts of local entities, company websites, and so on.

• The lack of comparable information is a major constraint faced in effectively applying transfer pricing legislation based on the arm's-length principle. A range of possible solutions and alternative approaches exists that can help address the dearth of information in practice.

• Most countries prescribe the five transfer pricing methods detailed in the *OECD Transfer Pricing Guidelines* as the applicable methods for determining consistency with the arm's-length principle, and numerous countries have included illustrative examples of the application of the methods in their administrative guidelines.

• Application of one-sided transfer pricing methods requires the selection of a tested party, which will generally be the party to the transaction with the least complex functional profile and for which the most reliable information is available.

• In practice the application of the most appropriate methods will typically give rise to a range of arm's-length results (an arm's-length range).

Transfer Pricing and Developing Economies • http://dx.doi.org/10.1596/978-1-4648-0969-9

Annex 4A: Sample Functional Analysis Questionnaire

The following questionnaire is from the IRS (2006, exhibit 4.61.3–4).

Analysis of Functions

I. Manufacturing

A. Materials Purchasing
   1. What materials or partly finished goods are purchased?
   2. From whom are purchases made?
   3. Are any purchases made from related companies?
   4. Where and how are raw materials purchased?
   5. Who performs the purchasing function?
   6. Who plans purchasing schedules?
   7. Who negotiates purchasing arrangements?
   8. Who approves the vendor as being of acceptable quality?
   9. Do purchasing decisions require head office approval?
   10. What are the other approvals required? Who makes these approvals?
   11. Are any purchases made on consignment?
   12. What are your major risks?

B. Inventory
   1. Where is inventory held?
   2. Who controls the levels of inventory?
   3. How are inventory levels controlled?
   4. Is there a computer system?
   5. Are any purchases made on consignment?
   6. How many days of inventory are on hand?
   7. Has there ever been a case, for whatever reason, where you were stuck with excess inventory?
   8. Who bears the cost of obsolete inventory?
   9. What are your major risks?

C. Production Equipment
   1. Who determines the purchasing budget?
   2. Who negotiates purchasing?
   3. Who maintains the plant?
   4. Who has expenditure authority for capital equipment?
   5. Who writes specifications for the plant?
   6. From whom is production equipment purchased?
   7. Are any purchases made from related companies?
   8. Do you have discretion over the equipment used?
   9. Can you modify the equipment?
   10. What decisions require head office approval?
   11. What are the approvals required?

D. Production Scheduling
1. Who is responsible for production scheduling decisions?
2. What factors enter the decisions?
3. When are the decisions made?
4. Is a computer system used?
5. What decisions require head office approval?
6. What are the approvals required?
7. What are your major risks?
8. Does your distributor buy everything you manufacture?

E. Manufacturing and Process Engineering
1. What products are produced?
2. Who designed the products and who owns the technology?
3. What is the manufacturing process?
4. Who developed the original process?
5. Have any improvements been made locally?
6. Is it possible to compare productivity between the subsidiaries in the group?
7. Have you ever utilized a third party to produce your products?

F. Package and Labeling
1. What packaging and labeling is done?
2. Where is it done?
3. Who makes the decisions in relation to packing and labeling?
4. Have you complete autonomy to make such decisions?

G. Quality Control
1. What form does quality control take?
2. Who sets finished product quality standards and procedures?
3. Who performs the quality control and who bears the cost?
4. Who provides the equipment and techniques for quality control?
5. How much product is lost because it fails quality and control checks?
6. What are your major risks?
7. What decisions require head office approval?
8. What are the approvals required?

H. Shipping of Products
1. Who pays freight charges for product in and out?
2. Who arranges shipping of products?
3. Who ships your products?
4. Where are the products shipped?
5. How are they shipped?
6. Who is responsible for the selection of shippers?
7. Who is responsible for shipping deadlines?
8. What are your major risks?
9. What decisions require head office approval?
10. What are the approvals required?

II. Research and Development

1. What research and development do you carry out?
2. Is any research and development carried out on your behalf by related companies?
3. Do you commission third parties to carry out research and development on your behalf?
4. Where are products designed?
5. What input do distributors have on manufacturing, product design or product modifications?
6. How important is the development of patents in the industry?
7. What patents do you own? Describe the unique products created by each patent.
8. What unpatented technical know-how have you developed that might differentiate your products from competitors, create import-cost efficiencies, or give you an advantage in increasing your market share?
9. What decisions require corporate head office approval?
10. What are the approvals required?
11. Who formulates the budget?
12. Are license agreements in existence between you and related companies or third parties?
13. Is there a cost-sharing agreement in force and if so, what are the details?
14. Provide a copy of the cost-sharing agreement and the relevant details.

III. Marketing

A. Strategic

1. Do you carry out your own marketing?
2. Are market surveys performed? Do you monitor market demand?
3. What decisions require head office approval?
4. What are the approvals required?
5. Who are your competitors?
6. Who assesses demand in foreign markets?
7. What are the risks related to demand for your products?
8. Who formulates the marketing budget?
9. Does your distributor always buy what your manufacturer produces?
10. Has your manufacturer ever refused to fill an order?
11. Do related companies carry out marketing on your behalf?
12. Are third-party distributors used?
13. Who chooses, authorizes, and controls third-party distributors?

B. Advertising, Trade Shows, etc.

1. What forms of marketing do you utilize?
2. What forms of advertising are used? Who pays for it?
3. Are trade shows used and, if so, who organizes them and who pays for them?

4. Are samples provided to distributors?
5. Who produces product brochures, specification sheets, etc.?
6. What marketing assistance do you receive?
7. What decisions require head office approval?
8. What are the approvals required?

IV. Sales and Distributions

A. Sales

1. How are sales made and who is involved?
2. Who issues the invoice to the customer?
3. Who issues the invoice to you?
4. Who formulates the projections and sets targets?
5. Where are sales orders received?
6. Who is responsible for the achievement of sales targets?
7. Who negotiates sales contracts? Do they operate autonomously?
8. Does your distributor always buy what your manufacturer produces?
9. How much is sold to related companies?
10. Are only finished goods shipped from here?
11. Who are your competitors?
12. What are the risks related to demand for your products?
13. What decisions require corporate head office approval?
14. What are the approvals required?
15. Are products exported? If so, who is responsible for the export function?
16. What are the major risks in selling products in foreign countries?

B. Quality Control

1. What form does quality control take?
2. Who sets finished product quality standards and procedures?
3. Who performs the quality control and who bears the cost?
4. Who provides the quality control and who bears the cost?
5. How much product is rejected by customers as below standard?
6. Who bears the loss on defective products?
7. What are your major risks?
8. What decisions require head office approval?
9. What are the approvals required?

C. Freight

1. Who pays freight charges for product in and out?
2. Who arranges shipping of products?
3. Who ships your products? To where? How?
4. Who is responsible for the selection of shippers?
5. Who is responsible for shipping deadlines?
6. What are your major risks?
7. What decisions require head office approval?
8. What are the approvals required?

D. Inventory
1. Do you actually receive the goods and hold stock?
2. Where is stock held?
3. Who controls the levels of inventory?
4. How are inventory levels controlled? Is there a computer system?
5. Are any purchases made on consignment?
6. How many days of inventory are on hand?
7. Has there ever been a case, for whatever reason, where you were stuck with excess inventory?
8. Who bears the cost of obsolete inventory?
9. What are your major risks?

E. Installation and After-Sales Services
1. Do you install your products?
2. Do you provide after-sales services? If so, describe the service.
3. Does any company carry out product repairs and who bears the cost?
4. Who bears the cost of installation and after-sales service?
5. Do you provide product guarantees?
6. Who bears warranty costs?

V. Administration and Other Services

A. General Administration
1. Is there a complete administration function?
2. Do related companies perform any administration for you?
3. What decisions require corporate head office approval?
4. What are the approvals required?
5. Who is responsible for administrative codes of practice?

B. Pricing Policy
1. Who determines the product pricing?
2. What is the pricing policy for the various goods and services?
3. What are your major risks?
4. What decisions require corporate head office approval?
5. What are the approvals required?

C. Accounting
1. What accounting functions are carried out? By whom?
2. Where are the financial reports prepared?
3. What decisions require head office approval?
4. What are the approvals required?
5. Is a bank account maintained? For what purpose?
6. Who has check signatory authority? What are the authority limits?
7. Do you bear the credit risk on sales to customers?
8. Who pays product liability insurance premiums?
9. Who arranges and pays for other insurance?

D. Legal

1. Who is responsible for legal matters?
2. What decisions require head office approval?
3. What are the approvals required?

E. Computer Processing

1. Is computer processing and programming done here? If not, by whom and where?
2. Who developed the software and is any charge made for it?
3. Who has expenditure authority for capital equipment?
4. What decisions require head office approval?
5. What are the approvals required?

F. Finance/Loans/Credit

1. Are there any intercompany loans or long-term receivables and, if so, is interest charged?
2. What trade credit terms are received and given?
3. Is interest paid or charged if credit periods are exceeded?
4. Who is responsible for borrowing requirements?
5. What are your major risks?
6. What decisions require head office approval?
7. What are the approvals required?

G. Personnel

1. Is there any compensation to or from overseas affiliates?
2. What positions do they hold in the company?
3. What training do you provide your employees?
4. What is the length of the training period?
5. Is there on-the-job training?
6. Where is management training done?
7. What is the staff turnover rate?
8. Are all employees on your payroll?
9. Who is responsible for the employment of staff?
10. What decisions require head office approval?
11. What are the approvals required?

H. Use of Property/Leasing

1. Is property owned or leased from affiliates?
2. Do you lease property to affiliates?
3. Who is responsible for this function?

VI. Executive

1. To whom does the general manager report?
2. Does anyone report to the parent company besides the general manager?
3. Who is responsible for dealing with government agencies?
4. What are some of the regulatory requirements?

5. Has the parent ever told you to use more procedures than you have developed?
6. How does manufacturing site selection occur?
7. Where does the initial impetus in relation to corporate decisions come from?
8. What decisions require head office approval?
9. What are the approvals required?

Analysis of Risks

I. Market Risk
1. What are the market risks?
2. Do you bear the market risks? If not, who does?
3. How significant are the market risks?

II. Inventory Risk
1. Does inventory become obsolete?
2. Who bears the cost of obsolete inventory?
3. Do you provide warranties in relation to finished goods?
4. Who bears the cost of returns under warranty?

III. Credit and Bad Debt Risk
1. What credit terms are given and received?
2. Do you bear the cost of bad debts? If not, who does?
3. Is this a significant risk?

IV. Foreign Exchange Risk

A.
1. Are you exposed to foreign exchange risk? If so, explain the risks.
2. How significant is the risk?
3. What steps do you take to minimize foreign exchange risk?
4. Do you have a manual that outlines your procedures/policies for dealing with foreign exchange risk? If so, provide a copy.
5. Do you engage in hedging of foreign exchange risk? If so, provide an explanation of your hedging activities.

Analysis of Intangibles
I. Manufacturing

A. Research and Development
1. Have you developed your own products? Are they unique?
2. Have you developed manufacturing processes?
3. How important are these processes to your business? Are they unique?

B. Manufacturing Processing/Technological Know-How
1. Do you possess technological know-how?
2. If so, what is its nature?

   3. How important to your business is the know-how?

   4. Is the know-how unique?

C. Trademarks/Patents, etc.

   1. Do you own any trademarks/patents?

   2. How significant are they to your business?

D. Product Quality

   1. Within your industry, and as compared to your competition, how would you rate the quality of your product?

E. Other

   1. Are there any other manufacturing intangibles?

   2. Request copies of all licensing agreements.

II. Marketing

A. Trademarks/Trade Names

   1. Do you own any trademarks/trade names?

   2. How significant are they to your business?

B. Corporate Reputation

   1. Do you consider that you have a corporate reputation?

   2. What is the nature of this reputation?

   3. Is corporate reputation significant in your business?

C. Developed Marketing Organization

   1. Do you have a developed marketing organization?

D. Ability to Provide Service to Customers

   1. Within your industry, and as compared to your competitors, how would you rate the quality of the services you provide to customers?

Annex 4B: Examples of Commercial Databases Used for Transfer Pricing

Table 4B.1 Common Commercial Databases

Provider	Database	Geographical Coverage	Content Coverage
Bloomberg[a]	Bloomberg Reference Data Services	Worldwide	Financial markets data
Bureau van Dijk[b]	Osiris	Worldwide	Company financial information (listed)
	Orbis	Worldwide	Company financial information (private and listed)
	Amadeus	Europe	As above
	Oriana	Asia-Pacific	As above
	Aida	Italy	As above
	Bel-first	Belgium-Luxembourg	As above
	Dafne	Germany	As above
	Diane	France	As above
	Fame	United Kingdom and Ireland	As above
	Icarus	United States and Canada	As above
	Odin	Nordic and Baltic	As above
	Mint Korea	Korea, Rep.	As above
	Reach	Netherlands	As above
	Ruslana	Russian Federation, Ukraine, and Kazakhstan	As above
	Sabi	Spain and Portugal	As above
	Sabina	Austria	As above
	Zephyr	Worldwide	Mergers and acquisitions information
Capital Market Publishers India	Capitaline TP[c]	India	Company financial information (private and listed)
Centre for Monitoring Indian Economy[d]	Prowess[e]	India	Company financial information (private and listed)
Dun & Bradstreet	Company360[f]	Australia	Company financial information (private and listed)
	Mergent Million Dollar Directory[g]	United States	Company information (private and listed)
Hedge Fund Research	HFR Database	United States	Hedge fund information
IBISWorld	IBISWorld	Australia	Company financial information (private and listed)
InfoCredit	Teigil	Poland	Company financial information (private and listed)
Intangible Spring[h]	Intangible Spring	Worldwide (United States and Canada)	Invotex Group[j]
Interfax	SPARK	Russia, Ukraine, and Kazakhstan	Company financial information (private and listed)
Invotex Group[j]	Royalty Connection	Worldwide (United States)	Intangibles license agreements (sourced from U.S. SEC)
KIS-Line[k]	KIS-Line	Korea, Rep.	Company financial information (private and listed)
Kompass[l]	Kompass	Worldwide	Company information (private and listed)

table continues next page

Table 4B.1 Common Commercial Databases *(continued)*

Provider	Database	Geographical Coverage	Content Coverage
ktMine[m]	ktMine IP[n]	Worldwide (United States)	Intangibles license agreements and royalty rates
Moody's Analytics[o]	RiskCalc Plus	Worldwide (29 models)	Risk of default models (credit score)
Rimes[p]	Rimes	Worldwide	Financial markets data, commodities, hedge funds and properties/REITs
Range royalty[q]	Range royalty	Europe	Intangibles license agreements and royalty rates
Onecle[r]	Business Contracts	United States	Business contract filings (SEC)
Royaltystat[s]	Licence Agreements Database	Worldwide (United States)	Intangibles license agreements (sourced from U.S. SEC)
RoyaltySource	RoyaltySource	Worldwide (United States)	Intangibles license agreements (sourced from U.S. SEC)
Standard and Poor's	Capital IQ—Financials[t]	Worldwide	Company financial information (private and listed)
	Compustat—North America	North America	Company financial information (listed)
	Compustat Global	Worldwide	Company financial information (listed)
	Credit Analytics	Worldwide	Risk of default models (credit score)
Thompson Reuters[u]	Dealscan[v]	Worldwide	Financial transactions data (loans)
	Eikon	Worldwide	Financial markets data
	Lipper	United States	Fund management data
	Worldwide public company data	Worldwide	Company financial information (listed)
	Worldwide private company data	Worldwide	Company financial information (private and listed)
	Worldwide intangibles data	Worldwide	Intangibles license agreements and royalty rates

Source: Based on mimeo by Christ, Cooper, and Loeprick 2015, information as of January 2014.

Note: List is not intended to be exhaustive. There is a range of other providers. REIT = real estate investment trust; SEC = Securities and Exchange Commission.

a. For more information, see Bloomberg's website at http://www.bloomberg.com/enterprise/data/reference-data-services/.

b. For more information, see Bureau van Dijk's website at http://www.bvdinfo.com/en-gb/products/product-selector/product-recommendations.

c. For more information, see Capitaline TP's website at http://www.capitaline.com/new/tp.asp.

d. For more information, see Centre for Monitoring Indian Economy's website at http://www.cmie.com/.

e. For more information, see Centre for Monitoring Indian Economy's website on Prowess at http://www.cmie.com/kommon/bin /sr.php?kall=wcontact&page=prowess.

f. For more information, see Company360's website at http://www.company360.com.au/.

g. For more information, see Mergent Million Dollar Directory's website at http://www.mergent.com/solutions/private-company-solutions /million-dollar-directory-(mddi).

h. For more information, see Intangible Spring's website at http://www.intangiblespring.com/pages/data.

i. For more information, see Invotex Group's website at https://www.royaltyconnection.com/.

j. For more information, see Invotex Group's website at https://www.royaltyconnection.com/.

k. For more information, see KIS-Line's website at http://www.kisline.com/.

l. For more information, see Kompass's website at http://rs3.kompass.com/en.

m. For more information, see ktMine's website at http://www.ktmine.com/.

n. For more information, see ktMine's website at http://www.ktmine.com/products/ktmine-ip/.

o. For more information, see Moody's Analytics's website at http://www.moodysanalytics.com/riskcalc2013.

p. For more information, see Rimes's website at http://www.rimes.com/.

q. For more information, see Range royalty's website at http://www.rangeroyalty.com/.

r. For more information, see Onecle's website at http://www.onecle.com/.

s. For more information, see Royaltystat's website at https://www.royaltystat.com/.

t. For more information, see S&P Global's website at https://www.capitaliq.com/home/what-we-offer/information-you-need/financials-valuation /financials.aspx.

u. For more information, see Thompson Reuters' website at https://tax.thomsonreuters.com/products/brands/onesource/onesource-transfer -pricing/comparable-databases/.

v. For more information, see Dealscan's website at http://www.loanconnector.com/dealscan/LPC_WEB_DS_SecurID.html.

Annex 4C: Example of Comparables Search Process

The following section sets out an example of a search process for the identification, analysis, and selection of external comparables using commercial databases and supplementary information sources. As depicted in figure 4C.1, the process is not necessarily linear, since steps may have to be revised and repeated as required.

Step 1: Database Selection and Screening

Determine and apply search parameters based on significant comparability factors to narrow the pool of potential comparables.

Examples of search parameters that may be used when searching for entities carrying out comparable transactions are set out in table 4C.1. Where the search is for a specific transaction type, such as loans or royalties, a different approach will likely be required.[30]

When determining the appropriate search parameters in practice, a balance between being too specific and being too general is required so as to sufficiently limit the results returned to results that are highly likely to be potential comparables, while at the same time not ruling out potential comparables that may not meet the initial search criteria.

Application of the search parameters to the relevant information source(s) will ideally result in a pool of potential comparables being identified. In practice, however, it is quite common that a search based on the search parameters

Figure 4C.1 Example of External Comparable Search Process

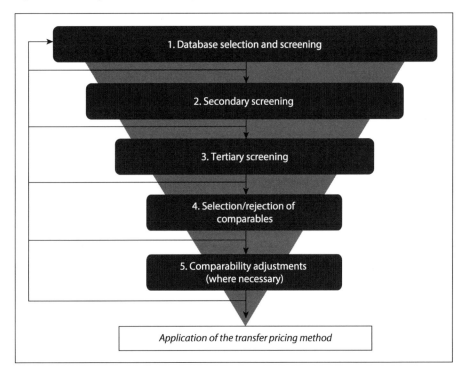

Table 4C.1 Example of Search Parameters

Industry	Commercial databases usually assign one or more industry classifications to entities that can be used to identify entities operating in the same entity and at the same level in the supply chain. These industry classifications are generally based on international or national coding systems, such as ISIC, United Nations; SIC, United States; NACE, European Union, and other country-specific codifications such as UKSIC, United Kingdom; OKVED, Russian Federation, etc.
Geographic location	A search parameter based on geographic location can assist with the identification of comparables that face similar economic circumstances. The appropriate search parameter may be country-specific, subregional, regional, or global depending on the facts and circumstances.
Size	Search parameters that limit the results to entities of a particular size (based on turnover, net assets, or number of employees, etc.) can assist with the identification of functionally comparable entities.
Independence	Commercial databases often allow for the application of independence thresholds (generally based on ownership percentages) that can be used to limit the results to independent enterprises. This can assist with identifying independent enterprises (or those not engaging in controlled transactions). In practice, some flexibility may be required, however, since the relevant threshold for determining whether or not entities are acceptable as comparables will generally depend on the relevant domestic law and practices. For example, in some countries entities engaging in a small (immaterial) percentage of transactions with related parties may be considered acceptable.
Availability of information	For an entity to be a potentially useful comparable, sufficient financial information must be publicly available for the relevant period (years) under review.
Year of incorporation or trading status	Search parameter that excludes recently established entities or entities that have gone into administration or liquidation can be used, if necessary, to eliminate startup entities and failed entities from the search results.
Keywords	Keyword searches that reflect economically important characteristics of the controlled transaction (that target business descriptions) may be used to narrow the search results.

Note: The examples are for illustrative purposes only. In practice, the appropriate search criteria will depend on the facts and circumstances. ISIC = International Standard Industrial Classification of All Economic Activities; SIC = Standard Industrial Classification; NACE = Nomenclature statistique des activités économiques dans la Communauté européenne; OKVED = Russian Economic Activities Classification System; UKSIC = United Kingdom Standard Industrial Classification of Economic Activities.

initially determined will return insufficient results. Where this is the case, it may be necessary to modify the search parameters, thus widening the initial stage of the search (see figure 4C.2).

While modification of the initial search parameters is often required in practice, the need to ensure that transactions (or entities) are sufficiently comparable remains. Thus, care should be taken so as to modify search parameters without materially affecting the comparability of the pool of potential comparables. How the search criteria can be modified will depend

Figure 4C.2 Modifying the Initial Search Parameters

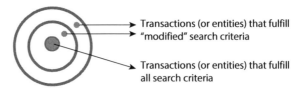

Transactions (or entities) that fulfill "modified" search criteria

Transactions (or entities) that fulfill all search criteria

on the facts and circumstances of the case, and requires experience and judgment. For example, for certain transaction types, expanding the geographical search parameters (i.e., inclusion of similar countries or an entire region) may be acceptable. This will, however, depend on the market within which the controlled transactions take place and thus the impact that differences in location may have on the condition being examined. Other examples of modifications include expanding the scope of the industries in which uncontrolled transactions may take place, or loosening constraints on the size of the entities under review (i.e., the range of acceptable turnover levels or number of employees).

Step 2: Secondary Screening

Where the pool of potential comparables identified from the primary screening is large, additional quantitative screening may be required to narrow down the pool of potential comparables. Where the pool of potential comparables is not very large, this additional screening may not be required.

Additional quantitative screening may involve

- Basic screening of financial information to ensure sufficient data are reported (i.e., relevant turnover, gross margin, net margin data, etc.)
- Use of diagnostic ratios to further reduce the pool of potential comparables (see box 4C.1)

Step 3: Tertiary Screening

To further narrow the pool of potential comparables, qualitative screening may be required. This will often involve a review of various sources of qualitative information, such as

- Business descriptions in database[31]
- Company homepages
- Internet (business directories and associations, etc.)

These sources of information are used to identify information (such as that regarding business strategies, new business activities, and so on) that may indicate that an entity is not comparable.

Box 4C.1 Use of Diagnostic Ratios to Reduce the Pool of Potential Comparables

Diagnostic ratios are financial ratios against which the financial data of potential comparables can be tested to narrow the pool of potential comparables. According to Gommers, Reyneveld, and Lund (2007), the application of diagnostic ratios is based on the assumption that a diagnostic ratio constitutes a reflection of the companies functional and risk profile. Examples of diagnostic ratios include

- Intangible assets over total assets
- Days of inventory (average)
- Days receivable (average)
- Days payable (average)
- Turnover per employee
- Fixed assets over total assets
- Inventory over sales
- Fixed assets to number of employees
- Fixed assets to total sales
- R&D expense over sales

These ratios may be applied using cutoff criteria and or statistical tools (such as ranges).

The selection of appropriate diagnostic ratios will depend on the facts and circumstances, including the nature of the business activities and the information available.

When applying diagnostic ratios, caution must be exercised since potentially comparable transactions may be rejected. In this regard, Gommers, Reyneveld, and Lund (2007, 222) note that "the rationale for applying diagnostic ratios is a compromise between accuracy and efficiency."

Step 4: Selection or Rejection of Comparables

The final set of potential comparables should be subject to a comparability analysis, taking into account all five of the comparability factors and identifying any economically important similarities or differences between the uncontrolled transactions and the controlled transactions.

Where commercial databases are relied upon to identify comparables, all of the information necessary to perform a comprehensive comparability analysis will generally not be available through the database. It is, therefore, often necessary to obtain and review copies of the original statutory accounts and to undertake further research to confirm and refine the comparables. This will generally involve detailed research on the Internet, reference to trade journals and news articles, sourcing and review of annual reports, and, in some instances, interviews with personnel. Company websites can provide information regarding the comparability factors and may provide access to copies of statutory accounts, particularly where shares in the company are publicly traded. These sources of information may be supplemented by information obtained from other sources, such as trade journals, newspaper articles, company brochures, and interviews. Further analysis may also be required to identify differences in accounting treatment and determine appropriate adjustments.

Where information is not available regarding comparability factors, judgment may be required regarding the deficiency; and where differences that may materially impact the condition being examined are identified, comparability adjustments may be required (see step 5). If crucial information is not available and judgment cannot be exercised regarding the deficiency, or if reasonably accurate comparability adjustments cannot be made, the potential comparable may need to be rejected as a comparable. In this regard, the Australian Taxation Office has published a decision tree that can assist with assessing the reliability of comparables. A copy of this decision tree is in annex 4B. In this regard, it is also important to note that the size of the sample pool (i.e., a larger number of "comparables") does not make up for poor quality data (OECD 2011a).

Step 5: Comparability Adjustments (where necessary)

Where differences exist between the comparable transactions and the controlled transactions, comparability adjustments may be required before the applicable transfer pricing method can be applied. Where accurate and reliable comparability adjustments that neutralize the impact of the difference that is materially impacting the condition being examined cannot be made, the transaction or entity will need to be rejected as a comparable.

Step 6: Apply the Transfer Pricing Method

Once the final pool of comparables or single comparable is identified, the applicable transfer pricing method is then applied to establish an arm's-length price or margin or range of arm's-length prices or margins.

Annex 4D: Steps in the Comparability Analysis

Comparability analysis (3.4)

	Step 1	Step 2	Step 3	Step 4	Step 5	Step 6	Step 7	Step 8	Step 9
	Years	Broad-based analysis	Controlled transaction(s)	Internal comparables	External comparables	Transfer pricing method	Potential comparables	Comparability adjustments	Arm's-length nature
	Determine years to be covered (3.75–79)	Analyze industry sector (1.34) Analyze MNE group's business strategies, markets, products, supply chain and key function, assets and risks (1.34)	Identify MNE members' operations (1.35) Identify commercial or financial relations with associated enterprises (1.36), consider: Contractual terms (1.42–50) Functional analysis (1.51–106) Characteristics of property or service (1.107–109) Economic circumstances (1.110–113) Business strategies (1.114–118)	Review existing internal comparables, if any (3.27, 28)	Determine available sources of information on external comparables, if needed (3.29–36)	Select most appropriate transfer pricing method (2.2), e.g.: CUP (2.13–20) RPM (2.21–38) CPM (2.39–55) TNMM (2.58–107) PSM (2.108–145) Consider options realistically available (1.40) Select tested party (3.18, 19) and net profit indicator (2.76–102), if needed	Identify (select or reject) potential comparables (3.40–46) Consider comparability factors (1.36, 39)	Determine and make comparability adjustments, if appropriate (3.47–54) Consider comparability factors (1.36, 39)	Interpret and use collected data (3.4) Determine arm's-length pricing (3.55–66)

Start (3.4) → Identification/delineation (1.33) → Comparison/pricing (1.33, 1.36 together with Ch 1-10)

Special framework for analyzing risk (1.60)

1. Identify key risks with specificity (1.71–76)
2. Contractual assumption of risk (1.77–81)
3. Functional analysis in relation to risk (1.82–85)
4. Interpret the information (1.86–97)
5. Allocation of risk (1.98, 99)
6. Pricing (1.100–106) or non-recognition (1.119–128) of transaction

Special framework for analyzing intangibles (6.34)

1. Identify, with specificity, intangibles (6.5–31) and key risks associated with DEMPE (6.65)
2. Contractual arrangements (6.35–46)
3. Functional analysis in relation to intangibles (6.47–72)
4. Confirm consistency (6.34)
5. Delineate the transaction (6.34)
6. Pricing (6.73, 74) or non-recognition (1.119–128) of transaction

Source: Good and Hedlund 2015.
Notes: MNE: Multinational Enterprise; Numbers in parentheses reference OECD guidelines.

Annex 4E: Comparability Adjustment Examples

The following examples are provided for illustrative purposes only and simply represent one possible approach to such adjustments, which may or may not be appropriate in a particular case.

Adjustments for Accounting Differences

In practice, different accounting standards and approaches may be adopted by entities and this can impact the financial information that is reported, resulting in timing differences (i.e., due to different depreciation or amortization methods, or different inventory accounting systems[32]), permanent differences (due to the recognition of certain income or expense), or classification differences (e.g., capitalization of certain expenditures or inclusion in cost of goods sold). These differences can have a material impact on the condition being examined, depending on the transfer pricing method being applied.

Differences in accounting treatment that give rise to classification differences and permanent differences can require adjustments to ensure comparability. The type of adjustments and the acceptability and appropriateness will depend on the particular facts and circumstances. One such adjustment that is sometimes made in practice, however, is adjustment for employee stock-based compensation.

Example: Employee Stock-Based Compensation Adjustment

The basic premise for making a stock-based compensation adjustment is that employee stock-based compensation is a form of employee remuneration (i.e., similar to wages and bonuses). As employee stock-based compensation is not always subject to uniform accounting treatment, this can lead to distortions in a company's financials that have a material impact on the condition being examined (e.g., the net margin) that may require adjustment,[33] as is illustrated by the following example.

A comparison is being made of the net margins earned in controlled transactions entered into by Enterprise A and the net margins earned in uncontrolled transactions entered into by Enterprise B.

- Enterprise A has booked employee stock option compensation as an expense.
- Enterprise B has disclosed that it awarded its employees stock-based compensation during the relevant year of US$3.25 million after tax, but that no employee stock-based compensation expense has been booked.

This difference in treatment has a material impact on the net margin reported by Enterprise B, since its expenses are understated as compared to Enterprise A. To adjust for this material difference, assuming a statutory tax rate of 35 percent, the reported US$3.25 million after-tax stock-based compensation is first grossed up to a before-tax amount of US$5 million (US$3.25/(1−0.35),[34] and Enterprise B's net margin is adjusted accordingly (table 4E.1):

Table 4E.1 Adjustment for Employee Stock-Based Compensation

	Enterprise B (before adjustment)	Enterprise B (after adjustment)
Revenue	100	100
Cost of goods sold	(65)	65
Gross profit	35	35
Selling, general, and administrative expenses	(20)	(25)
Depreciation	(5)	(5)
Net profit	10	5
Net margin (%)	10	5

Working Capital Adjustments

When applying the transaction net margin method, adjustments to take into account differences in the level of working capital of the tested party and the comparables may be appropriate. Such adjustments are referred to as "working capital adjustments," and they are commonly seen in practice.

The basic premise for making a working capital adjustment is the time value of money. For example, if an enterprise offers its customers extended payment terms of net 180 days and, therefore, carried high accounts receivable as compared to other enterprises that offer payment terms of net 30 days, in a competitive market this difference would likely be reflected in the price charged by the enterprise providing extended payment terms, since it will charge a higher price to cover its cost of financing these longer credit terms or for the opportunity cost of not being able to invest any surplus. The opposite applies for enterprises with high accounts payable, which will have lower costs of finance or can invest any cash surplus. Working capital adjustment seeks to adjust for such differences to take into account the time value of money, on the basis that differences should be reflected in the enterprises' profitability.

Example: Working Capital Adjustment

TestCo (the tested party) has been identified as having significantly higher levels of working capital as compared to CompCo (a comparable entity). To adjust for this, first the differences in the levels of working capital as between the tested party and the comparables are identified and measured against an appropriate base. In this example, trade receivables, trade payables, and inventories are considered, and the differences are applied against a sales base (on the basis that the TNMM is being applied using a sales-based financial indicator) (table 4E.2).[35]

The differences between TestCo and CompCo are then calculated, and the time value of money is reflected by multiplying the difference by an appropriate interest rate. This adjustment is then applied to CompCo's EBIT/sales ratio to produce a working capital adjusted EBIT/sales ratio (table 4E.3).

Table 4E.2 Working Capital Adjustment

TESTCO	Year 1	Year 2	Year 3	Year 4	Year 5
Sales	$1 79.5m	$182.5m	$187m	S195m	$198m
EBIT	$1.5m	$ 1.83m	$2.43m	$2.54m	$1.78m
EBIT'/sales (%)	0.8	1	1.3	1.3	0.9
Working capital (at end of year)					
Trade receivables (R)	$30m	$32m	$33m	$35m	$37m
Inventories (I)	$36m	$36m	$38m	$40m	$45m
Trade payables (P)	$20m	$21m	$26m	$23m	$24m
Receivables (R) + inventory (I) −payables (P)	$46m	$47m	$45m	$52m	$58m
(R + I − P)/sales (%)	25.6	25.8	24.1	26.7	29.3

COMFCO	Year 1	Year 2	Year 3	Year 4	Year 5
Sales	$120.4m	$121.2m	$121.8m	$126.3m	$130.2m
EBIT	$1.59m	$3.59m	S3.15m	$4.18m	$6.44m
EBIT/sales (%)	1.32	2.96	2.59	3.31	4.95
Working capital (at end of year)					
Trade receivables (R)	$17m	$18m	$20m	$22m	$23m
Inventory (I)	$18m	$20m	$26m	$24m	$25m
Trade payables (P)	$11m	$13m	$11m	$15m	$16m
Receivables (R) + inventory (I) − payables (P)	$24ra	$25m	$35 m	$31m	$32m
(R + I − P)/sales (%)	19.9	20.6	28.7	24.5	24.6

Note: EBIT = earnings before interest and tax.

Table 4E.3 Working Capital Adjustment Results
percent

Working Capital Adjustment	Year 1	Year 2	Year 3	Year 4	Year 5
TestCo's (R + I − P)/sales	25.6	25.8	24.1	26.7	29.3
CompCo's (R + I − P)/sales	19.9	20.6	28.7	24.5	24.6
Difference (D)	5.7	5.1	−4.7	2.1	4.7
Interest rate (i)	4.8	5.4	5.0	5.5	4.5
Adjustment (D*i)	0.27	0.28	−0.23	0.12	0.21
CompCo's EBIT/sales (%)	1.32	2.96	2.59	3.31	4.95
Working capital adjusted EBIT/sales for CompCo	1.59	3.24	2.35	3.43	5.16

Note: EBIT = earnings before interest and tax.

It is important to note that this is just one way in which working capital adjustments can be calculated. Alternative approaches include adjusting the tested parties' results to reflect those of the comparables and adjusting both the tested party and the comparables' results to reflect zero working capital. Different measures of working capital may be considered appropriate so as to give a better reflection of working capital levels in the relevant period (since average values are often used). Another important issue is the selection of the appropriate interest rate. Generally, this rate should reflect the commercial borrowing rate of the entity. However, where net working capital is negative (i.e., trade payable exceeds inventory and trade receivables) a different interest rate may be appropriate.

Country-Specific Risk Adjustments

Differences in the risk profiles of enterprises may have material effects on the condition being examined, and thus may require adjustments to be considered comparable. For example, country-specific risk adjustments are of particular importance in developing countries, where foreign comparables are often relied upon out of necessity.

For example, assume that the tested party is located in Country A, and the only possible sources of comparable information are enterprises located in Country B, which has a different level of country risk. In this situation, it may be necessary to adjust for this difference in country-specific risk. Such an adjustment would likely be based on the generally accepted notion that "[u]sually, in the open market, the assumption of increased risk would also be compensated by an increase in the expected return."[36]

There are numerous ways that such risk can be adjusted for in practice,[37] ranging from the very complex to the relatively simple, all of which have relative advantages and disadvantages. However, identifying good indicators to capture country-specific effects when using comparable information for transfer pricing studies is challenging, if not unrealistic. Recent analysis has broadly established that country-level determinants are relevant to understanding firm performance dynamics (Hawawini et al. 2004; Makino, Isobe, and Chan 2004). Proxies to adjust for these differences are, however, not readily available, and the approaches put forward for adjustments in day-to-day transfer pricing practice are exposed to a range of empirical challenges.

The following is an example of a simplified country-specific risk adjustment.

Example: Simplified Country Risk Adjustment[38]

The tested party (TestCo) is a contract manufacturer operating in Country A, and the only available comparable (CompCo) is contract manufacturer operating in Country B (table 4E.4).

The country risk in Country A is considered to be considerably higher than that in Country B, and thus it is considered necessary to adjust for this country risk. The adjustment is calculated by adjusting the operating profit of CompCo to reflect the additional return on operating asset in accordance with the country-specific risk premium. The average long-term government bond yield is used as a proxy for the country-specific risk premium.

The adjustment for country-specific risk is then calculated as follows:

> [Operating assets of CompCo] x [country-specific risk premium]
> = [100] x [4 percent]
> = 4

This additional 4 of profit, which reflects the increased return for the notional country-specific risk borne by CompCo for the purposes of the comparability analysis, is then added to the operating margin of CompCo. One shortcoming of this type of adjustment is that it increases the operating margin in order to take into account a return for increased risk, but does not take into consideration that with increased risk comes the possibility of a loss or lower operating margin.

Table 4E.4 Country Risk Adjustments

	TestCo (Country A)	CompCo (Country B)
Sales	100	120
Total costs	80	90
Operating profit	20	30
Operating assets	80	100

	Country A	Country B
Average long-term government bond yield (%)	9	5
Government bond yield gap (%)	4	

	TestCo (Country A)	CompCo (Country B)
Sales	100	120
Total costs	80	90
Adj. operating profit	20	34
Operating assets	80	100

Notes

1. See further, chapter on comparability analysis in the *UN Practical Manual on Transfer Pricing for Developing Countries* (2013).

2. Under the Incoterm standard published by the International Chamber of Commerce, FOB designates that the passing of risks occurs when the goods pass the ship's rail at the port of shipment; CFR and CIF, on the other hand, designate that the risk is transferred to the buyer once the goods are loaded on the vessel, and that the seller pays costs and freight (and insurance in the case of CIF) to bring the goods to the port of destination.

3. Simply performing more functions, bearing greater risks, and employing greater assets do not necessarily lead to high profitability. However, implicit in bearing more risk is the possibility of that risk materializing, resulting in decreased profitability or even losses.

4. See revisions to chapter 1, section D 1.59-1.106. Amendments in October 2015 by the Final Reports on BEPS Actions 8-10: "Aligning Transfer Pricing Outcomes with Value Creation."

5. See for example: *Commissioner of Taxation v. SNF Australia Pty Ltd. 2011 ATC 20-265* (Australia) where Ryan, Jessup, and Perram found that the evidence "pointed to the existence of a global market" and that "standing back from the evidence that conclusion should hardly be surprising: the products in question were high-volume industrial chemicals used in worldwide industries and inherently transportable. It is difficult to see how the market could not be a global one."

6. See further, chapter 1 of the *OECD Transfer Pricing Guidelines* (2010a) (revised in October 2015) and chapter on comparability analysis in the *UN Manual*.

7. For example, in its announcement and report concerning Advance Pricing Agreement (March 29, 2011) the U.S. IRS disclosure that the following sources of comparable information were used (with varying degrees of frequency): Compustat, Disclosure;

Mergent; Worldscope; Amadeus; Moody's; Australian Business Who's Who; Capital IO; Global Vantage; SEC; Osiris; Japan Accounts and Data on Enterprises (JADE); and "others." See the IRS website at http://www.irs.gov/pub/irs-utl/2010statutoryreport.pdf.

8. In Austria, for example, in the early 2000s Austrian tax administrators were confronted with the submission of an increasing number of transfer pricing studies based on commercial databases. Without having access to the same data source, options for the evaluation of the quality of the studies received were limited. This was particularly challenging regarding information on foreign comparables included in the studies (information regarding domestic comparables could at least be cross-checked with Austrian tax data, although this information could later not be relied on in a case due to tax secrecy). A cost-benefit analysis following a one-year pilot subscription showed that additional audit findings based on adjusted studies outweighed the cost of subscription.

9. See for, example, the Australian Securities and Investment Commission and the U.S. SEC.

10. See *OECD Transfer Pricing Guidelines* (2010a, paragraph 3.37).

11. The issue of a lack of comparable data for transfer pricing analyses was highlighted in a report to the Group of Twenty (20) major economies Development Working Group on the Impact of BEPS in Low Income Countries. To provide guidance on this challenge, the G20 mandated international organizations (the IMF, OECD, UN, and WBG) to develop a toolkit on "Addressing Difficulties in Accessing Comparables Data for Transfer Pricing Analysis." The toolkit is forthcoming in 2016/17.

12. For simplicity, for the purposes of the survey no distinction was made between "foreign comparables" and the use of "other markets data" (as outlined earlier). Thus in the presentation of the survey results the term *foreign comparables* encompasses the use of both (Christ, Cooper, and Loeprick 2015).

13. See OECD's website at http://www.oecd.org/dataoecd/41/4/45765363.pdf.

14. In other words, first in first out (FIFO), last in first out (LIFO).

15. *OECD Transfer Pricing Guidelines* (2010a), chapter 3, section 3.36.

16. See further OECD Secretariat note on "comparability adjustments" (2011), available at the OECD website, http://www.oecd.org/dataoecd/41/3/45765353.pdf, and the draft of the comparability analysis chapter of *UN Manual*.

17. See *OECD Transfer Pricing Guidelines* (2010a, paragraph 3.50).

18. Where operating costs are included, the condition being examined is based on the net margin (i.e., a full cost markup). Hence it is the TNMM that is being applied (see "Transactional Net Margin Method") as opposed to the cost-plus method.

19. With the exception of the Berry ratio, where reliable gross profit information is needed.

20. See Final Reports on BEPS Actions 8-10: "Aligning Transfer Pricing Outcomes with Value Creation."

21. The first step is to determine the relevant profit/losses the parties that relate to the controlled transactions. This requires a normalization of accounting treatment among other considerations.

22. See further Gonnet and Fris (2007).

23. *Comparable profit split* is not a term used in the *OECD Transfer Pricing Guidelines* (2010a). However, in paragraph 2.119 reference to the use of market data in applying the contribution analysis is made: "[t]his division can be supported by comparables data where available."

24. Note that when applying profit split method using a residual analysis (see "Residual Analysis"), more than one method is being applied in the broadest sense.

25. See further paragraphs 2.1–2.10 of the OECD *Transfer Pricing Guidelines* (2010a).

26. Paragraph 2.83 of Australian Taxation Ruling TR 97/20.

27. The main difference relates to whether or not the upper or lower quartile must be an actual observation from the dataset itself, or whether they can fall between observations, as is the case under IRC section 482 regulations (which require that the average between two observations be used if exactly 25 percent of observations are at or below the observation).

28. See SARS Practice Note 7, paragraph 11.4.7.

29. INTM467150. http://www.hmrc.gov.uk/manuals/intmanual/intm467150.htm#IDAXJJHG.

30. For example, the search criteria will need to focus on the significant comparability factors that are particular to those transaction types (i.e., for loans, the currency, term, and credit rating of the lender may be relevant search parameters, among others).

31. Where possible these descriptions should be corroborated against other sources (such as company homepages), as, for various reasons, descriptions lifted from public filings can often be outdated or inaccurate.

32. That is, first in first out (FIFO), last in first out (LIFO).

33. On employee stock option plans and transfer pricing see further, OECD *Employee Stock Option Plans: Impact on Transfer Pricing*, available at http://www.oecd.org/dataoecd/35/37/33700408.pdf.

34. Implicit in this adjustment is the assumption that the US$3.25 million after-tax amount disclosure by Company B has been determined based on similar principles to those adopted by Company B (i.e., fair value or cost basis) and that 35 percent statutory rate is appropriate for grossing up the after-tax amount to determine a before-tax amount.

35. Based on the example in OECD Secretariat Note on "Comparability Adjustments" (2010)—http://www.oecd.org/dataoecd/41/3/45765353.pdf.

36. OECD *Transfer Price Guidelines* (2010a, paragraph 1.45).

37. See, for example, Cody and Fickling (2003), Curtis and Ruhashyankiko (2003), Scholz (2006)), Scholz (2004), and Young (2000).

38. Based on example in presentation by Büttner (2010).

Bibliography

Ansoff, I. 1957. "Strategies for Diversification." *Harvard Business Review* 35: 113–24.

Büttner, W. 2010. "Use of Foreign Comparables and Comparability Adjustments for Economic (Market) Differences." Presented at a workshop on Transfer Pricing and Exchange of Information, OECD, Quito, Ecuador, August 24–27.

CFFR (Centre for Financial Reporting Reform). 2016. *Mission Statement*. Washington DC, World Bank. http://siteresources.worldbank.org/EXTCENFINREPREF/Resources/CFRR_brochure_spreads.pdf.

Christ, D., J. Cooper, and J. Loeprick. 2015. *Transfer Pricing Challenges in the Absence of Comparable Information*. Mimeo.

Cody, B. J., and S. R. Fickling. 2003. *Using Real Options to Design Transfer Pricing Policies*. 11 Transfer Pricing Report 990, March 19.

Cooper, J., and R. Agarwal. 2011. "The Transactional Profit Methods in Practice: A Survey of APA Reports." *International Transfer Pricing Journal* 18 (1).

Curtis, S. L., and J. F. Ruhashyankiko. 2003. *Risk Adjustments to the Comparables Range* (12 Transfer Pricing Report 176, July 9).

E-Gain Communications Private Limited (Pune Tribunal) (India). http://itatonline.org /archives/index.php/e-gain-communication-vs-ito-itat-pune-53-mb/.

EuropeAid and PricewaterhouseCoopers. 2011. Transfer Pricing and Developing Countries. Appendix D: Country Case Study Kenya. Brussels: EuropeAid and Pricewaterhouse Coopers. http://ec.europa.eu/taxation_customs/sites/taxation/files/resources/documents /common/publications/studies/transfer_pricing_dev_countries.pdf.

Gommers, E., J. Reyneveld, and H. Lund. 2007. "Pan-European Comparable Searches: Enhancing Comparability Using Diagnostic Ratios." *International Transfer Pricing Journal* 4: 219–27.

Gonnet, S., and P. Fris. 2007. "Contribution Analysis under the Profit Split Method." *International Tax Review Intellectual Property Supplement.* http://www.nera.com /extImage/PUB_ContributionAnalyses_ITR_Dec2007.pdf.

Good, O., and J. Hedlund. 2015. "Implications of BEPS for the Swedish Tax Administration." Internal presentation for the Swedish Tax Administration.

Hawawini, G., V. Subramanian, and P. Verdin. 2004. "The Home Country in the Age of Globalization: How Much Does It Matter for Firm Performance?" *Journal of World Business* 39 (2): 121–35.

Makino, S., T. Isobe, and C. M. Chan. 2004. "Does Country Matter?" *Strategic Management Journal* 25 (10): 1027–43.

OECD (Organisation for Econmomic Co-operation and Development). 2010a. OECD *Transfer Pricing Guidelines*. Paris: OECD.

———. 2010b. "Transfer Pricing Methods." OECD Secretariat Note.

———. 2011a. *Comparability Adjustments*. http://www.oecd.org/dataoecd/41/3 /45765353.pdf.

———. 2011b. "Transfer Pricing Legislation: A Suggested Approach." http://www.oecd .org/dataoecd/41/6/45765682.pdf.

———. 2012. "Dealing Effectively with the Challenges of Transfer Pricing." http://www .oecd-ilibrary.org/taxation/dealing-effectively-with-the-challenges-of-transfer -pricing_9789264169463-en

———. 2015. *Aligning Transfer Pricing Outcomes with Value Creation: Final Reports on BEPS Actions 8–10*. http://www.oecd.org/tax/aligning-transfer-pricing-outcomes -with-value-creation-actions-8-10-2015-final-reports-9789264241244-en.htm.

Scholz, C. M. 2004. *A Real Options Approach to Transfer Pricing.* 12 Transfer Pricing Report 979, March 3.

———. 2006. *Adjusting Operating Margins for Risk and Growth*. 14 Tax Management Transfer Pricing Report 23, v.14, n. 1014.

UN (United Nations). 2013. *UN Practical Manual on Transfer Pricing for Developing Countries*. New York: UN. http://www.un.org/esa/ffd/documents/UN_Manual_ Transfer Pricing.pdf.

Young, P. 2000. "Broadening the Concept of Geographic Market Adjustments." *International Transfer Pricing Journal* 7 (3).

Selected Issues in Transfer Pricing

The application of the arm's-length principle can, and often does, create issues for certain transaction types and in specific situations. In some areas, a level of international consensus (and guidance) exists regarding the application of the arm's-length principle to a specific transaction type or situation. In others, the approach varies from country to country, in particular where a country has introduced specific simplification measures. This chapter provides a high-level overview of 12 selected transaction types and situations, and their varying treatment in practice:

- Intragroup services
- Financial transactions
- Intangibles
- Cost contribution arrangements
- Loss-making entities and start-up operations
- Business restructurings
- Location savings
- Government regulation
- Set-off arrangements
- Transfer pricing and customs valuations
- Transfer pricing and value-added tax (VAT)
- Attribution of profits to permanent establishments

Intragroup Services

Unlike tangible goods, international services transactions cannot be intercepted, or even observed, at a country's borders. As a result, these are traditionally recognized as hard to tax, especially where a country's tax administration fails to progress beyond heavy reliance on physical controls (IMF 2011). As payments for intragroup services—such as management, administrative, marketing, and technical services—are, in most countries, considered deductible when determining the taxable base and are generally not subject to withholding taxes,

when such transactions take place between associated parties there is a high risk
to a country's tax base from mispricing. Mispricing of services transactions is an
issue of particular concern for many developing countries because under the
business model of many multinational enterprises (MNEs), local subsidiaries
often rely on management and technical expertise from foreign affiliates.
Moreover, it is also not uncommon in developing countries to observe the use of
invoices for intragroup services that are based on a percentage of the recipient's
revenue, instead of being based on the actual cost of providing the services.

Internationally, chapter 7 of the *OECD Transfer Pricing Guidelines for
Multinational Enterprises and Tax Administrations* (2010c) and the recent
inclusion of a simplified approach for low value-adding services[1] provides
specific guidance on the transfer pricing aspects of intragroup services. The
Organisation for Economic Co-operation and Development (OECD)
Secretariat's suggested approach to transfer pricing legislation also contains a
specific article on intragroup services. At the regional level, the European
Union Joint Transfer Pricing Forum (EUJTPF) has released a report on low
value-adding intragroup services (EUJTPF 2010); and at the country level,
various countries, including Australia, New Zealand (see box 5.1), Singapore,
and the United States, provide substantial guidance regarding the transfer
pricing aspects of intragroup services. Other countries, such as South Africa,
simply make specific reference to chapter 7 of the *OECD Transfer Pricing
Guidelines* in their administrative guidance.[2]

Guidance or legislation concerning intragroup services typically identifies and
addresses two main issues: (a) whether chargeable services were in fact provided;
and (b) if so, whether the remuneration for the services is consistent with the
arm's-length principle.

To determine whether chargeable services have in fact been provided, specific
issues typically require examination, such as shareholder services (where activities are performed by an entity in their capacity as a shareholder), on-call services, duplicate services, and passive association benefits (where associated
parties receive a benefit simply from being part of the larger MNE).

Many of the countries that have introduced specific guidance or legislation
concerning intragroup services have also introduced specific safe harbors or simplification measures. These safe harbors or simplification measures are generally
applicable to low value added services or de minimis service transactions, and
often provide for safe harbor markups on costs.

Low value added services transactions typically include routine services such
as legal, accounting, administrative, and certain information technology services.[3] The compliance burden for MNEs, which may be confronted with a
requirement to justify the benefit and remuneration of support provided by
headquarters or shared group service centers for each entity of the group, can
be significant in the absence of a simplified approach. The costs incurred in
providing these types of services when the arm's-length principle is applied are
generally marked up only modestly when priced with reference to the cost-plus
method or the transactional net margin method (TNMM), using a cost-based

Box 5.1 New Zealand Inland Revenue's Checklist for Service Transactions

To assist New Zealand taxpayers with the transfer pricing aspects of services charged, the New Zealand Inland Revenue has published a checklist of considerations on its website.[a]

Checklist for international service charges

To assist companies operating internationally, including in particular a large number of New Zealand small to medium enterprises, we have compiled the following checklist based on our long experience in reviewing international service charges:

1. Understand the charge, go behind the label and document it (the actual services provided, the benefits arising, the basis of the charge, etc).
2. The cost plus method is generally best, but never rule out the possibility of internal comparables (where similar services are being provided to third parties by the provider).
3. Watch out for "duplicated services" - in particular, does the enterprise have an infrastructure in New Zealand which can and does provide the type of services for which charges are also being made from overseas?
4. Be wary of charges for directors/chief executives (doing no more than investment monitoring), and overseas regulatory costs (for instance, Sarbanes Oxley compliance costs) - these are most probably non-chargeable "shareholder services".
5. Get the cost base right (including New Zealand tax deductibility of items included in cost sharing arrangements) and apply a sanity check - does it make sense, especially in relation to the bottom line?
6. Mark-ups must be fair and reasonable in relation to the nature of the service and the risks assumed - for example:
   • no mark-up for simply on-charging third party costs;
   • minimal mark-ups for low risk supporting services;
   • higher mark-ups where specialist knowhow or expertise is involved.
7. An allocation key should result in a charge proportionate to expected benefits - in this regard, turnover can be too simplistic and arbitrary (don't just assume a close relationship between services provided and sales without further analysis).
8. For outbound direct investment/New Zealand exporters, management and other support services provided to offshore associates (including controlled foreign companies) must be identified and fully charged.
9. A branch is not legally distinct from the rest of the enterprise - service charges should therefore be allocated on an actual cost basis only (ie no mark-ups).
10. Keep in mind other tax obligations such as withholding on services performed in New Zealand by offshore associates and royalties ("knowhow and connected services").

For a more detailed analysis, the most authoritative source is the *OECD Transfer Pricing Guidelines* at Chapter VII (Special Considerations for Intra-Group Services).

a. See Inland Revenue (2015).

financial indicator (see "Cost-Plus Method" and "Transactional Net Margin Method" in chapter 4; see also table 5.1). It is, therefore, often the establishment of an appropriate cost base that is more important when determining consistency with the arm's-length principle (EUJTPF 2011).

Other countries that have simplification measures for certain intragroup services include Austria, Japan, the Netherlands, New Zealand, and, more recently, Hungary (see box 5.2). Such simplification measures and safe harbors typically represent a compromise between the risk to revenue and the compliance burden imposed on taxpayers and tax administrations that would otherwise be required to determine and support appropriate markups. Recognizing the benefit of adopting a common approach with broad coverage, the concept of a safe harbor (named "elective simplified approach") for low value-adding services is now being added to the OECD *Transfer Pricing Guidelines*. Guidance is given on a broad range of relevant service categories, allocation keys that provide for an equal treatment of associated enterprises in similar conditions, and specific reporting requirements.

Table 5.1 Treatment of Markup on Routine Intragroup Services in Selected Countries

Country	Guidance	Source
Australia	7.5 percent markup (or a markdown of 5 percent [up to 10 percent in certain circumstances]) on "noncore services" and in de minimis cases, provided that certain conditions are met.	ATO Taxation Ruling TR 1999/1 (see annex)
New Zealand	7.5 percent markup (or a markdown of 5 percent [up to 10 percent in certain circumstances]) on "noncore services," provided that certain conditions are met.	Paragraph 558 of Inland Revenue 1997
Singapore	5 percent markup on "routine services" provided by the parent or a group service company for "business convenience and efficiency reasons."	IRAS 2009
United States	Under "services cost method," certain "low-margin" services may be compensated on the basis of cost without a profit (markup), provided a range of conditions is met.	§1.482-9(b) IRC section 482 regulations

Note: ATO = Australian Taxation Office; IRAS = Inland Revenue Authority of Singapore; IRC = Internal Revenue Code.

Box 5.2 Hungary's Regulations on Low Value-Adding Services

Based on EUJTF's work on low value-adding intragroup services (adopted by the European Commission in January 2011), at the end of 2011 Hungary revised its transfer pricing regulations to include special treatment for low value-adding intragroup services (a nonexhaustive list that is annexed to the regulations). The main features of these new regulations provide for simplified documentation requirements; application of the [full] cost-plus method, without the need for a separate analysis; and a safe harbor range of markups of 3–7 percent for transactions that do not exceed Ft 150 million, 5 percent of the service provider's net income, and 10 percent of the recipient's operational costs and expenditures in the relevant year (Ernst and Young 2012, 79).

Box 5.3 Selected Resources on Intragroup Services

- *OECD.* Chapter 7, *OECD Transfer Pricing Guidelines* as amended in October 2015.
- *EUJTPF. Guidelines on Low Value-Adding Intra-Group Services* (2011).
- *Australia.* Australian Taxation Ruling TR1999/1, "Income Tax: International Transfer Pricing for Intragroup Services)."
- *New Zealand. Transfer Pricing Guidelines* (2000, 512–70).
- *Singapore.* IRAS e-tax guide on transfer pricing guidelines for related party loans and related party services.
- *United Kingdom. HMRC International Manual.*[a] *United States.* IRC section 482 regulations.[b]

a. See the United Kingdom government's website, available at http://www.hmrc.gov.uk/manuals/intmanual/INTM464000.htm.
b. See the United States' IRS website, available at http://www.irs.gov/taxpros/article/0,,id=98137,00.html#26cfr.

The approach is based on a general agreement on the cost base composition and a markup of 5 percent. Introduction of the elective simplified method is envisaged by many OECD countries before 2018. However, further guidance on the implementation of the approach will need to be developed to inform, for instance, the design of application thresholds that would disqualify an entity.[4] These have been requested by countries involved in the base erosion and profit shifting (BEPS) discussions that are concerned about the risk of base erosion through service charges.[5] Box 5.3 lists selected resources on intragroup services.

Financial Transactions

Most MNE groups have intragroup financial arrangements in place, and the amounts involved are often substantial. Debt levels of individual entities can be relatively easily manipulated within an MNE group, and since financing costs (that is, interest and guarantee fees) are generally deductible and subject to limited or no withholding taxes,[6] the risk to revenue posed by non–arm's-length intragroup financial arrangements can be significant. This risk is arguably increased at the global level through the use of hybrid mismatch arrangements aimed at obtaining less than single taxation.[7] Research by Fuest, Hebous, and Riedel (2011) suggests that developing countries are particularly vulnerable to debt shifting. Transfer pricing legislation and rules to limit the deductibility of interest expenses can help provide a tax administration with the necessary legal basis to ensure that a country's tax base is not eroded through non–arm's-length financial arrangements.

Transfer Pricing Aspects of Financial Transactions

In recent years, tax administrations around the world have sharpened their focus on the transfer pricing aspects of financial transactions. For many MNE groups, their intragroup financial arrangements are limited to intragroup loans and guarantees, although it is increasingly common for MNEs to engage in more complex intragroup financial transactions, such as cash pooling, derivatives, and centralized treasury functions (for example, involving currency hedging). A primary concern among tax administrators is the use of MNE entities located in low-tax jurisdictions that provide funding without any other meaningful economic activity and receive returns exceeding a basic risk-free rate. The proposed response of the OECD/G20 BEPS project is guidance on the allocation of risks to parties that have the capacity to assume and control them (revisions to chapter 1 of the *OECD Transfer Pricing Guidelines*), combined with interest deductibility and controlled foreign corporation (CFC) rules.

Ensuring that intragroup financial arrangements are in accordance with the arm's-length principle requires an in-depth understanding of financial transactions and markets, and may require access to specialized market data. As a result, the compliance costs for private enterprises can be significant and potentially disproportionate—particularly with respect to smaller loans—and introducing simplification measures may therefore be appropriate. In this regard, numerous countries, such as Austria, Japan, New Zealand (see box 5.4), Slovenia, South Africa, and the United States (OECD 2011), for example, have introduced simplification measures for loans that provide for safe harbor interest rates or simplified transfer pricing methods.

Specific guidance on the transfer pricing treatment of financial arrangements other than intragroup loans is scarce at both the international and country levels. With respect to guarantee fees, a 2010 court case in Canada (*The Queen v. General Electric Capital Canada Inc.*, 2010 FCA 34) provides insights into the application of the arm's-length principle to guarantee fees. Most notably, the court ruled that the parent-subsidiary relationship should be recognized and

---

Box 5.4 New Zealand's Simplified Approach to Financing Costs[a]

Recognizing the need to strike a balance between protecting the tax base and containing compliance costs, in 2009 the New Zealand Inland Revenue Department adopted the following simplified approach:

> "For small value loans (that is, less than NZ\$2 million principal), we currently consider 300 basis points (3 percent) over the relevant base indicator is broadly indicative of an arm's-length rate in the absence of a readily available market rate for a debt instrument with similar terms and risk characteristics.
>
> For loans up to NZ\$10 million principal, independent banker quotes are generally acceptable, but once again considerable care is required. In particular, such quotes are generally accepted as indicative only and do not involve a full due diligence process, nor is the bank making any funding commitment. For all loans in excess of NZ\$10 million principal, we expect far more science and benchmarking to support interest rates applied."

a. See: http://www.ird.govt.nz/transfer-pricing/practice/transfer-pricing-practice-financing-costs.html.

Box 5.5 Selected Resources on Transfer Pricing Aspects of Financial Transactions

- *Australia.* Australian Taxation Office (ATO) Ruling (TR92/11) on application of Australia's transfer pricing legislation to loan arrangements and credit balances.[a]
- *New Zealand.* Inland Revenue Department guidance on financing costs.[b]
- *Singapore.* Inland Revenue Authority of Singapore (IRAS) e-tax guide on transfer pricing guidelines for related party loans and related party services.
- *United States.* Internal Revenue Service (IRS) regulations.[c]

a. For more information, see the ATO website, http://law.ato.gov.au/pdf/pbr/tr1992-011.pdf.
b. For more information, see the New Zealand Inland Revenue website, http://www.ird.govt.nz/transfer-pricing/practice
/transfer-pricing-practice-financing-costs.html.
c. For more information, see the IRS website, http://www.irs.gov/taxpros/article/0,,id=98137,00.html#26cfr.

---

considered as an economically relevant characteristic when pricing intragroup guarantees. Whether or not this position will be accepted in other countries remains to be seen. See box 5.5 for examples of guidance on transfer pricing aspects of financial transactions.

Rules to Limit Deductibility of Interest Expenses

To limit the erosion of the tax base from excessive interest payments, many countries have enacted thin capitalization provisions (see table 5.2). These provisions seek to protect a country's tax base by limiting the deductibility of financing costs, generally by

- Determining a maximum amount of debt on which deductible interest payments are available
- Determining a maximum amount of interest and other financing costs that may be deducted by reference to the ratio of interest paid or payable to another variable

Historically, thin capitalization rules have tended to focus on determining a maximum amount of debt on which deductible interest payments are available. However, where the focus is solely on the level of debt, tax planning involving the rate of interest, and involving guarantee fees can be employed to circumvent such measures (that is, by inflating the cost of the debt, as opposed to the amount). Therefore, recently there has been an increased focus on the level of interest that may be deducted, either through "earnings stripping" type rules (see table 5.2) or an increased focus on ensuring arm's-length pricing of the financial arrangements. Following the approach of limiting deductions for interest expenses to a percentage of earnings before interest, taxes, depreciation, and amortization (EBITDA) applied in a number of countries (for example, Germany, Italy, Spain), the OECD (under the BEPS action addressing base erosion through interest deductions) recommends an earnings stripping rule. The recommendation is to

Table 5.2 Thin Capitalization Provisions in Selected Countries

Test	Example
Predefined (or safe harbor) debt-to-equity ratio	*Pakistan:* Does not allow deductions for interest expenses incurred by foreign-controlled resident companies or branches of foreign companies that exceed a 3:1 debt-to-equity ratio.[a] *SARS:* Regards any debt-to-equity ratio in excess of 3:1* as breaching the arm's-length standard. However, it will accept a higher ratio if it can be justified as arm's-length.[b]
Arm's-length debt-to-equity ratio (or the "independent banker approach")	*United Kingdom:* Regulation of thin capitalization falls within transfer pricing legislation; an arm's-length standard as to the level of debt is thus imposed.
Specified percentage of profits (or "earnings stripping approach")	*Germany:* Limits deductions for interest expense to 30 percent of EBITDA earnings before interest, taxes, depreciation and amortization.[c] *Norway:* Net interest expense paid to a related party is deductible only to the extent that internal and external interest expense combined does not exceed 30 percent of taxable EBITDA. If the interest is under 5MNKr the whole amount could be deducted.[d]
Worldwide debt-to-equity ratio	In addition to the "safe harbor" and the "arm's-length" limits applicable to all taxpayers, Australia imposes the "worldwide gearing" limit for outward investors, which allows gearing to the level of the worldwide group of which the entity is a member. *Australia:* In 2013, the government announced the worldwide gearing ratio would be reduced from 120 percent to 100 percent of the gearing of its worldwide investment.

Note: Similar safe harbors are applied in many other countries, often with exemptions or differential treatment for financial institutions. Ratios are 3:1 in Australia, 3:1 in Chile, 1.5:1 in France, 3:1 in Hungary; 3:1 in Poland, 3:1 in the Russian Federation (12.5:1 for companies engaged in banking or leasing activities), and 4:1 in Slovenia (IBFD n.d.). EBITDA = earnings before interest, taxes, depreciation, and amortization.

a. See section 106, Income Tax Ordinance 2001.

b. See SARS Practice Note 2, 1996.

c. See IBFD 2011.

d. For more information, see "Norway Issues Regulations on Exemptions to the New Interest Deduction Limitation Rules" at http://www.ey.com/GL/en/Services/Tax/International-Tax/Alert--Norway-issues-regulations-on-exemptions-to-the-new-interest-deduction-limitation-rules.

rely on fixed ratio (between 10 percent and 30 percent) limiting net deductions to a percentage of EBITDA, which can be complemented by a worldwide group ratio rule to allow members of highly leveraged MNEs to deduct interest up to the ratio of the group.[8]

Determining whether to implement thin capitalization rules, and how such rules should be designed, involves careful balancing of the needs to protect the tax base and ensure an attractive investment climate, taking into account the country's investment and taxation policies.[9] Based on a study of data from OECD and European countries for the period 1996–2004, Büttner et al. (2008) conclude that thin capitalization rules are effective in curbing tax planning through intercompany loans, but that investment is adversely affected.

Intangibles

Intangible assets are increasingly critical to value creation and can account for a significant proportion of added value. Many companies have decreased their investment in physical or working capital assets (for example, by outsourcing manufacturing) and now focus their resources on developing the company's

Figure 5.1 Traditional, Tangible-Intensive Company and Intangible-Intensive Company Business Models

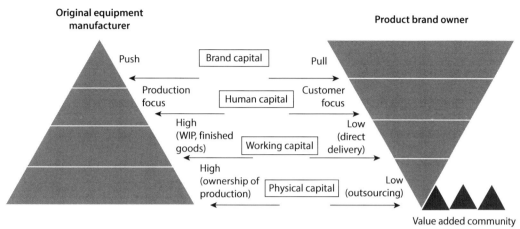

Source: Verlinden and Smits 2002.

brand and other intangible or intellectual property assets (see figure 5.1). Common examples of intangibles include trademarks, trade names, patents, know-how, models, designs, copyrights, customer lists, unique names and symbols, and trade secrets, some of which may be protected by the law.

Understanding the transfer pricing aspects of intangibles and the issues that can arise in practice is crucial to ensuring that the tax base is not eroded through non–arm's-length payments for the use or purchase of intangible property or through locally owned or generated intangibles not being sufficiently rewarded. However, transactions involving intangible property can be extremely difficult to evaluate from a transfer pricing perspective and, as a result, have been the source of complex disputes, often involving substantial sums of money. Difficulties typically involve

- Identification and ownership of intangibles (legal versus economic)
- Identification of transactions that require compensation
- Determination of arm's-length compensation
- Attribution of income from intangibles to the appropriate taxpayer

Recognizing the difficulties faced by tax administrations and taxpayers in relation to transfer pricing and intangibles, in 2011 the OECD initiated a project on the transfer pricing aspects of intangibles, which has turned into a core component of the BEPS project. As part of the project, the emphasis of guidance is on valuation challenges facing administrators, recognizing that uncertainty may require tailored approaches, including the consideration of ex post outcomes due to information asymmetries, which put administrators at a disadvantage in valuing hard-to-value intangibles. Box 5.6 provides examples of resources on transfer pricing and intangibles.

Box 5.6 Selected Resources on Transfer Pricing and Intangibles

- *International.* Chapters 6 and 7 of the *OECD Transfer Pricing Guidelines* as revised in October 2015.[a]
- *Australia.* ATO guidelines on marketing intangibles.[b]
- *United Kingdom. HMRC International Manual.*[c]
- *United States.* IRS regulations.[d]

a. For more information, see the OECD website, http://www.oecd.org/tax/aligning-transfer-pricing-outcomes-with-value -creation-actions-8-10-2015-final-reports-9789264241244-en.htm.
b. For more information, see the ato website, http://www.ato.gov.au/content/downloads/LBI_68495_marketing_intangibles .pdf.
c. For more information, see the U.K. government website, http://www.hmrc.gov.uk/manuals/intmanual/Index.htm.
d. For more information, see the IRS website, http://www.irs.gov/taxpros/article/0,,id=98137,00.html#26cfr.

Cost Contribution Arrangements

The OECD *Transfer Pricing Guidelines*, as revised in October 2015, define a *cost contribution arrangement* (CCA) as "a contractual arrangement among business enterprises to share the contributions and risks involved in the joint development, production or the obtaining of intangibles, tangible assets or services with the understanding that such intangibles, tangible assets or services are expected to create benefits for the individual businesses of each of the participants."[10]

In practice, CCAs are normally entered into between MNE group members, although arrangements with third parties also exist. Parties may decide to enter into a CCA for a variety of reasons, including the following

- Allows members of an MNE to share the costs, and therefore the risks, of research and development
- Provides a framework for leveraging the combined expertise within an MNE
- May yield cost savings and increased efficiencies though economies of scale
- May yield taxation benefits (for example, CCAs can be used to reduce future royalty flows or to migrate intellectual property)

From a transfer pricing perspective, CCAs can give rise to specific issues, such as

- Valuation of buy-in and buy-out payments
- Valuation of participants' contributions, both Intellectual Property (IP) and services
- Determination of participants' expected benefits
- Determination of the cost base (for example, inclusion of the costs of employee share options)

Box 5.7 Selected Resources on Cost Contribution Arrangements (CCAs)

- *International.* Chapter 7 of the *OECD Transfer Pricing Guidelines.*
- *Australia.* Taxation Ruling TR2004/1.[a]
- *EU.* EUJTPF Secretariat discussion document JTPF/16/2010/EN on Cost Contribution Arrangements.[b]
- *EU.* EUJTPF business members' example of CCA (JTPF/14/2010/EN).[c]
- *United States.* IRS regulations.[d]

a. For more information, see the ATO website, http://law.ato.gov.au/pdf/pbr/tr2004-001.pdf.
b. For more information, see the EU website, http://ec.europa.eu/taxation_customs/resources/documents/taxation /company_tax/transfer_pricing/forum/jtpf/2010/jtpf_016_2010_en.pdf.
c. For more information, see the EU website, http://ec.europa.eu/taxation_customs/resources/documents/taxation /company_tax/transfer_pricing/forum/jtpf/2010/jtpf_014_2010_en.pdf.
d. For more information, see the IRS website, http://www.irs.gov/taxpros/article/0,,id=98137,00.html#26cfr.

- Treatment of tax incentives and government subsidies
- Acceptance of different types of ownership of intangibles (that is, legal, beneficial, and economic)
- Tax treatment (for example, withholding obligations) of contributions and balancing payments

Most countries have issued only limited, if any, guidance on the treatment of CCAs. In fact, some countries' tax administrations do not even formally recognize CCAs for tax purposes (Australia and the United States are examples of countries that *have* issued detailed guidance on CCAs). As part of its current project on the transfer pricing aspects of intangibles, the OECD has revised its guidance on CCAs to ensure that these do not become an instrument to circumvent new guidance on the transfer pricing aspects related to risk assumption and transactions involving intangibles. The objective is to ensure that CCAs are assessed on the basis of actual arrangements as opposed to mere contractual terms. Box 5.7 presents selected resources on CCAs.

Loss-Making Entities and Startup Operations

Tax administrations generally scrutinize loss-making entities, especially where the local subsidiary is incurring ongoing losses and the MNE as a whole is profitable on a consolidated basis. Although such scrutiny is warranted, tax administrations should be careful not to automatically assume that transfer mispricing is the underlying cause.

Before it reaches such a conclusion, the tax administration needs to identify the associated party transaction and examine the cause of the losses to rule out legitimate causes, such as unfavorable economic conditions, inefficient

Box 5.8 Selected Resources on Loss-Making Entities and Start-Up Operations

• *International.* Chapter 1 of the *OECD Transfer Pricing Guidelines.*
• *International.* Comparability analysis chapter in the *United Nations Practical Manual on Transfer Pricing for Developing Countries.*[a]
• *New Zealand.* Internal Revenue guidance.[b]

a. For more information, see the United Nations' website, http://www.un.org/esa/ffd/documents/UN_Manual _TransferPricing.pdf.
b. For more information, see New Zealand's Internal Revenue website, http://www.ird.govt.nz/transfer-pricing /practice/transfer-pricing-practice-losses.html.

management, increased competition, or a business strategy. For example, a market penetration strategy may require the local entity to incur increased expenditures or reduced revenues while introducing a new product or service. However, an independent party would not bear such losses without the expectation of future profits. As Wright (2002, 174) notes, with reference to U.S. transfer pricing practice, "as a general rule, selling affiliates are allowed to report start-up losses for a period of three years or less." A business strategy, such as market penetration, should be considered part of the comparability analysis; the strategy and the expected future benefits should be contemporaneously documented by the taxpayer to provide the tax administration some support regarding the arm's-length nature of the strategy.

Tax administrations' transfer pricing audit plans generally target entities incurring sustained losses over several years (see chapter 8). Tax administrations should consider developing an internal policy toward the treatment of loss-making entities, taking into account local economic conditions. In China, for example, enterprises reporting losses in two or more consecutive years are likely targeted for a transfer pricing audit[11]; in New Zealand, the Inland Revenue has stated that "a constant period of losses may suggest commercially unrealistic transfer pricing policies".[12] Box 5.8 presents selected resources on loss-making entities and start-up operations.

Business Restructurings

Business restructurings typically involve the centralization of functions, assets (intangible assets in particular), and risks, as well as the related profit potential. The conversion of fully fledged manufacturers into contract or toll manufacturers, and the conversion of fully fledged distributors into limited risk distributors or commissionaires are typical examples of business restructurings that have become increasingly common over the last decade. Of particular concern to tax authorities is the impact these conversions have on the local tax base as a result of the profit potential, and therefore potential

---

Box 5.9 Selected Resources

- *International.* "Transfer Pricing Aspects of Business Restructurings," *OECD Transfer Pricing Guidelines* (2010, chapter 9).[a]
- *Australia.* ATO Ruling (TR2011/1) on application of transfer pricing aspects of business restructurings.[b]
- *Germany.* Summary of the rules on business restructurings.[c]
- *United Kingdom. HMRC International Manual.*[d]

a. For more information, see the OECD website, http://www.oecd.org/dataoecd/22/54/45690216.pdf.
b. For more information, see the ATO website, http://www.ato.gov.au.
c. For more information, see the OECD website, http://www.oecd.org/dataoecd/0/3/42273589.pdf.
d. For more information, see the see the U.K. government website, http://www.hmrc.gov.uk/manuals/intmanual/INTM465000.htm.

---

tax revenue, that is attached to these reallocated functions, assets, and risks. Box 5.9 presents selected resources on transfer pricing aspects of business restructuring.

To address countries' concerns about tax base erosion and private enterprises' concerns about uncoordinated responses by tax administrations, the OECD embarked on a project that considered the transfer pricing aspects of business restructurings. This project resulted in the addition of a new chapter—chapter 9, "Transfer Pricing Aspects of Business Restructurings"—to the *OECD Transfer Pricing Guidelines*. The chapter addresses some of the difficulties encountered in applying the arm's-length principle to business restructurings. It provides guidance on the following issues:

- Special considerations for risks
- Arm's-length compensation for the restructuring itself
- Remuneration of controlled transactions after restructuring
- Recognition of the actual transactions undertaken

In addition, some countries have adopted their own guidelines or enacted legislation on the transfer pricing aspects of business restructurings. German laws governing the transfer pricing treatment of cross-border business restructurings went into effect in 2008; the ATO explained its views regarding the application of Australia's transfer pricing laws to business restructurings in its Taxation Ruling TR2011/1.

In addition to the transfer pricing aspects of business restructurings, disputes regarding the existence of permanent establishments (PEs) can arise relating to the restructured operations (see table 5.3). The prevalence of such issues depends on the domestic law of the countries involved and the definitions of *PE* used in any applicable tax treaties (Cooper and Law 2010).

Table 5.3 Selected High-Profile Cases on Existence of Permanent Establishments

Country	Case	Ruling
France	*Société Zimmer Ltd.*	Overturning the decisions of the Court of Appeals, on March 31, 2010, the Administrative Supreme Court ruled that a French commissionaire did not give rise to a permanent establishment of the principal entity, located in the United Kingdom.
Norway	*Dell Products (Europe) BV v. Skatt Øst*	Both the Court of First Instance and the Supreme Court (December 2, 2011) found that the Norwegian commissionaire did not give rise to a permanent establishment of the Irish principal under the definition provided in Article 5(5) of the Norway-Ireland Income and Capital Tax Treaty (2000).
Spain	*Roche Vitamins Europe Ltd.* (appeal number 1626/2008)	In a decision handed down January 12, 2012, the Spanish Supreme Court found that the manufacturing and promotional activities undertaken by the Spanish affiliate of Roche Vitamins Europe Ltd. (a Swiss company) gave rise to a permanent establishment of Roche Vitamins Europe Ltd. in Spain.

Location Savings

Location savings can arise when an MNE achieves cost savings, such as reduced labor and materials costs, as a result of relocating certain activities. The saving is generally considered to be the net benefit to the MNE of the relocation (that is, the savings from the relocation less any costs of relocation and any increased costs associated with the new location). An example of a costs savings resulting from relocation of some of the company's business activities is illustrated in figure 5.2. In this case, the company's manufacturing activities are relocated, transferred, or moved from Country A to Country B. Despite incurring additional transport costs of 50, the company decreases its production costs by 200, resulting in a location saving of 150 (costs of relocation are negligible).

Where location savings are significant, an issue arises as to how they should be allocated between parties—that is, whether the savings should be allocated to the taxpayer in the jurisdiction with the lower costs, to the party or parties purchasing the goods or services, or proportionally among all parties. Ensuring the appropriate allocation of location savings can be of particular concern in developing countries, especially countries that have attracted foreign investment as a result of lower labor and materials costs. The OECD *Transfer Pricing Guidelines* take the view that how any location savings should be allocated depends on what independent parties would agree to in similar circumstances. Consequently, no specific adjustments for location savings are needed in cases where reliable local market comparables exist.

A few countries have issued specific guidance on the treatment of location savings. One example is U.S. IRC section 1.482-1(d)(4)(ii)(c), which states:

> If an uncontrolled taxpayer operates in a different geographic market than the controlled taxpayer, adjustments may be necessary to account for significant differences in costs attributable to the geographic markets. These adjustments must be based on the effect such differences would have on the consideration charged or

Figure 5.2 Location Savings Resulting from Relocation of Manufacturing Operations

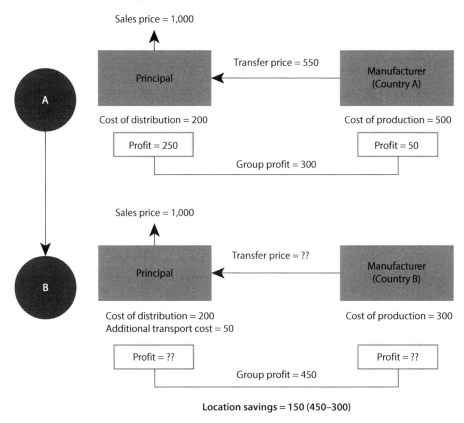

Location savings = 150 (450–300)

paid in the controlled transaction given the relative competitive positions of buyers and sellers in each market. Thus, for example, the fact that the total costs of operating in a controlled manufacturer's geographic market are less than the total costs of operating in other markets ordinarily justifies higher profits to the manufacturer only if the cost differences would increase the profits of comparable uncontrolled manufacturers operating at arm's-length, given the competitive positions of buyers and sellers in that market.

Government Regulation

In determining whether a controlled transaction and an uncontrolled transaction are comparable, the economic circumstances surrounding the transactions must be taken into account (see chapter 3). Doing so requires consideration of the market within which the transaction takes place, including the nature and extent of government regulation. Government regulation may also have an impact on the functional profile of an entity where, for example, specific regulatory requirements impose particular compliance obligations in certain industries.

In some countries, government regulations unrelated to transfer pricing—such as price controls, payment restrictions, interest rate controls, market regulation, subsidies or increased duties (antidumping), and exchange rate policies—can have a significant impact on the pricing of particular goods and services. Accordingly, such regulations must be considered when comparing transactions subject to such regulation with transactions not subject to the regulation. The *OECD Transfer Pricing Guidelines* provide a general rule in this regard:

> As a general rule, these government interventions should be treated as conditions of the market in the particular country, and in the ordinary course they should be taken into account in evaluating the taxpayer's transfer price in that market. The question then presented is whether in light of these conditions the transactions undertaken by the controlled parties are consistent with transactions between independent enterprises.

OECD Transfer Pricing Guidelines Chapter 1, Sec 1.132

Recognizing the impact that government regulations can have on the pricing transactions, transfer pricing legislation in the Russian Federation specifies in chapter 14.2(9)(5) that the degree of government intervention in market processes should be taken into account when assessing comparability.

In countries where price controls exist, the transactions subject to the price controls will generally be considered arm's-length for transfer pricing purposes or will fall outside the scope of the transfer pricing legislation. In Ukraine, for example, prices in transactions in which the state regulates pricing are viewed as arm's-length under Article 1.20.5 of the Corporate Profits Tax Law 1994 (IBFD 2010). In Vietnam, Transfer Pricing Circular 66 states that transactions subject to government price control under 2001 Price Ordinance and its implementing regulations are not subject to the transfer pricing regulations (IBFD 2010).

Set-Offs

Set-offs occur when one entity provides a benefit to an associated entity that is offset by the provision of a benefit back to that entity, as opposed to pricing and charging for the separate transactions. They may be intentional or unintentional. An example of a set-off between two companies is illustrated in figure 5.3.

In this example, Enterprise B provides know-how to Enterprise A (patent owner) and, in return, Enterprise A grants Enterprise B the right to use the patent.

As the arm's-length price for the use of patent (100) is equal to the arm's-length price for the use of know-how (100), this is an arm's-length arrangement and no payment is required by either of the parties. If, however, the arm's-length price for the use of the patent is not equal to the arm's-length price for the use of the know-how, a payment may be required by one entity to the other so as to ensure an equitable set-off.

Figure 5.3 Example of a Set-Off between Two Associated Enterprises

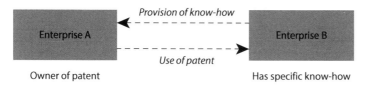

- Arm's-length price for use of know-how = 100
- Arm's-length price for use of patent = 100
→ No payments, as set-off is relied upon

While the acceptability of set-off arrangements can vary between countries, most countries tend to accept set-offs provided that consistency of the arrangement with the arm's-length principle is adequately documented. Characterization and quantification of the underlying transactions are generally also necessary, not only for determining consistency with the arm's-length principle but also for ensuring the correct treatment of the arrangement for other purposes, such as determination of withholding tax liability or any customs duties impacts.

In practice, taxpayers sometimes claim unintentional set-offs (offsets) during a transfer pricing audit or following the imposition of a transfer pricing adjustment. Whether or not a tax administration accepts such claims will generally depend on a country's transfer pricing legislation, the facts and circumstances, and the position adopted by the tax administration. In the United States, §1.482-1(g)(4) provides the possibility for a taxpayer subject to a transfer pricing adjustment to request that the commissioner of the IRS take into account other non–arm's-length transactions that will result in a set-off against the adjustment, provided certain conditions are met. The ATO considers similar requests, but only in the context of a mutual agreement procedure (TR97/20).

Transfer Pricing and Customs Valuations

The rules governing the determination of customs values are similar in principle to the transfer pricing regulations for direct tax purposes in that they seek to ensure that the relationship between the parties has not unduly influenced the price. The determination of appropriate customs values is important because duties may be levied on an ad valorem basis and the values are generally used to determine trade statistics.

Article 1 of the Agreement on Implementation of Article VII of the General Agreement on Tariffs and Trade (GATT) 1994, which provides the international legal framework for the determination of customs values, provides that

> The customs value of imported goods shall be the transaction value, that is the price actually paid or payable for the goods when sold for export to the country of importation adjusted in accordance with the provisions of Article 8, *provided … that the*

buyer and seller are not related, or where the buyer and seller are related ... that the relationship did not influence the price.

In practice, most values declared for customs purposes rely on the transaction value, which is defined in Article 1 of the GATT Valuation Code as the price actually paid or payable for the goods when sold for export to the country of importation, with adjustments made in accordance with Article 8.[13] Only where the relationship influenced the price do the other customs valuation methods need to be considered in the following prescribed hierarchical order:

- Transaction value
- Transaction value of identical goods
- Transaction value of similar goods
- Deductive method
- Computed method
- Fallback method

Some similarities exist between the customs valuation methods and transfer pricing methods described in the *OECD Transfer Pricing Guidelines*. Some commentators have drawn analogies between the deductive method and the resale price method. However, there are also significant differences in both objective and application. Customs valuation methods (aside from the transaction value method) are very prescriptive and, therefore, do not necessarily result in an arm's-length price. This divergence between the methods can, and does, lead to different values and prices being applied to the same goods under the two regimes, which in some countries has raised concerns over whipsawing.

Detailed guidance aimed at customs officials in charge of valuation policy or conducting audits of MNEs is provided in the recently published *World Customs Organization Guide to Customs Valuation and Transfer Pricing* (See box 5.10 for resources about customs valuation and transfer pricing).

Box 5.10 Selected Resources

- *World Customs Organization Guide to Customs Valuation and Transfer Pricing.*[a]
- World Customs Organization Commentary 23.1.[b]
- Australian Customs and Border Protection Service practice statement on applying for valuation advice on transfer pricing.[c]
- OECD and World Customs Organization, "Transfer Pricing, Customs Duties and VAT Rules: Can We Bridge the Gap?"[d]

a. For more information, see World Customs Organization's website, http://www.wcoomd.org/en/topics/key-issues/revenue-package/~/media/36DE1A4DC54B47109514FFCD0AAE6B0A.ashx.
b. For more information, see World Customs Organization's website, http://www.wcoomd.org/files/1.%20Public%20files/PDFandDocuments/Valuation/Commentary_23.1.pdf.
c. For more information, see OECD's website, http://www.oecd.org/dataoecd/44/62/44070404.pdf.
d. For more information, see OECD's website, http://www.oecd.org/dataoecd/40/54/39265412.pdf.

Transfer Pricing and Value Added Tax

Indirect taxes, such as value added tax (VAT), are usually calculated based on subjective values (that is, the values agreed and used by the parties) or, for imported goods, the customs value declared. In most circumstances, the calculation of VAT thus does not require a valuation based on objective criteria, such as the arm's-length principle, except, for example, where special valuation rules for related-party transactions exist (see chapter 3).

Where provisions do exist that require the determination of an "open market value,"[14] questions can arise over whether this value is equivalent to an arm's-length price. This is unclear because unlike for customs and transfer pricing for direct taxation purposes, there is no international (or supranational) guidance on the calculation of open market value for VAT purposes. This concern has been raised by the European Economic and Social Committee regarding the introduction of the subjective valuation rules in the European VAT Directive (77/388/EEC). Several countries, including Japan and Spain, have addressed this lack of guidance by making reference to the methods used for transfer pricing for direct tax purposes in their legislation. Other countries, such as Australia and New Zealand, have developed hybrid rules for their goods and services tax regimes that borrow from both their customs and their direct tax regimes (IBFD 2009).

Figure 5.4 Example of Revenue Neutrality of VAT Where Both Parties are Subject to VAT at the Full Rate

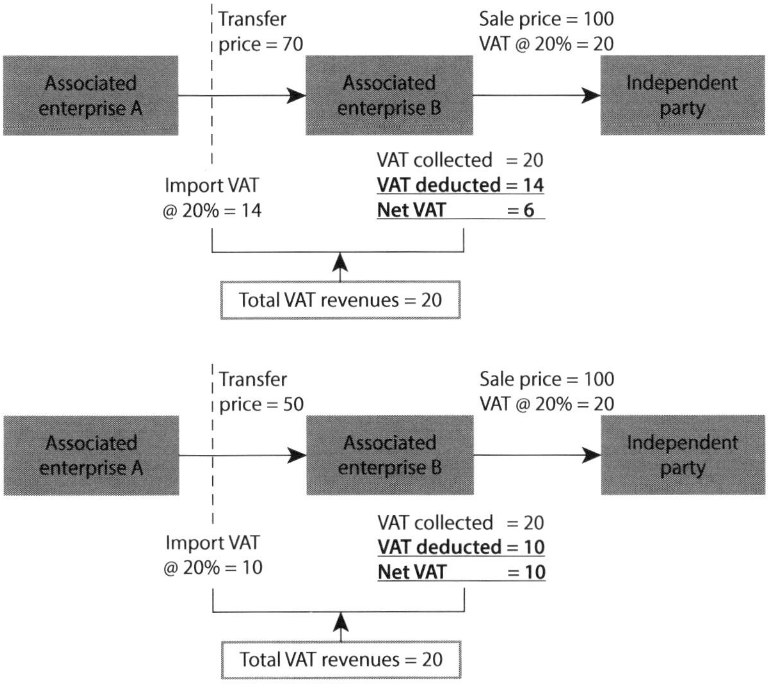

Note: VAT = value added tax.

Transfer Pricing and Developing Economies • http://dx.doi.org/10.1596/978-1-4648-0969-9

Similar to the issues regarding the interaction of transfer pricing for direct tax purposes and customs valuations, issues can arise regarding the value used for VAT purposes where a transfer pricing adjustment is made. Where the adjusted transaction takes place between two parties subject to the full rate of VAT, the outcome will be revenue neutral since any VAT paid will be deductible for both parties (see figure 5.4). The only corollary issue that may remain is the timing of the collection of the VAT and any applicable penalties and interest. Revenue issues can arise where one of the parties to the transaction cannot deduct some or all of the VAT paid.

Attribution of Profits to Permanent Establishments

Where a tax treaty that includes an article equivalent to Article 7 of the OECD and UN model tax conventions is applicable, the business profits of an enterprise are taxable in its country of residence, unless it has a PE (as per the definition in the relevant treaty [see Article 5 of the OECD and UN model tax conventions]) in the other country. The domestic law of most countries adopts this approach, although the definition of *PE* (or *branch*) can differ significantly. Where a PE exists, the business profits attributable to that establishment are taxable in that country.

From the perspective of the international legal framework, the arm's-length principle is applicable to the determination of the business profits attributable to a PE where a tax treaty containing an equivalent article to Article 7 of the OECD and UN model tax conventions is in force. Although the transfer pricing principles discussed in chapter 4 apply to transactions between associated parties that are attributable to a PE of one of the enterprises (provided the scope of the domestic law is drafted in a way that captures such transactions), the recognition and determination of appropriate transfer prices for so-called internal or intra-entity dealings by a PE can raise some challenging issues, particularly given the different approaches adopted in the various versions of articles in the OECD and UN model tax conventions and their commentaries (see table 5.4).

The wording of Article 7 of the UN model differs slightly from that in the pre-2010 versions of the OECD model and commentaries, and significantly from the current (2010) version of the OECD model. The differences in wording—in particular regarding the current version of the OECD model, which, after a substantial update to the text of the article and the commentary fully reflects the OECD's authorized approach (see box 5.11)—reflect different approaches to the recognition and treatment of internal or intra-entity dealings.

Depending on the wording of the articles in the applicable tax treaty and domestic law, different approaches may apply across countries or even within a country. As part of a review of a country's transfer pricing regime, the domestic law concerning the attribution of profits to PEs (or similar) and the policy adopted toward the negotiation and interpretation of tax treaties should be considered to reduce uncertainty and, where possible, ensure the consistency of the approach adopted.

Table 5.4 Models on Appropriate Transfer Prices for Internal and Intra entity Dealings of Permanent Establishments

Article	Key feature
Article 7 of United Nations model (2011)	• Taxing right of PE country covers profit attributable to PE and profit from same or similar goods or merchandise or business activities sold or carried out in the PE country. • Article 7(2) contains the separate entity concept and arm's-length principle, but it specifically restricts its application (that is, it cannot recognize intra-entity dealings for royalties or similar payments); services (unless standard charge exists or provision of services is main activity of the PE); or interest (except in the case of banking enterprises). • Through reference to selected paragraphs to the 2008 OECD model, the commentary provides for limited application of transfer pricing principles to certain intra-entity dealings (such as transfer of trading stock for resale and certain services transactions).
Article 7 of OECD model (pre-2010)	• Taxing right of PE country covers profit attributable to PE only. • Article 7(2) contains separate entity concept and arm's-length principle, but the commentary to Article 7(3) restricts its application; that is, it cannot recognize intra-entity dealings for royalties or similar payments, services (unless standard charge exists or provision of services is main activity of the PE), or interest (except in the case of banking enterprises). • Limited application of transfer pricing principles to certain intra-entity dealings (such as transfer of trading stock for resale and certain services).
Article 7 of OECD model (2010)	• Taxing right of the PE country covers profit attributable to the PE only. • Fully adopts the authorized OECD approach (AOA) and extensive application of transfer pricing principles for both step 1 and step 2. • May recognize intragroup dealings, such as tangible goods, interest, royalties, and services, but guarantee fees are not recognized since the PE is considered to have the same credit rating as the MNE (except in exceptional circumstances).

Note: AOA = authorized OECD approach; MNE = multinational enterprise; OECD = Organisation for Economic Co-operation and Development; PE = permanent establishment.

Box 5.11 Attribution of Profits under Article 7 of the OECD Model Tax Convention, 2010

As a result of a project that began in the 1990s, in June 2008 the OECD published its *Report on the Attribution of Profits to Permanent Establishments*, which proposed a new approach to the attribution of profits to PEs, branded AOA for short. Changes to Article 7 of the OECD model were made in 2010; the report was republished to reflect these changes (although the substantive conclusions reached in the 2008 report remain the same) (OECD 2010c).

The AOA is based on the premise that the profits attributable to a PE should be the profits the PE would have earned if it had been a distinct and separate enterprise performing the same or similar functions under the same or similar conditions and dealing wholly independently.

Application of the AOA involves a two-step analysis:

1. Identification of the activities carried on through the PE by way of a functional and factual analysis. This analysis is undertaken by hypothesizing the PE as a separate and independent enterprise capable of undertaking functions, owning or using assets, assuming risks,

box continues next page

Box 5.11 Attribution of Profits Under Article 7 of the OECD Model Tax Convention (2010)
(continued)

entering into transactions with other related and unrelated enterprises, and entering into dealings with the enterprise of which it is a part (intragroup dealings).

2. Where intragroup dealings are capable of being recognized, the pricing of such dealings should be determined by applying the arm's-length principle.

The detail in the report on both steps 1 and 2 makes reference to using the principles in the *OECD Transfer Pricing Guidelines*, thus making transfer pricing principles relevant to the determination of the profits attributable to a PE.

Chapter 5 Main Messages

• Mispricing of services transactions is a concern for many developing countries. Guidance concerning intragroup services typically identifies and addresses whether chargeable services were provided and, if so, whether the remuneration for the services is consistent with the arm's-length principle.

• Many countries have introduced specific safe harbors or simplification measures, which are typically applicable to low value added services or de minimis service transactions.

• Developing countries are particularly vulnerable to debt shifting. Transfer pricing legislation, tailored simplification measures, and rules to limit the deductibility of interest expenses can help provide a tax administration with the necessary legal basis to ensure that a country's tax base is not eroded through non–arm's-length financial arrangements.

• Understanding the transfer pricing aspects of intangibles and the issues that can arise in practice is crucial to ensuring that the tax base is not eroded through non–arm's-length payments for the use or purchase of intangible property or through locally owned or generated intangibles not being sufficiently rewarded.

Notes

1. Revisions to chapter 7 of the *OECD Transfer Pricing Guidelines*. See Final Reports on BEPS Actions 8–10: "Aligning Transfer Pricing Outcomes with Value Creation," 141–60.

2. See paragraph 18.1 of Practice Note No. 7 (South African Revenue Service).

3. It is, however, important that not the type of services, but their nature (routine), is critical. For instance, accounting services would be supportive for most MNEs, but relate to the core for an accounting firm.

4. Based on ratios determined for the recipient party or the group. Proposed examples include the share of intragroup services in total costs, turnover, and pre-intragroup service charge profit. See section 7.63 of the revised guidelines.

5. See Final Reports on BEPS Actions 8–10: "Aligning Transfer Pricing Outcomes with Value Creation," revisions to chapter 7 of the *Transfer Pricing Guidelines*, October 2015.

6. It is quite common that MNEs use countries with favorable tax treaties to reduce the withholding obligations.

7. Neutralizing the effects of these arrangements has been the focus of Action 2 in the BEPS project. See OECD's website, http://www.oecd.org/tax/neutralising-the-effects -of-hybrid-mismatch-arrangements-action-2-2015-final-report-9789264241138-en .htm.

8. See final report on Action 4 of the BEPS project, October 2015, at OECD's website, http://www.oecd-ilibrary.org/taxation/limiting-base-erosion-involving-interest -deductions-and-other-financial-payments-action-4-2015-final-report_9789264 241176-en.

9. In August 2012, OECD Tax and Development published a draft paper on thin capitalization legislation: "Thin Capitalization Legislation: A Background Paper for Country Tax Administrations," which can be a useful reference for policy makers. http://www.oecd.org/ctp/tax-global/5.%20Thin_Capitalization_Background.pdf.

10. See OECD (2015) Actions 8-10 - 2015 Final Reports: Aligning Transfer Pricing Outcomes with Value Creation, page 163. http://www.oecd.org/tax/aligning-transfer -pricing-outcomes-with-value-creation-actions-8-10-2015-final-reports-9789 264241244-en.htm.

11. See China, Article 29 2009 Special Measures.

12. See: Inland Revenue 2010. Guidance on Losses. Wellington: Inland Revenue. http:// www.ird.govt.nz/transfer-pricing/practice/transfer-pricing-practice-losses.html.

13. Adjustments include compulsory adjustments for commissions and brokerage (except buying commissions); the cost of containers and packaging; the value of assists; royalties and license fees related to the goods; proceeds of resale; and optional adjustments for the costs of transportation, loading, unloading, handling charges, and insurance.

14. See, for example, Article 73 of the EU VAT Directive.

Bibliography

Büttner, T. H., M. Overesch, U. Schreiber, and G. Wamser. 2008. "The Impact of Thin Capitalization Rules on Multinationals' Financing and Investment Decisions." Bundesbank Discussion Paper, Series 1: Economic Studies, 03/2008. Deutsche Bundesbank, Frankfurt. http://www.bundesbank.de/Redaktion/EN/Downloads/Publications/Discussion _Paper_1/2008/2008_02_25_dkp_03.pdf?__blob=publicationFile.

CCRA (Canada Customs and Revenue Agency). 2001. *Memorandum D13-4-5, Transaction Value Method for Related Persons (Customs Act, Section 48)*, Ottawa: CCRA. http:// www.cbsa-asfc.gc.ca/publications/dm-md/d13/d13-4-5-eng.pdf.

Cooper, J., and S. Law. 2010. "Business Restructuring and Permanent Establishments." *International Transfer Pricing Journal* 17 (4): 249–256.

Ernst and Young. 2012. *Transfer Pricing Global Reference Guide*. London: Ernst and Young.

EUJTPF (European Union Joint Transfer Pricing Forum). 2011. *Communication from the Commission to the European Parliament, the Council and the European Economic and Social Committee on the Work of the EU Joint Transfer Pricing Forum in the Period April*

2009 to June 2010 and Related Proposals: Guidelines on Low Value Adding Intra-group Services and Potential Approaches to Non-EU Triangular Cases. Brussels: EUJTPF. http://ec.europa.eu/taxation_customs/resources/documents/taxation/company_tax /transfer_pricing/forum/c_2011_16_en.pdf.

———. 2010. *Guidelines on Low Value-Adding Intragroup Services.* Brussels: EUJTPF. http://ec.europa.eu/taxation_customs/resources/documents/taxation/company_tax /transfer_pricing forum/jtpf/2010/jtpf_020_rev3_2009.pdf.

Frotscher, G., and A. Oestreicher. n.d. *Comment on the OECD Discussion Draft Regarding Transfer Pricing Aspects of Business Restructurings.* Göttingen: Georg-August-Universität Institut für deutsche und internationale Besteuerung.

Fuest, C., S. Hebous, and N. Riedel. 2011. "International Debt Shifting and Multinational Firms in Developing Economies." *Economic Letters* 113.

IBFD (International Bureau of Fiscal Documentation). n.d. *Corporate Taxation Country Surveys Database.* Amsterdam: IBFD.

———. 2009. *Transfer Pricing and Customs Valuation: Two Worlds to Tax as One.* Amsterdam: IBFD.

———. 2010. *Corporate Taxation Country Survey: Vietnam.* Amsterdam: IBFD.

———. 2011. *Corporate Taxation Country Survey: Germany.* Amsterdam: IBFD.

IMF (International Monetary Fund). 2011. *Revenue Mobilization in Developing Countries.* Washington, DC: Fiscal Affairs Department, IMF.

Inland Revenue. 1997. *New Zealand Transfer Pricing Guidelines.* Wellington: Inland Revenue. http://www.ird.govt.nz/resources/2/b/2b59ab004bbe5827b784f7bc87554 a30/trans-price-guidelines.pdf.

———. n.d. *Transfer Pricing. Guidance on Financing Costs.* Wellington: Inland Revenue. http://www.ird.govt.nz/transfer-pricing/practice/transfer-pricing-practice-financing -costs.html.

———. 2010. *Guidance on Losses.* Wellington: Inland Revenue. http://www.ird.govt.nz /transfer-pricing/practice/transfer-pricing-practice-losses.html.

———. 2015. *Guidance on Service Charges.* Wellington: Inland Revenue. http://www.ird .govt.nz/transfer-pricing/practice/transfer-pricing-practice-service-charges.html.

IRAS (Inland Revenue Authority of Singapore). 2009. *Transfer Pricing Guidelines for Related Party Loans and Related Party Services.* Singapore: IRAS. http://www.iras.gov .sg/irasHome/uploadedFiles/Quick_Links/e-Tax_Guides/TP-IRAS%20eTaxGuide %20-%20TP%20Guidelines%20for%20RPL%20RPS.pdf.

IRS (Internal Revenue Service). 2011. "Methods to Determine Taxable Income in Connection with a Cost Sharing Arrangement." *IRS Bulletin.* T.D. 9568, December 16. http://www.irs.gov/irb/2012-12_IRB/ar06.html.

OECD (Organisation for Economic Co-operation and Development). 2010a. *Location Savings.* Paris: OECD. http://www.oecd.org/dataoecd/41/5/45765521.pdf.

———. 2010b. *Report on the Attribution of Profits to Permanent Establishments.* Paris: OECD. http://www.oecd.org/dataoecd/23/41/45689524.pdf.

———. 2010c. *OECD Transfer Pricing Guidelines for Multinational Enterprises and Tax Administrations.* Paris: OECD. http://www.keepeek.com/Digital-Asset-Management /oecd/taxation/oecd-transfer-pricing-guidelines-for-multinational-enterprises-and-tax -administrations-2010_tpg-2010-en.

————. 2011. OECD *Releases a Scoping Document for Its New Project on the Transfer Pricing Aspects of Intangibles*. Paris: OECD. http://www.oecd.org/document/44/0,3746,en_26 49_45675105_46988012_1_1_1_1,00.html.

————. 2012. *Hybrid Mismatch Arrangements: Tax Policy and Compliance Issues*. Paris: OECD. http://www.oecd.org/dataoecd/20/20/49825836.pdf.

UN (United Nations). 2013. *UN Practical Manual on Transfer Pricing for Developing Countries*. New York: UN. http://www.un.org/esa/ffd/documents/UN_Manual_ TransferPricing.pdf.

U.S. Department of Homeland Security. n.d. *What Is Reconciliation?*. Washington, DC: U.S. Department of Homeland Security. http://www.cbp.gov/xp/cgov/trade/trade _programs/reconciliation/reconciliation.xml.

Verlinden I., A. Smits, and B. Lieben (Landwell). 2002. *Intellectual Property Rights from a Transfer Pricing Perspective*. Brussels: PricewaterhouseCoopers.

Wright, D. 2002. "Transfer Pricing When Losses Arrive." *International Transfer Pricing Journal* 9 (5): 174–79.

Zhabbarov, A., and A. Kulisheva. 2004. "Income Tax: International Transfer Pricing—Cost Contribution Arrangements." ATO. TR 2004/1. Australian Tax Office, Canberra. http://law.ato.gov.au/pdf/pbr/tr2004-001.pdf; http://www.irs.gov/Businesses/Checkli st-for-Cost-Sharing-Arrangements.

————. 2010. "Kazakhstan: New Transfer Pricing Law in Force." *International Transfer Pricing Journal* 17 (4).

Promoting Taxpayer Compliance through Communication, Disclosure Requirements, Transfer Pricing Documentation, and Penalties

This chapter discusses various forms of building awareness and promoting compliance among taxpayers through effective communication and outreach campaigns, and requirements to disclose transfer pricing-related information as part of the tax return or additional schedules. It also examines issues to consider when introducing transfer pricing documentation rules and provides an overview of international, regional, and country approaches to transfer pricing documentation requirements.

Communication and Outreach

Promoting taxpayer compliance with a new or amended transfer pricing regime requires clear communication of obligations and expectations. Where new legislation or disclosure requirements are introduced, the tax authority needs to (a) engage in consultations with the private sector during the development phase to achieve buy-in at all levels, and (b) provide taxpayers with timely notice of proposed changes and sufficient guidance (and training where possible) to generate awareness and buy-in. Ways to engage and inform the private sector include

- Consultation with the business community (including tax advisors)
- Staged implementation
- Consideration of a fiscal amnesty program
- Provision of guidance (formal and informal)
- Hosting of or speaking at seminars and conferences
- Establishment of working groups

Consultation with the Business Community

Ensuring buy-in from the private sector and ownership within the tax administration are important conditions for the successful implementation of reform. Where new transfer pricing legislation or compliance obligations are being developed, engaging the business community in the reform process—by, for example, allowing for public comments on legislation or proposed compliance obligations (such as disclosure schedules)—promotes awareness and increases the likelihood that the expectations of policy makers and the tax administration are met.

A consultative process allows potential (practical) issues with the proposed legislation or compliance obligations to be identified and provides timely notice of the proposed reforms, thus reducing the compliance burden and facilitating compliance. Formal private sector consultations, encompassing both the legislative and administrative aspects of reform, should be integrated into any program of transfer pricing reform.

Staged Implementation

Providing a time lag between the introduction or reform of the transfer pricing regime and its enforcement provides taxpayers time to develop and implement new transfer pricing policies. It also provides the tax administration time to develop its own capacity, thereby limiting any negative impact on the investment climate arising from increased obligations, low-quality audits, or both. A time lag can be achieved by delaying the formal start date for the application of new legislation or compliance requirements, announcing that the tax authority will not conduct audits for a set period of time, or implementing a legislative or informal approach in stages.

Honduras, for example, delayed the implementation of new transfer pricing legislation. Transfer Pricing Law No. 32,691 of December 10 was passed in 2011, but went into effect on January 1, 2014, thus giving taxpayers and the tax administration time to become familiar with new transfer pricing principles and compliance obligations.

Similarly, the Russian Federation incorporated aspects of the staged approach when introducing its legislation. The scope of transactions over which transfer pricing control is applicable increased over a three-year period, during which a Rub 3 billion (about US\$94 million) threshold applied for certain domestic-related-party transactions. The threshold decreased to Rub 2 billion in 2013 (about US\$63 million) and Rub 1 billion in 2014 (about US\$31 million) (EY 2011).

Where a delayed or staged implementation approach is adopted, policy makers should, however, consider the risk of increased noncompliance during the period in which the law is not applicable or has limited application and ensure that appropriate safeguards are in place.

Consideration of a Targeted Fiscal Amnesty Program

Where legislation dealing with transfer pricing has been in force for several years but guidance, clarity, or enforcement have been lacking, a carefully designed fiscal amnesty program may help promote future compliance by providing taxpayers the opportunity to revise their transfer pricing practices without fear of triggering an audit of prior years. Albania enacted a fiscal amnesty law on May 31, 2011 which gave taxpayers until December 31, 2011 to settle undeclared tax liabilities, including ones resulting from failure to adhere to the arm's length principle (provided the relevant tax audit had not started). Taxpayers making such declarations had to pay only half the tax liability and were not subject to interest or penalties (Karakitis and Jasini 2011).

International experience suggests that "the perceived benefits of tax amnesty programs are, at best, overstated and often unlikely to exceed the program's costs—of administration and of reduced taxpayer compliance—which are rarely measured" (Baer and Le Borgne 2008, vii). Nevertheless, a well-designed program that is combined with reforms to address the underlying reasons for noncompliance may be appropriate in specific cases, particularly since a tax amnesty can "be an expedient and effective way to break with a culture of non-compliance and prepare citizens for a regime of strong tax enforcement" (Baer and Le Borgne 2008, 57).

Provision of Guidance (Formal and Informal)

The provision of guidance to taxpayers on the expectations, views, and approach of a country's tax administration toward transfer pricing can increase awareness and reduce uncertainty, both of which promote taxpayer compliance. Guidance may be provided in an informal manner during public appearances or in a more formal manner, such as by publishing information on the website of the tax administration.

Informal guidance is less burdensome to produce and may therefore be appropriate for addressing specific issues on an interim basis. In Australia, for example, uncertainty had arisen regarding the interaction of the thin capitalization and transfer pricing legislation. To provide guidance while a final position was being developed, a deputy commissioner of the Australian Taxation Office (ATO) announced the office's interim position in a speech delivered at the Annual Corporate Tax Forum in Sydney on May 18, 2009.

Formal guidance provides taxpayers with a higher degree of certainty and may be more accessible. However, it can also be more resource intensive to produce. Detailed administrative guidelines, publications, or guidance on the tax administration's website detailing the expectations and approach of the tax administration, and checklists that taxpayers can use to self-assess their compliance, can help generate awareness and promote compliance with transfer pricing legislation.

Australia, Japan, New Zealand, and South Africa, for example, all provide written guidance. The ATO published an overview entitled "International Transfer Pricing: Introduction to Concepts and Risk Assessment" (ATO 2012). The Japanese National Tax Administration has a "Check Sheet for Confirmation of Efforts and Achievements on Transfer Pricing," which taxpayers can use to evaluate their efforts to manage their transfer pricing positions (PwC 2012).

The New Zealand Inland Revenue published explanations of its transfer pricing approach and details of its enforcement program. Transfer pricing questionnaires are available online allowing taxpayers to use them to evaluate their transfer pricing risk (New Zealand Inland Revenue 2009).

Hosting or Speaking at Seminars and Conferences

Having policy makers and senior tax officials give talks at seminars or conferences or provide awareness training on the application of a country's transfer pricing regime can be an excellent tool for communicating underlying policy rationale and reducing uncertainty.

Establishment of Working Groups

Countries' transfer pricing regimes and the approaches adopted by both the tax administration and taxpayers generally evolve as experience develops, the economy changes, new international practices appear, and new types of transactions and business models arise. To address the uncertainty that can be generated by this natural evolution and provide a forum for candid discussion of issues, it can be useful to establish a formal working group comprising relevant stakeholders (private sector representatives, tax officials, and policy makers) dedicated to transfer pricing or international tax matters.

The appropriate scope and mandate of the working group will differ across countries. The ATO, for example, has established the National Tax Liaison Group (NTLG), a consultative body comprising tax officials, policy makers, tax professionals, and representatives of professional bodies. The group has a formal charter (ATO 2013a). It operates through subgroups (each with its own charter and membership), which deal with a range of tax issues, including transfer pricing. The Swedish Tax Agency has a similar transfer pricing and permanent establishment project with subgroups for risk assessment, valuation of intellectual property, financial transactions, legal issues, and information to the public.

Disclosure Requirements: Collecting Information and Promoting Widespread Compliance

Requiring taxpayers to disclose specific information related to ownership and associated party transactions can provide the tax administration with the information necessary to identify and assess transfer pricing risks. It can also generate awareness and promote compliance.

To ensure the most productive use of resources and limit compliance costs, tax authorities need to develop and use risk-based assessment systems for selecting taxpayers for transfer pricing audits (see chapter 8). But many countries lack the basic information necessary to identify and assess potential transfer pricing risks. This information deficit can be addressed in the initial stages of developing a transfer pricing regime. Requirements to make transfer pricing-related disclosures can also promote awareness of transfer pricing risks and, as a result, compliance by taxpayers, since the introduction of transfer pricing-related disclosure requirements is a clear indication that transfer pricing has become a focus area of the tax administration.

Tax administrations have adopted various approaches to collecting the information needed to identify transfer pricing risks, ranging from requiring basic disclosures in the annual tax return to requiring taxpayers to complete specific schedules detailing their associated party transactions. When considering the appropriate approach for a particular country, policy makers must balance the need for information against the compliance burden that disclosures can impose on taxpayers. They need to consider

- What information should be gathered (i.e., the disclosures required) and how that information should be used
- How and when the information should be collected
- Which taxpayers should be required to provide such information and whether compliance burdens are appropriate

The following sections address these considerations by drawing on examples from a range of countries (see annex 6A for a detailed summary).

In addition to the general disclosure requirements, tax administrations may wish to collect more detailed information or information on selected topics and transaction types from specific taxpayers or categories of taxpayer. Targeted questionnaires can be used to do so.[1]

What Information Should Be Gathered and How Should It Be Used?

The information tax administrations may find useful to collect and have readily available includes the following:

- Type of taxpayer (resident or nonresident)
- Ownership information
- Economic classification and business activities
- Transactional information (e.g., transactions falling within the scope of the legislation, transactions for nonmonetary consideration, and details of the transaction)
- Methodologies applied
- Existence or level of documentation

Annex 6A summarizes the information that may be useful to collect and how it can be used. Some of this information, such as type of taxpayer, ownership information, and details of economic activities, may already be collected for purposes other than transfer pricing. Many countries, however, do not collect this information or collect it but lack ready access to it.

When considering the information that may be useful to collect, the tax authority should refer to the transfer pricing risk indicators used to identify and select taxpayers for a transfer pricing audit (see chapter 8).

How and When Should Information Be Collected?

The approaches adopted by countries can be broadly grouped into three main categories (see table 6.1). The appropriate method depends on such factors as the level of disclosure currently required, the potential imposition of an additional compliance burden, the country's investment policy for attracting foreign direct investment (FDI), the compliance culture, the capacity of the tax administration (including the resources to process the information), and the perceived level of transfer pricing risk.

Recognizing that requiring taxpayers to submit detailed information, such as complete transfer pricing documentation, at the time of filing the tax return may impede international trade and development, the OECD *Transfer Pricing Guidelines for Multinational Enterprises and Tax Administrations* (2010, paragraph 5.15) provide the following guidance:

> Any documentation requirement at the tax return filing stage should be limited to requiring the taxpayer to provide information sufficient to allow the tax administration to determine approximately which taxpayers need further examination.

Approach 1: Limited Disclosures in the Tax Return

Under this approach, the disclosures required in annual tax returns are limited to basic ownership information, the existence of transactions that fall within the scope of the country's transfer pricing legislation, and the existence of a documented transfer pricing policy. Countries that have adopted this approach include New Zealand (see figure 6.1) and South Africa (see figure 6.2).

The potential compliance burden imposed on taxpayers under this approach will be minimal to insignificant, but so will be the information collected by the

Table 6.1 Advantages and Disadvantages of Different Approaches to Transfer Pricing Disclosure Requirements

Approach	Advantages and disadvantages	Examples
Limited disclosures in the tax return (may be supplemented with targeted questionnaires)	• Insignificant additional compliance burden on taxpayers • Minimal information available to tax administration for risk assessment • Specific action required to obtain detailed information • Limited impact on compliance	Georgia, New Zealand, South Africa, Sweden
Additional form or schedule with detailed disclosures	• Potential increase in compliance burden on taxpayers • Detailed information available to tax administration for risk assessment • Potentially significant impact on compliance	Albania, Australia, Canada, Colombia, Finland, Ghana, Kenya, Norway, Russian Federation, Turkey
Additional form or schedule and independent sign-off requirements	• Substantial compliance burden on taxpayers • Detailed or independently reviewed information available to tax administration for risk assessment • Potentially significant impact on compliance	Denmark, India, Mexico

Figure 6.1 Extract from Corporate Income Tax Return in New Zealand

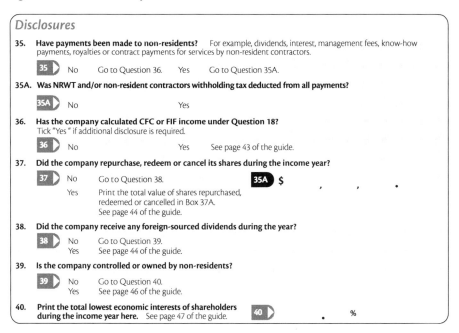

Source: Income Tax Return: Companies 2013 IR 4 April 2013, http://www.ird.govt.nz/resources/0/4/04a305804eb941c493b9f3b6c72de7d5/ir4-2013.pdf.

tax administration; on its own, this approach is likely not sufficient for identifying and assessing transfer pricing risks. The tax administration will need to rely on additional sources of information, such as financial reports, the media (newspapers, journals), and the Internet to obtain the information necessary for identifying and assessing transfer pricing risk. Other sources of information include patent and registration offices, and databases such as Zephyr[2] regarding business restructurings.

Tax administrations adopting this approach may need to supplement the information collected through targeted questionnaires periodically sent to taxpayers or through a desk review of tax returns and other available information, such as financial accounts.

Approach 2: Additional Form or Schedule with Detailed Disclosures
Under the second approach, detailed disclosures are required as part of the annual filing requirements, usually through an additional schedule. This approach has been adopted or is in the process of being adopted by numerous countries, including Australia, Canada, Colombia, Denmark, Finland, Ghana, Kenya,[3] Norway, Russia, and Turkey.

Disclosure requirements vary across countries. Generally, however, disclosure of ownership and transactional information (e.g., type and value) is required. Many countries also require disclosure of the transfer pricing

Figure 6.2 Extract from Corporate Income Tax Return in South Africa

INTERNATIONAL RELATED

Does the company, together with any connected person in relation to the company, hold at least 10% of the participation rights in any controlled foreign company?   7022

   If YES, did the company complete an IT10 that must be retained for a period of five years after date of submission of this return?   70C8

Did the company enter into any cross-border transactions, i.t.o. an international agreement, as defined in s 31?   7052

Does the company have a transfer pricing policy document in support of the transfer pricing policy applied in the current year in relation to the transactions as defined in s 31?   7054

Did the company receive any financial assistance from a non-resident connected person or from an investor as defined in s 31(3) and Practice Note 2?   7053

   If YES, were the provisions of s 31(3) and Practice Note 2 adhered to?   7333

Has the company provided goods, services or anything of value (including transactions on capital accounts) to a nonresident connected person for no consideration? (Please note that goods and services include a loan.)   7057

Has the company entered into a back-to-back arrangement with any other party which has resulted in an offshore connected person being granted financial assistance?   70C9

Source: ITR14 form available for companies registered with eFiling system at www.sarsefiling.co.za.

methods applied and whether or not transfer pricing documentation has been prepared. A summary of selected countries' disclosures requirements is provided in annex 6B. As a result of the increased compliance burden imposed by this approach, it may be appropriate that the requirement to complete the detailed schedule is limited to taxpayers passing a certain threshold (annexes 6C–6E provide copies of the schedules used by the tax authorities in Australia, Denmark, and Kenya).

Approach 3: Additional Form or Schedule and Independent Specialist Signoff Requirements

Some countries, including Denmark, India, and Mexico, have implemented requirements that require disclosures be certified by certified independent accountants or similar professionals.

From January 1, 2013, and upon request from the Danish tax authority, SKAT, a taxpayer must submit an independent auditor's statement regarding compliance with the arm's length principle within 90 days.

SKAT can only request an independent auditor's statement on companies that have

- Intercompany transactions with residents in non–European Union (EU) or non–European Economic Area (EEA) member states that do not have a double tax treaty with Denmark
- Realized a negative operating profit in earnings before interest and taxes (EBIT) for four consecutive years on average

The request may be made retroactively, i.e., under the statute of limitation rules, and the Danish tax authority may request an independent auditor's statement for the income year 2007 up until May 1, 2013.[4]

Section 92E of India's Income Tax Act 1961 requires the preparation and submission of an accountant's report that is signed by a registered chartered accountant or person entitled to be appointed as an auditor of companies (a copy of the required form is provided in annex 6F).

In Mexico, certain taxpayers are required to file a *dictamen fiscal*, which is essentially a statutory tax audit report carried out by a certified independent accountant. As part of the dictamen fiscal, information regarding the taxpayer's transfer pricing practices must be disclosed and certified by an independent accountant. The accountant's report must indicate that the taxpayer transactions were made at arm's length, list any transfer pricing adjustments and advance pricing agreements (APAs), and confirm the existence of transfer pricing documentation.

Which Taxpayers Should Be Required to Provide Such Information?

Where detailed disclosure requirements are put in place, it is important for the tax administration to balance the need for information against the potential compliance burden imposed. To do so, most countries that have detailed disclosure requirements limit the requirements to taxpayers that pass a certain threshold (see table 6.2). The appropriate threshold for a particular country depends on the approach to tax administration, tax policy, and broader economic factors.

In addition to the use of disclosures and specific schedules, various countries have undertaken specific initiatives that promote compliance and provide the tax administration with additional information, including detailed and targeted questionnaires. The tax authorities in New Zealand and South Africa use such questionnaires on a regular basis to collect detailed information regarding specific taxpayer's transfer pricing.[5] In 2011, Malaysia's Inland Revenue Board began issuing new forms to selected taxpayers, a move that changed taxpayer behavior (see box 6.1) (Goh 2012).

Table 6.2 Thresholds for Requiring Disclosure in Selected Countries

Country	Threshold	Requirement if threshold met
Albania	Taxpayers engaging in controlled transactions (including loan balances), which in aggregate, within the reporting period, exceed lek 50,000,000. When determining the aggregate transactions, income and expenses cannot be offset.	Required to complete and submit an "Annual Controlled Transactions Notice" to the Regional Tax Directorate with which they are registered.
Australia	Nonindividual taxpayers with aggregate international related party transactions of more than $A 1 million (including loan balances); threshold increased to $A 2 million for the new international dealings schedule.	Had to complete schedule 25A (replaced from 2012).[a]
Denmark	Aggregate of all controlled transactions during the income year exceeds DKr 5 million.	Must complete controlled transactions form.[b]
Canada	Reporting taxpayer or partnership with combined reportable transactions with nonresidents of more than Can$1 million.	Must complete Form T106.[c]
Colombia	Taxpayer engaged in transactions with foreign-related parties that at year end exceed the established caps of gross equity of 100,000 TUs (roughly US$1.2 million) or had gross income equal to at least 610,000 TUs (roughly US$7.3 million) and all taxpayers that engage in transactions with tax havens.[d]	Must complete individual informative return or consolidated information return and comparables information pursuant to Resolution 011188 (2010).[e]

Note: TU = taxable unit.
a. See annex 6C.
b. See annex 6D.
c. See annex 6B.
d. PwC 2011.
e. See annex 6B.

As part of its strategic compliance initiative, the ATO has used targeted mailings requesting taxpayers to provide specific information on particular situations or transaction types (such as economic performance, business restructurings, and financial transactions). A template example of a questionnaire is included in annex 6I. In 2001, the South African Revenue Service (SARS) undertook a similar initiative, sending a questionnaire entitled "Information Request: Interest-Free Loans to Non-Resident Individuals, Trusts or Companies" to 100 of the leading financial publication's list of the top 200 companies in South Africa as well as to 50 randomly selected companies (SARS 2001).

There has also been a recent trend toward requiring taxpayers to report uncertain tax positions. In the United States, for example, corporations that issue or are included in audited financial statements and have assets that equal or exceed US$100 million must complete an "uncertain tax position statement" as part of their annual filing requirement (IRS 2010). This statement requires that uncertain tax positions relating to transfer pricing be disclosed and ranked, with distinct disclosure required regarding transfer pricing positions and general positions; for details on the schedule, see IRS (2010). The ATO has introduced a "reportable tax position schedule" applicable for certain taxpayers beginning in 2011/12 (ATO 2012).

Box 6.1 Promoting Transfer Pricing Compliance in Malaysia

Malaysia's Inland Revenue Board began issuing new forms to selected taxpayers in 2011. The forms, Form MNE (PIN 1/2012), "Information on Cross-Border Transactions," and Form JCK (JCK/TP/1/2011), "Information on Related Company Transactions," are generally required to be completed and returned within 30 days of receipt.

The MNE form requires disclosure of substantially more comprehensive information than required in the annual income tax return (Form C). It entails disclosure of details of cross-border transactions with associated enterprises and confirmation of the existence of contemporaneous transfer pricing documentation.

Form JCK requires disclosure of transactions with associated enterprises within Malaysia and with foreign-associated enterprises. Information to be disclosed is similar to that required by the MNE Form, including confirmation of the availability of contemporaneous transfer pricing documentation.

According to Goh (2012, 223–24), a change in taxpayer practice has been observed since the introduction of these forms:

> "… many taxpayers (both domestic and multinational enterprises) have recognized the importance of preparation of transfer pricing documentation on a contemporaneous basis, and as such have initiated the process of preparation of such documentation. Taxpayers that have already prepared transfer pricing documentation in previous years are moving on to update their documentation on a more regular basis. Taxpayers have begun to diligently factor in the transfer pricing implications in their day-to-day transfer pricing decisions, as well as any discussions with related entities. Similarly, where fundamental changes are being made to the business operation such as a business restructuring, transfer pricing implications now take a front seat."

Transfer Pricing Documentation

Transfer pricing documentation provides tax administrations with information to identify transfer pricing risks and assess taxpayer compliance with a country's transfer pricing legislation. It can help prevent unnecessary transfer pricing disputes and resolve disputes should they arise. The tax administration should establish rules that balance its legitimate needs while limiting the investment climate impact of imposing overly burdensome compliance requirements on taxpayers.

All tax administrations emphasize the importance of obtaining transfer pricing documentation as part of the fact-finding process. The extent to which specific requirements are spelled out in the countries' legislation varies significantly, with some providing specific legislative record-keeping requirements and others opting to refrain from introducing statutory requirements and being comfortable with providing general guidance. A more formal approach increases certainty, but it can come with a higher overall compliance burden.

Transfer Pricing and Developing Economies • http://dx.doi.org/10.1596/978-1-4648-0969-9

A range of international institutions provide guidance on documentation requirements, and it is one of the most prominent initiatives of the base erosion and profit shifting (BEPS) action plan. Members of the Organisation for Economic Co-operation and Development (OECD) reexamined transfer pricing documentation obligations under Action 13 of the BEPS project and agreed in October 2015 on the need to introduce a minimum standard covering an obligation for country-by-country (CbC) reporting. The proposed three-tiered approach is aimed at increasing global consistency and transparency, requiring (a) a local file with information on all relevant intercompany transactions of a particular entity, (b) a master file with global information on the multinational enterprise (MNE) group activities, and (c) a CbC report with aggregate information for all entities and tax jurisdictions.

Issues to Consider in Developing Transfer Pricing Documentation Rules

A variety of considerations need to be addressed when crafting transfer pricing documentation rules (see table 6.3).

Burden of Proof Allocation and Its Impact on Transfer Pricing Documentation Obligations

In most countries, burden of proof rests initially with the tax administration, which has to demonstrate that the taxpayer's pricing is inconsistent with the arm's length principle. The tax authority, however, can demand from the taxpayer documentation that will support the company's transfer pricing policies and allow the tax administration to examine the controlled transactions. In some countries,

Table 6.3 Issues to Consider When Developing Transfer Pricing Documentation Rules

Issue	Considerations
Burden of proof	• Does the taxpayer or the tax administration bear the burden of proof? • How does the existence of transfer pricing documentation impact the burden of proof?
Requirements and incentives to prepare documentation	• What are the requirements and incentives for taxpayers to prepare documentation, such as penalties for failure to fulfill requirements or waived or reduced penalties for taxpayers who comply?
Scope of requirements (where applicable)	• Where penalties exist for nonfulfillment, are certain taxpayers or transactions excluded from documentation requirements?
Timing and submission	• When should the transfer pricing documentation be prepared: at the time of the transaction, at the time of filing, or upon request?
Content	• What information should be included in the documentation? • Are there different requirements for specific taxpayers (such as) or transactions?
Language and form	• What language should the documentation be in? • What form should the documentation be maintained in and where?

Note: SMEs = small and medium enterprises.

including Canada, India, South Africa, and the United States, the burden of proof is shifted to the taxpayer.

The burden of proof should be clearly defined in the law specifying whether the taxpayer or tax administration ought to prove that the pricing is in accordance with the arm's length principle since this impacts the information and documentation that need to be produced and submitted by the companies.

Requirements and Incentives to Prepare Documentation

Tax administrations need access to information to identify transfer pricing risks and assess taxpayers' compliance with a country's transfer pricing legislation. To provide them with this information, countries have introduced requirements or incentives for taxpayers to prepare and maintain transfer pricing documentation. In formulating documentation rules, they typically consider the impact on the burden of proof, the interaction with penalties, the risk of transfer pricing audit, and the reduced time and cost of such audits.

To encourage taxpayers to prepare transfer pricing documentation, numerous countries have established a link between their penalty regime and transfer pricing documentation. Some countries have introduced specific penalties for failing to fulfill the documentation requirements; others impose penalties only if a transfer pricing adjustment is made, with the documentation potentially providing relief from or a reduction in the applicable penalty, or, in cases of failure to meet documentation requirements, increased penalties.

The existence and quality of transfer pricing documentation are often two of the factors considered as part of the risk-based assessment process (see chapter 8). Evidence that a taxpayer has prepared transfer pricing documentation may reduce the risk of a transfer pricing review proceeding to a full-blown transfer pricing audit. If a transfer pricing audit is undertaken, the time and cost of managing the process is likely to be significantly reduced if transfer pricing documentation has been prepared and maintained.

In South Africa, for example, there is no explicit statutory requirement for taxpayers to prepare and maintain transfer pricing documentation. However, for a variety of reasons, SARS considers it to be in the taxpayer's best interests to document how prices have been determined[6]:

- Adequate documentation is the best way to demonstrate that transfer prices are consistent with the arm's length principle, as required by Section 31.
- It is more likely that the Commissioner will examine a taxpayer's transfer pricing in detail if the taxpayer has not prepared proper documentation.
- If the Commissioner, as a result of this examination, substitutes an alternative arm's length amount for the one adopted by the taxpayer, the lack of adequate documentation will make it difficult for the taxpayer to rebut that substitution, either directly to the Commissioner or in the Courts.
- If taxpayers have not maintained appropriate records, the process of checking compliance with the arm's length principle becomes far more difficult and the

Commissioner's officials are forced to rely on less evidence on which to apply a method, thus requiring a greater degree of judgment.

• The income-tax return for companies (IT 14) requires taxpayers to supply certain specific information regarding transactions entered into between connected persons. It is not possible for a taxpayer to comply with these requirements if the taxpayer has not addressed the question of whether its dealings comply with the arm's length principle.

Scope of Requirements

To avoid imposing disproportionate or unnecessary burdens on taxpayers, many countries limit the scope of reporting requirements (see table 6.4).

Timing and Submission

Countries' documentation rules include different requirements regarding the timing of the preparation and production of documentation, including requirements to prepare documentation at the time of the transaction, at the time of filing, or upon request. The most common approach is to oblige taxpayers to prepare and maintain the documentation at the time of filing. Australia, Denmark, India, and Italy require that disclosures indicating whether such documentation exists be submitted with the tax return. Submission of the documentation package, regardless of the time of its preparation, should, however, be done only upon the tax administration's request. Some countries do, however, require certain documentation (disclosures) to be submitted on an annual basis (see annex 6B).

There are two main approaches to applying the arm's length principle: setting prices in accordance with the arm's length principle and testing whether the outcome is arm's length. In practice, a combination is often used, with documentation focusing on whether the outcome is arm's length. When designing documentation requirements, policy makers should consider the practical constraint that information needed to apply the arm's length principle (external comparables information) is often not available until sometime after year end—in many instances even after the filing date.[7]

Content

From an investment climate perspective, it is important to ensure that a country's documentation requirements do not impose an unnecessary or disproportionate compliance burden on taxpayers. Detailed and prescriptive documentation requirements may reduce uncertainty for taxpayers regarding the tax administration's expectations and help ensure the availability of certain information to the tax administration. But overly prescriptive requirements—particularly ones that differ significantly from those of other countries—create unnecessary compliance costs. Where compliance with documentation requirements is linked to penalties, detailed guidance on the content of the documentation is necessary.

Table 6.4 Limitations on the Scope of Transfer Pricing Documentation Requirements in Selected Countries

Taxpayer or transaction type	Limitation
SMEs	Some countries exempt SMEs from documentation requirements (Denmark and Germany) or subject them to simplified requirements (Australia and Italy). In the United Kingdom and Ireland, SMEs that meet certain requirements are completely exempt from transfer pricing requirements.
Enterprises with minimal controlled transactions	Some countries, including Poland,[a] India,[b] and Portugal,[c] exempt or exclude enterprises that engage in only limited transactions from documentation requirements.
Insignificant or de minimis controlled transactions	Some countries, including Denmark,[d] Finland,[e] Hungary, Spain,[f] and Sweden exempt or exclude economically insignificant transactions from documentation requirements or subject them to simplified requirements.
Controlled transactions subject to simplification measures	Where simplification measures for specific types of transactions, such as low value added services or de minimis loans and services transactions have been introduced, weaker documentation requirements apply.
Domestic transactions	Some countries, including China and Turkey, exempt or exclude certain domestic transactions from documentation requirements.

Source: IBFD library.

Note: SMEs = small and medium-size enterprises.

a. The Polish documentation requirements "apply to transaction(s) between related entities in which the total amount (or its equivalent) resulting from the contract or the total amount actually paid in a tax year, relating to transactions enforceable in the tax year, is higher than the equivalent of EUR100,000 if the value of the transaction does not exceed 20 percent of the share capital, determined in accordance with relevant tax regulations; EUR30,000 in the case of performance of services, sale or making available of intangible assets and legal values; or EUR50,000 in the remaining cases" (IBFD 2011a).

b. In India, enterprises with aggregate related party transactions worth less than Rs100 million are subject to relaxed requirements (IBFD 2011a).

c. Only taxpayers with turnover and other income in excess of €3million the previous year are required to prepare and maintain a broad set of contemporaneous documentation (IBFD 2011b).

d. "Isolated transactions of limited economic significance" are excluded from the documentation requirements (IBFD 2011a).

e. "In case the total arm's length value of the transactions between two legal entities does not exceed EUR500,000, no functional analysis, economic analysis or financial analysis needs to be prepared concerning these transactions. Sec. 2 of Art. 14c of the VML stipulates that only: a description of the business; a description of related-party relationships; and details of controlled transactions have to be included in the transfer pricing documentation concerning these transactions" (IBFD 2011a).

f. One of Spain's exemptions from the general documentation requirements is "transactions with the same related individual or entity when the total market value of the same does not exceed EUR250,000. This exception does not apply in the following circumstances:

– transactions with individuals or entities resident in a tax haven for Spanish purposes (except those located in the European Union and carried out for sound economic reasons in the context of a business activity);
– transactions carried out by individuals in the context of a business activity taxable in accordance to the objective estimation method, with entities participated by themselves or by their relatives with a stake of at least 25 percent;
– transfers of businesses, stocks, or nontradable shares; and
– transfers of real estate or intangible assets" (IBFD 2011a).

Language and Form

Depending on the capacity of and resources available to the tax administration, requirements regarding the language and form of documentation (electronic or paper) may be necessary.

Although many countries prefer or formally require that documentation be submitted in the local language (or translated into the local language in a certified translation), countries are increasingly willing to accept documentation in English or a regional language, at least on an exceptional basis. This type of flexibility can help reduce compliance costs and avoid delays. Examples of countries accepting multiple languages include the following (Deloitte 2011):

- Belgium: English, Dutch, French, German
- Denmark: Danish, English, Norwegian, Swedish
- Hungary: Hungarian, English, French, German
- Kazakhstan: Kazakh, Russian
- Malaysia: Malay, English
- The Philippines: Filipino, English, Spanish
- Sweden: Swedish, Danish, Norwegian, English

The EU Code of Conduct recommends that country-specific documentation be prepared in the language or languages prescribed by the member states concerned (paragraph 6), but that tax administrations should be prepared to accept the master file when it is prepared in a commonly understood language in the member states concerned, and to require translation only if strictly necessary and upon specific request (paragraph 23). Other countries, such as the Arab Republic of Egypt, have taken a different approach, requiring that where documents are provided in a language other than Arabic, translation may be required at the taxpayer's expense.

Requirements regarding the form of the documentation depend on the needs, capacity, and document management practices of the tax administration. Where a tax administration is highly reliant on electronic document management, requirements for electronic filing of documentation (in searchable format) may be appropriate. In Italy, for example, documentation must be prepared in electronic format; if documentation is provided in hard copy (paper format), it must be converted to electronic format upon request of the tax administration. In other countries, providing flexibility for taxpayers may be a priority or the tax administration may prefer paper filings.

Transfer Pricing Documentation: International and Regional Guidance

The OECD, the European Council, the Pacific Association of Tax Administrators (PATA), and the International Chamber of Commerce (ICC) have all issued guidance on transfer pricing documentation.[8] Guidance on transfer pricing documentation is also included in the United Nations' (UN's) *Transfer Pricing: Practical Manual for Developing Countries* (2013). An overview of each of these sources of guidance is provided below.

OECD: *Chapter 5 of the* OECD Transfer Pricing Guidelines

Chapter 5 of the *OECD Transfer Pricing Guidelines*, which has been completely revised as part of the BEPS project, provides guidance for tax administrations on developing and enforcing documentation requirements and for taxpayers on the type of documentation that would be helpful in demonstrating compliance with the arm's length principle. The basic premise of the guidelines is that taxpayers are expected to make reasonable efforts to prepare and maintain documentation on their transfer prices and that tax administrations should have the right to obtain this documentation.

Regarding the content of the documentation, and in response to diverse documentation rules across countries and ensuing compliance costs for taxpayers in meeting each jurisdiction's specific rules, the revised guidelines provide directions for the development of the rules with the overall aim of more consistency among countries. In combination with the objective of addressing concerns of tax administrators regarding insufficient information on global operations of MNEs, this has led to the development of a standardized three-tiered approach covering

- A *local file*, covering all material transactions of the local taxpayer, thus largely containing the information typically included in existing documentation obligations
- A *master file* providing a detailed picture of the MNE's global operations, including an overview of the MNE's global transfer pricing policies and agreements with tax authorities
- A *CbC report*, providing high-level data with respect to the global allocation of the MNE's income, taxes, and other broad economic indicators (allocation of profits, revenues, employees, and assets).[9]

Annexes to chapter 5 of the revised guidelines spell out the detailed information that should be included in each tier. See box 6.2 below.

The proposed new approach to documentation extends the information available to administrators and will thus enhance the ability for comprehensive transfer pricing risk assessment. While the introduction of a master file follows an earlier recommendation by the EU Joint Transfer Pricing Forum (EUJTPF) on "Code of Conduct on Transfer Pricing Documentation"), the proposed contents of the new chapter 5 of the OECD *Transfer Pricing Guidelines* do provide a much broader picture on global activities of MNEs.

Regarding the timing of submission, the guidelines recognize different country practices and suggest as a best practice that the local file should be required to be submitted at the time of filing the local entity's tax return and the final master file at the due date of the ultimate parent's tax filing. The local and master file will normally be submitted by local taxpayers to its domestic administration or kept. The CbC report is filed by the parent in its country of residence.

The introduction of the CbC report is aimed at improving tax administrator's information for risk assessment purposes. By adding important information on global group performance, the CbC report is offering to tax administrators comprehensive insight into the location of earnings and tax payments of an MNE, and an understanding of inconsistent allocation of the jurisdictions of value creation and revenue recognition. Consequently, CbC reporting has

Box 6.2 OECD Guidelines Chapter 5: Proposed Contents of Master and Local Files

The following extracts are from G20/OECD Action 13, Final Report: "Transfer Pricing Documentation and Country-by-Country Reporting."

Master file

Organizational structure

- Chart illustrating the MNE's legal and ownership structure and geographical location of operating entities.

Description of MNE's business(es)

- General written description of the MNE's business including:
  - Important drivers of business profit;
  - A description of the supply chain for the group's five largest products and/or service offerings by turnover plus any other products and/or services amounting to more than 5 percent of group turnover. The required description could take the form of a chart or a diagram;
  - A list and brief description of important service arrangements between members of the MNE group, other than research and development (R&D) services, including a description of the capabilities of the principal locations providing important services and transfer pricing policies for allocating services costs and determining prices to be paid for intra-group services;
  - A description of the main geographic markets for the group's products and services that are referred to in the second point above;
  - A brief written functional analysis describing the principal contributions to value creation by individual entities within the group, i.e., key functions performed, important risks assumed, and important assets used;
  - A description of important business restructuring transactions, acquisitions, and divestitures occurring during the fiscal year.

MNE's intangibles (as defined in Chapter VI of these Guidelines)

- A general description of the MNE's overall strategy for the development, ownership, and exploitation of intangibles, including location of principal R&D facilities and location of R&D management;
- A list of intangibles or groups of intangibles of the MNE group that are important for transfer pricing purposes and which entities legally own them;
- A list of important agreements among identified associated enterprises related to intangibles, including cost contribution arrangements, principal research service agreements, and license agreements;
- A general description of the group's transfer pricing policies related to R&D and intangibles;
- A general description of any important transfers of interests in intangibles among associated enterprises during the fiscal year concerned, including the entities, countries, and compensation involved.

box continues next page

Box 6.2 OECD Guidelines Chapter 5: Proposed Contents of Master and Local Files *(continued)*

MNE's intercompany financial activities
- A general description of how the group is financed, including important financing arrangements with unrelated lenders;
- The identification of any members of the MNE group that provide a central financing function for the group, including the country under whose laws the entity is organized and the place of effective management of such entities;
- A general description of the MNE's general transfer pricing policies related to financing arrangements between associated enterprises.

MNE's financial and tax positions
- The MNE's annual consolidated financial statement for the fiscal year concerned if otherwise prepared for financial reporting, regulatory, internal management, tax, or other purposes;
- A list and brief description of the MNE group's existing unilateral advance pricing agreements (APAs) and other tax rulings relating to the allocation of income among countries.

Local file
Local entity
- A description of the management structure of the local entity, a local organization chart, and a description of the individuals to whom local management reports and the country(ies) in which such individuals maintain their principal offices;
- A detailed description of the business and business strategy pursued by the local entity, including an indication whether the local entity has been involved in or affected by business restructurings or intangibles transfers in the present or immediately past year and an explanation of those aspects of such transactions affecting the local entity;
- Key competitors.

Controlled transactions
For each material category of controlled transactions in which the entity is involved, provide the following information:
- A description of the material controlled transactions (e.g., procurement of manufacturing services, purchase of goods, provision of services, loans, financial and performance guarantees, licenses of intangibles, etc.) and the context in which such transactions take place;
- The amount of intragroup payments and receipts for each category of controlled transactions involving the local entity (i.e., payments and receipts for products, services, royalties, interest, etc.) broken down by tax jurisdiction of the foreign payor or recipient;
- An identification of associated enterprises involved in each category of controlled transactions, and the relationship amongst them;
- Copies of all material intercompany agreements concluded by the local entity;
- A detailed comparability and functional analysis of the taxpayer and relevant associated enterprises with respect to each documented category of controlled transactions, including any changes compared to prior years;

box continues next page

Box 6.2 OECD Guidelines Chapter 5: Proposed Contents of Master and Local Files *(continued)*

- An indication of the most appropriate transfer pricing method with regard to the category of transaction and the reasons for selecting that method;
- An indication of which associated enterprise is selected as the tested party, if applicable, and an explanation of the reasons for this selection;
- A summary of the important assumptions made in applying the transfer pricing methodology;
- If relevant, an explanation of the reasons for performing a multiyear analysis;
- A list and description of selected comparable uncontrolled transactions (internal or external), if any, and information on relevant financial indicators for independent enterprises relied on in the transfer pricing analysis, including a description of the comparable search methodology and the source of such information;
- A description of any comparability adjustments performed, and an indication of whether adjustments have been made to the results of the tested party, the comparable uncontrolled transactions, or both;
- A description of the reasons for concluding that relevant transactions were priced on an arm's length basis based on the application of the selected transfer pricing method;
- A summary of financial information used in applying the transfer pricing methodology;
- A copy of existing unilateral and bilateral/multilateral APAs and other tax rulings to which the local tax jurisdiction is not a party and which are related to controlled transactions described above.

Financial information
- Annual local entity financial accounts for the fiscal year concerned. If audited statements exist they should be supplied and, if not, existing unaudited statements should be supplied;
- Information and allocation schedules showing how the financial data used in applying the transfer pricing method may be tied to the annual financial statements;
- Summary schedules of relevant financial data for comparables used in the analysis and the sources from which that data was obtained.

drawn significant public attention and some criticism related to the high exemption threshold for entities with consolidated group revenue below €750 million (the threshold will be reconsidered in a review of the reporting standards scheduled for 2020), which may exclude critical taxpayers in many emerging and developing economies. Moreover, some countries have indicated a preference for a wider scope for the CbC report than what is currently covered in the agreed reporting template, for instance, covering additional transaction data such as interest and royalty payments.

UN: Practical Manual on Transfer Pricing for Developing Countries
Chapter 9 on documentation cites some existing international guidelines, provides a more in-depth discussion of selected topical issues, and contains summaries of selected countries' transfer pricing documentation requirements (UN 2013).

European Council: "Code of Conduct on Transfer Pricing Documentation for Associated Enterprises in the European Union"

In 2006, the European Council adopted the "Code of Conduct on Transfer Pricing Documentation for Associated Enterprises in the European Union" (hereafter, "the Code"), developed by the EUJTPF.[10] The Code proposes a standardized and partially centralized documentation package and recommends that if MNEs operating in the EU satisfy the requirements, member states should not impose documentation-related penalties. The Code is not legally binding on member states. As a result, member states have adopted it to varying degrees, with some member states, such as Hungary and Italy, adopting the recommendations in their domestic documentation requirements and others making no reference to it in either their legislation or their general guidance.

The Code is based on the "master file" (paragraph 4.2) and "country-specific documentation" (paragraph 5.2) concepts, which have now been incorporated in the revised OECD *Transfer Pricing Guidelines*. The Code aims to reduce compliance costs by reducing the need to replicate certain aspects of transfer pricing documentation in multiple member states (see box 6.3). Together, the master file and country-specific documentation constitute the documentation package to be provided to the tax administration of an interested member state.

Box 6.3 Master File and Country-Specific Documentation Required by the EU "Code of Conduct on Transfer Pricing Documentation"

The following extracts are from the annex to the "Code of Conduct on Transfer Pricing Documentation for Associated Enterprises in the European Union."[a]

Master file
- a general description of the business and business strategy, including changes in the business strategy compared to the previous tax year;
- a general description of the MNE group's organizational, legal, and operational structure (including an organization chart, a list of group members, and a description of the participation of the parent company in the subsidiaries);
- the general identification of the associated enterprises engaged in controlled transactions involving enterprises in the EU;
- a general description of the controlled transactions involving associated enterprises in the EU, that is, a general description of:
  – flows of transactions (tangible and intangible assets, services, financial),
  – invoice flows, and
  – amounts of transaction flows;
- a general description of functions performed, risks assumed, and a description of changes in functions and risks compared to the previous tax year, for example, change from a fully fledged distributor to a commissionaire;

box continues next page

Box 6.3 Master File and Country-Specific Documentation Required by the EU "Code of Conduct on Transfer Pricing Documentation" *(continued)*

- the ownership of intangibles (patents, trademarks, brand names, know-how, etc.) and royalties paid or received;
- the MNE group's intercompany transfer pricing policy or a description of the group's transfer pricing system that explains the arm's length nature of the company's transfer prices;
- a list of cost contribution agreements, Advance Pricing Agreements, and rulings covering transfer pricing aspects as far as group members in the EU are affected; and
- an undertaking by each domestic taxpayer to provide supplementary information upon request and within a reasonable time frame in accordance with national rules.

Country-specific documentation

- a detailed description of the business and business strategy, including changes in the business strategy compared to the previous tax year;
- information, that is, description and explanation, on country-specific controlled transactions, including:
  - flows of transactions (tangible and intangible assets, services, financial),
  - invoice flows, and
  - amounts of transaction flows;
- a comparability analysis, that is:
  - characteristics of property and services,
  - functional analysis (functions performed, assets used, risks assumed),
  - contractual terms,
  - economic circumstances, and
  - specific business strategies;
- an explanation of the selection and application of the transfer pricing method(s), that is, why a specific transfer pricing method was selected and how it was applied;
- relevant information on internal and/or external comparables if available; and
- a description of the implementation and application of the group's intercompany transfer pricing policy.

a. See (EU TPD), C 176/4 EN Official Journal of the European Union 28.7.2006.

The Code recommends that the country-specific documentation be prepared in a language prescribed by the member state concerned (paragraph 9); it is more flexible regarding the master file (paragraph 23):

> It may not always be necessary for documents to be translated into a local language. In order to minimize costs and delays caused by translation, Member States should accept documents in a foreign language as far as possible. As far as the EU Transfer Pricing Documentation is concerned, tax administrations should be prepared to accept the master file in a commonly understood language in the Member States concerned. Translations of the master file should be made available only if strictly necessary and upon specific request.

PATA: Transfer Pricing Documentation Package

The members of PATA—Australia, Canada, Japan, and the United States—have published a set of principles (henceforth, "PATA Documentation Package") that provides a penalty protection to taxpayers in all member countries.[11] The package is voluntary for taxpayers and does not impose any additional legal requirements beyond those imposed by the member's domestic documentation requirements. The PATA Documentation Package is interesting because each member country agreed that taxpayers in compliance with all of the principles contained in it avoid the imposition of transfer pricing penalties. Compliance with the principles does not, however, preclude a tax administration from making transfer pricing adjustments or imposing interest on unpaid taxes.

The PATA Documentation Package is based on three principles:

- Taxpayers need to make reasonable efforts to establish their transfer pricing in accordance with the arm's length principle.
- Taxpayers need to reasonably and contemporaneously document their efforts to comply with the arm's length principle.
- Taxpayers need to produce the foregoing documentation in a timely manner upon request of a PATA member tax administration to benefit from the penalty protection.

The schedule to the PATA Documentation Package specifies 10 broad categories of documents and lists specific documents for each. The 10 categories are

- Organizational structure
- Nature of the business or industry and market conditions
- Controlled transactions
- Assumptions, strategies, and policies
- Cost contribution arrangements
- Comparability, functional, and risk analysis
- Selection of the transfer pricing method
- Application of the transfer pricing method
- Background documents
- Index to documents

ICC: Practical Manual on Transfer Pricing for Developing Countries

Recognizing the increasing and diverse transfer pricing documentation requirements facing its members, in 2003, the ICC Commission on Taxation released a policy statement on transfer pricing documentation (*Transfer Pricing Documentation: The Case for International Cooperation*).[12] This document recognizes that it is legitimate for tax authorities to expect taxpayers to document their transfer pricing, draws attention to the increasing and diverse documentation requirements resulting from separate and uncoordinated responses by tax authorities, and the significant compliance burden it can impose on business, and calls for a common set of rules for transfer pricing documentation.

In 2008, the ICC developed this policy further, publishing a transfer pricing documentation model.[13] The model proposes "a set of rules allowing MNEs to prepare a single uniform package of documentation that would be considered reasonable by all involved tax authorities."

The set of rules proposed is based on three key principles:

- The documentation package should be based upon information that is readily available in the bookkeeping and management reports of the MNE concerned. External assistance to provide documentation should not be necessary.
- Common documentation rules should not merely cumulate all requirements of all countries. Rather, a reasonable and balanced reflection of the various national approaches should be taken into account.
- Once an MNE fulfills the proposed documentation requirements, it should be relieved of any liability for penalties.

The model also outlines the elements of the documentation package, as envisaged in the 2003 policy statement, and provides a sample documentation package. It proposes a single report for the group parent company, which is then adapted to local country requirements.

Transfer Pricing Documentation: Selected Country Examples

This section provides brief overviews of transfer pricing documentation requirements in Australia, China, Colombia, Denmark, Hungary, Italy, Kenya, Malaysia, the Russian Federation, South Africa, Turkey, and the United States.

Australia

Australia currently has no explicit statutory requirements for taxpayers to prepare and maintain transfer pricing documentation beyond the general record-keeping requirements in section 262A of the Income Tax Assessment Act 1936.[14] The ATO does, however, expect that taxpayers will prepare and maintain contemporaneous transfer pricing documentation that records the application of the arm's length principle. These expectations are set out in Taxation Ruling TR 98/11 ("Income Tax: Documentation and Practical Issues Associated with Setting and Reviewing Transfer Pricing in International Dealings"). Paragraph 2.1 cites the main reasons for maintaining such documentation:

- Statutory requirements to keep records
- Relevance to penalty considerations
- The burden of proof, which rests with taxpayers in the event of dispute
- Practical advantages in reducing the risk of tax audits and adjustments and in communicating [one's] position to the ATO

TR 98/11 provides a four-step process for applying the arm's length principle, including detailed guidance on each of the four steps (see figure 6.3).[15] This process is not mandatory or prescriptive and may need to be tailored to the facts

Figure 6.3 Australia's Four-Step Process for Testing International Transfer Prices

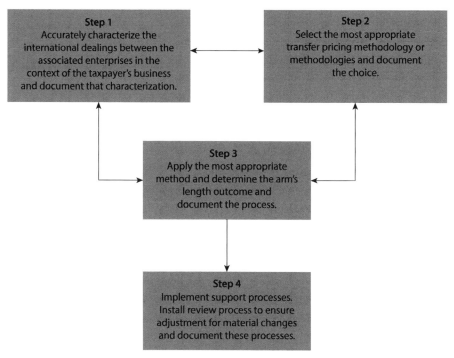

and circumstances. However, taxpayers who implement and document the four steps are less likely to be exposed to transfer pricing adjustments and penalties.

Recognizing the need for balance between the appropriate level of documentation and the compliance burden imposed, TR 98/11 states that "detailed analysis is not required in every case and the level of detail required varies, subject to the size of the business and the complexities involved." Regarding small and medium-size enterprises SMEs, chapter 6 of TR 98/11 recognizes the need for taxpayer judgment in determining the level of documentation to be prepared and maintained and provides the following example (paragraphs 6.3–6.4):

> For example, a small business which has turnover of $10 million and international dealings with associated enterprises of $500,000 may not deem it prudent business management to undertake extensive analysis and documentation of its transfer pricing practices to demonstrate compliance with the arm's length principle. This is an exercise of commercial judgment made by a manager having regard to the particular circumstances of the taxpayer's business, the complexity of the dealings and the risk of an ATO review.

> On the other hand, if the particular example above involves a dealing that is narrowly focused and can be benchmarked against arm's length outcomes by

reference to readily available data, then a prudent manager, at little cost and with little effort, could document the process used and the comparison with arm's length outcomes.

The ATO has issued specific guidance on a "simplified approach to documentation and risk assessment" to assist SMEs. Failure to maintain transfer pricing documentation will not lead to a penalty, but may affect the size of any penalty imposed if a transfer pricing adjustment is made. According to paragraph 2.10 of TR 98/11 (chapter 2): "The existence of adequate contemporaneous documentation is an indicator that the efforts of a taxpayer are such that penalties should be remitted in the event of a transfer pricing adjustment."

China

In January 2009, China released "Tentative Implementation Rules for Special Tax Adjustments" (Guo Shui Fa 2 9 no. 2), which set out detailed transfer pricing documentation requirements for the first time (IBFD 2011a, China chapters of PwC 2011, and Yang 2009). In addition to the nine forms that must be filed with the annual tax return, upon request taxpayers who are not exempt from the obligation to prepare transfer pricing documentation must prepare and submit transfer pricing documentation covering 25 specific items (see table 6.5).[16] The documentation must be prepared in Chinese.

Taxpayers are exempt from the documentation requirements under the following conditions:

- The annual amount of related party purchases and sales is less than Y 200 million (about US$31.5 million) and the annual amount of other related-party transactions (services, interest, royalties, and so forth) is less than Y 40 million (about US$6.3 million) (excluding amounts covered by an advance pricing agreement)
- Related-party transactions are covered by an advance pricing agreement
- The foreign shareholding in the enterprise is less than 50 percent and the enterprise engaged in only domestic related-party transactions.

Failure to provide the relevant documentation may result in the imposition of penalties of Y 2,000 to Y 50,000. Where documentation is prepared and produced upon request, the 5 percent penalty interest usually levied on transfer pricing adjustments may be waived. Refusal to provide documentation, or submission of false information, may empower the tax administration to deem an amount of taxable income and impose adjustments accordingly.

Colombia

In addition to filing the individual (or consolidated) informative return and Form 1525 (Resolution 011188), taxpayers with foreign related parties that at year end exceed the established caps of gross equity of Col$100,000 (about US$1.2 million in 2009) or gross income equal of at least Col$610,000 (about US$7.3 million in 2009),

Table 6.5 Content of China's Contemporaneous Transfer Pricing Documentation Package

Area	Documentation required
Organizational structure	• Relevant organizational structure and shareholding structure of the enterprise group the tested enterprise is related to • Change and development of the relationships between the tested enterprise and its related parties • Information about related parties, including their names, legal representatives, senior management personnel, registered addresses and actual operation places, and so forth • Each related party's applicable type of tax, tax rates, and possible tax incentives
Description of business operations	• Major economic and legal issues affecting the taxpayer and the industry, such as a summary of the enterprise's development, a summary of the industry's development, the enterprise's business strategy, and industrial policy or industrial restrictions • Description of the enterprise group's supply chain arrangement and the position of the enterprise on the chain • Summary showing the percentage of the enterprise's revenues and profits per business line as well as market and competition analysis • Information regarding the enterprise's functions, risks, and assets • The consolidated financial report prepared at the end of the enterprise's year
Information about the related-party transactions	• Types, participants, timing, amounts, currency, and contractual terms • Description of the transactional model, terms applied, and changes to the mode • Operational flows, including information, product, and cash flows at different stages and flow comparisons with transactions with unrelated parties • Intangible assets utilized and their influence on the pricing of the transactions • Copies of intercompany agreements and their execution status • Analysis of the main legal and economic factors affecting the pricing of the related-party transactions • Segmented financial analysis
Comparability analysis	• Factors considered in performing the comparability analysis • Information related to the functional profiles (functions performed, risks assumed, and assets employed) of the comparable enterprises • Explanation of the comparable transaction, such as the physical character, quality and use of tangible property, proper interest rate, amounts, currency, period, guarantee, the credit of borrower, the form of repayment, the calculation of interest, and so forth; the extent and nature of the service; and the type and transaction form of intangible property, the right to use intangible property by trading, and the income from using intangible property • Source, selection criteria, and rationale for selection of comparables
Section and application of transfer pricing methods	• Rationale and support for selection of transfer pricing method, including information on the contribution to the total group profit or residual profit by the tested enterprise • Whether the comparable information can support reliable application of the selected method • Assumptions and judgments when determining comparable prices or profits • Description of the determination of comparable prices or profits by applying a reasonable transfer pricing method and comparability analysis and justification of the arm's length principle • Other documents that can justify the selection of transfer pricing methods

Source: Guo Shui Fa 2009, no. 2.

Transfer Pricing and Developing Economies • http://dx.doi.org/10.1596/978-1-4648-0969-9

and any taxpayers who engage in transactions with tax havens are required to prepare and maintain transfer pricing documentation for all transactions exceeding Col$10,000 (about US$120,000 in 2009) (PwC 2011, Colombia chapter). This documentation should be made available to the tax authorities upon request no later than June 30 of the year following the relevant fiscal year. The documentation should contain the information set out in the table 6.6.

Documentation should be submitted in Spanish. Some annexes may be acceptable in English, although the tax authorities may request a translation

Table 6.6 Content of Colombian Transfer Pricing Documentation

Area	Documentation required
General information	• Description of the taxpayer's organizational and functional structure • General description of the business • Equity composition, including name, income-tax identification, and ownership percentage of partners or shareholders • General description of the company's industry, indicating the company's position in it • Name, income tax identification, domicile, and description of the business purpose and activity of related parties, including ownership details and subsidiaries. The facts that give rise to the relationship should also be provided
Specific information	• Detailed description of each type of transaction • Parties, purpose, terms, and prices of all contracts and agreements • For transactions with residents or entities domiciled in tax havens, a copy of the documentation that certifies that the transaction took place • Functional analysis by type of transaction, including a short description of the activities, classification of used assets, and inherent risks of the transactions • General information about commercial strategies • Information about the industry and description of substitute goods or services • Political or normative changes that could affect the result of the transaction • Method used by the taxpayer in the transfer pricing analysis, selected in accordance with the best-method rule • Profit-level indicator used in the analysis • Identification and determination of comparable companies, information sources, and inquiry dates and indication of the criteria by which comparable companies were rejected • Description of technical adjustments and, when needed, generic description of the principal differences between Colombian accounting practice and accounting practices in countries where the comparable companies are domiciled • Detailed conclusions of the level of compliance with arm's length standard
Annex information	• Financial statement (general purpose) • Balance sheet, profit and losses statement, production costs statement, and sales costs statement, segmented by type of transaction • Copy of contracts or agreements • In economic or special business situations, pertinent supporting information, such as marketing studies, projections, and reports

Source: PwC 2011.

(Deloitte 2011). Penalties are imposed for failure to fulfill documentation requirements (see annex 6J).

Denmark

Denmark introduced new statutory rules in 2006. Statutory Order 42 sets forth a basic requirement for transfer pricing documentation (IBFD 2011a, Denmark chapter; Ottosen and Nørremark 2006; PwC 2011, Denmark chapter).[17] To fulfill this requirement, taxpayers must maintain contemporaneous documentation that includes the following:

- Description of the group and commercial activities
- Description of controlled transactions
- Comparability analysis
- Implementation of arm's length principle
- Catalog of written agreements concerning controlled transactions

The documentation must not necessarily follow the structure and description set out in the statutory order, which recognizes that the extent of the analyses will depend on the size and complexity of the transaction. Documentation may be prepared in Danish, English, Norwegian, or Swedish.

The documentation requirements apply to domestic and international transactions. SMEs are required to prepare documentation only with respect to controlled transactions with parties in countries outside the EU or EEA with which Denmark has not entered into a tax treaty (see figure 6.4).

Failure to provide adequate documentation within 60 days upon the requests of the tax authority can give rise to substantial penalties.

Failure to provide acceptable transfer pricing documentation within 60 days of request from the tax administration or not submitting an independent auditor's statement may result in a fixed penalty of DKr 250,000 (€35,000) per company, per year. The penalty can be reduced by 50 percent if compliant transfer pricing documentation is subsequently submitted.[18]

Where a transfer pricing adjustment is imposed, the minimum penalty is increased by 10 percent of the profit adjustment. These penalties have not been applied in practice to date.

Hungary

Transfer pricing documentation requirements were first introduced in Hungary in 2003. They were amended in 2009 (effective January 1, 2010). The amendment introduced the possibility for taxpayers to prepare their documentation using a master file approach as an alternative to separate documentation (similar to that found in the EU Code).

Taxpayers other than individuals and small and microenterprises (as defined in section 3 Act XCV of 1999) are required to document all transactions with related parties, subject to some exceptions (e.g., transactions that do not exceed Ft 50 million in value, net of VAT, are subject to simplified documentation requirements).

Figure 6.4 Document Requirements under Denmark's Statutory Order 42

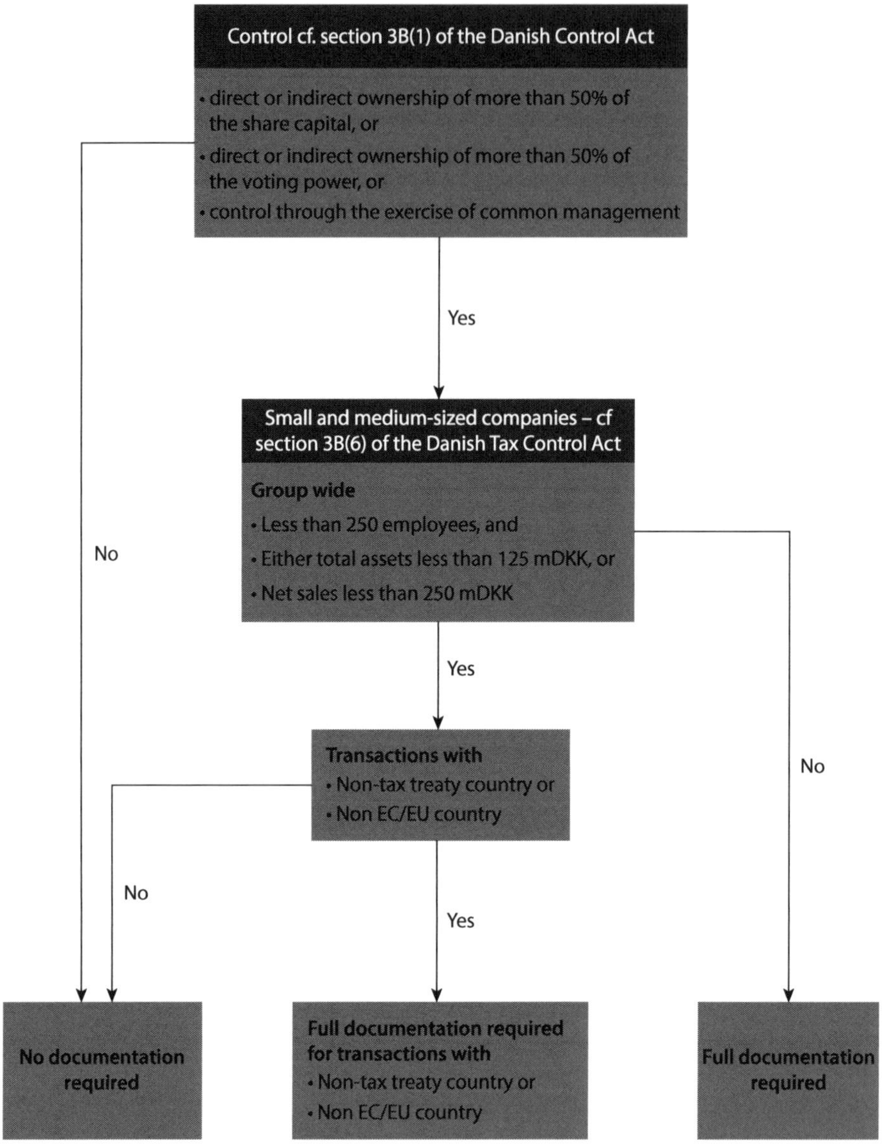

Source: Deloitte 2010.
Note: EC = European Community; EU = European Union.

Where separate documentation is prepared, the transfer pricing documentation should include the following information (Hungary chapter of IBFD 2011a):

• Name, seat, tax number or equivalent identification number (or registration number), and name and seat of court (authority) keeping the commercial register (record) of the related party
• Subject, date of conclusion and modification, and duration of contract

- Details of characteristics of the property, service, and method and terms of performance
- Functional analysis: analysis of activity performed, resources used, and business risk undertaken
- Description and characteristics of possible relationship
- Method used to determine arm's length price
- Reasons for selecting the applied method
- Source of comparable data, method of selecting comparable data, and explanation of selection
- Facts and conditions relating to comparable products and services
- Price, margin, profit, other value or range (arm's length price) calculated on the basis of comparable assets and services
- Arm's length price and determination of difference in factors influencing arm's length price and consequent adjustments
- Date of preparation and modification of documentation
- Reason and explanation for aggregation of transactions or contracts, if applicable
- Details of pending or closed administrative actions or judicial proceedings regarding the related party transaction covered by the documentation

The documentation may be prepared in Hungarian, English, French, or German.[19] Documentation should be prepared before submission of the tax return and provided to the tax administration upon request. Failure to fulfill the documentation requirements can result in the imposition of a penalty of up to Ft 2 million per transaction for which adequate documentation has not been prepared. Between 2006 and 2010, the tax administration was active in enforcing these documentation rules and imposing penalties (see figure 6.5).

Figure 6.5 Penalties Imposed by Hungarian Tax Authority for Missing or Incomplete Documentation, 2006–10, in Euros

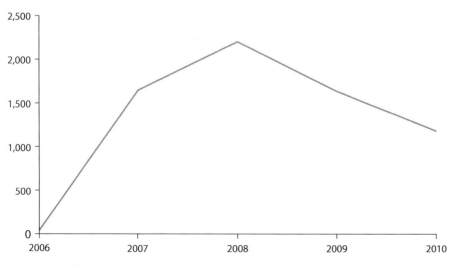

Source: Mekler and Sethi 2012.

Italy

Italy introduced transfer pricing documentation provisions in 2010 that provide protection from administrative penalties in the event of a transfer pricing adjustment for taxpayers who submitted the appropriate documentation during an audit or within 10 days of a request by the tax administration and communicated to the tax authorities in their tax return that such documentation was prepared (see annex 6A) (IBFD 2011a, Italy chapter; Musselli and Musselli 2011).[20] The form of the appropriate documentation is in a decision of the commissioner issued September 29, 2010. The requirements, based on the EU "Code of Conduct on Transfer Pricing Documentation" and the *OECD Transfer Pricing Guidelines* (2010), specify different documentation requirements for Italian holding companies, subholding companies, and controlled enterprises (see figure 6.6). The decree specifies the content of the master file and the country-specific documentation (see box 6.4).

Figure 6.6 Italy's Documentation Requirements

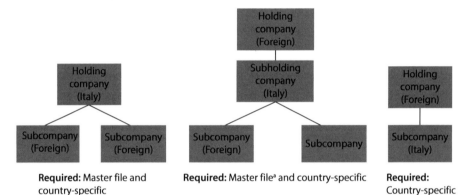

Required: Master file and country-specific

Required: Master file[a] and country-specific

Required: Country-specific

Note: EU = European Union.
a. Can be based on subgroup activity or master file for entire group may be submitted if prepared by EU resident company in accordance with EU "Code of Conduct."

Box 6.4 Master File and Country-Specific Documentation Required by Italian Tax Authority

The following extract is an unofficial English translation of the Decision of the Commissioner of Italy Revenue Agency (2010).[a]

Master file
Multiple master files may be prepared if the multinational enterprise is active in different industries.

• General description of the multinational group
• Group structure (organizational structure and operational structure) of the MNE
• Business strategies pursued by the MNE group
• Transaction flows

---

box continues next page

Box 6.4 Master File and Country-Specific Documentation Required by Italian Tax Authority *(continued)*

- Intragroup transactions; sale of tangible or intangible assets, provision of services, financial services transactions; intragroup services; cost contribution arrangements
- Functions performed, assets used, and risks assumed
- Intangible assets
- Transfer pricing policy of the MNE
- APAs with EU tax authorities and rulings obtained from EU tax authorities

Country-specific documentation
- General description of the enterprise
- Identification of business sector
- Organization chart
- General business strategies pursued
- Information on controlled transactions (sale of tangible and intangible assets, provision of services, and financial services transactions)
- Cost contribution arrangements
- Transaction flow chart
- Copies of written agreements

a. See Agenzia Entrate's website, September 29, 2010 (ref.2010/137654 29.09.2010), available at http://www.agenziaentrate
.gov.it/wps/wcm/connect/407e6800444f85af891ceb536ed3dbc9/ItalyCommissionerDecision_29_09_2010_transfer_pricing
.pdf?MOD=AJPERES&CACHEID=407e6800444f85af891ceb536ed3dbc9.

Documentation must be prepared annually if there are no substantial changes in the economic circumstances affecting the taxpayer; SMEs (businesses with annual revenues of less than €50 million) are required to update their comparability analysis (if a search of external comparables was relied on) and the selection of method only every two years. Documentation must be prepared in Italian, with the exception of the master file, which is prepared in English when presented by a subholding company (see figure 6.6). Documentation should be prepared electronically; if it is provided in paper format, it must be converted to electronic format if requested by the tax administration.

Kenya

The Kenya Revenue Authority has not published any detailed transfer pricing documentation requirements or guidelines to date. However, Rule 9(1) of the Income Tax (Transfer Pricing) Rules 2006 states that the tax commissioner may request certain information, including books of accounts and other documents relating to transfer pricing. Rule 9(2) specifies that documents referred to in paragraph (1) shall include documents relating to the following issues[21]:

(a) Selection of the transfer pricing method and the reasons for the selection;
(b) Application of the method, including the calculations made and price adjustment factors considered;
(c) Global organization structure of the enterprise;

(d) Details of the transaction under consideration;
(e) Assumptions, strategies, and policies applied in selecting the method; and
(f) Such other background information as may be necessary regarding the transaction

Rule 9(3) requires that the books of accounts and other documents be prepared in or translated into English at the time the transfer price is determined. Rule 10 provides that taxpayers should develop a transfer pricing policy, determine the arm's length price, and provide evidence thereof to the tax commissioner upon request.

Malaysia

In 2012, the Income Tax Transfer Pricing Rules (2012) were published (effective January 1, 2009).[22] Rule 4 states that a person who enters into a controlled transaction must prepare contemporaneous transfer pricing documentation, including records and documents that provide a description of the following:

- Organizational structure, including an organization chart identifying people involved in controlled transactions;
- The nature of the business or industry and market conditions;
- The controlled transaction;
- Strategies, assumptions, and information regarding factors that influence the setting of any pricing policies;
- Comparability, functional, and risk analysis;
- Selection of the transfer pricing method;
- Application of the transfer pricing method;
- Documents that provide the foundation for or otherwise support or are referred to in developing the transfer pricing analysis;
- Index to documents; and
- Any other information, data, or document considered relevant to determining an arm's length price.

For the purposes of satisfying this rule, transfer pricing documentation is considered "contemporaneous" where it is brought into existence.

Russia

Russia introduced new transfer pricing legislation in July 2011 (effective January 1, 2012). The legislation identifies documentation requirements for taxpayers engaging in controlled transactions that, if satisfied, provide relief from penalties in the event a transfer pricing adjustment is made (as defined in chapter 105.14 of the Tax Code, which includes certain thresholds).

To satisfy the requirements, the taxpayer must produce the documentation within 30 days of a request from the authorities. Requests cannot be made until June 1 of the year after the year audited. Although no specific format is specified, the documentation must include the following (Starkov 2011):

- Description of taxpayer's business;
- List of related parties, including their countries of residence;

- Description of controlled transactions and their terms, including transfer pricing method or methods used (if any), payment terms, and other relevant conditions;
- Functional analysis of controlled parties, including risks taken and assets used by each party;
- Description of method or methods used to test arm's length nature of transfer prices, including discussion of why method was selected;
- Description of the sources used;
- Calculation of arm's length range, including description of selection of comparable transactions;
- Tested party's profit and loss statement;
- Profit of tested party associated with use of valuable intangibles obtained in controlled transaction;
- Other relevant information, such as market strategy;
- Adjustments to reported tax liability made by taxpayer, if any; and
- Any other information confirming the arm's length nature of transactions that taxpayer considers relevant.

South Africa

There is no explicit requirement for taxpayers in South Africa to maintain transfer pricing documentation. However, in paragraph 10.1 of Practice Note 7, the South African Revenue Service (SARS) notes that "it is in the taxpayer's best interest to document how transfer prices have been determined, since adequate documentation is the best way to demonstrate that transfer prices are consistent with the arm's length principle." The note highlights various advantages.

Paragraph 10.3 of Practice Note 7 sets out the tax commissioner's expectations regarding documentation, making reference to the principles in chapter 5 of the *OECD Transfer Pricing Guidelines*, in particular prudent business management. It lists items that are generally expected to be addressed (paragraph 10.3.6):

- Identification of transactions in terms of international agreements entered into with connected persons and the extent of any other commercial or financial relations with connected persons, which fall within the scope of Section 31;
- Copies of the international agreements entered into with connected persons;
- A description of the nature and terms (including prices) of all the relevant transactions (including a series of transactions and any relevant offsetting transactions);
- The method that has been used to arrive at the nature and terms of the relevant transactions (including the functional analysis undertaken and an appraisal of potential comparables);
- The reasons why the choice of method was considered to be the most appropriate to the relevant transactions and to the particular circumstances;

- An explanation of the process used to select and apply the method used to establish the transfer prices and why it is considered to provide a result that is consistent with the arm's length principle;
- Information relied on in arriving at the arm's length terms such as commercial agreements with third parties, financial information, budgets, forecasts, etc.; and
- Details of any special circumstances that have influenced the price set by the taxpayer.

According to the 2005 addendum to Practice Note 7, where taxpayers have prepared a formal transfer pricing policy and made a disclosure to that effect in their tax return, this policy document should be submitted with the tax return:

> SARS hereby confirms that its policy remains that there is no statutory requirement that taxpayers compile a formal transfer pricing policy document. The requirement for submission of a formal transfer pricing policy document in terms of the annual return of income must, therefore, be read as a requirement to submit such a policy document where a taxpayer has in fact already compiled one. In the event that a taxpayer has not compiled such a policy document, it is sufficient to formally confirm that one has not been compiled.

Turkey

Turkey introduced comprehensive transfer pricing documentation (so-called annual transfer pricing report) requirements effective 2007 (January 1, 2008, for transactions involving Turkish free trade zones) (Biçerm 2011; Deloitte 2009; IBFD 2011a, Turkey chapter; PwC 2011, Turkey chapter). Under these requirements:

- Corporate taxpayers registered with the Large Taxpayers Office must prepare an annual transfer pricing report for both their domestic and their cross-border related-party transactions;
- Corporate taxpayers registered with other tax offices must prepare an annual transfer pricing report for their cross-border related-party transactions and transactions with related parties operating in a Turkish free-trade zone; and
- Corporate taxpayers operating in Turkish free-trade zones must prepare an annual transfer pricing report for their domestic transactions with other corporate taxpayers not operating in a Turkish free-trade zone.

The annual transfer pricing report must be prepared in line with the general communiqué on transfer pricing (annex C to Communiqué 1), which requires five main sections: general overview, details of related parties, details of related-party transactions, transfer pricing analysis, and conclusion. Documents and data referred to in the report must also be included with the report. New guidelines issued by the revenue authority in 2010 provide details regarding the preparation of the annual transfer pricing report.[23]

Documentation should be prepared in Turkish. However, original documents may be included that require translation only upon the request of the tax authorities. The annual transfer pricing report does not need to be submitted with the tax return, but it must be made available within 15 days of a request from the tax authorities. There is no specific penalty regime for transfer pricing.

United States

In the United States, taxpayers must prepare contemporaneous transfer pricing documentation to obtain protection from the penalties otherwise applicable for underpayment of tax arising as a result of transfer pricing adjustment. Protection from penalties is available where:

- It is established that the taxpayer determined such price in accordance with a specific pricing method set forth in the regulations prescribed under Section 482 and that the taxpayer's use of such method was reasonable;
- The taxpayer has documentation (which was in existence as of the time of filing the return), which sets forth the determination of such price in accordance with such a method and which establishes that the use of such method was reasonable; and
- The taxpayer provides such documentation to the Secretary within 30 days of a request for such documentation (Section 6662 (e)(3)(b)(i) USC).

The documentation requirements are set out in §1.6662-6 of the Regulations.[24] Ten principal documents must be included in a taxpayer's documentation:

- An overview of the taxpayer's business, including an analysis of the economic and legal factors that affect the pricing of its property or services.
- A description of the taxpayer's organizational structure (including an organization chart) covering all related parties engaged in transactions potentially relevant under Section 482, including foreign affiliates whose transactions directly or indirectly affect the pricing of property or services in the United States.
- Any documentation explicitly required by the regulations under Section 482.
- A description of the method selected and an explanation of why that method was selected.
- A description of the alternative methods that were considered and an explanation of why they were not selected.
- A description of the controlled transactions (including the terms of sale) and any internal data used to analyze those transactions. For example, if a profit split method is applied, the documentation must include a schedule providing the total income, costs, and assets (with adjustments for different accounting practices and currencies) for each controlled taxpayer participating in the relevant business activity and detailing the allocations of such items to that activity.
- A description of the comparables that were used, how comparability was evaluated, and what (if any) adjustments were made.

- An explanation of the economic analysis and projections relied upon in developing the method. For example, if a profit split method is applied, the taxpayer must provide an explanation of the analysis undertaken to determine how the profits would be split.
- A description or summary of any relevant data that the taxpayer obtains after the end of the tax year and before filing a tax return, which would help determine if a taxpayer selected and applied a specified method in a reasonable manner.
- A general index of the principal and background documents and a description of the record-keeping system used for cataloging and accessing those documents.

Any background documents that support the assumptions, conclusions, and positions in the principal documents must also be included.

Penalties Related to Transfer Pricing

Penalties can play a very important role in promoting and ensuring taxpayer compliance. Their purpose is to make the cost of noncompliance higher than the cost of compliance. The appropriate approach for a country depends on a range of factors, including the overall tax system, the compliance culture, and the allocation of burden of proof. Some countries have introduced specific penalty regimes for transfer pricing; others rely on the general penalty provisions in the tax law.

The type and size of penalties also varies (see table 6.7). Although some countries impose criminal penalties, only civil (administrative) penalties are applied in practice.

Penalties related to transfer pricing fall into two broad categories: adjustment-related penalties and documentation and compliance penalties. Where a transfer pricing adjustment gives rise to an underpayment of a tax liability, some countries, including China, impose an interest payment in addition to specific penalties.

Adjustment-Related Penalties

Most countries impose penalties only if a transfer pricing adjustment is made. The penalty may be levied on the amount of the adjustment or, more commonly, on the unpaid tax liability arising from the adjustment. The penalty rates imposed range from 5 percent to 300 percent. In many countries in which specific provisions regarding transfer pricing have been introduced (including Australia, China, Hungary, Italy, Russia, and the United States), penalties may be waived or reduced if adequate transfer pricing documentation is maintained. This potential protection from or reduction in penalties provides an incentive for taxpayers to prepare transfer pricing documentation.

Documentation and Compliance Penalties

Numerous countries have introduced penalties that may be imposed if a taxpayer does not comply with documentation requirements. Such penalties are

Table 6.7 Transfer Pricing Penalties in Selected Countries

Country	Fault	Penalty
Australia	Adjustment	10–50 percent of additional taxes (higher in cases of fraud)
India	Failure to maintain prescribed documentation	2 percent of transaction value
	Failure to furnish documents or information during audit	2 percent of transaction value
	Adjustment	100–300 percent of additional taxes
	Failure to produce accountants report	Rs 100,000 (about US$1,800)
Hungary	Failure to comply with documentation requirements	Ft 2 million per transaction per year
	Additional tax liability	Up to 50 percent
Malaysia	—	No specific transfer pricing penalties, but general penalty regime may result in penalties of 10–45 percent of additional taxes
Sweden	—	No specific transfer pricing penalties, but general penalty regime may result in penalties of 10–40 percent of additional taxes.
United States	Price for any property or service or for use of property in a related-party transaction is 200 percent or more (or 50 percent or less) of the amount determined under Section 482 to be correct price or the net section or Section 482 transfer pricing adjustment for taxable year exceeds the lesser of USD5 million or 10 percent of the taxpayer's gross receipts	20 percent of underpayment of tax
	Price used by taxpayer is 400 percent or more (or 25 percent or less) of price determined under Section 482 or net Section 482 transfer pricing adjustment exceeds the lesser of US$20 million or 20 percent of the taxpayer's gross receipts	40 percent of underpayment of tax

Source: Country-specific legislation.
Note: — = not applicable.

often applicable regardless of whether a transfer pricing adjustment is made (as is the case in Colombia, Denmark, and Hungary). The amounts differ across countries and can be significant.

Penalties for failure to comply with a country's documentation requirements can help ensure that taxpayers prepare transfer pricing documentation. Where the penalties are significant, they can provide low-hanging fruit for the tax administration in the early years of its transfer pricing enforcement program.

Introduction of documentation-related penalties should, however, be balanced against the potential compliance costs imposed on taxpayers and the possibility that taxpayers may be required to prepare levels of documentation that are not consistent with the level of risk posed by the transactions. Ensuring that the scope of the documentation requirements is appropriate, through the use of thresholds, is critical.

Transfer Pricing and Developing Economies • http://dx.doi.org/10.1596/978-1-4648-0969-9

Chapter 6 Main Messages

- Taxpayer compliance can be promoted through various forms of building awareness, effective communication, and outreach campaigns, as well as requirements to disclose transfer pricing-related information as part of the tax return or additional schedules.
- Many countries lack the basic information necessary to identify and assess potential transfer pricing risks. Requiring taxpayers to disclose specific information related to ownership and associated-party transactions can provide the tax administration with this information. It can also generate awareness and promote compliance.
- Transfer pricing documentation provides the information needed to assess taxpayer compliance with transfer pricing legislation. It can help prevent unnecessary transfer pricing disputes and resolve disputes should they arise.
- In formulating documentation rules, policy makers need to consider the impact on the burden of proof, the interaction with penalties, and the risk of transfer pricing audits. To avoid imposing disproportionate or unnecessary burdens on taxpayers, limitations to the scope of reporting requirements can be useful.
- A range of international institutions has provided detailed guidance on documentation requirements and has been one of the most prominent component of the OECD's BEPS action plan.

Annex 6A: Overview of Information Collected through Transfer Pricing–Related Disclosures

Disclosure/ Information collected	Rationale	Selected country examples
Type of taxpayer	• Provides the tax administration with the information necessary to identify the residence status of the taxpayer	• *Status of company (resident/nonresident/ nonresident permanent establishment/...)* [Australia] • *Resident status* (resident/nonresident) [India] • *In the case of a nonresident is there a permanent establishment (PE) in India?* (y/n) [India] • *Residential status of company* (resident/ nonresident) [Kenya]
Ownership information	• Allows the tax administration to easily identify taxpayers that are foreign owned or controlled, or own or controlled foreign subsidiaries. This is important as these are the taxpayers most likely to be party to transactions that fall within the scope of a countries' transfer pricing legislation.[a]	• *Name and country code of ultimate holding company* [Australia] • *Percentage of foreign shareholding (%)* [Australia] • *Does the corporation have any nonresident shareholders?* (y/n) [Canada] • *Did the corporation have any controlled foreign affiliates?* (y/n) [Canada] • *Names of holding company and subsidiaries* [India] • *Do you have related/associated enterprises outside Kenya? (y/n + name and address)* [Kenya]

table continues next page

Annex 6A: *(continued)*

Disclosure/ information collected	Rationale	Selected country examples
		• *Is your company controlled or owner by nonresidents? (y/n)* [New Zealand] • Exerts decisive influence on legal persons or has a permanent establishment abroad (y/n) [Denmark] • Is subject to decisive influence from individuals or legal persons or is an individual or legal person with a permanent establishment in Denmark (y/n) [Denmark]
Economic classification/ business activities	• Allows the tax administration to obtain a high-level understanding of taxpayer's business activity(s), which can provide a basis for classification for peer comparisons	• *Description of main business activity and industry code* [Australia] • *Specify the principal product(s) mined, manufactured, sold, constructed, or services provided, giving the approximate percentage of the total revenue that each product or service represents* [Canada] • *Nature of three main business activities/ products (code and description)* [India] • *State nature of business and related turnover* [Kenya]
Transactional information • **Party to transactions falling within the scope of the legislation**	Allows the tax administration to easily identify taxpayers who have entered into transactions that fall within the scope of the transfer pricing legislation	• *Did you have any transactions or dealings with international related parties (irrespective of whether they were on revenue or capital account)?* [Australia] • *Was the aggregate amount of the transactions or dealings with international related parties (including the value of property transferred or the balance outstanding on any loans) greater than AUD1m? (y/n)* [Australia] • *Has the corporation had any non–arm's-length transactions with a nonresident? (y/n)* [Canada]
Transactional information • **Transactions for no or nonmonetary consideration**	Allows the tax administration to easily identify taxpayers who have entered into transactions that fall within the scope of the transfer pricing legislation, but are not reflected in the accounts	• *Have you received from or provided to an international related party any nonmonetary consideration for the performance of services, transfer of property (tangible or intangible), processes, rights, or obligations during the income year?* [Australia] • *Have you provided to an international related party any services, transfer of property (tangible or intangible), processes, rights, or obligations for which the consideration was nil during the income year?* [Australia] • Provision or receipt of nonmonetary consideration for transfer of service, tangible or intangible asset, or anything else (y/n) [Canada]

table continues next page

Annex 6A: *(continued)*

Disclosure/ information collected	*Rationale*	*Selected country examples*
Transactional information • **Transaction details (type and value)**	Provides detailed information that the tax administration can use to risk assess taxpayers, in particular allowing them to identify large, abnormal, and/or high-risk transactions	• Aggregate purchases/expenditure and sales/revenue for specified transaction categories (see Appendix 6.4) [Australia] • Transactional information, including aggregate amounts of transactions, distinguished between income and expense for 19 categories of transaction type across five categories (tangible property; rents, royalties and intangible property; services; financial; and other) • Profit and loss and balance sheet transactions (by category — see Appendix 6.5), specifying for each category if < DKK10m, between DKK10–100m or > DKK100m, whether transactions in that category exceed 25 percent of total transactions and where the parties to the transactions were located (Denmark, EU/EEA, DTA countries and non-DTA countries) [Denmark] • Value of related-party transactions aggregated by sales and purchases per specified category (19 categories) [Turkey]
Transfer pricing methodologies	• Provides detailed information that the tax administration can use to risk assess taxpayers, in particular allowing them to identify abnormalities. Requires taxpayers to consider application of methodology and commit to a disclosure at time of lodging the tax return, thereby promoting compliance	• The four principal methodologies in descending order of total dollar value [Australia] • The transfer pricing method used for each category of transaction disclosed (see above) [Canada] • Aggregate values of sales and purchases for each transfer pricing method used [Turkey]
Documentation	• Provides tax administration with information as to whether taxpayer has documentation justifying application of the arm's length principle available	• Approximate percentage of the total dollar value of related party international dealings disclosed for which you have documented the processes involved in Steps 1 and 2 of TR 98/11 and Step 3 of TR 98/11[b] [Australia] • Whether appropriate transfer pricing documentation has been prepared as required by law for each nonresident transacted with (i.e. per detailed T106 slip)[c] [Canada]

Note: EEA European Economic Area; EU = European Union.
a. Whilst some countries require a list of all associated parties, the majority restricts such information to those which the taxpayer has transacted with. Requirements to list all associated parties, regardless of transactions, may impose an unnecessarily large compliance burden, particularly for large MNE groups that can comprise 100s of entities worldwide.
b. See Section 5.3.3.1 on TR 98/11.
c. See Appendix 6.1.

Annex 6B: Summary of Selected Countries' (Transfer Pricing) Disclosure Requirements

Country	Form	Who	Disclosures	Notes
Australia	Separate schedule (Schedule 25A)[a]	All non-individual taxpayers with aggregate international related party transactions > AUD1m (including loan balances)	Disclosures in Part A (which deals with transfer pricing), include: • Three primary business activities, along with three primary locations for each and aggregate values of international related party transactions • Purchases/expenditures and income/revenue amounts (not netted off) for various specified international related party transaction types falling under the general categories of tangible property; royalties, rent and intangible property; services; other and loan balances (interest-bearing and interest-free) • Whether or not any non-monetary consideration was received or provided to an international related party for goods, services, or property (y/n) • Whether or not any goods, property, or services were provided to international related parties for no consideration(y/n) • Approximate percentage of dollar value of transaction for which transfer pricing documentation has been prepared in accordance with TR 98/11 • The four main transfer pricing methods used to price revenue transactions by dollar value of transactions and approximate percentage of transactions for which each was used • Disclosures regarding capital (non-revenue) transactions, such as sales of assets, etc., including methods used • Whether or not a nonresident participated in the capital, management, or control • Number of international related parties with which taxpayer had dealings during the year	Used by the Australian Taxation Office for risk assessment purposes — transfer pricing reviews/audits will generally commence with a request for information supporting the disclosures made
Canada	Separate form (Form T106)[b]	Reporting taxpayer or partnership with combined reportable transactions with nonresidents > CAD1m	*T106 Summary Form,* detailing: • Total amounts from T106 slips (see below) • Gross revenue of reporting person • Main business activities (up to four) using NAICS codes • Any amounts reported affected by completed, outstanding, or anticipated requests for competent authority assistance (y/n) • Any amounts reported adjusted to reflect assessment or proposed assessment by a foreign tax administration (y/n)	Information is used by the CRA as part of its audit selection process

table continues next page

Annex 6B: *(continued)*

Country	Form	Who	Disclosures	Notes
			• Any amounts reported covered by an APA or similar agreement between nonresident and foreign tax administration (y/n) • Provision or receipt of non-monetary consideration for transfer of service, tangible or intangible asset or anything else (y/n) For each nonresident transacted with a *Detailed T106 slip* is required to be completed, detailing: • Contact information and country of nonresident (and whether or not that is a country with which Canada has a tax treaty) • Type of relationship • Main business activities for reported transactions • Whether appropriate transfer pricing documentation has been prepared as required by law • Transactional information, including aggregate amounts of transactions, distinguished between income and expense for 19 categories of transaction type across five categories (tangible property; rents, royalties and intangible property, services, financial and other) and the transfer pricing method used for each category • Loan balances and investment amounts • Information regarding derivatives, including number of contracts, notional amount, revenue and expenditure for eight categories of contract • Current account balances (payables and receivables)	

table continues next page

Annex 6B: *(continued)*

Country	Form	Who	Disclosures	Notes
Colombia[c]	Individual informative return (Form 120)[d] (or Consolidated informative return in the case of affiliates not required to file — Form 130)[e] Form 1525 (Resolution 011188)	Taxpayers with foreign-related parties that at year end exceed the established caps of gross equity greater than or equal to TU100,000[f] or gross income equal to or higher than TU610,000 and any taxpayers that engage in transactions with tax havens.	*Informative return* • Taxpayer's fiscal identification • Income-tax ID and country of domicile of the parties to the controlled transactions • Transfer pricing method(s) used • Interquartile range obtained in the application of the transfer pricing method(s) • Assessment of sanctions, where necessary *Comparables information (Resolution 011188)* • Information on comparables (document type code, tax identification number, name, type of transaction, internal v. external, etc.) – Internal comparables: name, country, value, amount or margin, profitability, adjustment etc. – External comparables: acceptance and rejection matrix, name, country, adjustment margin, source, date, etc.	Must be filled electronically
Denmark	Separate form 05.021/05.022[g]	All taxpayers with controlled transactions during the year the sum of which is > DKK5m	Basic information: • Whether taxpayer exerts or is subject to decisive influence on or by a nonresident or a permanent establishment (or is a permanent establishment), or is otherwise associated with legal persons • Principal field of activity • Number of units with which there have been controlled transactions Detailed information: • Profit and loss disclosures (sales and purchases of goods, services, leasing, intangibles, financing + more) indicating amount of each type if < DKK10m, between DKK10-100m or > DKK100m and whether total of type is > 25 percent of total controlled transactions • Balance sheet (capital transactions, including intangibles, tangibles, capital participation sales or purchases, financial assets, loans + more) indicating is amount of each type if < DKK10m, between DKK10-100m or > DKK100m and whether total of type is > 25 percent of total controlled transactions	A disclosure is also required in the corporate tax return as to whether taxpayer has controlled transactions during the year the sum of which is > DKK5m Used for risk assessment

table continues next page

Annex 6B: *(continued)*

Country	Form	Who	Disclosures	Notes
India	Separate form (Form No. 3CEB)	Every person who entered into an international transaction	• List of associated enterprises with whom international transactions were entered into, including name, relationship, brief description of business carried on • Particulars with respect to transactions, including: - tangible property (raw materials or consumables, finished goods and other property) - intangible property - providing services - lending or borrowing money - mutual agreement or arrangement - any other transaction including name and address of associated party(s), description of transaction and quantity sold/purchased, total amount paid/receivable or payable/ received per books and as computed per arm's length price, transfer pricing method used	Form must be signed off by a chartered accountant or other person eligible to audit companies
Kenya	Additional schedule to tax return[h]	Companies having transactions with related/associated enterprises outside Kenya	• Annex to income-tax return for companies IT2C requires disclosure of: - Whether or not taxpayer has related/associated enterprises outside of Kenya - Whether taxpayer has documented its transfer pricing policy - A list of nonresident-related/associated enterprises (including address and nature of relationship) - Details of aggregate monetary value of sales and purchase transactions grouped by transaction type (tangible goods, services, etc.) and including details of TPM used and amount of any transfer pricing adjustment made - Details of loan balances (interest-bearing and interest-free)	Introduced in 2010, but only as part of electronic filing

table continues next page

Annex 6B: *(continued)*

Country	Form	Who	Disclosures	Notes

New Zealand	Limited disclosures required in tax return	n/a	• Tax return (IR4) requires taxpayers to disclose:
			  - Whether payments were made to nonresidents
			  - Whether the company was controlled or owned by nonresidents
				Used for risk-assessment purposes
				Completion of a detailed questionnaire may be required post lodgment[i]

Russia	Controlled Transactions Notice	Taxpayers engaged in controlled transactions[j]	• Information on controlled transactions, including:
			  - the calendar year over which the controlled transactions took place
			  - the subjects of the controlled transactions
			  - particulars of the parties to the controlled transactions
			  - the sum of income earned and/or expenses incurred with respect to controlled transactions (may be grouped for homogenous transactions)
				Failure to submit the notice may result in a fine of RUB5,000

South Africa	No separate form, but disclosures required in tax return (IT14)[k]		• Did the company enter into any cross-border transactions in terms of an international agreement, as defined in Section 31? • Does the company have a transfer pricing policy document in support of the transfer pricing policy applied in the current year in relation to the transactions as defined in Section 31? • Has the company provided goods, services, or anything of value (including transaction on capital accounts) to a nonresident connected person for no consideration? (Please note that goods and services include a loan).	Instructions state that if the answer is "yes" to either of the first two questions, then taxpayers need to furnish the following in respect of each transaction: • Copy of agreement entered into; • Copy of transfer pricing policy document; applicable to the current year. Unless documentation already submitted applies to the current year's transactions.[l] *Completion of a detailed questionnaire may be required post lodgment[m]*

table continues next page

Annex 6B: *(continued)*

Country	Form	Who	Disclosures	Notes
Turkey	Form related to transfer pricing, controlled foreign corporation and thin capitalization (attachment to corporate tax return)	Corporate taxpayers	• General information about the company (tax identification number, trade registry number, name of corporation, activity code, telephone and fax number, taxation period) • Name and details (residency) of related parties • Details of transactions carried out with related parties (i.e. aggregate purchases and sales by classification — assets, services, financial transactions, other transactions, etc.) • Methods used (by aggregate value for sales and purchases) • Details about foreign subsidiaries (name, location, ownerships percentage, and gross income) • Information regarding thin capitalization (total assets, total debt, total equity, total amount of debt to shareholders and related parties)	

Note: APA = advance pricing agreement; CRA = Canada Revenue Agency; n.a. = not applicable; NAICS = North American Industry Classification System; SARS = South Africa Revenue Service.

a. The Australian Taxation office is currently in the process of introducing a new schedule ("International Dealings Schedule"). It was introduced in 2011 for financial institutions, and will be introduced for all taxpayers in 2012 (See Appendix 6.3).

b. http://www.cra-arc.gc.ca/E/pbg/tf/t106/t106-11e.pdf.

c. Source: Based on information in PWC International Transfer Pricing 2011.

d. Available in Spanish at http://www.dian.gov.co/descargas/Formularios/2010/120-2010.pdf.

e. Available in Spanish at http://www.dian.gov.co/descargas/Formularios/2010/130-2010.pdf.

f. In FY2009 one TU was equivalent to COP23,763 (roughly USD12.51USD).

g. See Appendix 6.4.

h. See Appendix 6.5.

i. See Appendix 6.7.

j. Which when aggregated are greater than RUB100m in 2012 and RUB80m in 2013. It is understood this threshold will be removed in later years. See Starkov, V., "The New Russian Transfer Pricing Regulations: An Overview," BNA Tax Management Transfer Pricing Report, Vol. 20 No. 7, 7/28/2011 at http://www.nera.com/nera-files/PUB_BNA_Tax_0711.pdf.

k. http://www.sars.gov.za/Tools/Documents/DocumentDownload.asp?FileID=59719.

l. In practice, SARS does not actually require submission of a copy of transfer pricing policy unless one has been prepared by the taxpayer as there is no statutory obligation for taxpayers to prepare such documentation, see Section 6.3.3.10. Transfer Pricing: Addendum to SARS Practice Note 7 Dated 6 August 1999: Submission of Transfer Pricing Policy Document (http://www.sars.gov.za/Tools/Documents/DocumentDownload.asp?FileID=57375).

m. See Appendix 6.7.

Annex 6C: Australia: Schedule 25A (2011)[a]–Part A[b]

Australian Government
Australian Taxation Office

Schedule 25A

Print neatly in BLOCK LETTERS with a black or blue ballpoint pen only.

2011

Refer to *Schedule 25A instructions 2011*, available on our website www.ato.gov.au for explanations and instructions on how to complete this schedule.

Tax file number (TFN)

This schedule forms part of the tax return of:

Name of entity and Australian business number (ABN)

ABN

Section A	Overseas transactions information

Show whole dollars only (rounded down to the nearest dollar).

1   List the industry codes that best describe the business activity undertaken by you to which the international dealings relate, in descending order of total dollar value. For each industry code specify the three principal foreign locations of these international related parties in descending order of total dollar value and the total dollar value of related party dealings (excluding loans).

	Industry code		Amount				Foreign locations		
A		**B**	.00	**C**		**D**		**E**	
F		**G**	.00	**H**		**I**		**J**	
K		**L**	.00	**M**		**N**		**O**	F

2   For items 2a to 2d, write at Column A the amounts of purchases/expenditure and at Column B the amounts of sales/revenue in respect of related party international dealings.

For items 2e and 2f, write at Column A the amount of opening balances and at Column B the amount of closing balances of the interest bearing loans and interest free loans in respect of international related parties.

			Column A Purchases/expenditure		Column B Sales/revenue	
2a	Tangible property	Stock in trade and raw materials	**A**	.00	**B**	.00
		All other tangible property	**C**	.00	**D**	.00
2b	Royalties, rent and intangible property	Royalties	**E**	.00	**F**	.00
		Rent other than royalties	**G**	.00	**H**	.00
		All other intangible property	**I**	.00	**J**	.00
2c	Services	Management, financial, administrative, marketing, training	**K**	.00	**L**	.00
		Technical, construction	**M**	.00	**N**	.00
		Research and development	**O**	.00	**P**	.00
		Other	**Q**	.00	**R**	.00 F
2d	Other	Interest, discounts	**A**	.00	**B**	.00
		Insurance	**C**	.00	**D**	.00
		All other payments, expenses, sales and revenue not included elsewhere	**E**	.00	**F**	.00

			Opening balance		Closing balance	
2e	**Loans** – interest bearing	Amounts borrowed	**G**	.00	**H**	.00
		Amounts loaned	**I**	.00	**J**	.00
2f	**Loans** – interest free	Amounts borrowed	**K**	.00	**L**	.00
		Amounts loaned	**M**	.00	**N**	.00 F

NAT 1125–6.2011   IN CONFIDENCE – when completed   PAGE 1

3a Have you received from or provided to an international related party any non-monetary consideration for the performance of services, transfer of property (tangible or intangible), processes, rights or obligations during the income year?   **B** ☐   Print **Y** for yes or **N** for no.

3b Have you provided to an international related party any services, transfer of property (tangible or intangible), processes, rights or obligations for which the consideration was nil during the income year?   **C** ☐   Print **Y** for yes or **N** for no.

---

4 For items 4a and 4b select one of the codes listed in the instructions for item 4. Use the approximate percentage of the total dollar value of related party international dealings referred to in items 2a to 2d for which you have documented the processes involved in:

4a Step 1 and step 2 of Taxation Ruling TR 98/11   **F** ☐

4b Step 3 of Taxation Ruling TR 98/11   **G** ☐

---

5 What are the arm's length pricing methods used to set or review consideration in related party international dealings of a revenue (non-capital) nature (referred to in items 2a to 2d)? Work out the four principal methods used, in descending order (most to least) of total dollar value of revenue derived and expenses incurred.

Column A   Column B

Column A: List the four principal methodologies in descending order of total dollar value. The methodologies should be identified using the codes in the instructions at item 5.   **H** ☐   **I** ☐

J ☐   **K** ☐

Column B: For each of the methods shown at Column A, list the codes to indicate the approximate percentage of the total dollar value of revenue derived and expenses incurred that the methodology covers – see item 5 of the instructions.   **L** ☐   **M** ☐

N ☐   **O** ☐

6a During the income year did you have any related party international dealings of a non-revenue (capital) nature referred to in questions 2a to 2d in which:
- you acquired an interest in an asset, OR
- a CGT event occurred (including disposal)?   **P** ☐   Print **Y** for yes or **N** for no.

The words **acquired**, **CGT event**, **disposal** and **asset** are used in this item within the context of Part 3-1 of the *Income Tax Assessment Act 1997* (ITAA 1997). The question does not refer to trading stock held in the ordinary course of business.

Only answer items 6b and 6c if the answer to 6a is yes.

6b Use the codes listed in the instructions for item 6 to list the four principal methods used for pricing acquisitions and disposals, in descending order of total dollar value.   **Q** ☐

6c Use the codes listed in the instructions for item 6 to indicate the total dollar value of the related party international dealings of a non-revenue (capital) nature included at item 6a as a percentage of total dollar value of related party international dealings of a revenue and non-revenue (capital and non-capital) nature referred to in items 2a to 2d.   **R** ☐

---

7 Did a non-resident participate directly or indirectly in your capital, management or control during the income year?   **S** ☐   Print **Y** for yes or **N** for no.

---

8 Show the number of international related parties with which you had dealings during the year.   **T** ☐   F

PAGE 2   www.ato.gov.au

Section B   Interests in foreign companies or foreign trusts

9 Show the number of controlled foreign companies and controlled foreign trusts in which you had either a direct or indirect interest at the start and end of the accounting period.

	Listed country	Section 404 country	Unlisted country
Start	**A**	**B**	**C**
End	**D**	**E**	**F**

10 Show the amounts of attributable income of controlled foreign companies (CFC) and controlled foreign trusts (CFT) included in your assessable income against the following sections of the *Income Tax Assessment Act 1936* (ITAA 1936).

	Listed country	Section 404 country	Unlisted country	Total
Section 456 – CFCs attributable income	**G** ·00	**H** ·00	**I** ·00	**J** ·00
Section 457 – CFCs change of residence			**K**	·00
Section 459A – interposed Australian entities			**N**	·00

11 Show the amounts of foreign non-assessable non-exempt income derived by you against the following sections of ITAA 1936.

	Listed country	Unlisted country and Section 404 country	Unlisted country
Section 23AH – foreign branch profits of Australian companies	**O** ·00	**P** ·00	
Section 23AI – amounts paid out of attributed CFC income	**Q** ·00	**R** ·00	**S** ·00
Section 23AJ – non-portfolio dividend from foreign countries	**T** ·00	**U** ·00	**V** ·00

Section 23AK – amounts paid out of attributed foreign investment fund (FIF) income **W** ·00 **F**

12a If applicable, what is the amount of the reduction in capital gains determined in accordance with Sub-division 768-G of the *Income Tax Assessment Act 1997* (ITAA 1997)? **L** ·00

12b If applicable, what is the amount of capital losses, as reduced in accordance with Sub-division 768-G of the ITAA 1997, that may be utilised or carried forward? **G** ·00

13 Has any controlled foreign company or controlled foreign trust of an unlisted country transferred any asset (excluding trading stock transferred in the normal course of business) or amounts of accumulated profits, capital, or other assets/reserves to a related entity in a listed country at any time during the income year?

Accumulated profits	**S**	Print **Y** for yes or **N** for no.
Accumulated losses	**T**	Print **Y** for yes or **N** for no.
Paid up capital	**U**	Print **Y** for yes or **N** for no.
Other assets/reserves	**V**	Print **Y** for yes or **N** for no.

14 Have you ever, directly or indirectly, caused the transfer of property, including money or services, to a non-resident trust estate? **W** Print **Y** for yes or **N** for no.

15 Were you a beneficiary of a non-resident trust estate at any time during the income year? **X** Print **Y** for yes or **N** for no.

16 Did you have an interest in, or an entitlement to acquire an interest in, either the income or capital of a non-resident trust estate at any time during the income year? **Y** Print **Y** for yes or **N** for no.

17 If the answer is yes to items 14, 15 or 16, were any of the non-resident trusts discretionary? **Z** Print **Y** for yes or **N** for no.

18 Were you able to directly or indirectly control or direct a non-resident trust at any time during the income year? **A** Print **Y** for yes or **N** for no. **F**

www.ato.gov.au   PAGE 3

If the schedule is not lodged with the income tax return you are required to sign and date the schedule.

Important
Before making this declaration check to ensure that all the information required has been provided on this form and any attachments to this form, and that the information provided is true and correct in every detail. If you are in doubt about any aspect of the tax return, place all the facts before the ATO. The income tax law imposes heavy penalties for false or misleading statements.

TAXPAYER'S DECLARATION

DECLARATION

I declare that all the information on this form is true and correct.

Signature

Date [ ] [ ] / [ ] [ ] / [ ] [ ] [ ] [ ]
(Day / Month / Year)

Contact person

Daytime contact number (include area code)   **F**

Important notes about *Schedule 25A 2011*

If you printed **Y** for yes at a question concerning overseas transactions on the partnership, trust, company or fund tax return, complete Section A of this schedule and attach it to the appropriate tax return.

If you printed **Y** for yes at a question concerning interest in a foreign company, foreign trust, foreign investment fund or foreign life assurance policy on the partnership, trust, company or fund tax return, complete all items in Section B of this schedule and attach it to the appropriate tax return.

If you printed **Y** for yes at both questions, complete Sections A and B and attach the schedule to the appropriate tax return.

The ABN is to be completed by corporate taxpayers and foreign companies with registered businesses in Australia.

Please note: If you are a financial service provider you may need to complete the *International dealings schedule – financial services 2011* instead of the Schedule 25A.

The International dealings schedule – financial services must be completed by all financial service providers who are:

- a foreign bank,
- a foreign bank branch,
- general or life insurance entity, or
- financial service providers (except superannuation funds) who reported an annual turnover of $250 million or more on their current year's income tax return.

For more information, refer to *International dealings schedule – financial services instructions 2011* available on **ato.gov.au**.

Terms used in this schedule

Related party international dealings means international transactions, agreements or arrangements between related parties. The term includes all transactions between an Australian resident and international related parties.

Participate(s) includes a right of participation, the exercise of which is contingent on an agreed event occurring.

International related parties means persons who are parties to international dealings that can be subject to Division 13 Part III of the ITAA 1936 or the associated enterprises article of a relevant double tax agreement. The term includes the following:

- any overseas entity or person who participates directly or indirectly in your management, control or capital
- any overseas entity or person in respect of which you participate directly or indirectly in the management, control or capital
- any overseas entity or person in respect of which persons who participate directly or indirectly in its management, control or capital are the same persons who participate directly or indirectly in your management, control or capital.

Person has the same meaning as in subsection 6(1) of ITAA 1936 and section 995-1 of ITAA 1997.

Capital means an equity interest of 10% or greater.

Refer to the *Schedule 25A instructions 2011* for detailed instructions and explanations.

Note: The instructions for completing the Schedule 25A can be accessed here: http://www.ato.gov.au/taxprofessionals /content.aspx?menuid=0&doc=/content/00277668.htm&page=2&H2. Part B of Schedule 25A requires disclosures relevant to, inter alia, compliance with Australia's controlled foreign companies' legislation. The full schedule can be accessed here: http:// www.ato.gov.au/content/downloads/TP00277665nat11252011.pdf.
a. The instructions for completely the Schedule 25A can be accessed here: http://www.ato.gov.au/taxprofessionals/content. aspx?menuid=0&doc=/content/00277668.htm&page=2&H2.
b. Part B of Schedule 25A requires disclosures relevant to *inter alia* compliance with Australia's controlled foreign companies' legislation. The full schedule can be accessed here: http://www.ato.gov.au/content/downloads/TP00277665nat11252011.pdf.

Annex 6D: Denmark: Controlled Transactions Form

SKAT

Controlled transactions
1(3)
Appendix to tax return

Income year

Name

Business reg.no. (CVR)	or	Civil reg. no. (CPR)

Appendix to the income tax return concerning controlled transactions, see section 3 B of the Danish Tax Control Act (Skattekontrolloven)

All points 1-33 must be completed	Yes (tick)	No (tick)
1. Exerts decisive influence on legal persons or has a permanent establishment abroad		
2. Is subject to decisive influence from individuals or legal persons or is an individual or legal person with a permanent establishment in Denmark		
3. Is otherwise associated with a legal person		
4. Is covered by section 3 B(6) of the Tax Control Act		

5. The taxable entity's principal field of activity:

Tick appropriate boxes	Production	Trade	Finance	Service	Other

6. Exact number of entities with which there have been controlled transactions

in Denmark:

in the EU/EEA: of which are permanent establishments:

in states outside the EU/EEA with which Denmark has signed a double tax convention:

of which are permanent establishments:

in states outside the EU/EEA with which Denmark has not signed a double tax convention:

of which are permanent establishments:

7. Are the foreign entities comprised by joint taxation in Denmark? Yes No

---

Guidance

Point 2
The expression 'legal persons' also includes the so-called tax-transparent entities, i.e. companies and associations etc. that according to the Danish tax rules are not in themselves single taxpayers but entities regulated by corporate laws, a company agreement, regulations of the association or the like, e.g. a limited partnership (K/S) or a partnership (I/S). Foreign individuals and legal persons that are taxable in Denmark from a hydrocarbon allied company according to section 21(1) or (4) of the Danish Hydrocarbon Act (Kulbrinteskatteloven) are also subject to the information and documentation requirements of section 3 B of the Tax Control Act even if they do not have a permanent establishment according to the standard definition.

Point 3
Tick "yes" if the taxable entity is subject to decisive influence from the same shareholders or the same management as another legal person. A legal person can also be a tax-transparent entity, see the above paragraph.

Point 4
Tick "yes" if the taxable entity belongs to a group of companies with less than 250 employees and either a balance sheet below DKK 125 million or a turnover below DKK 250 million. These taxable entities must only produce transfer pricing documentation for controlled transactions with entities resident in states with which Denmark has not signed a transfer pricing-relevant double tax convention (DTC) and which are not members of the EU/EEA, see section 3 B(6) of the Tax Control Act. The states with which Denmark has transfer pricing-relevant DTCs, are described in Danish in section C.F.9 of SKAT's legal guide. The agreements with Hong Kong, Iran, Jordan, Lebanon and the CIS countries do not cover the question of associated companies and are therefore not considered to be transfer pricing-relevant DTCs.

Point 5
The taxable entity's principal field of activity should be stated in general and not limited to controlled transactions.

Point 6
An entity is an associated party as defined in point 1-3. Legal persons in point 2 and 3 can also be tax-transparent entities. Enter "0" if there has not been any controlled transactions with the entities resident in one or more of the geographical areas indicated. The states with which Denmark has a transfer pricing-relevant DTC are described in Danish in section C.F.9 of SKAT's legal guide, see also guidance for point 4.

05.022

Guidance *(continued)*

The types of transactions are stated on page 3 of the form. Information should be given about the taxable entity's total controlled transactions. Types of transactions not comprised by the specific types in the table should be listed under "other".

For each individual type of transaction the total gross value of all the controlled transactions with all the affiliated entities is stated as precisely as possible (nearest thousand DKK). Transactions equal to a value of 0 DKK is stated with a 0.

Instead of the precise value, one of the following ranges can be stated:

1 = (1 DKK – 1 million DKK),
2 = (1 million DKK – 5 million DKK),
3 = (5 million DKK – 25 million DKK),
4 = (25 million DKK – 100 million DKK),
5 = (100 million DKK – 250 million DKK),
6 = (250 million DKK – 500 million DKK),
7 = (500 million DKK – 1 billion DKK)
8 = more than 1 billion DKK.

If there have been no transactions of a specific type, tick off in the column "No transactions".

If controlled transactions of a specific type exceed 25 % of the taxable entity's total transactions of the type in question, tick off in the column "above 25 %".

For each type of transaction write in which state(s) the entity(s) with which there have been controlled transactions is/are resident.

Put either A, B, C or D on the line, where
A = only in Denmark
B = only in states within the EU/EEA. This might include Denmark
C = also in states outside the EU/EEA with which Denmark has signed a double tax convention. This might include both Denmark and states within the EU/EEA.
D = also in states outside the EU/EEA with which Denmark has not signed a double tax convention. This might include both Denmark and states within and outside the EU/EEA with which Denmark has signed a double tax convention.

Example: If there have been transactions with associated entities in Denmark and Iran write "D" in the box.

Points 8, 22, 24, 26 and 28	The term "Sales" includes tranfers without any consideration or payment.
Points 9, 23 25, 27 and 29	The term "Purchase/Aquisition" includes reception without any consideration or payment.
Points 10-11	Incomes and expenses relating to services cover any allocation and distribution of costs among the entities in question regardless of their designation.
Points 14-15	Incomes and expenses relating to intangible assets comprise royalties and similar payments for the use of intellectual property.
Points 16-17	Financing incomes and expenses also comprise profits and losses in connection with financial contracts.
Points 20-21	Other incomes and expenses comprise income and expenses related to captives,
Point 22	Sales of intangible assets comprise assets acquired against remuneration as well as sales of intangible assets developed within the company whether the research and development costs have been capitalised or carried as expenses.
Points 30-31	The total maximum loans calculated as the sum of the maximum loan to or from each entity assessed on the day of the income year when it was largest.
Points 32-33	Options, futures, swaps and forward rate agreements etc. are considered as financial contracts.

3(3)

	Income year	Business reg.no. (CVR)	or	Civil reg. no. (CPR)

Type of controlled foreign transactions

Profit and loss account:

	No trans-actions (tick off)	Gross value in DKK	Above 25%	State: (A, B, C or D)
8. Sale of goods and other current assets				
9. Purchase of goods and other current assets				
10. Incomes from services, including management fees, and cost sharing				
11. Expenses for services, including management fees, and cost sharing				
12. Rental and leasing incomes				
13. Rental and leasing expenses				
14. Incomes deriving from intangible assets				
15. Expenses relating to intangible assets				
16. Financing incomes				
17. Financing expenses				
18. Subsidies received, including waivers of loans				
19. Subidies given, including waivers of loans				
20. Other incomes				
21. Other expenses				

Balance sheet:

22. Sale of intangible fixed assets				
23. Purchase of intangible fixed assets				
24. Sale of tangible fixed assets				
25. Purchase of tangible fixed assets				
26. Sale of capital participation in associated companies				
27. Purchase of capital participation in associated companies				
28. Sale of other financial fixed assets				
29. Purchases of other financial fixed assets				
30. Loans from legal persons or individuals (max. in the income year)				
31. Loans to legal persons or individuals (max. in the income year)				
32. Other financing granted, including financial contracts				
33. Other financing received, including financial contracts				

Please note that submission by e-mail is **not** secure unless you either **encrypt** or attach a **digital signature** to your message and the attached data file.

[Send data via e-mail]

Annex 6E: Kenyan Revenue Authority: Disclosure of Transfer Pricing Transactions

KENYA REVENUE AUTHORITY

ISO 9001:2000 CERTIFIED
LARGE TAXPAYERS OFFICE

Disclosure of Transfer Pricing Transactions: Proposed Amendment to IT2C
(This part is to be filled by companies having transactions with related/ associated enterprises outside Kenya)

Part I: Reporting person information

Name:
PIN No:
Do you have related/ associated enterprises outside Kenya

| YES | | NO |

Have you documented your transfer pricing policy?

| YES | | NO |

Part II: Non –Resident information

Enterprise name	Address / Location/ country of residence	Nature of Relationship

Part III: Transactions between reporting person and non-resident

Enter in the appropriate box the monetary consideration in Kenya shillings derived or incurred for the following transactions with the non-resident. Enter the appropriate transfer pricing methodology (TPM) codes from the list in the instructions.

description	Sold to non-resident	TPM	Purchased from non-resident	TPM	Transfer Pricing Adjustment (if any)
Tangible Property					
Stock in trade/raw materials					
Other (specify):					

Page 1 of 3

Rents, Royalties and Intangible Property				
Rents				
Royalties				
License or franchise fees				
Intangible property or rights (acquired or disposed of)				
Services				
Management, financial, administrative, marketing, training, etc.				
Engineering, technical, construction, etc				
Research and development				
Commissions				
Financial				
Interest				
Dividends				
Sale of financial property (including factoring, securitizations and securities)				
Lease payments				
Insurance				
Others				
Other				
Reimbursement of expenses				
Other				
Please enter the total of all entries made in each column of part III				

Part IV: Loans, advances, investments, current account and similar amounts

Description	Beginning balance	Increase	Decrease	Ending balance
Interest bearing loans				
Amounts borrowed				
Amounts loaned out				
Interest free loans				

Page 2 of 3

Amounts borrowed				
Amounts loaned out				
Current accounts				
Amount of account receivables				
Amount of account payables				

Page 3 of 3

Tatipo Ushuru Tujitegemee

Annex 6F: India: Form 3CEB (Transfer Pricing—Accountants Certificate)

FORM NO. 3CEB

[*See* rule 10E]

Report from an accountant to be furnished under section 92E relating to international transaction(s) and specified domestic transaction(s)

1. *I/We have examined the accounts and records of _____ (name and address of the assessee with PAN) relating to the international transaction (s) and the specified domestic transaction(s) entered into by the assessee during the previous year ending on 31st March, _____

2. In*my/our opinion proper information and documents as are prescribed have been kept by the assessee in respect of the international transaction(s) and the specified domestic transactions entered into so far as appears from *my/our examination of the records of the assessee.

3. The particulars required to be furnished under section 92E are given in the Annexure to this Form. In*my/our opinion and to the best of my/our information and according to the explanations given to *me/us, the particulars given in the Annexure are true and correct.

**Signed

Name

Address : Membership No. :

Place :

_____

Date :

_____

Notes :

1. *Delete whichever is not applicable.

2. **This report has to be signed by—

    (*i*) a chartered accountant within the meaning of the Chartered Accountants Act, 1949 (38 of 1949); or

    (*ii*) any person who, in relation to any State, is, by virtue of the provisions in sub-section (2) of section 226 of the Companies Act, 1956 (1 of 1956), entitled to be appointed to act as an auditor of companies registered in that State.

ANNEXURE TO FORM NO. 3CEB

Particulars relating to international transactions and specified domestic transactions required to be furnished under section 92E of the Income-tax Act, 1961

PART A

1. Name of the assessee _____

2. Address _____

3. Permanent account number _____

4. Nature of business or activities of the assessee* _____

5. Status _____

6. Previous year ended _____

7. Assessment year _____

8. Aggregate value of international transactions as per books of accounts _____

Transfer Pricing and Developing Economies • http://dx.doi.org/10.1596/978-1-4648-0969-9

9. Aggregate value of specified domestic transactions as per books of accounts_____

* Code for nature of business to be filled in as per instructions for filling Form ITR 6

PART B
(International Transactions)

10.	*List of associated enterprises with whom the assessee has entered into international transactions, with the following details :*	
	(*a*) Name of the associated enterprise.	
	(*b*) Nature of the relationship with the associated enterprise as referred to in section 92A(2).	
	(*c*) Brief description of the business carried on by the associated enterprise	
11.	Particulars in respect of transactions in tangible property.	
	A. Has the assessee entered into any international transaction(s) in respect of purchase/sale of raw material, consumables or any other supplies for assembling or processing/manufacturing of goods or articles from/to associated enterprises?	
	If 'yes', provide the following details in respect of each associated enterprise and each transaction or class of transaction :	Yes/No ____
	(*a*) Name and address of the associated enterprise with whom the international transaction has been entered into.	
	(*b*) Description of transaction and quantity purchased/sold.	
	(*c*) Total amount paid/received or payable/receivable in the transaction—	
	(*i*) as per books of account;	
	(*ii*) as computed by the assessee having regard to the arm's length price.	
	(*d*) Method used for determining the arm's length price [*See* section 92C(1)]	
	B. Has the assessee entered into any international transaction(s) in respect of purchase/sale of traded/finished goods?	
	If 'yes' provide the following details in respect of each associated enterprise and each transaction or class of transaction :	Yes/No ____
	(*a*) Name and address of the associated enterprise with whom the international transaction has been entered into.	
	(*b*) Description of transaction and quantity	

	purchased/sold.	
	(c) Total amount paid/ received or payable/ receivable in the transaction	
	(i) as per books of accounts;	
	(ii) as computed by the assessee having regard to the arm's length price.	
	(d) Method used for determining the arm's length price [*See* section 92C(1)]	
	C. Has the assessee entered into any international transaction(s) in respect of purchase, sale, transfer, lease or use of any other tangible property including transactions specified in Explanation (i)(a) below section 92B(2)?	Yes/No ____
	If 'yes' provide the following details in respect of each associated enterprise and each transaction or class of transaction:	
	(a) Name and address of the associate enterprise with whom the international transaction has been entered into.	
	(b) Description of the property and nature of transaction.	
	(c) Number of units of each category of tangible property involved in the transaction.	
	(d) Amount paid/received or payable/receivable in each transaction of purchase/sale/transfer /use, or lease rent paid/received or payable/receivable in respect of each lease provided/entered into —	
	(i) as per books of account;	
	(ii) as computed by the assessee having regard to the arm's length price.	
	(e) Method used for determining the arm's length price [*See* section 92C(1)]	
12.	Particulars in respect of transactions in intangible property :	
	Has the assessee entered into any international transaction(s) in respect of purchase, sale, transfer, lease or use of intangible property including transactions specified in Explanation (i)(b) below section 92B(2)?	
	If 'yes' provide the following details in respect of each associated enterprise and each category of intangible property :	Yes/No ____
	(a) Name and address of the associated enterprise with whom the international transaction has been entered into.	
	(b) Description of intangible property and nature of	

Transfer Pricing and Developing Economies • http://dx.doi.org/10.1596/978-1-4648-0969-9

	transaction.	
	(c) Amount paid/received or payable/receivable for purchase/sale/transfer/lease/use of each category of intangible property—	
	(i) as per books of account;	
	(ii) as computed by the assessee having regard to the arm's length price.	
	(d) Method used for determining the arm's length price [*See* section 92C(1)]	
13.	Particulars in respect of providing of services :	
	Has the assessee entered into any international transaction(s) in respect of Services including transactions as specified in Explanation (i)(d) below section 92B(2)?	
	If 'yes' provide the following details in respect of each associated enterprise and each category of service :	
	(a) Name and address of the associated enterprise with whom the international transaction has been entered into.	Yes/No ____
	(b) Description of services provided/availed to/from the associated enterprise.	
	(c) Amount paid/received or payable/receivable for the services provided/taken—	
	(i) as per books of account;	
	(ii) as computed by the assessee having regard to the arm's length price.	
	(d) Method used for determining the arm's length price [*See* section 92C(1)]	
14.	Particulars in respect of lending or borrowing of money :	
	Has the assessee entered into any international transaction(s) in respect of lending or borrowing of money including any type of advance, payments, deferred payments, receivable, non-convertible preference shares/ debentures or any other debt arising during the course of business as specified in Explanation (i)(c) below section 92B (2)?	Yes/No ____
	(a) Name and address of the associated enterprise with whom the international transaction has been entered into.	
	(b) Nature of financing agreement.	
	(c) Currency in which transaction has taken place	
	(d) Interest rate charged/paid in respect of each lending/borrowing.	
	(e) Amount paid/received or payable/receivable in the transaction—	

		(*i*) as per books of account;	
		(*ii*) as computed by the assessee having regard to the arm's length price.	
		(*f*) Method used for determining the arm's length price [*See* section 92C(1)]	
15.	Particulars in respect of transactions in the nature of guarantee:		
	Has the assessee entered into any international transaction(s) in the nature of guarantee?	Yes/No ____	
	If yes, provide the following details:		
	(*a*) Name and address of the associated enterprise with whom the international transaction has been entered into.		
	(*b*) Nature of guarantee agreement		
	(*c*) Currency in which the guarantee transaction was undertaken		
	(*d*) Compensation/ fees charged/ paid in respect of the transaction		
	(*e*) Method used for determining the arm's length price [*See* section 92C(1)]		
16.	Particulars in respect of international transactions of purchase or sale of marketable securities, issue and buyback of equity shares, optionally convertible/ partially convertible/ compulsorily convertible debentures/ preference shares:		
	Has the assessee entered into any international transaction(s) in respect of purchase or sale of marketable securities or issue of equity shares including transactions specified in Explanation (i)(c) below section 92B (2)?	Yes/No ____	
	If yes, provide the following details:		
	(*a*) Name and address of the associated enterprise with whom the international transaction has been entered into.		
	(*b*) Nature of transaction		
	(*c*) Currency in which the transaction was undertaken		
	(*d*) Consideration charged/ paid in respect of the transaction.		
	(*e*) Method used for determining the arm's length price [*See* section 92C(1)]		
17.	Particulars in respect of mutual agreement or arrangement :	Yes/No ____	
	Has the assessee entered into any international transaction with an associated enterprise or enterprises by way of a mutual agreement or arrangement for the allocation or apportionment of, or any contribution to, any cost or		

Transfer Pricing and Developing Economies • http://dx.doi.org/10.1596/978-1-4648-0969-9

	expense incurred or to be incurred in connection with a benefit, service or facility provided or to be provided to any one or more of such enterprises?	
	If 'yes' provide the following details in respect of each agreement/arrangement:	
	(*a*) Name and address of the associated enterprise with whom the international transaction has been entered into.	
	(*b*) Description of such mutual agreement or arrangement.	
	(*c*) Amount paid/received or payable/receivable in each such transaction—	
	(*i*) as per books of account;	
	(*ii*) as computed by the assessee having regard to the arm's length price.	
	(*d*) Method used for determining the arm's length price [*See* section 92C(1)].	
18.	Particulars in respect of international transactions arising out/ being part of business restructuring or reorganizations:	
	Has the assessee entered into any international transaction(s) arising out/being part of any business restructuring or reorganization entered into by it with the associated enterprise or enterprises as specified in Explanation (i) (e) below section 92B (2) and which has not been specifically referred to above?	Yes/No _____
	If 'yes', provide the following details:	
	(*a*) Name and address of the associated enterprise with whom the international transaction has been entered into.	
	(*b*) Nature of transaction	
	(*c*) Agreement in relation to such business restructuring/reorganization.	
	(*d*) Terms of business restructuring/ reorganization.	
	(*e*) Method used for determining the arm's length price [*See* section 92C(1)].	
19.	Particulars in respect of any other transaction including the transaction having a bearing on the profits, income, losses or assets of the assessee:	
	Has the assessee entered into any other international transaction(s) including a transaction having a bearing on the profits, income, losses or asset , but not specifically referred to above, with associated enterprise?	
	If 'yes' provide the following details in respect of each associated enterprise and each transaction :	Yes/No _____
	(*a*) Name and address of the associated enterprise with whom the international transaction has been entered	

Transfer Pricing and Developing Economies • http://dx.doi.org/10.1596/978-1-4648-0969-9

	into.	
	(*b*) Description of the transaction.	_____
	(*c*) Amount paid/received or payable/receivable in the transaction—	
	(*i*) as per books of account;	
	(*ii*) as computed by the assessee having regard to the arm's length price.	_____
	(*d*) Method used for determining the arm's length price [*See* section 92C(1)].	_____
20.	Particulars of deemed international transactions:	
	Has the assessee entered into any transaction with a person other than an AE in pursuance of a prior agreement in relation to the relevant transaction between such other person and the associated enterprise?	
	If yes, provide the following details in respect of each of such agreement	Yes/No ____
	(*a*) Name and address of the person other than the associated enterprise with whom the deemed international transaction has been entered into.	_____
	(*b*) Description of the transaction.	
	(*c*) Amount paid/received or payable/receivable in the transaction—	
	(*i*) as per books of account;	_____
	(*ii*) as computed by the assessee having regard to the arm's length price.	_____
	(*d*) Method used for determining the arm's length price [*See* section 92C(1)].	_____
	PART C (Specified domestic transaction)	
21.	List of associated enterprises with whom the assessee has entered into specified domestic transactions, with the following details:	
	(*a*) Name, address and PAN of the associated enterprise.	_____
	(*b*) Nature of the relationship with the associated enterprise	_____
	(*c*) Brief description of the business carried on by the said associated enterprise.	_____
22.	Particulars in respect of transactions in the nature of any expenditure:	
	Has the assessee entered into any specified domestic transaction (s) being any expenditure in respect of which payment has been made or is to be made to any person referred to in section 40A(2)(b)?	Yes/No ____
	If "yes", provide the following details in respect of each of	

Transfer Pricing and Developing Economies • http://dx.doi.org/10.1596/978-1-4648-0969-9

	such person and each transaction or class of transaction:
	(*a*) Name of person with whom the specified domestic transaction has been entered into.
	(*b*) Description of transaction along with quantitative details, if any
	(*c*) Total amount paid or payable in the transaction—
	(*i*) as per books of account;
	(*ii*) as computed by the assessee having regard to the arm's length price.
	(*d*) Method used for determining the arm's length price [*See* section 92C(1)]
23.	Particulars in respect of transactions in the nature of transfer or acquisition of any goods or services:
	A. Has any undertaking or unit or enterprise or eligible business of the assessee [as referred to in section 80A(6), 80IA(8) or section 10AA)]transferred any goods or services to any other business carried on by the assessee? Yes/No ____
	If yes, provide the following details in respect of each unit or enterprise or eligible business:
	(*a*) Name and details of business to which goods or services have been transferred
	(*b*) Description of goods or services transferred
	(*c*) Amount received/receivable for transferring of such goods or services –
	(*i*) as per the books of account;
	(*ii*) as computed by the assessee having regard to the arm's length price.
	(*d*) Method used for determining the arm's length price [*See* section 92C(1)].
	B. Has any undertaking or unit or enterprise or eligible business of the assessee [as referred to in section 80A(6), 80IA(8) or section 10AA] acquired any goods or services from another business of the assessee? Yes/No ____
	If yes, provide the following details in respect of each unit or enterprise or eligible business:
	(*a*) Name and details of business from which goods or services have been acquired
	(*b*) Description of goods or services acquired
	(*c*) Amount paid/payable for acquiring of such goods or services–
	(*i*) as per the books of account;
	(*ii*) as computed by the assessee having regard to

Transfer Pricing and Developing Economies • http://dx.doi.org/10.1596/978-1-4648-0969-9

	the arm's length price	
	(d) Method used for determining the arm's length price [*See* section 92C(1)].	
24.	Particulars in respect of specified domestic transaction in the nature of any business transacted:	Yes/No ____
	Has the assessee entered into any specified domestic transaction(s) with any associated enterprise which has resulted in more than ordinary profits to an eligible business to which section 80IA(10) or section 10AA applies?	
	If "yes", provide the following details:	
	(a) Name of the person with whom the specified domestic transaction has been entered into	
	(b) Description of the transaction including quantitative details, if any.	
	(c) Total amount received/receivable or paid/ payable in the transaction -	
	(i) as per books of account;	
	(ii) as computed by the assessee having regard to the arm's length price.	
	(d) Method used for determining the arm's length price [*See* section 92C(1)].	
25.	Particulars in respect of any other transactions :	
	Has the assessee entered into any other specified domestic transaction(s) not specifically referred to above, with an associated enterprise ?	
	If 'yes' provide the following details in respect of each associated enterprise and each transaction :	
	(a) Name of the associated enterprise with whom the specified domestic transaction has been entered into.	Yes/No ____
	(b) Description of the transaction.	
	(c) Amount paid/received or payable/receivable in the transaction—	
	(i) as per books of account;	
	(ii) as computed by the assessee having regard to the arm's length price.	
	(d) Method used for determining the arm's length price [*See* section 92C(1)].	

Signed _____

Name : _____

Address : _____

Transfer Pricing and Developing Economies • http://dx.doi.org/10.1596/978-1-4648-0969-9

Place : _____

Date : _____

Notes :**This annexure has to be signed by -

(*i*) a chartered accountant within the meaning of the Chartered Accountants Act, 1949 (38 of 1949); or

(*ii*) any person who, in relation to any State, is, by virtue of the provisions in sub-section (2) of section 226 of the Companies Act, 1956 (1 of 1956), entitled to be appointed to act as".

Annex 6G: New Zealand: Transfer Pricing Questionnaire (Foreign-Owned)

Inland Revenue
Te Tari Taake

**TRANSFER PRICING QUESTIONNAIRE:
FOREIGN-OWNED MULTINATIONALS**

Please complete the following questions based on the latest completed **tax** year. In responding to the questions you may provide separate written comments if you wish to give clarification on any issue or identify assumptions made. Consolidated group information (Qu 12 – 19 below) can be in the currency of the parent company. All other values must be in NZ dollars (as indicated by the column headings).

1   Name of the company
2   IRD Number
3   Address

4   Contact name
5   Telephone number
6   E-mail
7   Tax representative
8   Ultimate parent company
9   Tax residence of ultimate parent company

10   Describe the principal activities of the company

11   Describe the principal activities of the ultimate parent company and its consolidated group

The following information is required for the purpose of calculating various accounting ratios for comparison purposes. The intention is to compare the performance of the New Zealand company with that of the consolidated group of the ultimate parent company. If your company is performing below consolidated group levels you may wish to provide an explanatory note.

		This Company NZ$000	Consolidated Group $m
12	Shareholders funds (net assets)		
13	Total assets		
14	Total Revenue (excluding interest)		
15	Gross Profit		
16	Total expenses (excluding interest and expenses taken into account in calculating gross profit)		
17	Earnings Before Interest & Tax (exclude extraordinaries)		
18	Gross interest expense		
19	Gross interest income		

Transfer Pricing and Developing Economies • http://dx.doi.org/10.1596/978-1-4648-0969-9

Inland Revenue
Te Tari Taake

		Supplied by associated persons NZ$000	Supplied to associated persons NZ$000
Property:			
20	Raw materials		
21	Processed goods		
22	Other (specify)		
23	Rents, royalties, licence or franchise fees		
24	Intangible property (acquired or disposed of)		
Services:			
25	Management and administration		
26	Technical		
27	Research and Development		
28	Commissions		
Financial:			
29	Interest		
30	Dividends		
31	Insurance		
32	Others (specify)		
Other transactions:			
33	Reimbursement of expenses		
34	Cost sharing/contribution arrangements		
35	Other (specify)		
36	**Total associated party transactions**		

New Zealand tax legislation sets out 5 methods (listed below) for calculating an arms length consideration for setting transfer prices. Please set against each of the methods the value of transactions where prices have been confirmed by that method (the "Tested transactions"). Where more than one method was used, allocate the value to the predominant method. In addition to the method fields an additional field has been included for untested prices. The "Total Transactions" (fields 43) must equal the "Total associated party transactions" (fields 36) above.

		Supplied by associated persons NZ$000	Supplied to associated persons NZ$000
Tested transactions:			
37	Comparable uncontrolled price method		
38	Resale price method		
39	Cost plus method		
40	Profit split method		
41	Comparable profits methods		
42	Untested transactions		
43	**Total Transactions**		

44   Has the company provided any goods or services or anything else of value to a non-resident associated person for no consideration?
(Tick the box if the answer is YES)

For more information, please visit our
Website at www.ird.govt.nz/transfer-pricing/

Page 2

Inland Revenue
Te Tari Taake

If the answer is yes please provide details.

45 What is the value of transactions with associated persons tax resident in low tax jurisdictions or territories as listed on page 4? Total value for all such associated party transactions - $000

46 Have there been any material structural changes in the last five years which have resulted in a reduction of business functions, assets held and risks borne by the New Zealand operations? If so, please provide full details.

47 If the company has entered into a partnership, a joint venture or a profit or revenue sharing arrangement with a non-resident associated person, please supply details of the arrangement.

48 If there are a number of companies in New Zealand which, together with this company, form a group for tax purposes, please provide a list of the names of the other group companies on a separate schedule and state whether they have any material cross-border associated party transactions or dealings.

49 How many staff does this company employ?
50 How many staff earn more than $150,000 pa (including benefits)?

For this company (including the New Zealand group if there is one) and the consolidated group please provide the following information:

	This Company NZ$000	Consolidated Group $m
51 Total group debt		
52 Total group assets		

The detailed basis for calculating these amounts is contained in section FG 4 of the Income Tax Act 1994 (subpart FE of the Income Tax Act 2007).

53 Has transfer pricing documentation been produced in support of your transfer prices in accordance with the Transfer Pricing Guidelines? *(Tick the box if the answer is YES)*

The Transfer Pricing Guidelines can be found in the appendix to the IRD Tax Information Bulletin: Volume 12, No 10 (October 2000) and are available online. Online link: http://www.ird.govt.nz/forms_guides/number/forms-unnumbered/guide-transfer-pricing.html

54 Have any associated party transactions been the subject of an advance pricing agreement in another jurisdiction? *(Tick the box if the answer is YES)*

55 Are you giving consideration to applying for an advance pricing agreement in New Zealand? *(Tick the box if the answer is YES)*

56 Name of officer providing this information:

57 Position:

Inland Revenue
Te Tari Taake

Low tax jurisdictions or territories

Andorra	Liechtenstein
Angola	Luxembourg
Anguilla	Macau
Antigua and Barbuda	Madeira
Aruba	Maldives
Bahamas	Marshall Islands
Bahrain	Monaco
Barbados	Montserrat
Bermuda	Nauru
British Channel Islands	Nevis
British Virgin Islands	New Caledonia
Campione	Norfolk Island
Cayman Island	Oman
Cook Islands	Palau
Costa Rica	Panama
Curacao	Puerto Rico
Cyprus	Saint Helena
Djibouti	Saint Kitts
Dominica	Saint Lucia
Ecuador	Saint Vincent
French Polynesia	San Marino
Greece	Seychelles
Grenada	Sint Maarten
Gibraltar	Solomon Islands
Guatemala	Sri Lanka
Hong Kong	Switzerland
Isle of Man	Turks and Caicos Islands
Jamaica	United Arab Emirates
Jordan	Uruguay
Kuwait	Vanuatu
Lebanon	Venezuela
Liberia	

Transfer Pricing and Developing Economies • http://dx.doi.org/10.1596/978-1-4648-0969-9

Annex 6H: South Africa: Transfer Pricing Questionnaire (South African–Owned)

TRANSFER PRICING QUESTIONNAIRE:
SOUTH AFRICAN-OWNED MULTINATIONAL GROUPS

1. Please complete the following questions based on the latest completed IT14 tax return for the latest year submitted.

2. In responding to the questions you may provide separate written comments if you wish to give clarification on any issue or identify assumptions made.

3. All values should be stated in South African Rands.

a. Name of Company	
b. Company registration number	
c. Company tax reference number	
d. Company VAT reference number	
e. Registered address of company	
f. Name, telephone number and email address of the public officer	
g. Name and contact details of the tax advisors	
h. Total value of international related party transactions undertaken	

4. Please provide a description of the principle activities of the South African company.

5. The following information is required to understand the nature and quantum of the transactions with non-resident related parties.

	Received from non-resident related parties	Supplied to non-resident related parties
Goods		
Raw materials		
Processed or finished goods		
Other (specify)		
Rents, royalties, license fees or franchise fees		
Intangible property		

SARS Large Business Centre

transferred	

Services

Management and administration	
Technical	
Research and development	
Commissions	

Financial

Interest	
Insurance	
Other (specify)	

Other

Reimbursement of expenses	
Cost sharing / cost contribution arrangements	
Employment costs for expatriate employees	
Other (specify)	
Total Value of transactions with non-	

▼SARS *Large Business Centre*

resident related parties		

6. The South African Revenue Service recognises the transfer pricing methods endorsed by the Organisation for Economic Development and Cooperation (OECD) in its Guidelines on Transfer Pricing for Multinational Enterprises and Tax Administrations (1995), the OECD Guidelines. These methods are outlined in Practice Note 7 issued on 6 August 1999. Please specify the transaction value for each of the transactions identified above, against each of the methods used to set or test the appropriateness of the pricing policy adopted. If more than one method was used please provide further details of such methods used and allocate the value against the primary method used. Please note that the total value of transactions should equal the total from the above table.

Method	Received from non-resident related parties	Supplied to non-resident related parties.
Comparable Uncontrolled price (CUP)		
Resale Price Method (RP)		
Cost Plus Method (CP)		
Transactional Net Margin Method (TNMM)		
Transactional Profit Split Method (TPSM)		
Other method (specify)		
Not tested		
Total Value of transactions		

SARS *Large Business Centre*

7. Has the company provided any goods or services (including the provision of financial assistance) to a non-resident related party for no consideration?

If so, please provide details

8. Have any of the transactions listed in above occurred with a non-resident related party which is tax resident in a tax haven or low tax country?

If so, please provide details

9. Has the company prepared transfer pricing supporting documentation for the transactions listed above?

If so, indicate (based on transaction value) the approximate percentage of the transactions supported by such transfer pricing documentation.

10. Please provide copies of the annual financial statements for the latest tax year for which an IT14 has been lodged for each of the international related parties with whom transactions have been concluded.

11. Please provide details of the representative from the company completing the questionnaire for future reference, should we require further information.

Name	
Position/Title	
Contact number	
E-mail address	

Annex 6I: Australia: ATO Draft Information Request—Transfer Pricing

The Public Officer
[Company_Name]
[Address_Line_1]
[Address_Line_2]
[SUBURB] [STATE/TERRITORY] [POSTCODE]

Our reference:	<insert_data>
Contact officer:	<contact_officer_name>
Telephone:	<insert_phone number>
Facsimile:	<insert_fax number>
Your reference:	
Issue date:	<insert_date>

Dear Sir/Madam

INFORMATION REQUEST - TRANSFER PRICING PROJECT

[COMPANY_NAME] - TFN: [XXXXXXXX]

As part of the Tax Office's Strategic Compliance Initiative, we are currently conducting an industry wide compliance risk assessment project on targeted international related party dealings and associated emerging transfer pricing risks.

We are approaching companies with significant international related party dealings with foreign jurisdictions. As one of those companies selected, could you please provide responses to the attached questions which explore the effect of the global recession on your economic performance, including any relevant financing or business restructuring.

Your response will assist us to determine your level of transfer pricing compliance risk in respect of this/these issues and we will advise you if any further action is required. We appreciate your co-operation in providing the information referred to in the enclosed attachment.

[Insert_additional_content_if_required]

Please provide your reply by [insert_date] to the following address:

        Attention: [Case_Officer_name]
                      Australian Taxation Office
                      Large Business & International
                      [Reply_Address_Line1]
                      [SUBURB] [STATE/TERRITORY] [POSTCODE]

We will contact you shortly to discuss this enquiry. Meanwhile, if you have any questions with regard to any aspect of this request, please call [Case_Officer_name] on [contact_number]

SCI TP PROJECT – DRAFT LETTERS AND ATTACHMENTS

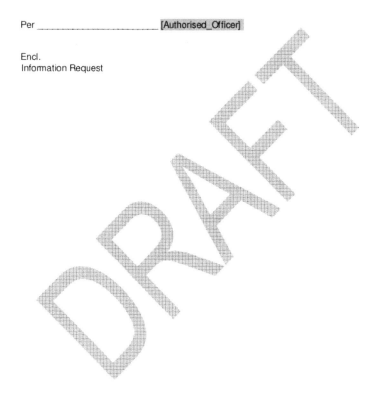

Thank you for your participation in this process.

Yours faithfully
Paul Duffus
DEPUTY COMMISSIONER OF TAXATION

Per _____ [Authorised_Officer]

Encl.
Information Request

PAGE 8 OF 10

INFORMATION REQUEST
TRANSFER PRICING - PROFITABILITY

1. Do you foresee that your profits and taxable income for 2009 income year will be higher or lower than your 2008 income year, and if so by how much? What do you perceive to be the business drivers for the difference?

2. What are the most significant internal drivers (in terms of income or costs) in your business operations that are likely to have the biggest impact on your revenue and profit levels for the 2009 year and how these are being managed? For example:

   - labour workforce (increase / decrease / employment mix – contractors, casuals)
   - pricing
   - volatility in the $AUD and the associated effects of hedging and derivative positions on your company's profitability
   - the tight credit markets and access to funding in the current or future year
   - the availability of losses to offset Australian profits
   - the likelihood of your bad debts increasing over coming years.

3. During the 2009 financial year, has there been a change to your transfer pricing policy, including your functions, assets and risks?

4. If there was a change to your transfer pricing policy, please detail.

5. Was this policy a consequence of the Global Recession?

6. Does your company enter into any end of year adjustments with an overseas related party to achieve your level of profitability?

7. If the answer to question 6 is yes, what transfer pricing method has been selected to ensure that any such adjustments will produce an arm's length outcome?

8. Please provide details of the calculations and reasoning for your belief that you have returned an arm's length outcome.

FINANCING

Set out below are specific questions in relation to your financing arrangements:

9. Please advise whether [Company_Name] or any other related Australian entity has any financial instruments such as:

   - debt interest
   - hybrid financial instrument
   - performance or financial guarantees

10. With respect to the instruments identified above:

a) Could you describe the financial instrument (e.g. loan, redeemable preference shares)?
b) Who is/are the counterparty/ies and what is the relationship of that/those party/ies to [Company_Name] ?
c) In what tax jurisdiction/s are the related party/ies located?
d) What are the key terms and conditions of the instrument/s? for example:

- all the charges associated with the facility (e.g. set up fees)

- rate of interest paid/received

- details of any financial or performance guarantees

- any other key terms (e.g. dividend rate, periodic payments, any contingencies)

- the purpose of the issue (e.g. to provide working capital for an existing business, to refinance maturing debt, to start up in a new location, etc)

- date of issue and tenor

- amount and currency of issue

- the rate and amount of any withholding tax withheld, if any

- details of any hedges, swaps, puts, calls or guarantees associated with that debt interest

11. What factors were considered in setting the interest rate and any of the associated charges?

11. How have you satisfied yourself the interest rate and any associated charges are in accordance with the arm's length principle?

13. In the case of non-interest bearing loans, how have you satisfied yourself this is in accordance with the arm's length principle?

BUSINESS RESTRUCTURING

14. Has the company or any related Australian entity been involved in business restructuring?

15. If yes, please detail the specific nature of the change, including:

- the commercial drivers and reasoning behind the business restructure
- details of all related parties involved (including country of residence)
- any amounts payable and receivable in connection with the change
- how you believe the arm's length principle has been applied to each of the amounts referred to above, including details of any arm's length pricing method used
- details of any financing arrangements entered into in connection with the change.

Annex 6J: Colombia: Penalty Matrix

Summary of Penalties

	Supporting documentation		Informative return		
Case	Inconsistent/After deadline/Not the requested/ Mistaken/Does not Permit verification	Not filed	Late filing	Amendment	Not filed
Rate	1%	1%	1% per month or month fraction	1%	20%
Base	Total value of transactions with related parties				
Cap	15,000 TU	20,000 TU	20,000 TU	20,000 TU	20,000 TU
Effect		Rejection of the cost or deduction			Could not be used as a proof
Different Base	0.5% of the net income reported in the income tax return of the same fiscal year or in the last income tax return filed. If there is no income, 0.5% of the total assests reported in the income tax return of the same fiscal year or in the last income tax return filed.				10% of the net income reported in the income tax return of the same fiscal year or in the last income tax return filed. If there is no income, 10% of the total assets reported in the income tax return of the same fiscal year or in the last income tax return filed.
Other Considerations			After tax notice, penalty will be doubled	Inconsistent information could be amended between the two years after the deadline established for the return and before the notification of the requirement.	

Notes

1. In this context, the future availability of CbC reports on large MNEs will need to be considered as well.

2. Bureau van Dijk's database, where all information worldwide is gathered regarding rumors, ongoing, and finalized restructurings.

3. Kenya introduced a "Disclosure of Transfer Pricing Transactions" (proposed amendment to IT.2.C Form) for companies having transactions with related or associated enterprises outside Kenya.

4. See PwC's website, http://www.pwc.com/gx/en/international-transfer-pricing/assets /denmark.pdf.

5. Both authorities have different questionnaires for foreign- and domestically owned MNEs. A copy of New Zealand's questionnaire for foreign-owned enterprises is in annex G; a copy of South Africa's questionnaire for enterprises owned by South Africans is included in annex H.

6. See chapter 10 of Practice Note 7 (SARS 1999).

7. In India, the practical difficulties arising from the fact that companies were required to file their financial accounts with the Ministry of Corporate Affairs by October 30 of the following year, but transfer pricing documentation was required to be completed by September 30, was recently acknowledged and the date by which transfer pricing documentation was required to be completed extended until November 30 (Finance Act 2011).

8. The ICC, a representative body for international business, has issued a policy statement that discusses business expectations with respect to transfer pricing documentation and published model transfer pricing documentation. See ICC's website, http://www .iccwbo.org/uploadedFiles/ICC/policy/taxation/Statements/Transfer%20Pricing%20 Documentation%20Model%20180-498-final.pdf.

9. An initial CbC report needs to be filed by December 31, 2017, for fiscal years beginning on January 1, 2016.

10. The Code is available at http://eur-lex.europa.eu/LexUriServ/LexUriServ .do?uri=OJ:C:2006:176:0001:0007:EN:PDF.

11. The document is available at the Canada Revenue Agency's website, http://www.cra -arc.gc.ca/tx/nnrsdnts/cmmn/trns/pt-eng.html.

12. A copy of the statement is available through the ICC's website, http://www.iccwbo.org.

13. Policy Statement, Transfer Pricing Documentation Model, Commission on Taxation, ICC, Document No: 180-498, 13/02/2008, available at http://www.iccwbo.org and in annex J.

14. The Australian Treasury is reviewing Australia's transfer pricing rules. As part of its review, it is considering introducing mandatory documentation requirements and specific penalties for failure to maintain contemporaneous documentation (see the Australian Treasury's website, http://www.treasury.gov.au/contentitem.asp?NavId =&ContentID=2219).

15. Numerous countries, including New Zealand and Thailand, have adopted the four-step process or variations of it.

16. The nine forms cover related parties, related transactions, purchases and sales transactions, services, trade of intangibles, trade of fixed assets, financing, foreign investment, and payments made abroad.

Transfer Pricing and Developing Economies • http://dx.doi.org/10.1596/978-1-4648-0969-9

17. The latest version of the guidelines was issued on January 24, 2013.

18. See PwC's website, http://www.pwc.com/gx/en/international-transfer-pricing/assets/denmark.pdf.

19. Amendments to the law in late 2011 removed the possibility for the tax administration to require translations where documentation is prepared in English, French, or German (KPMG 2012).

20. An unofficial English translation of the Decision of the Commissioner of Italy Revenue Agency, September 29, 2010 (ref.2010/137654 29.09.2010), is available at http://www.agenziaentrate.gov.it/wps/wcm/connect/407e6800444f85af891ceb536e d3dbc9/ItalyCommissionerDecision_29_09_2010_transfer_pricing.pdf?MOD=AJPE RES&CACHEID=407e6800444f85af891ceb536ed3dbc9.

21. Rule 9[2] of the Income Tax [Transfer Pricing] Rules 2006.

22. The rules are available at http://www.hasil.org.my/pdf/pdfam/Kaedah_Kaedah_Cukai _Pendapatan_Penentuan_Harga_Pindahan_2012.pdf.

23. The requirements are available in Turkish at http://gib.gov.tr/fileadmin/user_upload /yayinlar/transfer_fiyatlandirma2010.pdf.

24. The regulations are available at http://law.justia.com/cfr/title26/26-13.0.1.1.1.0.16.264 .html.

Bibliography

ATO (Australian Tax Office). 2009. "Assisting Compliance and Managing Tax Risks in the Large Market: Understanding ATO Approaches and Perspectives." Speech by Jim Killaly, deputy commissioner of Taxation, Large Business and International (Case Leadership) to the Fifth Annual Corporate Tax Forum, Sydney, 18 May 2009. ATO, Canberra. http://www.ato.gov.au/corporate/content.aspx?doc=/content /00194163.htm.

———. 2012. *International Dealings Schedule.* Canberra: ATO. http://www.ato.gov.au /content/00298236.htm.

———. 2013a. *The National Tax Liaison Group Charter.* Canberra: ATO. https://www.ato .gov.au/Tax-professionals/Cons ultation--Tax-practitioners/In-detail/NTLG-documents /About/National-Tax-Liaison-Group-charter/.

———. 2013b. *Reportable Tax Position Schedule.* Canberra: ATO. http://www.ato.gov.au /content/00279408.htm.

———. n.d. *International Transfer Pricing—Introduction to Concepts and Risk Assessment.* Canberra: ATO. http://www.ato.gov.au/General/International-tax/In-detail/Transfer -pricing/International-transfer-pricing—introduction-to-concepts-and-risk-assessment/.

Australian Department of Treasury. 2011. *Income Tax: Cross-Border Profit Allocation: Review of Transfer Pricing Rules.* Canberra: Australian Department of Treasury. http://www .treasury.gov.au/documents/2219/PDF/Review_of_transfer_pricing_rules_CP.pdf.

Baer, K., and E. Le Borgne. 2008. *Tax Amnesties: Theory, Trends, and Some Alternatives.* Washington, DC: International Monetary Fund.

Biçerm, R. 2011. "New Transfer Pricing Administrative Guidelines." *International Transfer Pricing Journal* 18 (3): 211–19.

Deloitte. 2009. *Turkey Transfer Pricing Matrix.* Istanbul: Deloitte. http://www.deloitte.com /assets/Dcom-Turkey/Local%20Assets/Documents/Turkey-tr_tax_tpmatrix2009 _08052009.pdf.

———. 2010. *Transfer Pricing in Denmark*. Copenhagen: Deloitte. http://www.deloitte .com/assets/Dcom-Denmark/Local %20Assets/Documents/Vores %20loesninger/Skat /TP %20in %20Denmark.pdf.

———. 2011. *2011 Global Transfer Pricing Desktop Reference: Planning for Methods, Documentation, Penalties and Other Issues*. New York: Deloitte Global Services. http:// www.deloitte.com/assets/Dcom-Global/Local%20Assets/Documents/Tax/dttl_tax _strategymatrix_2011_180211.pdf.

EY (Ernst & Young). 2011. *New Transfer Pricing Law in Russia*. London: EY. http://www .ey.com/Publication/vwLUAssets/EY_Russia_Transfer_Pricing_Russia%27s_new _transfer_pricing_law/$FILE/TP_Russia_new_transfer_pricing_law.pdf.

Goh, D. 2012. "Malaysia: New Transfer Pricing Forms to Increase Transfer Pricing Compliance." *International Transfer Pricing Journal* 19 (3): 222–26.

IBFD (International Bureau of Fiscal Documentation). 2011a. *Database*. Amsterdam: IBFD. http://www.ibfd.org.

———. 2011b. *IBFD Transfer Pricing: Features of Selected Countries*. Inland Revenue of New Zealand. http://www.ird.govt.nz/transfer-pricing. Wellington: IBFD.

IRS (Internal Revenue Service). 2010. *Instructions for Schedule*. Washington, DC: IRS. http://www.irs.gov/pub/newsroom/2010_instructions_for_sch_utp.pdf.

———. 2010. *Schedule UTP (Uncertain Tax Positions)*. Washington, DC: IRS. http://www .irs.gov/Businesses/Corporations/Uncertain-Tax-Positions—Schedule-UTP.

Karakitis, A., and A. Jasini. 2011. "Transfer Pricing: A Risk Management Challenge for Investors in Albania." *International Tax Review* 13 (61).

KPMG (Klynveld Peat Marwick Goerdeler). 2012. *Global Transfer Pricing Review*. Budapest: KPMG. http://www.kpmg.com/Global/en/IssuesAndInsights/ArticlesPublications /Documents/gtps-2012/hungary.pdf.

Mekler, A., and Z. S. Sethi. 2012. "Hungary: The Way Forward." Unpublished manuscript.

Musselli, A., and A. Musselli. 2011. "Italy: New Rules Provide Incentive for Associated Companies to Prepare Supporting Contemporaneous Documentation." *International Transfer Pricing Journal* 18 (1): 3–7.

OECD (Organisation for Economic Co-operation and Development). 2010. *OECD Transfer Pricing Guidelines for Multinational Enterprises and Tax Administrations*. Paris: OECD. http://www.oecd.org/ctp/transfer-pricing/transfer-pricing-guidelines .htm.

Ottosen, A. M., and M. Nørremark. 2006. "Denmark: New Transfer Pricing Documentation Regulation." *International Transfer Pricing Journal* 13 (3): 162–65.

PwC (PricewaterhouseCoopers). 2011. *International Transfer Pricing*. London: PwC. http://www.pwc.com/gx/en/international-transfer-pricing/assets/itp-full-2011.pdf.

———. 2012. *PKN Alert: Japan National Tax Agency Transfer Pricing Update: Introduction of Transfer Pricing Survey to Evaluate Taxpayer Efforts to Manage Transfer Pricing*. London: PwC. http://www.publications.pwc.com/DisplayFile.aspx?Attachmentid=5846&Mailinstanc eid=24966 July 10.

SARS (South African Revenue Service). 2001. *Transfer Pricing Questionnaire*. Cape Town: SARS. http://www.saica.co.za/integritax/2001/927_Transfer_pricing_questionnaire.htm.

Starkov, V. 2011. "The New Russian Transfer Pricing Regulations: An Overview." *BNA Tax Management Transfer Pricing Report* 20 (7). http://www.nera.com/nera-files/PUB_BNA _Tax_0711.pdf.

UN (United Nations). 2013. *UN Practical Manual on Transfer Pricing for Developing Countries*. New York: UN. http://www.un.org/esa/ffd/documents/UN_Manual _TransferPricing.pdf.

Yang, H. 2009. "A Comparative View of Transfer Pricing Documentation: New Chinese Rules and the EU Code of Conduct." *International Transfer Pricing Journal* 16 (5), 318–24. http://online.ibfd.org/kbase/#topic=doc&url=/collections/itpj/pdf/itpj050904.pdf.

Avoiding and Resolving Transfer Pricing Disputes

Disputes arise for a number of reasons already discussed in this handbook. These include differences in the interpretation of domestic and international law, differences in the assessment of facts and economic circumstances when reviewing company information, aggressive tax administrations under pressure to generate additional tax revenue, or taxpayers aggressively trying to avoid or limit taxation.

Avoiding Transfer Pricing Disputes

The cost of transfer pricing disputes can be substantial given the need for intensive factual development of cases. It is thus efficient for tax administrations to consider how to avoid disputes and encourage voluntary compliance. Various mechanisms may help achieve this objective. These can be specified in binding rules or sometimes even be a mere administrative practice. Dispute avoidance can be coordinated between two or more states or implemented unilaterally. Finally, measures vary in their degree of cooperation with the taxpayer.

General Measures

This handbook has already discussed several ways a tax administration can proactively avoid disputes. At the outset, clear, sufficiently detailed guidance surrounding the application of the arm's-length principle can help ensure consistency, reduce uncertainty, and provide fast and effective resolution when disputes arise (see chapter 3). Similarly, releasing public statements regarding approaches to be taken for specific transfer pricing issues can provide transparency and assist businesses in proactively addressing potential issues with specific intercompany transactions. Increasing compliance costs, by requiring accountability from third-party auditors to ensure taxpayers' tax audit risk is reported, and allowing for tax preparers to be penalized under certain circumstances can also be a mechanism – albeit costly for the taxpayer – to ensure that defensible positions are filed with the tax return, thus limiting scope for dispute (see chapter 6).

Safe Harbors

As discussed in chapters 3 and 5, safe harbors are a simplification measure applying to a group of taxpayers and/or transactions providing certainty with respect to the appropriate applicable transfer pricing method and/or result. Safe harbors are suitable for entities, which do not assume important risks or make use of valuable intangibles. The majority of safe harbors are unilateral, meaning the government provides guidance in domestic legislation and regulations. However, there are also bilateral safe harbors (see box 7.1).

In 2013, the OECD published a revised version of chapter 4 of the *OECD Transfer Pricing Guidelines* on safe harbors[1] that changed its general position toward the instrument. While safe harbors were considered incompatible with the arm's-length principle before 2013 (paragraph 4.120, *OECD Transfer Pricing Guidelines* 2010), the 2013 revision states *"that the use of bilateral or multilateral safe harbors under the right circumstances should be encouraged."* In 2013 the OECD endorsed the introduction of bi- and multilateral safe harbors, as these decrease the risk of double taxation and disputes.[2]

It is important to note, however, that unilateral safe harbor instruments can also mitigate the risks of double taxation or double non-taxation by strictly defining the categories of transactions within its scope and by ensuring that specified margins for those transactions are in line with the arm's length principle. The risks are also reduced if taxpayers are able to opt out of a safe harbor if they consider that it does not produce an arm's length result. In addition, it

---

Box 7.1 Example: Pakistan–Germany Bilateral Safe Harbor

Agreement on the Use of the Resale Price Method in the Pharmaceutical Industry
Extract is from Mile 2004.

Officials from the German and Pakistani finance ministries met on 6 and 7 July 2004 for a mutual agreement discussion on the interpretation of the double tax treaty under particular circumstances. The agreement reached is documented in a joint memorandum, published by the German finance ministry on 8 September 2004. The terms of this memo are:

…

4. Transfer pricing in the pharmaceuticals industry is to be on the resale price method.
5. The parent company in the pharmaceuticals industry may ask its own tax authority to certify that its transfer prices are in line with its prices charged to third parties in other, similar countries. If there are no such transactions, the certificate may refer to transfer prices to related parties in other, similar countries. Such certificates will be accepted by the tax authorities in the other state.

---

is important for transfer pricing of transactions according to safe harbors to be within the scope of the MAP provision of a relevant tax treaty. For developing economies well-designed[3] safe harbor regimes have important potential, particularly in countries with limited or no publicly available domestic information to conduct a benchmarking analysis (See also discussion on "Dealing with the Dearth of Comparable Information" in Chapter 4).[4] The instrument can provide certainty to taxpayers and, by removing the need for providing an extensive benchmarking analysis, it can help reduce compliance and administrative burdens, thus releasing resources to focus on other areas of revenue risk. Importantly, the introduction of safe harbors may help targeting administrative efforts to manage compliance. For instance, in the context of safe harbors, audits of taxpayers or transactions would normally be focused on their eligibility for the regime, thus directing auditors toward a careful review of a taxpayer's functional profile.

Advance Pricing Agreements

An advance pricing agreement (APA) is an agreement, which specifies the transfer pricing approach that the taxpayer will use for intercompany transactions. An APA can be either unilateral, bilateral, or multilateral. Unilateral APAs are agreements between a taxpayer and tax authority. Bilateral APAs involve a taxpayer seeking an agreement with and between two tax authorities, which is then implemented domestically in each country. Multilateral APAs involve more than two tax authorities reaching an agreement. Without a tax treaty in place between two countries in which the parties to the transaction are tax residents, a unilateral APA is normally the only option available to taxpayers. An APA typically covers multiple years in the future, and allows multinational taxpayers and tax authorities to avoid or reduce the potential for audits, uncertainty, investor risk, and compliance costs. Many countries have decided to introduce an APA program. Importantly, however, the initiation of an APA program typically follows the establishment of a well-functioning transfer pricing audit team. As a result of effective compliance management by such a team, demand from taxpayers for APAs to minimize the risk of double taxation tends to increase.

Significant interest in APAs should be expected from taxpayers who have either been selected for audit in the past or who expect to be audited and want to avoid a contentious drawn-out process. Careful evaluation of cases should be conducted before acceptance into an APA program. APAs come with important potential benefits for both the government and taxpayers. They do, however, also have non-negligible cost and therefore often not a priority for countries building up a transfer pricing regime (see table 7.1).

Legal Basis

To be able to conclude either uni-, bi-, or multilateral APAs, a suitable legal basis, both in procedural and in substantive law, is needed. For unilateral APAs, the procedural basis can typically be found in the domestic procedural rules on tax

Table 7.1 Benefits and Shortcomings of APAs

Benefits

Certainty

Successful APAs bring certainty to both business and the tax administration. The tax administration will have comfort as to the intercompany pricing going forward, and once agreed can focus resources on different taxpayers and transactions. On the private sector side, business can also allocate fewer resources to the tax function, focusing more on the core business within the country.

Cooperative process

APAs are a voluntary process for taxpayers. To participate they must cooperate and provide detailed information on their business and financial dealings. In contrast to an audit, which can be contentious, APAs foster productive dialogue and cooperative exchanges between the public and private sectors.

Flexibility for the tax administration

Tax authorities have the option to either accept or reject an APA request. Simply because the administration establishes an APA program does not guarantee that the taxpayer will be granted access to the APA program. Likewise, even if accepted into the APA program, there is no guarantee of an APA reaching resolution. As such, APA programs provide flexibility and options for tax administrations as to whom and what strategically to allow into the program.

However, administratively it may be important to understand the interaction of an APA program with a country's constitution. For instance, certain countries have raised concerns that granting acceptance into an APA program to some taxpayers but not others could potentially be considered unfair treatment in the context of the constitution. The core concern for tax administrators in this context is that without full legal analysis they may confront legal action from taxpayers denied entry into the APA program based on a provision involving fair treatment of taxpayers.

Costs and limitations of APA programs

Despite the benefits of having a successful APA program within a tax administration, there are some limitations.

Not suitable for all transactions

Not all intercompany transactions are good candidates for APAs. For instance, a fast-moving industry with a rapidly evolving climate may not be able to establish set pricing for years into the future. Similarly, transactions with tax havens based on aggressive tax planning may be better handled as part of an audit. Moreover, some transactions might be too small to justify the significant investment required for the APA process.

Time-consuming process

An APA is a significant investment for both the tax administration and the taxpayer. First, the fact-gathering process can take time since care has to be taken to consider where the business is headed in the future, rather than simply evaluating past results. Second, the negotiation process with taxpayers or foreign tax authorities under the treaty can take a considerable amount of time before reaching agreement, and is therefore difficult to plan.

Resource constraints and miss-allocation of scarce resources

Certain APAs may involve compliant taxpayers who would not have been flagged for an audit. APA programs thus risk consuming resources, which could have been used to conduct an audit of a potentially noncompliant taxpayer. Consequently, it is very important to evaluate the suitability of a taxpayer's transactions for acceptance into an APA program before formal acceptance.

Difficulties in measurement and evaluation

The performance of the audit division is easily measured based on the amount collected as well as other potential measures. However, there are no easy ways to measure the effectiveness of an APA program. It is possible to look at the number of cases closed, but no two cases are alike. In addition, without knowing what the taxpayer would have filed in the absence of an APA, or what the adjustments would have been in a regular audit, there is no baseline to measure and evaluate the effectiveness of the APA cases.

law. For bi- and multilateral APAs it can be found either in domestic rules or in international law, or both. For example, paragraph 4.139 of the *OECD Transfer Pricing Guidelines* states that: *"APAs involving the competent authority of a treaty partner should be considered within the scope of the mutual agreement procedure under Article 25 of the OECD Model Tax Convention, even though such arrangements are not expressly mentioned there."* The substantive legal basis can be found for both bi- and multilateral APAs in the articles on business profits and on associated enterprises of the applicable tax treaty. For unilateral APAs, this is typically in the domestic provision implementing the arm's-length principle.

Unilateral Compared with Bi- and Multilateral

At the outset of creating any APA program, policy makers need to determine whether the program will allow either or both bi- and multilateral and unilateral APAs. The following lists benefits specific to *bilateral APAs*:

- *Elimination of double taxation.* Through mutual agreement between countries based on a tax treaty, the major business risk of double taxation from transfer pricing is effectively eliminated for multinational enterprises. Whereas with unilateral APAs, the taxpayer's audit risk is eliminated only in one country of the transaction.
- *Interaction and cooperation among governments.* To conclude a successful bilateral APA, a mutual agreement must take place, based on the tax treaty and between two governments, to alleviate double taxation regarding the multinational taxpayer's income. These bilateral negotiations can provide an avenue for countries to quickly get up to speed on international practices while also defending their tax base and increasing bilateral cooperation.

Given the benefits to bilateral cases, some countries accept unilateral APAs only in exceptional cases. Others bias APAs toward the conclusion of bilateral cases. In the United States, for instance, taxpayers must explain in a prefiling memorandum why a unilateral APA is appropriate to cover an issue that could be covered by a bi- or multilateral APA. Similarly, a prerequisite for acceptance of unilateral APAs could be specified along the following lines in a country's guidelines determining the APA process:

- No tax treaty is in place between home country and foreign country party to the intercompany transaction.
- If a treaty exists, the treaty partner has rejected the taxpayer's APA request.
- Intercompany volume threshold is not met (i.e., the case is too small for an investment in a bilateral APA process).

APA Guidelines

An APA guideline can provide government and taxpayers alike with a policy framework as well as a procedural roadmap. This section discusses the key policy considerations that should be clarified in an APA guideline to ensure transparency. Typical guidelines for conducting a bi- or multilateral APA can also be found in the annex to chapter 4 of the OECD *Transfer Pricing Guidelines*.

Eligibility. When considering APA program eligibility, the first step is to determine what kind of cases the tax administration wants to include. Country approaches vary greatly. In the United Kingdom Her Majesty's Revenue and Customs (HMRC), for instance, looks for one or more of the following characteristics: (a) the transfer pricing issues are complex rather than straightforward; (b) without an APA, there is a high likelihood of double taxation; and (c) the taxpayer seeks to implement a method that is highly tailored to its particular circumstances, but is not one that the HMRC (2010) considers treaty partners would regard as being overtly tax aggressive. In contrast, the U.S. approach allows most cases into the Internal Revenue Services' (IRS's) APA program. Whatever approach a government takes, it is good practice to have clear rules concerning taxpayer eligibility (i.e., that inform taxpayers of their options before making investments into an APA process) drafted into an APA guideline. That said, for an APA program to be efficient, there must be an element of discretion for tax administrations to determine whether a specific transaction is suitable for an APA.

Fees. Some countries charge taxpayers a user fee for undertaking the APA process, while others do not (see table 7.2). Administrations that charge a fee tend to justify this with the investment required to complete an APA. APAs are voluntary, require more fact-finding as well as potential travel to discuss with foreign component authorities (if bilateral), and may thus lead to additional costs when compared to a standard audit.

APA Type. The tax administration must decide whether to allow only unilateral, only bilateral, or both types of APAs at the outset. As previously discussed, there can be benefits and drawbacks to the different types, so a careful evaluation of the legal and treaty network should conducted before such a policy decision is made.

Term Maximum. Many countries also prefer to state a maximum term length in their APA guideline. At the outset of the program, it is advisable not to reach unilateral agreements longer than three to five years. A typical APA application length is five years, but the most appropriate term length will vary significantly by taxpayer and industry.

Rollbacks. An important advantage of an APA can be its use as a mechanism for resolving audit cases. It is thus also an important decision whether or not to allow rollback of an APA. A rollback involves a taxpayer requesting an APA term (going forward), but also for the agreed result to be "rolled back" multiplied by the

Table 7.2 Select APA Features and User Fees in the European Union

Country	APAs offered	Filing fee	Total number of APAs in force (2013)	Average time to negotiate with EU countries
Belgium	Unilateral and bi-/multilateral	None	10	24 months
Czech Republic	Unilateral and bi-/multilateral	CZK10,000	34	n.a.
Germany	Bi-/multilateral	User fees for APAs were introduced in 2007. A general fee for every APA application amounts to €20,000 (renewal: €15,000; change or modification: €10,000). Fees can be reduced for taxpayers with minor transactions to foreign-affiliated companies.	21	24 months
Hungary	Unilateral and bi-/multilateral	Unilateral: Ft 500,000 to Ft 5 million, if ALP determined with the CUP, resale price or cost-plus method and Ft 2 million to Ft 7 million if ALP determined using other methods. Bilateral: Ft 3 million to Ft 8 million. Multilateral: Ft 5 million to Ft 10 million.	58	n.a.
United Kingdom	Unilateral and bilateral	None	73	23 months

Source: EU JTPF 2014.
Note: ALP = arm's-length principle; APA = advance pricing agreement; CUP = comparable uncontrolled price; n.a. = not applicable.

number of years into already filed results. Many issues must be considered if roll-backs are to be allowed, including:

- Case control between the audit or examination team and APA team regarding years already filed
- Whether the rollback request is for a bilateral case where a treaty is in force
- Whether the facts of the case suggest a rollback making sense, or whether the fact pattern and comparables differ to an extend where the result applied forward would not be sensible for retroactive application
- The potential tax impact of the rollback (i.e., whether it is likely for a refund or additional tax to be collected)

Given the duration of average APA negotiations, it often can be of practical value to allow for rollbacks. At the end of many APA negotiations, the originally requested term may have already almost expired. In the final report to Action 14 of the BEPS project, recommendation 2.7 therefore states: "*Countries with bilateral advance pricing arrangement (APA) programs should provide for the rollback of APAs in appropriate cases, subject to the applicable time limits (such as statutes of limitation for assessment) where the relevant facts and circumstances in the earlier tax years are the same and subject to the verification of these facts and circumstances on audit."*[5]

Processing Deadlines. It is often helpful for taxpayers and the APA administration to set deadlines for processing. For example, Singapore's transfer pricing guidelines specify a timeline for the APA process that provides clarity for taxpayers (see table 7.3).[6]

At the same time, caution is needed when implementing processing deadlines since they can put unnecessary pressure on the involved tax administrations. Elaborate decisions will need time, particularly at an early stage in the implementation of a new APA program.

Collateral Issues. A prefiling conference is the ideal place to identify potential collateral issues associated with the proposed covered transactions for the APA. Examples of collateral issues that may be identified are (a) additional intercompany transactions (international or domestic); (b) thin capitalization; (c) permanent establishments; (d) withholding taxes; (e) customs duties; (f) deductibility of expenses under domestic law; or (g) beneficial ownership. It should be determined how these issues and others will be handled prior to accepting a taxpayer into the APA program. In addition, it may need to be decided how collateral issues will be handled if discovered as part of the APA due diligence process.

Withdrawal. Clear guidance is also needed in an APA guideline concerning withdrawal from the APA program for both taxpayers and the tax administration. Since APAs are voluntary for both sides, either party can exit the process at any time. This, of course, is subject to a tax administration's obligation to

Table 7.3 APA Timeline in Singapore

	Step 1	Step 2	Step 3	Step 4
Submission of prefiling materials	1st prefiling meeting	Submission of APA application	Review and negotiation	Implementation
Taxpayer submits prefiling materials ≥ 10 months before X (e.g., not later than 1 Mar 2016).	Taxpayer initiates prefiling meeting ≥ 9 months before X (e.g., not later than 1 Apr 2016).	IRAS indicates ≥ 4 months before X (e.g., not later than 1 Sep 2016) if application can be submitted. Taxpayer submits application within 3 months from receipt of IRAS' indication. IRAS issues acceptance letter within 1 month from receipt of the application.	IRAS informs taxpayer of the APA outcome within 1 month from reaching agreement by the CAs.	Taxpayer and IRAS implements the APA agreement.

Source: IRAS 2016, p. 58.
Note: APA = advance pricing agreement; CA = competent authority; IRAS = Inland Revenue Authority of Singapore. X refers to the first day of the APA covered period (for example, January 1 2017).

act in good faith. However, taxpayers will likely want to see clear criteria that must be met concerning when a taxpayer can be removed from the APA program.

Cancellation and Revocation. Further guidance should be stated as to the government's power to outright cancel an APA. The general rule is that an APA is an agreement that is in force unless the term has expired, a critical assumption is realized, or the taxpayer provided inaccurate information either as part of the evaluation of the APA or during the annual compliance review. If it is determined that the government was deliberately misled, it is recommended that the government reserve the right to retroactively cancel the APA and proceed with a case under domestic law. In practice, such instances are rare, and extreme caution needs to be exercised for a successful APA program to be built.

Transparency. Unilateral APAs have raised important concerns on both transparency and harmful tax practice in the recent past. When not reported to other affected states, they run the risk of allowing a taxpayer to report inconsistent tax positions that may result in double nontaxation. A policy of attracting investment by providing preferential rulings that offer taxation not in accordance with the arm's-length principle is now widely considered being a harmful tax practice. In 2015, the European Court of Justice considered such rulings as state aid according to European law.[7] As a consequence, international pressure and obligations on exchanging unilateral transfer pricing rulings have increased. For OECD countries, the final report on OECD BEPS Action 5[8] develops clear guidance on which rulings have to be exchanged.

Audit Coordination
Typically, international transfer pricing disputes arise after unilateral audits of cross-border transactions. To give a simple example, the practical application of the arm's-length principle often allows for a range of results. Tax administrations obviously have an incentive to opt for a point in that range that maximizes their revenue collection. Coordination between tax administrations at an early stage of an audit may thus help ensure that both tax administrations' audit teams take into account the position of the other country.

International coordination of transfer pricing audits can be achieved by conducting simultaneous or joint audits. Simultaneous audits do not necessitate a common solution of the case or a common audit team, but guarantee the exchange of information in the process of a jointly timed audit. A joint audit goes further, requiring the establishment of a common audit team with the objective of finding a common solution to the case. Both simultaneous audits and joint audits are recommended by the European Union's Joint Transfer Pricing Forum (EUJTPF) in its 2013 report on *Transfer Pricing Risk Management* (see box 7.2).

Box 7.2 EUJTPF *Transfer Pricing Risk Management,* 2013

In the European Union, Article 12 of the directive on administrative cooperation in the field of taxation of February 15, 2011 (2011/16/EU) provides a legal basis for conducting simultaneous controls. Bi- and multilateral controls (audits) are regularly implemented in the EU. Being aware of additional costs of bi- and multilateral controls, the EU Fiscalis 2020[a] program provides funding for these kinds of controls. It is not only open to EU member countries, but also to a group of associated countries (Albania, Bosnia-Herzegovina [the former Yugoslav Republic of Macedonia], Montenegro, Serbia, and Turkey).

a. Program Fiscalis 2020, available at http://ec.europa.eu/taxation_customs/taxation/tax_cooperation/fiscalis_programme /fiscalis_2020/index_de.htm.

Resolving Transfer Pricing Disputes

Disputes will arise no matter how well dispute avoidance strategies are being implemented. Transfer pricing is fact-based, and even a common understanding of the facts can result in multiple interpretations and a range of positions on the appropriate application of a method to determine arm's-length pricing. Therefore, a tax administration must also consider ways to resolve disputes. With more countries implementing transfer pricing regimes and the growing global attention to the risk of profit shifting, the inventory of transfer pricing disputes worldwide is expected to increase. At the same time, governments continue operating with limited human resources to resolve them. The first step the taxpayer must take when issued an audit assessment is to engage the tax administration in an effort to resolve the dispute. This can be done in various ways: the adjustment can be challenged by domestic appeal, a mutual agreement procedure (MAP) can be applied for, or both can be done in parallel.

Domestic Dispute Resolution

Domestic dispute resolution is the only available avenue to taxpayers when there is no tax treaty in place with the country where double taxation has occurred. The same applies in situations where the taxpayer does not want information to be shared with the other tax administration—a behavior that may indicate risk to both tax administrations.

Many countries have instituted an appeals division, which provides a double check on the auditor's work when a transfer pricing dispute arises. An appeals process involves a second look at the case that is not overly influenced by the first look taken by the tax administration.[9] A number of questions arise when designing an appeals process and country practices differ. Table 7.4 provides an overview of core principles and country approaches. Overall, it is critical that the appeals division has a reasonable level of independence from the audit division. If a case is upheld in appeals, the next step the taxpayer can usually pursue is to litigate. If a tax court exists, this is generally preferred since the tax court

Table 7.4 Approaches to Domestic Dispute Resolution

Design Elements	Suggested good practice and country examples in domestic dispute resolution
Single appeal path and progressive selection of cases	A single, defined stream for the progression of an appeals case: *First stage.* An internal administrative review by the revenue authority. The review should be as removed from the original auditor and assessor as much as possible. Some ways to achieve this could be to (a) create a separate appeals division with appeals officers who are tasked with this first-stage review; (b) assign the review to a senior official who does not directly supervise the original case auditor; or (c) assign the review to a new auditor with no previous knowledge of the case. *Second stage.* An independent appeals body, sitting outside the revenue authority. This body could be an administrative tribunal (*India, Kazakhstan, Uganda*) or a specialized tax court (*Turkey, Canada*). Often there is a provision to create a separate, procedurally informal, and efficient track for cases with small disputed values (*Canada, South Africa*). *Third stage.* Finally, cases can be appealed to the courts and proceed through the regular hierarchy of court levels. Most countries will limit appeals at the court stage to those dealing with matters of law only (as distinct from matters of fact) under the rationale that matters of fact are best resolved at the first and second stages. This is also a way to ensure there are only a few tax cases per year dealt with in the court system, especially at the appellate court and supreme court levels. Only those cases that address important points of law or are of strong precedential importance should be addressed at this level. However, it should be noted that many countries' constitutions grant taxpayers the right to appeal a case directly to court (*Ukraine, Uganda, Portugal*), but in many of these instances, taxpayers are required by law to exhaust administrative remedies before seeking judicial ones.
Independence of appeal body and decision makers	*Independence of institution.* The actual and perceived independence of the appeals body (usually second stage) is the cornerstone of an effective appeals system that is respected by taxpayers. It can send a powerful signal to domestic and international investors and provide confidence that the *rule of law* is adhered to. This means that the appeals function and the decision makers need to be as *independent from the tax authority*, and from the revenue and tax policy function, as possible. In countries where the second-stage appeal is to a specialized court, it is often the ministry of justice that has oversight. In countries where a tribunal or appeals committee is created, this is often under the authority of the ministry of finance, but in that case it is recommended that *a separate appeals directorate be created* that is distinct from the revenue and fiscal policy functions of that ministry, and that this be as *separately resourced* as possible. *Independence of decision makers.* It is critical to have clearly defined selection criteria for members to ensure that they are qualified and unbiased. As well, it is usually recommended that operational manuals are developed, decisions are published, and annual appeal statistics are reported to allow this independence to be adequately monitored. There should be sanctions and removal procedures in place, with adherence to due process, for improper behavior by tribunal or committee members or judges.
Reasoned decisions	Taxpayers should be given written reasons for judgment that clearly explain the relevant facts, the law on point, and the reasoning behind the decision. This is critical to ensure that there is appropriate record of the case to • Give guidance to other taxpayers on application of the law • Allow taxpayers to make an informed decision on whether to appeal • Allow higher appeal bodies to see how the lower court or tribunal reached its decision so that they can decide whether to affirm or overturn the decision • Document that decisions are arrived at after consideration of the law, and not as a result of arbitrary or discretionary measures

table continues next page

Table 7.4 **Approaches to Domestic Dispute Resolution** (continued)

Design Elements	Suggested good practice and country examples in domestic dispute resolution
Payment of disputed amount	It is essential to balance two competing principals when determining how much of the disputed value should be paid prior to appeal: *accessibility of the appeals system for taxpayers versus deterrence of frivolous appeals.* In many countries, taxpayers are not barred from appealing if they do not pay (and normal enforcement procedures are stayed), but they bear the risk of interest and, potentially, penalties continuing to accrue. This is not always the case, and frequently a portion of the disputed amount needs to be paid as a precondition to appeal (e.g., *Greece:* 20 percent, *Tanzania:* 30 percent). Additional payment considerations: *Security for payment.* Other modifications could be a requirement to pay the full amount, but with provision for taxpayers to provide security for payment (e.g., guarantee, pledge) rather than actual payment. *Waiver application.* Other countries require payment of the full amount, but then have provision for taxpayers to apply for a waiver of full or partial payment under prescribed circumstances. *Costs.* Courts may award costs against one party in exceptional cases to deter against the most frivolous appeals cases.
Reasonable timeframes	Most countries will impose timeframes on taxpayers for each stage, and in many countries timeframes are imposed on the state for the first and second appeals stage (sometimes legislatively and sometimes administratively). The goal is quick resolution of a tax dispute to give taxpayers certainty on the financial outcome of the case, while minimizing resources spent by the state. Examples: *Time to initiate an appeal. The Netherlands* (42 days), *Latvia* (30 days), *United Kingdom* (30 days), *United States* (30–90 days). *Time for first-stage decision at tax authority level. Lithuania* (30 days, extendable by 60 days), *Bulgaria* (45 days). *Time limits for appeal to court stage. The Netherlands* (six weeks), *Norway* (six months), *Romania* (six months), *Spain* (two months), *Cyprus* (75 days).
Consistent treatment	Regardless of whether strict rules of precedence exist or not, *taxpayers must be treated consistently.* It is, therefore, advisable to ensure that the principals emerging from appeals cases are recorded and reflected in the operating manuals followed by auditors and in the general interpretations published by the tax authority and the ministry of finance.
Publication	Most countries will publish key decisions from the second stage of appeals, often within a stated timeframe and often on an anonymous basis (*Ireland, Canada*), and will publish all decisions at the court stage. There is often access to information legislation in place to allow individuals to access first-stage appeals information on an anonymous basis, though these procedures are less routine. Dissemination of decisions is critical to ensuring *transparency of the appeals process* and to provide taxpayers with *guidance on the application of the law.*
Ombudsman office	Many countries establish an *independent office of an ombudsman* to address taxpayers' grievances relating to matters *other than the tax assessed,* such as conduct of revenue officials, delays in processes, perceived bias, and other errors of omission. The existence of an independent tax ombudsman, an institution pioneered in *Sweden,* provides an independent recourse for taxpayers who are dissatisfied with the way they have been dealt with by the tax authority. In some developing economies with tax ombudsmen, the office has been particularly effective in identifying cases of corruption in the tax authority. It also helps foster improved taxpayer relations and adopt a more client-service focus. The ombudsman, typically, has no power to determine a tax dispute on its merits or to act as an administrative appeals officer. Many countries have a taxpayers' charter or bill of rights that the ombudsman's office enforces: Canada (Taxpayers' Ombudsman), United Kingdom (Adjudicator's Office), United States (Taxpayers' Advocate).

Source: World Bank Group country reports.

will have familiarity and knowledge of tax concepts. Alternatively, tax administrations will allow taxpayers to go to general court to pursue the case. In this scenario, it will usually be important for both sides to present expert witnesses to be able to convey advanced transfer pricing concepts to those who may not be familiar with the context.

International Dispute Resolution

Where a tax treaty has been negotiated by two countries, it typically includes Article 9 of OECD and UN model conventions regarding the implementation of the arm's-length principle. Where a taxpayer is of the opinion that an adjustment results from a wrong interpretation of the arm's-length principle by a tax administration, application for a MAP can be made, according to Article 25 of the OECD and UN model conventions. The MAP is a mechanism under international law that provides for representatives (the "competent authority") of the contracting states to interact directly to avoid taxation not in accordance with the terms of the agreement. It is open to any person that considers that the actions of one or both of the contracting states of a treaty result or will result in taxation not in accordance with the provisions of the applicable treaty. The majority of current tax treaties contain a MAP article, but the legal basis for MAPs can also be found in other international agreements. For example, the EU Arbitration Convention provides for a MAP phase prior to the arbitration procedure.

When looking at transfer pricing disputes between treaty partners among OECD countries the increase in disputes from 2006 through 2014 is remarkable (see figure 7.1).

It is, however, important to note that figure 7.1 presents only a subset of all transfer pricing disputes. Not included are non-OECD countries and disputes handled outside of MAP, such as those resolved through domestic

Figure 7.1 OECD Countries' End-of-Year MAP Case Inventories

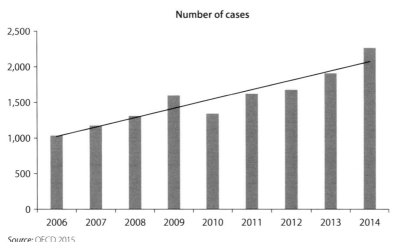

Source: OECD 2015.
Note: MAP = mutual agreement procedure.

dispute-resolution mechanisms discussed above. Moreover, the number of cases per jurisdiction varies significantly.[10] Differences are likely explained by legal, factual, and behavioral reasons:

- The scope of countries' treaty networks matters since treaties provide the legal basis for MAPs. Without a treaty, a MAP is simply impossible.
- The more integrated a country is into the global economy, with more cross-border activity of taxpayers, the higher the potential number of disputes and MAP cases.
- Where tax administrations give no clear guidance on the process of MAPs, some taxpayers may be reluctant to enter into such a procedure. And where taxpayers include corresponding adjustments "silently" (and in contradiction to accounting requirements) into their accounts, tax administrations will not even know about the potential for MAP cases (see box 7.3).

Historically, the majority of the MAP cases have involved requests for relief from economic double taxation arising as a result of transfer pricing adjustments.[11] However, as discussed previously, the MAP is also applicable for nontransfer pricing cases, such as issues of dual residency, permanent establishment issues (existence), the application of interest, royalty and dividend articles, and so forth. In addition to dispute resolution, the MAP may also be used to conclude bilateral and multilateral APAs and other agreements, such as bilateral safe harbors. MAP articles in tax treaties based on the OECD or UN

Box 7.3 "Silent" Corresponding Adjustments

In a number of countries, a "silent" inclusion of corresponding adjustments in the accounting by a taxpayer can be observed. Normally, this occurs in countries where transfer pricing audit activities are limited. In a typical case, a related party S1, resident of Country A, has been audited in Country A, which results in a transfer pricing adjustment for the year X with regard to transactions with the related Company S2 resident in Country B. Instead of asking Country B's tax administration for a corresponding adjustment, the Company S2 simply enters a reduced profit (based on the liability toward S1) into its books in the year X + 1 (the year X will already be closed) and therefore avoids double taxation. In this situation the tax administration in Country B will not even know of the potential case and thus has no opportunity to defend its position in a MAP. The same problem could occur in cases where no central coordination for transfer pricing has been established. If, for instance, S2 asks a regional tax office for a corresponding adjustment (with the regional tax office lacking sufficient transfer pricing know-how to evaluate the case) and no internal coordination mechanism is in place for involving a central group of transfer pricing experts, the regional tax office might simply implement the taxpayers' request. As a result, Country B would not defend its position in a MAP.

---

models will usually provide for the procedure to be used to address three areas of possible contention:

- *Taxation not in accordance with the provisions of the Convention.* See Article 25(1)-(2) of the OECD and UN models
- *Difficulties or doubts as regards the interpretation or application of the Convention.* See Article 25(3) of the OECD and UN models
- *Elimination of double taxation in cases not otherwise provided for in a convention.* See Article 25(3) of the OECD and UN models

The most common application of the MAP article involves situations where a taxpayer believes that the actions of one or both of the contracting states has resulted or will result *in taxation not in accordance with the provisions of the Convention.* In such situations, the taxpayer is entitled to present its case to the relevant "competent authority," which has an obligation, provided the case is justified and it cannot arrive at a satisfactory solution itself, to endeavor to resolve the case by mutual agreement with the *competent authority* of the other contracting state.

There is, however, no guarantee that a case will be resolved through a MAP. The only requirement is that the competent authorities must *endeavor* to reach a resolution. Where a resolution cannot be reached, the taxpayer will likely have to suffer economic double taxation unless access to arbitration is available. Efforts to strengthen the effectiveness of the MAP process have, therefore, also been a key element of the OECD BEPS process, which resulted in the adoption of commitment by member countries to implement specific measures aimed at the timely, effective, and efficient resolution of treaty-based disputes.

In the context of transfer pricing, the MAP plays a crucial role in helping avoid instances of economic double taxation, not only through its role as a mechanism for international dispute resolution and avoidance but also as a form of quality control for transfer pricing administration.

Accessing the MAP for Transfer Pricing Cases

There are a number of general conditions that must be met in order to seek relief from double taxation through a MAP:

- *Applicable legal basis for the MAP exists.* For relief through the MAP to be possible, a tax treaty or other international law instrument containing a legal basis for the MAP must be applicable to the situation. For example, where the transactions subject to a transfer pricing adjustment have taken place between two parties that are not residents of countries that have a tax treaty or similar agreement in force containing a MAP article, there will be no legal basis for the competent authorities to come together and resolve the issue.

- *Criteria for the MAP under the relevant article are fulfilled.* Where a legal basis for the MAP exists, for a taxpayer to be able to access the MAP provided for in a specific tax treaty or similar agreement, the relevant legal criteria must be fulfilled. Where the applicable MAP article is based on Article 25 of the OECD or UN models the following criteria must generally be fulfilled:
  - *The case is presented to the competent authority within the specified maximum time frame.* For example, Article 25(1) of the OECD model requires that the case be presented *"within three years from the first notification of the action resulting in taxation not in accordance with the provisions of the Convention."* In practice, countries have adopted differing views as to when there is a first notification of taxation not in accordance with the provisions of the convention (i.e., at time of amended assessment being issued, at time of reasons given, etc.)
  - *There is taxation not in accordance with the provisions of the relevant treaty.* While this is generally not an issue for cases involving requests for relief from economic double taxation arising from a transfer pricing adjustment, several countries have adopted the view that where the treaty does *not* contain an equivalent article to Article 9(2) of the OECD and UN models, the treaty does *not* express an intention to provide relief from economic double taxation.

- *Practical access to the MAP is available and any domestic law requirements have been met (where applicable).* Even where developing economies have developed tax treaty networks, experience with the MAP is often limited. As a result, taxpayers are practically impeded from making MAP requests due to there being no clear responsibility for the competent authority function, no publicly available contact details, and no procedural guidance. Ideally, a country will issue procedural guidance that specifies, for example, minimum information to be provided and specific formal requests to be made (i.e., to suspend a decision on an objection or similar). One of the outcomes of the BEPS Action 14 is a commitment of countries participating in the BEPS project to ensure that information is made available to taxpayers by publishing rules, guidelines, and procedures for access and use of the MAP (see box 7.4). MAP articles based on Article 25 of the OECD or UN models provide that cases may be presented for a MAP by the taxpayer regardless of the remedies available under domestic law; see, for example, Article 25(1) of the OECD and UN models. In this regard, the MAP is considered a special procedure that is additional to any remedies provided under domestic law. As a result, upon presenting a case for a MAP a taxpayer may be required to take action to protect its rights under domestic law while the MAP takes place. In some countries, access to the MAP is made available only once all remedies under domestic law have been exhausted (i.e., through final decision, waiver, or time lapse). A requirement to exhaust domestic remedies can, however, undermine the intention of the tax treaty since the taxpayer may be left with no avenue of recourse should the competent authorities fail to

---

Box 7.4 Outcomes of Action 14 of the OECD BEPS Initiative

As part of Action 14 of the BEPS initiative, OECD countries agreed to a minimum standard consisting of three broad principles (extract is from OECD/G20 Base Erosion and Profit Shifting (BEPS), Action 14 Final Report (2015): "Making Dispute Resolution Mechanisms More Effective."):

1. Countries should ensure that treaty obligations related to the mutual agreement procedure are fully implemented in good faith and that MAP cases are resolved in a timely manner:
   - The good-faith implementation of Article 25 of the OECD Model treaty is thus an integral part of the contracting parties' obligations.
   - Countries commit to seek to resolve MAP cases within an average time frame of 24 months.
   - Progress toward meeting the target will be reviewed by peers and be based on statistics, which should be prepared based on a common reporting framework.
2. Countries should ensure that administrative processes promote the prevention and timely resolution of treaty-related disputes:
   - Rules, guidelines, and procedures to access and use MAP should be published and adequate resources provided to MAP function.
   - Staff dealing with MAP need independent (from directions of tax administration staff involved in the initial assessment) authority to resolve MAP cases.
   - Performance indicators should provide the right incentives. Countries should thus refrain from measuring staff by sustained audit adjustments in the MAP.
3. Countries should ensure that taxpayers that meet the requirements of paragraph 1 of Article 25 can access the mutual agreement procedure.
   - Countries agree to review Article 25 to reduce barriers to access the MAP.

---

resolve the issue. The new minimum standard of the OECD requires countries to clarify the effects of such domestic requirements on the MAP with treaty partners and in the public guidance for taxpayers.

In countries at an early stage of implementing transfer pricing regimes, with no or only a few transfer pricing audit cases, a small number of staff with transfer pricing expertise, and a narrow tax treaty network, investments into the MAP process are often not an initial priority. Where a country has developed a network of tax treaties, investors may, however, have the reasonable expectation that those treaties will be implemented into domestic law and that access to relief provided for under the treaty will be available. Providing access will generally involve formalizing the competent authority function (see box 7.5) and developing procedures or guidance for taxpayers to follow when making MAP requests.[12]

Ensuring that field auditors are aware of the taxpayer's right to request a MAP can also help to avoid "poor," "nonreasoned," or "silent" (see box 7.3) adjustments being proposed or made. For example, a transfer pricing auditor with the knowledge that the taxpayer may request relief from double taxation

Box 7.5 Formalizing the Competent Authority Function

Key Steps in Formalizing the Competent Authority Function

1. Identify resources necessary for undertaking the competent authority functions and allocate responsibilities accordingly (exchange of information, APAs, MAP disputes, and MAP interpretation, etc.). Where necessary, formal delegation of responsibility may be required, and relevant treaty partners should be notified.
2. Ensure that persons with competent authority responsibilities are adequately trained (e.g., on the application and interpretation of tax treaties, transfer pricing, exchange of information procedures, and negotiation skills, as appropriate) and resourced (travel budget, etc.).
3. Make readily available the competent authority's contact details and procedures for making applications.
4. Put in place performance indicators and address ongoing resourcing and training and development needs.

through the MAP must consider that the adjustment the taxpayer proposes will be reviewed by its country's competent authority (potentially offering an additional level of quality control) and that, if upheld, the adjustment may have to be defended to the competent authority of the other contracting state. Knowledge of this can help to ensure that adjustments proposed are supportable in principle and substantiated with sound reasoning.

It is generally suggested to separate the auditing function from the function of conducting MAPs (see box 7.4). Field auditors who have worked for a long time on certain adjustments may find it more difficult to find compromise solutions that consider the position of another country as opposed to administrators not involved in the respective audit. Nevertheless, in practice, a MAP team will certainly need to draw on the experience and factual reports of field auditors with their detailed knowledge of a specific case.

A particular concern in many developing economies is that the separation of auditing and MAP teams is difficult in a tax administration that has just started implementing a transfer pricing regime. At an early stage, transfer pricing know-how is usually very much linked to the auditing teams, and other parts of a tax administration develop this expertise only over time.

The MAP Process
The negotiation of a case under the MAP between the competent authorities is a government-to-government process. Hence, taxpayers do not, as a general rule, participate or attend as observers at the negotiations or consultations between the competent authorities. Taxpayers may, however, be called upon to give clarification. Since the taxpayers concerned are also stakeholders, competent

---

Box 7.6 Bilateral Memorandums of Understanding

Certain treaty partners will have confidential bilateral memorandum of understanding (MOU) agreements. These agreements may be similar to safe harbors, but implemented at the competent authority level. For instance, the agreement may say to withdraw all adjustment below a certain threshold. Or it may provide a certain return to routine, standard functions.

Box 7.7 Key Documents

In 2007, the OECD produced a *Manual on Effective Mutual Agreement Procedures* (MEMAP), which, in addition to providing a general guide to the MAP process, contains guidelines for setting up competent authority operations.[a]

The UN Committee of Experts on International Cooperation in Tax Matters is currently preparing guidance on MAPs, which also provides guidance on providing access to them.[b]

a. The MEMAP can be accessed through the OECD's website, http://www.oecd.org/ctp/transferpricing/manualoneffectivemutualagreementprocedures-index.htm.
b. A draft, dated October 11, 2012, can be accessed through the UN's website, http://www.un.org/esa/ffd/tax/seventhsession/CRP_4_clean.pdf.

---

authorities will typically update them regularly regarding the outcome of consultations and the expected time frame to complete their cases.

The MAP process can take a long time, illustrated by the recent agreement among OECD countries to aim for an average of no more than 24 months.[13] Recognizing the potential cash-flow constraint as a result of double taxation while a MAP is ongoing, a hold on the requirement to pay can be introduced.[14] Most tax administrations will provide procedures for suspending taxes, with some of these procedures tailored for international disputes and others applying in all kinds of disputes.

Arbitration

As noted previously, the MAP does not require a solution, only that the parties endeavor to resolve double taxation. Although the majority of disputes are resolved, this is not always the case. Where available, taxpayers (or the competent authorities) may have access to arbitration can provide a solution where the competent authorities are unable to agree.

Arbitration involves an independent party assessing each treaty partner's case and determining a result to provide double taxation relief for the multinational taxpayer. There are two general kinds of arbitration: "baseball" arbitration (implemented between the United States and select treaty partners) and traditional arbitration (such as implemented in the EU). Each is discussed in box 7.8. In the course of the OECD BEPS project, 20 countries, including Australia, France, Germany, the United Kingdom, and the United States, have declared their commitment to provide for mandatory binding arbitration in their tax treaties. The Multilateral Instrument, which the OECD plans to finalize in 2016, will also include an optional provision on binding arbitration. Policy makers should carefully consider in treaty negotiations whether and when opting for mandatory arbitration reflects their interest.

Box 7.8 Traditional and "Baseball" Arbitration

Europe's Approach: Traditional Arbitration

Traditional arbitration has been applicable to transfer pricing in the EU since the 1990s. The EU Arbitration Convention forms the committee in similar ways, yet allows it to select a result that may not be equal to the positions put forth by each of the parties. In other words, it can select a point that resides between each position, resulting in no winners and losers, but something in between.

U.S. Approach: "Baseball" or "Final Offer" Arbitration

Baseball can be characterized as a game with one winner: each player seeking to maximize its chance of winning by balancing the reward of a better number for itself against the risk that that number is not chosen. Baseball arbitration is designed to eliminate a practice that has emerged in international arbitration, where arbitrators "split the baby." That is, arbitrators split the difference between the parties' positions in coming to a middle-of-the-road compromise. Anticipating this assumed practice, parties are inclined to adopt extreme positions, thereby potentially reducing the chances of successful settlement.

Baseball arbitration is adopted bilaterally in tax treaties between the United States and four separate treaty partners: Belgium, Canada, France, and Germany. The key feature of baseball arbitration is that the independent parties selected must choose which position is best. The process generally goes as follows:

1) The MAP goes unresolved for a certain number of years.
2) Mandatory arbitration is realized, and each side of the tax convention selects an arbitrator outside the tax administration. Each of those two selected arbitrators selects a third arbitrator to "chair" the three-person committee.
3) Each administration party to the MAP case drafts an arbitration paper for the committee to review.
4) The committee reviews each paper and requests additional information, if necessary.
5) The committee votes on which side has "won" the arbitration case to relieve double taxation, and the case is processed according to the results exactly as stated in the winning paper.

Alternative Dispute Resolution

While much less common, alternative dispute resolution mechanisms could theoretically contribute to solving disputes. In the OECD Commentary to Article 25 OECD MC, mediation is introduced as one supplementary dispute resolution mechanism. It is further suggested that: *"If the issue is a purely factual one, the case could be referred to an expert whose mandate would simply be to make the required factual determinations. This is often done in judicial procedures where factual matters are referred to an independent party who makes factual findings, which are then submitted to the court."* While these approaches necessitate a high level of mutual trust, they certainly can help tax administrations to overcome capacity problems in the short run.

Chapter 7 Main Messages

- Because the cost of transfer pricing disputes can be substantial, tax administrations need to consider how to encourage voluntary compliance. Various mechanisms can be relied upon to avoid disputes.
- Well-designed safe harbor regimes have important benefits, particularly in countries with limited or no publicly available domestic information to conduct benchmarking analysis.
- APAs can help multinational taxpayers and tax authorities to avoid or reduce the potential for audits, uncertainty, investor risk, and compliance costs. These programs, however, have a number of important costs, and the decision on their introduction should be based on a careful assessment of costs and benefits.
- In the context of transfer pricing, the MAP plays a crucial role in helping avoid instances of economic double taxation, not only through its role as a mechanism for international dispute resolution and avoidance but also as a form of quality control for transfer pricing administration.
- While many developing economies have broad tax treaty networks, familiarity with the MAP is often limited. As a result, taxpayers are often practically impeded from making MAP requests.

Notes

1. "Revised Section E on Safe Harbors in Chapter IV of the Transfer Pricing Guidelines" available at the OECD website, http://www.oecd.org/ctp/transfer-pricing/Revised -Section-E-Safe-Harbours-TP-Guidelines.pdf.

2. As an annex to its report, the OECD provides model agreements for safe harbors on low-risk distribution, manufacturing, and research and development. See annex 1 of OECD's guidelines at its website, http://www.oecd.org/ctp/transfer-pricing/Revised -Section-E-Safe-Harbours-TP-Guidelines.pdf.

3. Ensuring, for example, that the price or margin or the safe harbor approaches an arm's-length outcome by conducting a careful analysis of administrative data. In addition, where a regime requires taxpayers to apply the safe harbor to all transactions within the scope of the regime, there should be an option for taxpayers to opt out of the regime (the taxpayer then bearing the burden of proof that its alternative approach leads to an arm's-length result).

4. To provide guidance on this challenge, the Group of Twenty (20) major economies mandated international organizations (the IMF, OECD, UN, and WBG) to develop a toolkit on "Addressing Difficulties in Accessing Comparables Data for Transfer Pricing Analysis." The toolkit will include further guidance on the design of safe harbor regimes and is forthcoming in 2016/17.

5. "Making Dispute Resolution Mechanisms More Effective, Action 14—2015 Final Report," at the OECD website, http://www.oecd-ilibrary.org/taxation/making-dispute -resolution-mechanisms-more-effective-action-14-2015-final-report_97892 64241633-en.

6. Note that the review and negotiation phase does not have a timeline. This is by design since setting deadlines for negotiation of an APA can significantly alter its dynamics and results.

7. "Countering Harmful Tax Practices More Effectively, Taking into Account Transparency and Substance, Action 5 - 2015 Final Report." Available at the OECD website, http:// www.oecd.org/tax/countering-harmful-tax-practices-more-effectively-taking-into -account-transparency-and-substance-action-5-2015-final-report-9789264241190 -en.htm.

8. "Countering Harmful Tax Practices More Effectively, Taking into Account Transparency and Substance, Action 5 - 2015 Final Report." Available at the OECD website, http://www .oecd.org/tax/countering-harmful-tax-practices-more-effectively-taking-into-account- transparency-and-substance-action-5-2015-final-report-9789264241190-en.htm.

9. At times, a taxpayer will negotiate or simply pay the assessed amount. If an agreement can be reached bilaterally between the tax administration and taxpayer, no further steps are needed.

10. The OECD provides a country specific overview on reported MAP cases. http://www. oecd.org/ctp/dispute/map-statistics-2013.htm.

11. OECD MEMAP paragraph 1.2.1; http://www.oecd.org/ctp/transferpricing/1backg round-12whatisamutualagreementproceduremap-121.htm.

12. See, for example, the country profiles for MAPs at the OECD website, http://www .oecd.org/ctp/disputeresolution/disputeresolutioncountryprofiles.htm.

13. OECD/G20 BEPS, Action 14, 2015 Final Report. See also box 7.4 on the outcomes of Action 14.

14. For example, the ATO has specified such an approach:

> In cases where the ATO makes a transfer pricing or profit reallocation adjustment, the debtor may seek Competent Authority assistance, under the Mutual Agreement Procedure (MAP) article contained in Australia's double tax agreements, to attempt to have the matter resolved with the other tax jurisdiction involved. It is recognized that the collection of tax during MAP cases will, in some instances, impose temporary double taxation on the taxpayer whilst the MAP is in progress because the same profits have been subject to tax in both jurisdictions. Where the possibility of such double taxation arises, the ATO will agree to defer recovery action under Section 255-5 in Schedule 1 to the TAA, including the recovery of any GIC, until an agreed future date (which will usually be the date that the MAP process is concluded), unless there is a risk to the revenue; the taxpayer has other liabilities unpaid after the due date; or the taxpayer has failed to meet other tax obligations when required.

Bibliography

EUJTPF (European Union Joint Transfer Pricing Forum). 2013. *Report on Transfer Pricing Risk Management.* Brussels: EUJTPF. http://ec.europa.eu/taxation_customs/sites /taxation/files/resources/documents/taxation/company_tax/transfer_pricing/forum /jtpf/2013/jtpf_007_2013_en.pdf.

———. 2014 *Statistics on APAs at the End of 2013.* Brussels: EUJTPF. http://ec.europa.eu /taxation_customs/sites/taxation/files/resources/documents/taxation/company_tax /transfer_pricing/forum/final_apa_statistics_2013_en.pdf.

HMRC (Her Majesty's Revenue and Customs). 2010. *Policy Paper Statement of Practice 2,* (2010). London: HMRC. https://www.gov.uk/government/publications/statement -of-practice-2-2010/statement-of-practice-2-2010#who-may-apply-for-an-apa.

IRAS (Inland Revenue Authority of Singapore). 2016. *Transfer Pricing Guidelines,* 3rd edition. Singapore: IRAS. https://www.iras.gov.sg/irashome/uploadedFiles/IRASHome/e-Tax _Guides/etaxguide_CIT_Transfer%20Pricing%20Guidelines_3rd.pdf

IRS (Internal Revenue Service). 2015. *Procedures for Advance Pricing Agreements.* Washington, DC: IRS. https://www.irs.gov/pub/irs-drop/rp-15-41.pdf.

Mile, Andrew. 2004. "Germany: German Tax & Legal News—September 2004." *Mondaq* (blog), September 20. http://www.mondaq.com/article.asp?article_id=28493.

OECD (Organisation for Economic Co-operation and Development). 2007. *Manual on Effective Mutual Agreement Procedures (MEMAP).* Paris: OECD. http://www.oecd.org /ctp/38061910.pdf.

———. 2015. *Mutual Agreement Procedure Statistics for 2014.* Paris: OECD. http://www .oecd.org/ctp/dispute/map-statistics-2014.htm.

UN (United Nations). 2011. "Committee of Experts on International Cooperation in Tax Matters." Note on Dispute Resolution: Guide to Mutual Agreement Procedure, Seventh Session, October 24–28, Geneva, UN. http://www.un.org/esa/ffd/tax /seventhsession/CRP_4_clean.pdf.

Developing a Transfer Pricing Audit Program

As the preceding chapters demonstrate, a country's transfer pricing regime can be appropriately designed to protect the tax base, minimize compliance burdens, and limit instances of unrelieved economic double taxation. This can, however, be completely undermined by weak processes and administration.

Following the enactment of transfer pricing legislation and guidance, tax administrations need to develop, implement, and continuously update an effective transfer pricing audit program. This is a multifaceted process that needs to be based on a country's specific requirements, risk areas (see chapter 1 and table 1.4, specifically, regarding approaches for assessing a country's transfer pricing exposure), level of experience in dealing with large taxpayers and international tax issues, available resources (e.g., human, information technology, financial), private sector expertise, the legal system (including tax treaties), and the existing organizational structure and culture within the tax administration.

Typically, it is necessary to make a substantial investment in capacity building and the development of appropriate administrative policies and procedures to successfully implement a transfer pricing regime. Only with the appropriate training and experience can the tax administration be expected to make informed decisions and exercise discretion appropriately and consistently, thus limiting uncertainty and the incidence of unnecessary compliance costs.

Institutional Arrangements and Responsibility of Transfer Pricing Staff

At the outset of a reform program, policy makers need to decide on the institutional setup for implementing a transfer pricing regime. The selected organizational structure will depend on the environment within which the team will operate. The two main options are a centralized or a decentralized model, but there are a multitude of other viable alternatives, including hybrid structures. The approach ultimately chosen needs to be tailored to suit the individual country and be flexible enough to allow for changes and improvements as a transfer pricing regimes evolve.

Centralized Model

The most common approach observed in World Bank Group assistance programs is the establishment of a centralized team that is dedicated to improving transfer pricing compliance throughout the tax administration (see figure 8.1). Typically, tax administrations have either a large taxpayer office (LTO) or a large business and international (LB&I) division, which houses the transfer pricing team. The LTO or LB&I is predominately organized along industry specialization, which reflects the country's main economic activities. Most taxpayers in the scope of transfer pricing legislation will be classified as large taxpayers,[1] although in some countries with domestic transfer pricing legislation, which encompasses a very broad definition of associated enterprises, even taxpayers classified as small can have their transactions subjected to scrutiny under the transfer pricing rules (see chapter 3).[2]

A centralized structure may be most appropriate in situations where

- A country is in the start-up phase of implementing transfer pricing
- The number of transfer pricing cases is limited
- There is a refocusing of priorities or plans to concentrate on transfer pricing cases
- There are only a small number of transfer pricing experts within the organization

Figure 8.1 Centralized Approach to Transfer Pricing Administration in Singapore

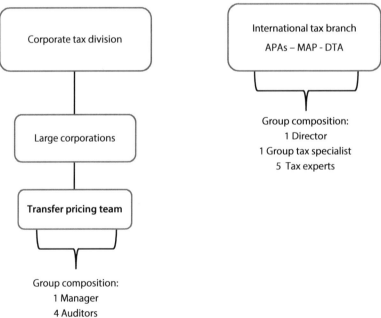

Group composition:
1 Manager
4 Auditors

Group composition:
1 Director
1 Group tax specialist
5 Tax experts

Source: Arcotia Hatsidimitris interview with principal tax auditor, IRAS, October 2011.
Note: APA = advance pricing agreement; DTA = Double Taxation Agreement; IRAS = Inland Revenue Authority of Singapore; MAP = mutual agreement procedure.

Centralizing allows for a core group to quickly build expertise through specialist training and often provides for economies of scale. The team can readily discuss relevant issues and arrive at agreed positions, which are then consistently applied, reducing the risk of communication breakdowns and allowing the group to have oversight of all the transfer pricing cases.

An additional benefit for the private sector is a clearly defined public sector counterpart on the interpretation and application of transfer pricing provisions.

For a transfer pricing team in a start-up phase, where experience and resources are limited and a country's transfer pricing regime might still be under development, a centralized approach will generally provide for the most effective allocation of resources.[3]

Irrespective of the approach, it is important to clearly define the responsibilities of the transfer pricing team members and their relationship with other tax auditors. Where a centralized approach is implemented, the central unit must try to keep in close communication with other tax officials involved in general auditing activities as well as policy makers.

As highlighted by the UN (2013), experience suggests that there are many risks in upsetting the institutional equilibrium in the initial stages of implementing a centralized transfer pricing team[4]:

> "*First*, there is the possibility of resentment against those involved with transfer pricing policy and administration by others in more 'established' areas. Because it is new, people within the organization do not always know exactly what it is about and feel uncertain and can be unwilling or dismissive about taking up transfer pricing issues. Further, setting up such a Transfer Pricing Unit may require the recruitment of outside expertise in key roles. Existing staff may feel it is a 'fashionable' area of work that draws resources and support away from their own equally important areas of work, or unduly rewards 'outsiders' and 'upstarts' who have not 'paid their dues [...]'"

In summary, a centralized team will have the benefit of economies of scale in developing experience and judgment and should aid in ensuring consistent application of the law. However, where a centralized team is understaffed or underfunded, it may ultimately lack the knowledge or ability to effectively implement the law.

Decentralized Model

In large economies with a high degree of decentralization, there may be a need to adopt a decentralized model to manage the sheer number of transfer pricing cases and to align the organizational transfer pricing design to fit into the existing institutional setup. This approach generally requires auditors to cover transfer pricing issues where relevant, though they can rely on regional specialists for support on specific issues (see figure 8.2). Larger economies with substantial multinational enterprise (MNE) activity tend to require major investments in maintaining sufficient numbers of transfer pricing experts.

Figure 8.2 Decentralized Approach to Transfer Pricing Administration in Japan's National Tax Agency

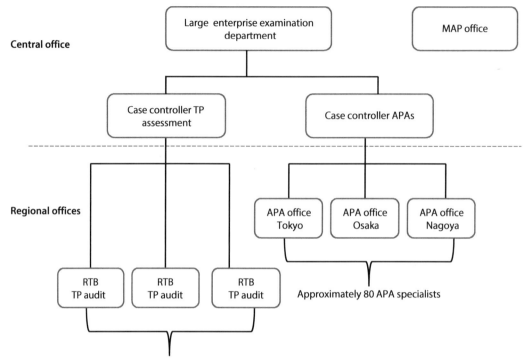

There are approximately 160 transfer pricing auditors spread across 12 (RTB); issues that are significant, of high value or complicated are referred to the Case Controller Assessment in the Central Office. RTB also reports directly to RTB directors.

Source: Hatsidimitris interview with senior tax official, NTA, October 2011.
Note: APA = advance pricing agreement; MAP = mutual agreement procedure; RTB = regional tax bureau; TP = transfer pricing.

A decision to centralize, decentralize, or opt for a hybrid model might be reconsidered at different times depending on policy priorities. For example, the U.S. Internal Revenue Service (IRS) and the U.S. Department of Treasury recently aimed to create a more efficient process for transfer pricing enforcement and compliance by realigning the existing structure and centralizing the transfer pricing practice under one director for Transfer Pricing Operations. This would allow for more coordination with the field examination teams (PwC 2012).

Douglas Shulman, commissioner of the IRS, explained the reasons for the new transfer pricing practice:

> In the past, our transfer pricing enforcement resources and compliance tools have been disaggregated [...] and this has made it impossible to operate strategically based on risk assessment and business insight [...] we needed to work transfer pricing as a single, fully-integrated program, where our experts are working together [...] to develop and coordinate our transfer pricing strategy, training and operational approaches to key transfer pricing matters arising in

field examination. We have also put our Competent Authority and the Advance Pricing Agreement program under the same executive to ensure that they are fully aligned.[5]

Further Considerations Regarding the Institutional Design

In applying a centralized, decentralized, or hybrid model, policy makers should decide how the relationship between the transfer pricing team and the competent authority (CA) will be managed. This is particularly relevant with regard to advance pricing agreements (APA) and mutual agreement procedure (MAP) cases (see chapter 7), since both procedures require detailed factual knowledge of a case. The necessary information can usually only be provided by field staff of a transfer pricing team. Members of the transfer pricing unit may be allocated with CA responsibilities or they may be required to provide expertise to the CA (e.g., managing or assisting with MAPs or bilateral APA negotiations). At a minimum, there should be open lines of communication between the CA and the transfer pricing unit to ensure that a consistent and principled approach is taken on all transfer pricing matters.

Once there is an institutional model, a transfer pricing audit program must have a core group of senior tax officials responsible for transfer pricing matters.[6] Where a centralized approach is chosen, the transfer pricing unit is then allocated responsibility for administration of the transfer pricing regime, including educating taxpayers and tax officials, undertaking transfer pricing reviews and audits, and liaising with policy makers on future developments. In this regard, the transfer pricing unit would typically be responsible for either undertaking the transfer pricing audits or taking an advisory role to the audit team.

The transfer pricing unit must also establish a good working relationship with stakeholders. Effective communication, both internal and external (with other agencies, taxpayers, intermediaries, and the business community), is critical. Educating and engaging in a dialogue with the private sector will also form part of building strong working relationships. In addition, since the judiciary is an important stakeholder, care should be taken to ensure that judges and other legal experts are familiar with transfer pricing concepts and their application in a business setting.

A transfer pricing unit must also consider that opportunities for corruption are a challenge, irrespective of the organizational model chosen. This issue is particularly acute with respect to transfer pricing given the large monetary amounts that are often the subject of transfer pricing disputes, the inherent need for a certain level of discretion, and, where applicable, the ability for taxpayers to enter into APAs. To address the potential for corruption, appropriate internal procedures and practices to manage this risk need to be implemented (see box 8.1).

Another area to consider is the level of participation in international forums. For example, the Organisation for Economic Co-operation and Development (OECD) Working Party 6; the United Nations (UN) Committee of Experts on

Box 8.1 Limiting Opportunities for Corruption in a Transfer Pricing Regime

The arm's-length principle requires the exercise of a level of subjectivity and discretion by the tax administration, which, if not properly controlled, may provide opportunities for corruption or result in the imposition of unnecessary compliance costs to the taxpayer. Transfer pricing cases can involve substantial amounts, so it is important to put in place appropriate safeguards (EuropeAid and PwC 2011; World Bank Group country reports).

A number of approaches can help minimize the possibility of corruption by reducing the level of subjectivity and discretion that can be exercised by tax officers, such as

- Annual independent compliance checks and random quality reviews by an internal audit division
- Development of a code of conduct
- Introduction of objective, risk-based audit selection criteria (see discussion in box 8.2) and the preparation of detailed audit plans
- Asset or wealth declarations for tax administration staff
- A central registry of taxpayer files, covering all records of client communications with access restricted to authorized staff
- Handling transfer pricing cases in a team, and instituting a rotation system for auditors and regular cross-checks of audits by several senior tax auditors
- A requirement for senior approval and sign-off on major decisions (e.g., before commencing audit, proposing an adjustment, and reviewing an objection).

International Cooperation in Tax Matters and its subcommittees, the Study Group on Asian Tax Administration and Research (SGATAR) and the Pacific Islands Tax Administrators Association (PITAA); regional meetings; working groups; conferences; and events. Appropriate representation within the global tax environment can contribute to administrative efficiency by enhancing a team's knowledge base and by building professional working relationships with other government officials, which can aid in discussing potential cross-border differences in the interpretation and application of each country's respective transfer pricing rules. However, international commitments can quickly absorb significant staff time and finances, thus reducing access to already scarce resources in the administration.

Human Resources

Where a country implements a transfer pricing audit program without securing all the necessary support and resources, including competent and confident auditors, taxpayers might assess the tax administration's capacity to effectively conduct transfer pricing audits as weak. Whether such a weakness is perceived or real, it likely has an undesirable negative effect on future tax collections.

A successful transfer pricing program requires the financial investment to prepare staff for specialized tasks, with a broad range of competencies typically required for successful implementation (see box 8.2).

Retaining Staff

Enterprises, governments, tax advisory and law firms worldwide recruit transfer pricing personnel at an ever-increasing rate. PricewaterhouseCoopers (PwC)

Box 8.2 Relevant Competencies for Transfer Pricing Implementation

Implementing a transfer pricing regime requires a range of competencies from various disciplines,[a] including

- *Accounting.* Interpretation of financial accounts and undertaking financial analysis.
- *Auditing.* Conducting transfer pricing documentation reviews and undertaking audits.
- *Communications*: Writing position papers and discussing complex tax issues with the taxpayer and their representatives or with other tax administrations.
- *Economics.* Conducting benchmarking and comparability analysis, determining economic ownership of intangibles, and calculating/advising on economic measures of profitability.
- *Industry and business experts.* Involving experts in, for example, the fields of banking, oil and gas, pharmaceuticals, financial services, and telecommunications. This expertise is imperative in the preparation of the business analysis, industry analysis, and parts of the functional analysis. Taxpayers have a distinct advantage regarding knowledge about how their business and industry operates. External expertise may sometimes be helpful to tax administrations especially where the industry or the nature or the transactions are complex.
- *IT.* To design the program for the transfer pricing risk-based assessment and a system for managing transfer pricing cases and a transfer pricing knowledge platform.
- *International taxation.* To report on tax treaty implications, in particular Articles 5, 7, 9, 25, 26 of the OECD and UN Model Tax Convention. Analysis of tax-planning structures and their potential impact on related party dealings.
- *Legal.* Review related party and third-party agreements their interpretation from a transfer pricing perspective; establish who has legal ownership of assets, especially intangibles; and litigate cases, i.e., defend the tax administration's position in a controversy.
- *Negotiation and conflict resolution.* The ability to negotiate and resolve conflicts will be required for most transfer pricing cases. In some complex cases a formal negotiation procedure will be required to settle a dispute or disagreement, either with the taxpayer or with another administration.
- *Valuation.* Expert valuation may be required in areas related to business restructuring and the transfer of intangibles assets.

a. Each competency lists only a few examples of transfer pricing activities that may be undertaken.

---

alone employs over 1,800 transfer pricing specialists in 70 countries (PwC 2011). As the demand for transfer pricing specialists surpasses supply, tax administrations face difficulties in attracting experienced people and struggle to retain talented staff.

One of the main reasons for this problem is the common differential between private and public sector salaries. Policy makers can attempt to mitigate this issue by reviewing their internal pay scales[7] and by providing attractive packages whose benefits could help to compensate for the salary disparity.

Nonsalary benefits offered by tax administrations could include

- Professional development opportunities coupled with a career path in line with the employees' expectation for growth and advancement. There are many different areas to specialize in within transfer pricing, which should strengthen career development prospects (risk assessment, audit, valuation, litigation, etc.)
- Work–life balance, flexible working hours, flexible working arrangements, and flexible leave entitlements
- Childcare and other family support provisions
- Challenging and satisfying work, which is supported, appreciated, and recognized with financial and nonfinancial rewards
- International exposure through forums, conferences, working groups, or an opportunity for a placement or training program abroad
- Attractive pension scheme or retirement plan

Even where such incentives are insufficient to keep all staff, some tax administrations see the departure of staff as an opportunity, since former staff will help spread knowledge and awareness of the administration's views.[8]

Knowledge Management

In light of the preceding discussion, one of the main challenges facing tax administrations is to preserve the knowledge, experience, and know-how that risks being lost as staff members leave or retire. One of the core responsibilities of experienced transfer pricing staff should thus be the specialized training of other selected tax officials and provision of general awareness training for all tax officials with relevant auditing responsibilities. Allocation of transfer pricing responsibilities to more junior staff is also important for maximizing on-the-job training opportunities, particularly given the practical nature of transfer pricing cases.

Another important element of knowledge management is the establishment of an internal library or knowledge center that contains, for instance, a dossier on each taxpayer that has been subject to transfer pricing analysis. In addition, court decisions, rulings, opinions, articles, and academic papers sorted by subject matter could be stored on such a platform, allowing transfer pricing staff to readily review a particular topic. Ideally, the knowledge management center would be available through the tax administration's intranet and, if virtual and interactive, it could act as a vehicle for transfer pricing experts to communicate across a geographically dispersed area. These platforms typically encompass transfer pricing research and analysis tools, external transfer pricing databases, manuals, guidance notes, training material, presentations, useful resource links, etc.

Commercial Database Access

As discussed in chapter 4, the application of the arm's-length principle based on a comparability analysis generally requires a comparison of the conditions in the controlled transactions with the conditions in comparable uncontrolled transactions. In practice, this will require identifying internal or external comparables. External comparables are often identified using commercial databases. Reliance on such databases is of particular importance where foreign information is relied upon due to a lack of local comparables information, which is the situation in many developing economies (see discussion in chapter 4).

As a result, the tax administration will generally require access to commercial databases—such as those offered by Thomson Reuters, Bureau van Dijk, Standard & Poor's—to identify and analyze external comparables so as to test or adjust the taxpayer's transfer prices in accordance with the arm's-length principle. A non-exhaustive list of available databases is provided in annex 4B along with details of the regions (and where applicable, transaction types) that they cover. Access to such databases can require a substantial investment. However, the tax administration's ability to access potential comparable data is necessary to undertake risk assessment, test transfer prices or profits, support transfer pricing adjustments, and design risk indicators.

Risk Management: Maximizing the Use of Scarce Audit Resources

Risk management concepts form the building blocks for modern tax administrations.[9] They are also an essential component for the implementation of an efficient and effective transfer pricing audit program. As stated by Douglas Shulman, commissioner of the IRS,[10] the objective is to try to develop a way of organizing international compliance programs to:

- Identify the highest compliance risks among the taxpayer base;
- Work cases as effectively and efficiently as possible;
- Not waste taxpayers' time on issues that do not pose compliance risk; and
- Find appropriate ways to resolve cases as soon as possible.

Tax administrations are faced with finite resources and limited time, which means they are unable to conduct audits on all taxpayers with related party dealings. They will, therefore, need to determine the potential tax revenue at stake to select the most suitable audit cases.[11] A core principle for selecting transfer pricing audit cases is the maximization of returns on limited audit resources.

A metric of the extra revenue expected from the audit resources deployed can be established by combining the quantitative analysis of the extra revenue that an audit might generate with a qualitative estimate of the time and resources to successfully conduct a specific audit (Khwaja et al. 2011).

Moreover, a well-structured risk analysis should increase the efficiency of tax administrations by improving the quality of actual audits conducted because it will provide auditors with the initial guidance on areas that require further investigation and prevent weak adjustment decisions, which risk being overturned in courts or being unsustainable in a MAP (OECD 2013).

Audit and Risk Review Selection Process for Transfer Pricing

Taxpayers should comply with both the letter and the spirit[12] of the transfer pricing legislation and regulations of the country in which they operate. Those who fail to do so should face a higher risk of being selected for a transfer pricing audit. Risk assessment is aimed at achieving this objective. It should assist in identifying the potential revenue at risk as a result of transfer mispricing and the degree of transfer pricing risks linked to a specific taxpayer's transfer pricing policy.

A precursor to risk assessment is for a tax administration to electronically collect and store the necessary information for developing, implementing, and assessing criteria to detect any potential deviation from its transfer pricing legislation and regulations. If this information is not readily available, the tax administration should determine the gaps and, where possible, amend the tax returns and related schedules to ensure that the required information is captured (see chapter 6 on documentation requirements). Once this information is collected, an administration should be in a position to analyze and interpret it efficiently and effectively.

The usual starting point for transfer pricing risk assessment will be the analysis of the tax return database. Risk assessment will, however, not be limited to tax return data and should be supplemented with information from other sources, including, for example:

- Publicly filed accounts at the stock exchange, chamber of commerce, or business registry
- Other government agencies or organizations, such as the customs agency or patent office
- News articles
- Stock broker reports
- Industry information (websites, reports, publications)
- Transfer pricing documentation prepared by the taxpayer
- Transfer pricing questionnaires
- Transfer pricing, commodity, business or credit agency databases
- Information published on a company website
- Case law
- Expert industry knowledge, including external experts

Depending on the information available to administrators, a range of structural risk indicators can be developed. Country practices vary, and the degree of precision and sophistication aimed for in the risk analysis is directly related to the amount of resources required to operate the system. It is thus important to recognize that risk assessment is not aimed at absolute precision, which is the objective of an actual audit (OECD 2013).

At the outset, a range of features implying high and low risk needs to be determined. Auditing taxpayers who share information and demonstrate compliance with the arm's-length principle risks wasting administrative and taxpayer resources. Similarly, independent minority shareholders can play a role in mitigating transfer mispricing risks since their interests tend to be aligned with those of domestic tax administrators. The prevalence of joint ventures in some sectors, such as oil and gas exploration, can thus lower profit shifting risks through transfer mispricing, although this does not need to apply to all entities and transactions along the hydrocarbon value chain.[13]

Designing Risk Indicators

The OECD "Draft Handbook on Transfer Pricing Risk Assessment," published as a discussion draft in 2013,[14] is a useful reference for the design of risk indicators. Broadly speaking, there are four types of risk indicators that will be used for risk assessment:

- Indicators that reflect the general tax risk potential of different taxpayer groups
- Indicators that relate to taxpayers' past behavior
- Indicators that relate to deviations of current performance from norms
- Information from paid or voluntary informants

Depending on a country's economy, legal and tax framework, transaction types, and industries may pose different levels of transfer pricing risk. A number of tax administrations communicate directly or indirectly with taxpayers on their areas of focus (see table 8.1).

A summary of high-level indicators is also provided by the OECD (table 8.2) and complemented in the UN transfer pricing manual, where the following risk flags are highlighted[15]:

- "Consistent and continued losses;
- Transactions with related parties in countries with lower effective/marginal tax rates, especially "secrecy jurisdictions" from which tax information is not likely to be shared;
- Local low-profit or loss-making companies with material cross-border transactions with related parties offshore with the offshore part of the group being relatively more profitable.
- The existence of centralized supply chain companies in favorable tax jurisdictions, i.e., centralized sourcing or marketing companies located in jurisdictions with low or no tax regimes and which are not located in the same country/region as the group's main customers and/or suppliers.

- Material commercial relationships with related parties in jurisdictions with aggressive/strict transfer pricing rules—the corporate group may be more likely to transfer price in favor of the more aggressive jurisdiction and at the cost of the less aggressive jurisdiction due to the higher likelihood of intense scrutiny in the former jurisdiction.

- The same applies in the case of material commercial relationships with companies located in the "home" jurisdiction of the MNE or where the holding company is listed.

- Similarly, material commercial relationships with companies in jurisdictions that employ safe harbors or similar rules that do not always align to the arm's-length principle."

Table 8.1 Summary of General Transfer Pricing Risks in the United Kingdom, New Zealand, and China

United Kingdom: HMRC general transfer pricing risk indicators[a]	New Zealand's core transfer pricing risks[b]	China's SAT transfer pricing audit triggers[c]
• Profit or losses inconsistent with business activity or the worldwide group results • Low or no royalties received by a domestic affiliate providing intangibles, whereas the transaction partner is making a high return (in comparison to its industry peers) • High debt ratios and high interest payments of affiliates when compared to other entities in the sector, possibly resulting in unsustainable debt burdens • Transactions with low tax jurisdictions and transactions lacking commercial sense (i.e., insertion of holding companies) • Debt-funded acquisitions by private equity firms and publicly available information on business restructurings • Disappearance or decline in stock	• Chronic recurring losses • Widely differing profits between the local company, other members of the group, the group as a whole, and the industry • Major downward shifts in profitability of a domestic company upon acquisition by an MNE • Domestic management accepting, without question, prices set by overseas associates • Transactions with low or no tax jurisdictions • Material levels of untested transactions • Lack of documentation to support transfer prices	• A failure to disclose or prepare contemporaneous documentation • Growing sales accompanied by losses • A substantial difference between related and unrelated sales margins • Significant related-party transactions or different types of such transactions • Profits that are not commensurate with the function or risk assumed • Business restructurings and share transfers • Recurring losses, marginal profits, or fluctuating profits • Significant related-party transactions with affiliates located in tax havens

Sources: Bell 2011; HMRC INTM482030; ITD 2007.
Note: HMRC = Her Majesty's Revenue and Customs; MNE = multinational enterprise; SAT = State Administration of Taxation.
a. HMRC, INTM482030, "Transfer Pricing: Risk Assessment: Transfer Pricing Indicators: General." See the HMRC website, http://www.hmrc.gov.uk/manuals/intmanual/INTM482040.htm.
b. Information published on the International Tax Dialogue Platform, available at http://www.itdweb.org/.
c. Information based on Bell 2011.

Table 8.2 OECD Checklist for Transfer Pricing Risk

Feature	Brief description
Significant transactions with related parties in low-tax jurisdictions	Where transactions take place with lowly taxed and related entities there is a risk that mispricing will incorrectly attribute excess profits to the lowly taxed jurisdiction.
Transfers of intangibles to related parties	Transactions of this nature raise difficult valuation questions, especially where the intangibles are unique and consequently there is a lack of comparables.
Business restructurings	The transfer pricing aspects of business restructuring were the subject of a specific OECD study published and incorporated as a new Chapter IX of the *OECD Transfer Pricing Guidelines* in July 2010.
Specific types of payments	Payments of interest, insurance premiums, and royalties to related parties because the underlying rights are highly mobile and consequently there is a risk that the payments do not reflect the true value being added by the related party.
Loss making	Year-on-year loss making, where there is no attempt made to change business operations or financing. Sustained losses may be evidence that the reported results do not reflect the true value of the business.
Poor results	Similarly, results that are not consistent with industry norms or with the functions carried out by the enterprise in the country concerned may be evidence that related party transactions have not been correctly priced.
Effective tax rate	Significant variations between the effective tax rate reported at group level and the nominal rates to which it is subject can be the result of transfer pricing that allocates too much profit to low-tax jurisdictions.
Poor/nonexistent documentation	Evidence that transfer prices and the methods used to compute them are inadequately recorded casts doubt on the reliability of the prices themselves.
Excessive debt	Debt that appears to be in excess of the amount that an entity could borrow if it were a freestanding entity, or interest rates that appear to be in excess of market rates.

Source: OECD 2012.

A subset of indicators of transfer pricing risk applied in most countries includes:

- Persistent loss making
- Inconsistent profit levels (persistently lower profitability compared to industry peers)
- Low tax jurisdictions in the value chain (transactions with offshores or tax havens or with taxpayers subject to tax exemptions)
- Inconsistent remuneration in the MNE group context
- Substantial payments of interest to nonresident related parties (particularly when made by an entity with low profitability or by a loss-making entity)

- Substantial payments of royalties to nonresident related parties (particularly when made by an entity with low profitability or by a loss-making entity)
- Substantial payments of services fees to nonresident related parties (particularly when made by an entity with low profitability or by a loss-making entity)
- Business restructurings (reduction in profitability post acquisition by MNE group)
- Lack of or low quality of documentation to support transfer prices
- Nontaxpayer-related risks

Persistent Loss Making

Published criteria typically suggest that entities reporting consistent losses over a three- to five-year period are likely to become the target of transfer pricing audit activities. This is in line with the OECD and UN's transfer pricing guidelines[16] and is particularly appropriate where the business activities carried on by the company are relatively routine (e.g., routine wholesale distribution activities; see also discussion in chapter 5). Depending on what functions and risks a wholesaler takes on, initial losses might be acceptable, but a rule of thumb is that independent wholesalers would not consistently return losses for more than three years without renegotiating with their suppliers, reorganizing their business, or going out of business.[17] Numerous countries thus use the reporting of persistent losses as a trigger for a transfer pricing review or audit (see box 8.3).[18]

Risk factors specific to transfer pricing are never determined on a stand-alone basis and always need to be assessed within the context of the legal, tax, business, and industry environment. For example, if a taxpayer reports consistent losses, several additional questions should be considered, including

- To what extent do similar independent companies incur losses during the same years as the company under examination?

Box 8.3 Persistent Losses in Vietnam as a Trigger for Transfer Pricing Audits

Consecutive losses or low profitability are a target for transfer pricing audit
Extract is from PwC (2012).

The General Department of Taxation (GDT) of Vietnam in its half yearly 2011 report has indicated that reported tax revenue losses have decreased by US$107 million as a result of its recent audits on 107 Foreign Invested Enterprises (FIEs). The GDT has instructed provincial tax offices to conduct tax audits on 870 FIEs, which reported consecutive losses for financial years 2008 to 2010, and companies that report very low profitability. In addition, GDT will also carry out inspection on 40 FIEs and 82 other local conglomerates based on a list furnished by the Ministry of Finance. Survey forms are being issued by the GDT to selected taxpayers as a means to obtain information on transfer pricing practices and whether transfer pricing documentation has been prepared. It is expected that the information will be used as a risk assessment tool for the GDT to select companies for an audit.

- Do the company's financial indicators deviate from what is observed in the general business cycle?
- How does the company perform in relation to the MNE group as a whole?
- What type of historical compliance profile does the company have?
- Are there any anomalies locally, regionally, or globally that should be taken into account?
- What is the relationship of any feature compared to one or more other features? For example, is there a nexus between dealings with tax havens and reported profitability (see figure 8.3)?

Inconsistent Profit Levels (Persistently Lower Profitability Compared to Industry Peers)

Most tax administrations rely on comparisons of companies' reported financial results with industry benchmarks or to the results of an MNE group at the global level. Performance indicators that can be used to establish these benchmarks include (a) gross profit-to-net sales, (b) operating profit-to-net sales, (c) operating expenses-to-net sales, (d) cost coverage ratio (sometimes referred to as a "Berry ratio," or a gross profit-to-operating expense), and (e) operating profit to average total assets (OECD 2013). The applicable indicator will depend on circumstances and industry characteristics. Asset-based indicators, for instance, are more appropriate where assets are consistently captured and an important driver operating profit, such as in capital-intensive industries like mining, construction, and telecommunication. In general, this tends to be more the case for manufacturing entities as opposed to distributors or service providers. For entities that do not employ significant assets, indicators using sales or cost as a base tend to be more appropriate. Obviously, profit trends that are contrary to market trends can be driven by a broad range of reasons and do not necessarily reflect a problem of transfer mispricing, but a constant review of trends against benchmarks can be helpful in uncovering outliers and systematic risk.

Low Tax Jurisdictions in the Value Chain

Substantial transactions with low tax jurisdictions are another common risk indicator. Incentives to shift profit increase the larger the tax differential between an entity and its affiliated group members. As a result, many administrations treat sizable transactions with affiliates in low tax jurisdictions as a general risk indicator. For example, as part of its compliance plan in 2011, Australia's tax office stated:

> We are concerned about the use of arrangements between Australia and offshore affiliates to shift or shelter profits, including: restructuring Australian-based operations to shift functions, assets, and risks on a non–arm's-length basis, such as the creation and use of marketing hubs or the sale of intellectual property at nominal prices; paying excessive royalties, interest, guarantee, and other fees; Australian-headquartered companies providing services to overseas affiliates for a non–arm's-length consideration; allocating to Australian businesses income and expenses not consistent with the economic activities conducted here.

Transfer Pricing and Developing Economies • http://dx.doi.org/10.1596/978-1-4648-0969-9

Figure 8.3 Reported Returns Comparing Similar Entities with Affiliates in a Low Tax Treaty Partner to Those Without

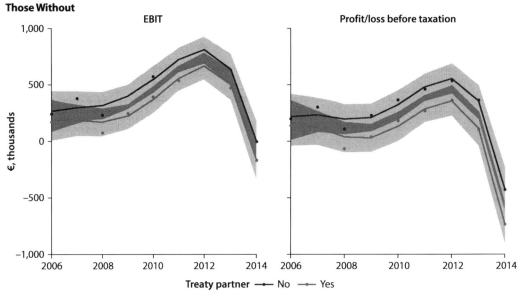

Sources: WBG country report.
Note: Data sourced from BvD's Orbis Database (September 2015). Only companies with complete information from 2006 to 2014 selected. Four hundred and eighty-nine companies' treaty partner affiliates were matched on fixed assets with MNE subsidiaries nonaffiliated to this specific treaty partner. EBIT = earnings before interest and taxes; MNE = multinational enterprise.

It may sometimes make sense to use industry comparisons to identify trends related to MNE structures and the role of specific low tax jurisdictions. Figure 8.3 provides the example of a country where access to an affiliate in a specific low tax jurisdiction (a double tax treaty had been concluded with the low tax jurisdiction) seems to be systematically correlated to lower reported earnings of domestic MNE affiliates.

Inconsistent Remuneration in the MNE Group Context

Another useful reference point considered by most tax administrators is the MNE group context. Where available, data regarding a group's global returns and effective tax rates paid are important indicators to determine risk. Reviews of the performance of a domestic entity in relation to the rest of its MNE will likely take a more prominent role with the widespread availability of country-by-country (CbC) reports (see chapter 6). This approach can be particularly useful as a high-level indicator when comparing activities and functional profiles with returns to highlight mismatches. Note that large differences in returns are not by themselves a problem. The question to answer where income is unequally distributed is whether functions, assets, and risks are equally tilted in a specific direction (OECD 2013).

Substantial Payments of Interest to Nonresident Related Parties

Excessive interest payments to nonresidents are of particular concern for many countries. These can significantly erode a country's tax base, especially where such payments are fully deductible and subject to low or no withholding taxes. A comparison of an affiliate entity's debt structure to nonaffiliated entities can help identify risks of excessive debt or interest payments. In addition to triggering thin capitalization rules, a high debt-to-equity ratio (or debt to earnings before interest, taxes, depreciation, and amortization [EBITDA] as suggested in BEPS Action 4, see chapter 5) can be a potential risk indicator of non–arm's-length debt. Another useful indicator of thin capitalization or non–arm's-length interest payments can be the interest coverage ratio of a company,[19] which indicates the number of times the interest payments made by a company to service its debt are exceeded by the company's earnings. The lower the ratio, the greater the risk that the entity will not be able to meet its interest payment obligations out of current income, with a ratio of less than 1 indicating that the entity has not generated sufficient profits to cover its interest expense for the period.

Royalty Payments

Similar to interest payments, non–arm's-length royalty payments to nonresidents can erode a country's tax base, particularly where such payments are deductible and are subject to no or reduced withholding tax rates. As a result, non–arm's-length royalty payments are often identified by tax administrations as an area of concern. For example, in its Transfer Pricing Enforcement Policy the New Zealand Inland Revenue (2007) specified royalties as an area that merited close attention:

"We are carrying out a special project on associated party royalties. In particular, we are examining:

- the quantum of the royalty in the context of the paying taxpayer's profitability;
- the transfer pricing methodology employed; and
- the supporting documentation."

A particular concern are payments going to low tax jurisdictions. With respect to the payment for the right to exploit intellectual property, the importance of considering effective tax rates is highlighted by the widespread use of preferential tax regimes for intellectual property ("patent boxes"), which have become a common instrument for many OECD countries to attract research and development (R&D) activities and affect the location of intangible assets.[20]

Intragroup Service Payments

Payments for intragroup services, such as management, administrative, consulting, and technical services, are generally deductible and usually subject to reduced or no withholding tax rates where there is an income tax treaty between the relevant countries. The risk to a country's tax base arising due to non–arm's-length service payments is generally considered to be high, as their provision can be hard to evidence. The identification of service transactions that are missing in the accounts is a core component of transfer pricing risk assessment (an observation applying to all transactions). As a result, intragroup service payments and, in particular, so-called management fees, are often the first issue examined in transfer pricing audits (Silberztein 2010) and should be looked at as part of a structural review of transfer pricing risks.

Business Restructurings

Major transactions, including business restructurings and significant asset sales or purchases, can have important impacts on a country's income tax base. Even when driven entirely by entrepreneurial decision making, say to move production facilities closer to markets, the tax consequences of business restructuring can be significant and thus often warrant a transfer pricing audit to look at the valuation and transfer pricing approaches taken in the process.[21] This is particularly important in cases that involve the movement of functions, assets, and risks from high tax to low tax countries. Many tax administrations routinely review performance indicators before and after a business reorganization. Important risk indicators to consider are a significant drop in returns for a domestic entity post-restructuring or the relocation of valuable assets into favorable tax environments.

Quality of Documentation

The quality of documentation provided by taxpayers regarding their transfer pricing arrangements is another potential risk indicator. In Australia, for instance, the quality of documentation received is ranked on a scale by the tax office (see table 8.3). Subsequently, the Australian Taxation Office (ATO) relies on a "Transfer Pricing Risk Rating" system that assesses the risk of two factors: (a) the quality of the business' processes and documentation; and (b) the commercial realism of the taxpayer's dealing and outcomes. For example, a business that consistently returns losses and has a low quality of process and documentation is at the highest risk of a transfer pricing audit. Conversely, a business that has commercially realistic outcomes and has a high quality of process and documentation is at the lowest risk.

Other, Including Nontaxpayer and Related Risks

As discussed in chapters 1 and 3, a number of nontax factors may drive price distortions. These include customs valuation, currency and price controls, internal management, and cash flow incentives. Another interesting aspect highlighted by a few tax administrations, IMF (2014) and the UN (2013), is the potential spillover effect of other countries' transfer pricing practices. Her Majesty's Revenue and Customs (HMRC 2016), for instance, explicitly notes the risk of overcompliance to the detriment of the U.K. tax base. This would be the case where another country is implementing an aggressive stance to counter transfer mispricing, relying on heavy sanctions that may lead to a non–arm's-length price in transactions involving the United Kingdom and

Table 8.3 Assessment of Quality of Documentation in Australia

1	2	3	4	5
Low quality	*Low to medium quality*	*Medium quality*	*Medium to high quality*	*High quality*
No analysis of functions, assets, risks, market conditions, and business strategies	No analysis of functions, assets, risks, market conditions, and business strategies	Inadequate analysis of functions, assets, risks, market conditions, and business strategies	Sound analysis of functions, assets, risks, market conditions, and business strategies	Sound analysis of functions, assets, risks, market conditions, and business strategies
No documentation or processes to enable a check on selection of methodologies	Insufficient documentation or processes to enable a check on selection of methodologies	Selection of method supported with some contemporaneous documentation	Selection of method fully supported with contemporaneous documentation	Selection of method fully supported with contemporaneous documentation
No comparables used	No comparables used	Broad inexact comparables used or comparability based on data from external related party comparables	Comparability based on limited data from independent dealings	Comparability based on adequate data from independent dealings
No documentation or processes to enable a check on application of methodologies	No documentation or processes to enable a check on application of methodologies	Application of method supported with some contemporaneous documentation	Reliability assessed	Reliability taken into account in choice of comparables
			Application of method fully supported with contemporaneous documentation	Application of method fully supported with contemporaneous documentation
No effort to implement and review arm's-length transfer pricing policies	Limited effort to implement and review arm's-length transfer pricing policies	Limited effort to implement and review arm's-length transfer pricing policies	Genuine effort to implement and review arm's-length transfer pricing policies	Genuine effort to implement and review arm's-length transfer pricing policies

Source: ATO.

Note: For more information, see the ATO website, https://www.ato.gov.au/Print-publications/International-transfer-pricing—introduction-to-concepts-and-risk-assessment/?page=9#Quality_of_processes_and_documentation. ATO = Australian Taxation Office.

that other country. Similar concerns may apply where countries do not recognize specific transfer pricing methods or rely on approaches that lead to non–arm's-length outcomes, and where MNEs have a strong preference to increase income in a parent's home country to pay dividends or fund investment.[22]

Chapter 8 Main Messages

- Following the enactment of transfer pricing legislation and guidance, tax administrations need to develop, implement, and continuously update an effective transfer pricing audit program. This requires substantial investment in capacity building and the development of appropriate administrative policies and procedures.
- A common approach is to establish a centralized team dedicated to improving transfer pricing compliance throughout the tax administration.
- To address the potential for corruption, appropriate internal procedures and practices to manage this risk need to be implemented.
- Tax administrations are faced with finite resources and limited time, which means that they are unable to conduct audits on all taxpayers with related party dealings. They will, therefore, need to determine the potential tax revenue at stake to select the most suitable audit cases.
- Depending on the information available, administrators can develop a range of structural risk indicators that draw on international guidance and published country experience.

Notes

1. For a comprehensive discussion on large taxpayers, refer to OECD (2009).
2. The EUJTPF released a report examining challenges for small- and medium-sized enterprises (SMEs). It made a series of recommendations concerning, inter alia, transfer pricing audits, encouraging member states to apply the principle of proportionality; see the EC website, http://ec.europa.eu/taxation_customs/taxation/company_tax/transfer_pricing/forum/index_en.htm#ach6.
3. See chapter 4 of UN (2013).
4. See chapter 4, paragraphs 4.6.1.2. and 4.6.1.4, of UN (2013).
5. Douglas H. Shulman, commissioner of the IRS, at the IRS and George Washington University 24th Annual Institute on Current Issues in International Taxation, December 2011; see IRS website, http://www.transferpricing.com/pdf/US_Commisioner_GWU_24th_Annual_Institute.pdf.
6. See chapter 4, paragraph 4.6.2 of UN (2013).
7. Though, when done selectively, this may create internal frictions between regular and targeted staff with "scarce skills."
8. In Sweden, for instance, employees are frequently returning to the tax administration, ensuring a continuous exchange of knowledge.

9. Regarding risk assessment, there is a vast body of knowledge publicly available, such as the *Risk Management Guide for Tax Administrations* (EC 2006), which addresses techniques to improve the tax administration's effectiveness in dealing with risks and a handbook on *Risk-Based Tax Audits* (World Bank 2011), which summarizes country experience in Eastern European economies.

10. Douglas H. Shulman, Commissioner of Internal Revenue Service, at the IRS and George Washington University 24th Annual Institute on Current Issues in International Taxation, December 2011. http://www.transferpricing.com/pdf/US_Commisioner _GWU_24th_Annual_Institute.pdf.

11. For a detailed discussion on selecting the right cases refer to chapter 2 of the OECD (2012).

12. An enterprise complies with the spirit of the tax laws and regulations if it takes reasonable steps to determine the intention of the legislature and interprets those tax rules consistent with that intention in light of the statutory language and relevant, contemporaneous legislative history (OECD 2011).

13. Beer and Loeprick (2015) provide evidence on observable profit shifting in the oil and gas sector.

14. The OECD expects to release a revised version in 2016 or 2017.

15. See chapter 8, paragraph 8.3.5, of UN (2013).

16. As quoted from paragraph 1.70 (OECD 2010): "*associated enterprises, like independent enterprises, can sustain genuine losses, whether due to heavy start-up costs, unfavorable economic conditions, inefficiencies, or other legitimate business reasons. However, an independent enterprise would not be prepared to tolerate losses that continue indefinitely.*"

17. Wright (2002, 174) observes that "[as] a general rule, selling affiliates are allowed to report start-up losses for a period of three years or less."

18. In China, for example, "an enterprise that reports losses in two or more consecutive years is a likely target for transfer pricing audits (Article 29 2009 Special Measures)" and in New Zealand, the Island Revenue Department (IRD) has stated that "a constant period of losses may suggest commercially unrealistic transfer pricing policies" (see "Transfer Pricing" at the IRD website, http://www.ird.govt.nz/transfer-pricing/practice /transfer-pricing-practice-losses.html) with "chronic losses" being specified by the IRD (2007).

19. In the United Kingdom, the interest coverage ratio is one of the ratios considered by the HMRC when considering thin capitalization. See further at the HMRC website: http://www.hmrc.gov.uk/manuals/intmanual/intm577040.htm.

20. Dischinger and Riedel (2011) find that intangible asset holdings are distorted toward MNE's low tax subsidiaries, accounting for patent box regimes by lowering the assumed corporate income tax rate in countries with preferential regimes. The development and ownership of intellectual property have become an important component of MNE tax planning strategies (Evers and Spengel 2014). With the effective income tax burden being substantially reduced by patent boxes, the incentive and risk of mispricing of license and royalty payments going to affiliates in these countries likely increases (Loeprick 2015).

21. A discussion of transfer pricing challenges and approaches related to business restructurings can be found in chapter 9 of OECD (2010).

22. Dischinger, Knoll, and Riedel (2014) provide some evidence that a disproportionate share of MNE profits accrues with the corporate headquarters.

Bibliography

ATO (Australian Taxation Office). 2015. *International Transfer Pricing: Introduction to Concepts and Risk Assessment.* Canberra: ATO. https://www.ato.gov.au/Business /International-tax-for-business/In-detail/Transfer-pricing/International-transfer -pricing---introduction-to-concepts-and-risk-assessment/.

Australian Department of Treasury. 2011. *Income Tax: Cross-Border Profit Allocation: Review of Transfer Pricing Rules.* Canberra: Australian Department of Treasury. http:// www.treasury.gov.au/documents/2219/PDF/Review_of_transfer_pricing_rules _CP.pdf.

Beer, S., and J. Loeprick. 2015. "Taxing Income in the Oil and Gas Sector—Challenges of International and Domestic Profit Shifting." WU International Taxation Research Paper Series No. 2015–18. WU International, Vienna.

Bell, K. A. 2011. "Local Tax Bureau Accepted Business Reasons for Shanghai Firm's Losses." *International Tax Monitor.*

Dischinger, M., B. Knoll, and N. Riedel. 2014. "There's No Place Like Home: The Profitability Gap between Headquarters and Their Foreign Subsidiaries." *Journal of Economics & Management Strategy* 23: 369–95. doi:10.1111/jems.12058.

Dischinger, M., and N. Riedel. 2011. "Corporate Taxes and the Location of Intangible Assets within Multinational Firms." *Journal of Public Economics* 95 (7–8): 691–707.

EC (European Commission). 2006. *Risk Management Guide for Tax Administrations.* Brussels: EC. http://ec.europa.eu/taxation_customs/resources/documents//taxation/tax _cooperation/gen_overview/Risk_Management_Guide_for_tax_administrations_en.pdf.

EuropeAid and PwC (PricewaterhouseCoopers). 2011. *Implementing the Tax and Development Policy Agenda: Transfer Pricing and Developing Countries: Final Report.* Brussels: EuropeAid and PwC. http://ec.europa.eu/taxation_customs/resources /documents/common/publications/studies/transfer_pricing_dev_countries.pdf.

Evers, L., and C. Spengel. 2014. "Effective Tax Rates under IP Tax Planning." ZEW Discussion Paper No. 14-111.

HMRC (Her Majesty's Revenue and Customs). 2016. *Transfer Pricing: Risk Assessment: Transfer Pricing Risk Indicators: Transfer Pricing Rules in Other Countries* (INTM482060). London: HMRC. https://www.gov.uk/hmrc-internal-manuals/international-manual /intm482000.

IMF (International Monetary Fund). 2014. *Spillovers in International Corporate Taxation.* Technical Report. Washington, DC: IMF.

Khwaja, M. S., R. Awasthi, and J. Loeprick, eds. 2011. *Risk-Based Tax Audits: Approaches and Country Experiences.* Washington, DC: World Bank.

New Zealand Inland Revenue. 2007. *Transfer Pricing Enforcement Policy.* http://www.itd-web.org/documents/NZ_Transfer_Pricing_Enforcement_Policy-10_Dec_2007.pdf

Loeprick, J. 2015. "Indirect Access to Intellectual Property Regimes—Effects on Austrian and German Affiliates." WU International Taxation Research Paper Series No. 2015–13, WU International, Vienna.

OECD (Organisation for Economic Co-operation and Development). 2009. *Forum on Tax Administration: Compliance Management of Large Business Task Group Guidance Note Experiences and Practices of Eight OECD Countries.* Paris: OECD.

———. 2011. *Commentary on Taxation OECD Guidelines for Multinational Enterprises.* Paris: OECD.

————. 2012. *Dealing Effectively with the Challenges of Transfer Pricing.* Paris: OECD. www .oecd.org/site/ctpfta/49428070.pdf.

————. 2013. "Draft Handbook on Transfer Pricing Risk Assessment." Released for public consultation on April 30, OECD, Paris. http://www.oecd.org/tax/transfer-pricing /Draft-Handbook-TP-Risk-Assessment-ENG.pdf.

PwC (PricewaterhouseCoopers). 2011. *International Transfer Pricing.* London: PwC. https://www.pwc.com/gx/en/international-transfer-pricing/assets/itp-2011.pdf.

————. 2012. *Pricing Knowledge Network: Focusing on the Impact of Major Transfer Pricing Issues.* London: PwC.

Runkel, M., and A. Haufler. 2008. "Multinationals' Capital Structures, Thin Capitalization Rules and Corporate Tax Competition." Paper prepared for the European Tax Policy Forum. http://www.ifs.org.uk/docs/etpf/hauflerrunkel.pdf.

Silberztein, C. 2010. "Transfer Pricing Disputes and Their Causes." *Asia-Pacific Tax Bulletin* (November/December).

UN (United Nations). 2013. *United Nations Practical Manual on Transfer Pricing for Developing Countries.* New York: UN. http://www.un.org/esa/ffd/documents/UN _Manual_TransferPricing.pdf.

Wright, D. 2002. "Transfer Pricing When Losses Arrive." *International Transfer Pricing Journal* 9 (5).

Environmental Benefits Statement

The World Bank Group is committed to reducing its environmental footprint. In support of this commitment, we leverage electronic publishing options and print-on-demand technology, which is located in regional hubs worldwide. Together, these initiatives enable print runs to be lowered and shipping distances decreased, resulting in reduced paper consumption, chemical use, greenhouse gas emissions, and waste.

We follow the recommended standards for paper use set by the Green Press Initiative. The majority of our books are printed on Forest Stewardship Council (FSC)–certified paper, with nearly all containing 50–100 percent recycled content. The recycled fiber in our book paper is either unbleached or bleached using totally chlorine-free (TCF), processed chlorine-free (PCF), or enhanced elemental chlorine-free (EECF) processes.

More information about the Bank's environmental philosophy can be found at http://www.worldbank.org/corporateresponsibility.